INVENTING WINE

ALSO BY PAUL LUKACS

The Great Wines of America:
The Top Forty Vintners, Vineyards, and Vintages

American Vintage: The Rise of American Wine

INVENTING
WINE

A NEW HISTORY OF
ONE OF THE WORLD'S
MOST ANCIENT PLEASURES

PAUL LUKACS

W. W. Norton & Company

New York • London

Copyright © 2012 by Paul Lukacs

For information about permission to reproduce
selections from this book, write to
Permissions, W. W. Norton & Company, Inc.,
500 Fifth Avenue, New York, NY 10110

For information about special discounts for bulk purchases,
please contact W. W. Norton Special Sales at
specialsales@wwnorton.com or 800-233-4830

Manufacturing by Courier Westford
Book design by Marysarah Quinn
Production manager: Devon Zahn

Library of Congress Cataloging-in-Publication Data

Lukacs, Paul (Paul B.)
Inventing wine : a new history of one of the world's most
ancient pleasures / Paul Lukacs. — 1st ed.
p. cm.
Includes bibliographical references and index.
ISBN 978-0-393-06452-0 (hardcover)
1. Wine and wine making—History—To 1500.
2. Wine and wine making—History. I. Title.
TP549.L85 2013
663'.2—dc23
                              2012027151

W. W. Norton & Company, Inc.
500 Fifth Avenue, New York, N.Y. 10110
www.wwnorton.com

W. W. Norton & Company Ltd.
Castle House, 75/76 Wells Street, London W1T 3QT

2 3 4 5 6 7 8 9 0

TO HELEN,
with love

CONTENTS

INTRODUCTION

Human beings have been inventing wine for some eight thousand years. Not the natural product, something that occurs on its own whenever the skins of ripe grapes split open, but rather the cultural and artisanal one. Or to be more precise, the cultural and artisnal ones, since men and women over those many years have defined what wine is, and why it matters, very differently. So while people in different times and places have long drunk the same basic chemical substance, they have done so for a wide array of social and cultural reasons, in the process coming up with very different uses for it. Through its extensive history, wine has played various roles, being everything from a vehicle for spiritual communion to a source of bodily nourishment to an object of aesthetic appreciation. In virtually all of them, it has brought pleasure, but pleasure conceived of in a wide range of ways. This is a book about those ways. As a history, it recounts wine's passage through time, emphasizing how the various pleasures it provided changed over the millennia.

Most previous accounts of wine's past, no matter when they were written, celebrate continuity. Their authors assume a fundamental correspondence between contemporary wines and those that people drank hundreds, even thousands of years ago. This book tells another story. It contends that while wine is old, wine as we know it is new. Far from being the end-point in an unbroken series of vintages stretching back to antiquity, today's wines are the product of a set of radical, even revolutionary changes involving both how wine was produced and why it was drunk. One crucial change involved its secularization, something that only occurred on a wide scale in Europe's Middle Ages. Another came during the Renaissance and Enlightenment, with wine's initial scientific and technological modernization, and then still another with its quite recent stylistic and qualitative globalization. This book tells the story of those changes, and so is marked as much by disruption as by continuity. It thus offers a new way to view the present as well as the past.

History exists not simply in the past, but more precisely in recollections or reports of the past. After all, history never just happens. Events do, but their significance—how much they matter and to whom—depends almost entirely on the people who recall and recount them. In this regard, it seems significant that the word "story" lies embedded within the word "history," which the *Oxford English Dictionary* defines first as "a relation of incidents . . . a narrative [or] tale," and only subsequently as an "aggregate of past events." Put another way, no matter the subject, those events, being past, necessarily remain finished and forgotten until they live again in the stories men and women tell about them.

Let me acknowledge here at the start that some people may consider the specific subject of this book trivial, and so not really worth reading (or writing) about anew. It's worth noting, however, that many commentators have venerated wine for a very long time. In the *Odyssey*, Homer characterized wine as something "descended from the bless'd abodes / A rill of nectar, streaming from the gods." This idea of wine as something sacred was very common in many ancient cultures, and as a consequence people long valued no foodstuff more highly. Wine provided men and women with both physical sustenance and psychological solace. Since it could help them stay or even become healthy, as well as win favor with their gods, they cared less about how it tasted than about what it represented or embodied. Some people held onto this view even in early modern times. Witness James Howell, an English Renaissance writer who, with tongue only partially in cheek, declared, "Good wine makes good blood, good blood causeth good humors, good humors cause good thoughts, good thoughts bring forth good works, good works carry a man to heaven, *ergo* good wine carrieth a man to heaven." Though that is not our twenty-first-century logic, many of us still consider wine to be one of life's great pleasures. And as the distinguished contemporary wine merchant and author Gerald Asher once noted wryly, "Only idiots take their pleasures frivolously."

For many thousands of years, people needed wine, or at least believed that they did. Their specific requirements shifted over time, but they considered wine necessary for their basic existence. That only started to change about five centuries ago, when wine began to assume new form as a cultural choice. Though it took many years for it to become something worth selecting for itself rather than for any alleged benefits it might bring, the shift from need to choice enabled wine to assume modern form. Why people choose it today depends largely on their circumstances—their desire for conviviality, for what is sometimes called "the good life," for sophistication, and, of course, for flavors they think are worth savoring. Less than a century ago, a great many commercial wines, some cheap but others quite costly, tasted spoiled or rotten. Few drinkers risk that sort of unpalatable disappointment today. There are places, parts of the former Soviet Union, for example, and countries in South Asia, where seriously flawed wine still exists in significant volume, but it rarely does for the rest of us. In most parts of the winemaking world, modern science and technology, coupled with a more demanding marketplace, have made bad wine little more than a remnant of times past. We personally may not like a particular bottle, but when we pour a glass, we usually can be certain that the wine in it will be at least chemically sound. Often, of course, it is much more than that. Wine can bring remarkable delights. This book tells the story of those delights, where they came from and how we came to value them. It focuses more on the origin and development of what we enjoy than on the relics of what in all probability we would not even tolerate.

Wine today is extremely popular. Characters in movies and on television drink it, just as newspapers and magazines cover it, and websites and blogs fill cyberspace with discussions about it. Shops specializing in wine carry literally thousands of different selections. Restaurants, cafés, and bars offering long lists of often esoteric choices have proliferated across the globe, and tourism in wine-producing regions has turned into a big business. Not all that long ago, caring about wine as anything more than a simple quaff was the almost exclusive provenance of the wealthy. This was not so much because they alone could afford something better as because very little quality wine was made anywhere. No more. We are blessed today with an abundance of excellent wines coming from every continent save Antarctica, and in much of the wine-drinking world, knowing something about them has become a middle-class passion. But then, the emergence of modern wine, something that began on a limited scale in Renaissance Europe, always accompanied the emergence of the modern bourgeoisie. When that social class expanded, so too did consumers' choices. A new market and a new sort of high-quality wine (made with freshly harvested rather than dried, raisined grapes) arrived together, changing forever how people perceived their own wants and desires when they drank it.

Paradoxically, though never more popular, with elite examples more than ever in demand (and fetching ever-higher prices), less wine actually is being drunk today than was consumed thirty, fifty, or a hundred years ago. The decline, however, has been almost entirely in two categories: cheap coarse wines, the sort that used to be guzzled by poor farmers or factory workers as part of their daily diet, and equally cheap fortified wines, the kind often hidden from respectable sight in brown paper bags. The rapidly waning demand for both of these reflects the final stage in the nearly five-hundred-year shift in wine's cultural status— from need to choice. Drinking wine today more often reflects cultural preferences than satisfies physical appetites. Enjoying it has become a mark of the kind of discernment that in a less self-consciously egalitarian age was called "good taste," and its current popularity is intimately related to people's perceptions of themselves.

That use of the word "taste" can carry with it connotations of snobbery, and so has fallen somewhat out of vogue. Yet the simple fact that we speak of "wine appreciation" much as we do music or art appreciation suggests that enjoying wine involves more than just liking it. With wine, full enjoyment comes from being able to know, judge, and discriminate—that is, from choosing, and choosing wisely. In turn, making sensible (and sensitive) choices necessitates paying attention to not just the thing tasted but also the individual tasting. Moreover, since the radically improved quality of wine worldwide has made such enjoyment possible for people of even fairly modest means, discernment and taste have become widely shared values. Wine appreciation sometimes still carries suggestions of exclusivity or elitism, but even a quick glance at the glasses being lifted at an American bistro or an Australian pub, an Argentinean café or Italian trattoria, suggests otherwise. High-quality wine today is hardly the exclusive province of any single social or economic group. It instead is being enjoyed by more and more different people, in more and more places, all the time.

Wine began to assume recognizable, modern form when vintners started to make, and drinkers started to demand, wines possessing particularly appealing aromas and flavors—wines, that is, worth choosing for themselves. Though the ancient Greeks and Romans had distinguished between special and ordinary wines, the fundamental difference then came from how the two types were made—the first by drying grapes in the sun until they shriveled into virtual raisins, the other by picking often under-ripe grapes and fermenting them immediately. Dried-grape wines remained popular for many centuries, but by the late Middle Ages and Renaissance another distinction was beginning to be drawn, this one involving where the grapes were grown. A fine wine, as opposed to an ordinary one, came from an especially fine grape-growing place. This marked the beginning of the originally French but now global idea of *terroir*, and from that point on, place became an important element in any quality wine's identity.

Yet since the grapes for wine are a cultivated, not a wild crop, equally integral to that identity are both the care taken by the vintner in a vineyard's management and the attention devoted to that vineyard or region by the person drinking the wine. The men and (occasionally) women who cultivated early modern vineyards improved their terroirs through craft and diligence, while the consumers who purchased the wines made with the fruit grown there did so with their purses. Terroir, then, is ultimately something invented by humans as well as discovered by them. And the power of such invention belongs as much to the people drinking the wine as to those producing it. As Roger Dion acknowledged in his celebrated history of French wine, "The role of the land in the making of a [fine wine] scarcely goes beyond that of the material used in making a work of art." Moreover, place is not the only material used. The choice of grape or grapes proves just as important to any wine's intrinsic character. Nearly nine thousand varieties of grapes grow in the world today. How a particular wine tastes depends to a considerable degree on which one, or which ones, have gone into it.

Modern wine emerged with the discovery of particular flavors stemming from both place and grape. But it flourished into an object of widespread desire only with the development of tastes that valued those flavors and wanted ever more of them. That desire for more has led to fine wines today that hail from all over the globe. As odd as it may seem, these come both in a myriad of forms and in one dominant style, thus representing the twin phenomena of specialization and globalization that define contemporary wine worldwide. For most of wine's history, style came naturally, certain grapes from a certain place yielding wines of a certain type. Now, however, it is as much a product of human vision and foresight, modern science and technology having enabled vintners to make very different wines from the same grapes grown in the same places. The choice of style, much like the choice of both grape and vineyard, may be motivated by everything from the pursuit of excellence to the need to meet market demands, but it remains at heart a human one. This book ends with the story of those choices, a story that again involves wine's pleasures as much as its production.

Many of modern wine's pleasures are sensual—its smell, taste, and feel, including the feel of its effects—but some also are cerebral. "Wine is the intellectual part of a meal," the nineteenth-century novelist Alexandre Dumas once remarked, meaning that a glass or two can stimulate contemplation and conversation. Yet pleasure, whether physical or mental, comes as much from the person who derives enjoyment from experiencing an object as from the object itself. Put another way, just as beauty is often said to be in a beholder's eye, delectability is on a taster's palate. And eye and palate always are informed by the twin forces of expectation and memory—what one hopes to experience and what one has experienced before. Twenty-first-century wines may not necessarily be better than wines made in earlier eras, but they are undoubtedly different, as are the likes and dislikes of those of us who care about them.

Wine and its appreciation have undergone great changes over the centuries. Those changes are ultimately what this history recounts.

—⁓—

Many people helped me during the six years it took to research and write this book. A year's sabbatical leave proved invaluable in getting started, and special thanks go to my colleagues at Loyola University Maryland for helping make that possible. My agent, Georges Borchardt, and my editors, Maria Guarnaschelli and Melanie Tortoroli, believed in the book even when I wasn't always sure that I did. I am grateful for their support and, even more, their patience. Different friends and associates read portions of the manuscript at various times, and their counsel always proved helpful. Finally, no one offered more encouragement or wiser advice than Marguerite Thomas. Her unfailing support gave me the courage to pursue my convictions, and as with so much else in my life over the past sixteen years, her presence by my side made all the difference.

Baltimore, Maryland
October 2012

INVENTING WINE

GOD'S GIFTS
Wine in Ancient Worlds

For thousands of years, the pleasures provided by wine were spiritual as well as sensory. Because people believed that wine came directly from their gods, they valued it less for its taste, or even its intoxicating effect, than for its apparently divine origin. In most ancient winemaking cultures, whether Greek or Roman, early Christian or Judaic, Anatolian, Egyptian, Mesopotamian, or Transcaucasian, wine was something mystifying, a liquid that came into being through a magical transformation, replete with bubbles, heat, and an invisible vapor that could make one faint. Moreover, it had a seemingly miraculous ability to raise spirits. Drinking it encouraged conviviality, friendship, and even love. "The gods made wine," declared the author of an early Greek epic, the *Cypria*, "[as] the best thing for mortal man to scatter cares." Beer, typically made with barley, also was popular in the ancient world, but it never inspired comparable reverence. While beer too could relieve worry, it quite clearly was created by human beings, who mashed grain in order to make it. By contrast, wine required divine, not human agency. It was not so much a mark of civilization as a gift from the heavens. Thus in the *Odyssey*, Ulysses visits the island of the Cyclops, a land in which nature proves so fecund that the inhabitants need not even till soil or sow crops. When there, he is amazed to find that "spontaneous wines

from weighty clusters pour / And Jove descends in each prolific show'r."
In this pre-civilized place, the most powerful of all gods lives literally
within the grapes. No one even needs to crush them since they yield
wine of their own accord.

Surely this is how fermented grape juice first came into being. A gust
of wind blew a cluster of ripe fruit off the vine. Or some force, perhaps a
passing animal, knocked it down to the ground. The skins then opened,
letting the sweet juice seep out. Almost immediately, the yeasts that had
been living on the grapes began to convert the sugar in the juice into
alcohol and carbon dioxide. Unlike other ancient beverages—barley
beer, for instance, and mead—this fermentation occurred spontaneously. Therefore in its most basic incarnation, wine was (and is) a wholly
natural product.

When and where would this have occurred? Many, many millions of
years ago, in any place with a sufficiently temperate climate for vines to
grow wild. Grapes belong to the Vitaceae plant family, fossil seeds of
which have been found in rocks dating from the late Tertiary geologic
period, some 50 million years ago. Some scientists have speculated that
this family's ancestry goes still farther back, to a climbing vine that may
have grown on the supercontinent of Pangaea before the different land
masses began to drift apart, some 300 to 500 million years ago. But
whenever grapevines first emerged in botanical history, fermentation
must have followed soon after. The earliest wines were not human artifice or invention. Instead, they were gifts from nature, or nature's gods.

But so too is vinegar, and any wine coming straight from nature had
to have been very short-lived. That's because exposure to oxygen following fermentation would have resulted in the rapid multiplication of
Acetobacter bacteria, which turn wine into vinegar. Stone Age men and
women most likely noticed wine, particularly when they saw bees buzz-
ing around fallen grapes. They may even have tasted it. Yet no history
of wine as we know it can start with its spontaneous fermentation in
some unsettled wilderness. Instead, it has to begin when human beings
first interfered with nature—for example, by collecting grape juice in a
container with some sort of stopper, thus intentionally delaying spoilage; or by deliberately crushing the fruit, and so encouraging rather
than waiting for fermentation. Wine certainly remained natural when

it became part of different human cultures. It did not, however, remain completely so. Instead, it also became a mark of those cultures, something that helped identify or distinguish them. And in ancient worlds, it did that primarily through the practice of faith—faith in the gods who first brought wine into being, the gods whose spirits so often were believed to live within it.

Because wine, so natural, also eventually became so civilized, any account of its history must center on the relationship between human agency and organic origin. That relationship changed significantly over time. More than anything else, the changes explain why today's wines are so different from their ancient antecedents—in taste, but even more important, in function.

In the modern world, men and women attempt to control and master nature when they make wine. But in ancient worlds, the mastery of nature, if even conceivable, would have been regarded as a sort of blasphemy. Within those different cultures, people did learn how to make wine—by planting vines, harvesting grapes, inducing fermentation, delaying spoilage, and more. Their methods of doing so are not radically different from those practiced by contemporary vintners. Yet ancient wine remains wholly foreign to us today, foreign to our minds as well as to our palates. The reason has more to do with changing tastes than with changing production methods. And tastes never exist in personal isolation. Instead, they too are marks of communal culture. Men and women in ancient worlds conceived of wine very differently from people today. When they drank it, they were not just consuming a beverage. Rather, they were imbibing something they considered magical or divine.

Other foodstuffs certainly were considered holy in various times and places, but across the millennia of antiquity only wine was imbued consistently with sacred qualities. Why? Perhaps it was the color—similar to human blood, suggesting some sort of connection between this particular drink and life itself. Possibly it was the vine, a plant that seems to die in autumn only to be reborn in spring, thus likely symbolizing the death and birth of the primeval gods of ancient myths. Maybe too the fact that the fruit of that vine, in the form of wine, was able to survive this autumnal death to provide both sustenance and pleasure in later seasons played an important part. Surely wine's inebriating effect, its ability to assuage anxiety and provoke a sense of transcendence, did so as well. But most important, wine wasn't invented or made by human beings so much as discovered by them. It came from the earth, and evidently from some power within or beyond the earth. That understanding of its origin explains why ancient winemakers did not think that they were commanding or compelling nature when they plied their craft. Instead, they were aiding it. More precisely, they were aiding or serving their gods. No wonder so many vineyards were owned by priests; no wonder so many wines were poured in temples; no wonder so many people in so many places viewed it with reverence and considered it the drink of privilege. As the prophet Tiresias says of Dionysus in Euripides's *Bacchae*:

> He it was who turned the grape into a flowing draft
> And proffered it to mortals . . .
> So when we pour libations out
> It is the god himself we pour out . . .
> And by this bring blessings on mankind.

—⁕—

Where did it begin? Where and when did people first do more than just observe fermentation and actually work to cultivate grapes and produce wine? No one knows for certain. Grapes still grow wild in many temperate regions of the globe, and the wild Eurasian species (*Vitis vinifera*, subspecies *sylvestris*), which is the living progenitor of the domesticated wine grape and its many thousands of varieties, can be found all the way from Central Asia to Iberia. In earlier geologic epochs, when the earth was alternately warmer and colder than it is now, grapevines may have grown elsewhere. Perhaps too, places with no demonstrable history of indigenous winemaking harbor long-lost traditions. North America, for instance, is home to more wild grapes than anywhere else. No archeological evidence exists of ancient Native Americans making wine, but that lack of proof does not mean that they never did so, even if only experimentally. Moreover, there is no need to suppose that there was just one beginning. Genesis proclaims Noah the initial vintner, and ample evidence locates an early wine culture near Mount Ararat in eastern Turkey, where he supposedly planted his vineyard. Different peoples in different places, however, may well have been making wine at about the same time, without knowing anything about each other. Again, no one can say for sure. Wine's beginnings are not demonstrable facts. Instead, they are the stuff of myth and fable—stories found, for example, in the Bible, and the Babylonian *Epic of Gilgamesh*, and the Persian story of Jamsheed. According to legend, that king or shah, who supposedly liked to eat fresh grapes in the fall, decided one year to store some in a jar so that he might enjoy them later. Come winter, when he opened the jar, he found the fruit split open and the juice bubbling and hissing. Concluding that this potion must be some sort of magic trick, Jamsheed ordered that no one drink it. His directive was ignored, however, by a sick consort in his harem who, after imbibing, fell fast asleep. The next day, when the young woman awoke, she found herself miraculously cured, leading the king to order more grapes put in more jars, and then to declare wine a sacred medicine.

This would have happened in what today is northwestern Iran, which is not that far from Mount Ararat. It would have been north of the Mesopotamian Fertile Crescent, so might well be the place that the Babylonian poet has Siduri tempting Gilgamesh with wine. In these and other early mythological accounts, wine's geographical origin is much the same—the region geographers now call Transcaucasia. Lying south of the Greater Caucasus Mountains, between the Black and Caspian Seas, Transcaucasia encompasses present-day Armenia, Azerbaijan, Georgia, northern Iran, and eastern Turkey. While other hypotheses about other places are certainly conceivable, no locale can make a stronger claim to be wine's first homeland. That's because Transcaucasia is not only where many old legends locate wine's origin, but also where the earliest archeological evidence of an ancient wine culture has been unearthed to date.

That culture was primarily a farming one, based in villages. It had mastered the craft of firing clay and producing pottery, thus giving its inhabitants a container with which to prevent wine's immediately souring into vinegar. Residue from a clay jar excavated from an archeological site in Georgia, now housed at the Georgian National Museum in

Tbilisi, proves that wine was being stored in pottery there as early as 6000 BCE. Similar jars from a site in Iran's northern Zagros Mountains indicate much the same thing. Evidence that Transcaucasian peoples harvested grapes goes still farther back, as seeds and stems, some evidently picked ten thousand years ago, have been found in eastern Turkey. The seeds from domesticated grapes tend to be larger than those from wild ones, and radiocarbon analysis of seeds found elsewhere in Georgia matches the date of the jar in Tbilisi. No one can say exactly where *the* first wine was made. Nonetheless, archeological and scientific investigations, most conducted over the past three decades, have made it clear that wine became part of Transcaucasian culture or cultures sometime during the Neolithic period (roughly 8000 to 4000 BCE). From there, wines and vines likely spread in virtually all directions—most notably, south to Mesopotamia, Egypt, and the Levant; west to Anatolia; and east to Central Asia.

Transcaucasian wine was not the initial alcoholic beverage invented by human beings. To date, the first identified by archeologists hails from Henan Province in north-central China. Also from the Neolithic period, but evidently made somewhat earlier, it was a blend of fermented honey, fruit juice (some possibly from wild grapes), and rice beer. The latter likely was made by people chewing the grains so as to convert their starch into sugar, which then could be fermented by the yeasts already at work in the juice and honey. Similar techniques evidently were employed, and similar mixed beverages made, in Transcaucasia as well. How, or even if, the idea of inducing the mystery of fermentation traveled across Central Asia remains unknown, but it seems clear that Neolithic drink makers, regardless of locale, used all sorts of ingredients—figs, berries, grapes, spices, honey, grains, herbs, and more—to produce early alcoholic beverages that their communities valued. Only later did specialized drinks, those made with single fermented ingredients, become common. When they did, grape wine led the way, though mead and barley beer did not lag far behind.

It is impossible to know what Neolithic wine tasted like. Archeologists can, however, make educated guesses. The excavated ancient Transcaucasian pottery with wine residue also contains evidence of terebinth resin. The terebinth tree, a member of the pistachio family, grows throughout the Middle East, and in some places wild grapevines climb among its branches. Resin from it most likely was used as a preservative. Ancient vintners may have noticed that the gooey liquid protects the tree, and so surmised that it also could protect the fermenting wine. (Ancient doctors, having observed the same thing, often used tree resin to help heal human wounds.) In Neolithic Transcaucasia, preserving wine would have been critically important. These early winemakers stored their wine in clay jars, which they sealed with clay stoppers. The stoppers kept most air out, but the seal was not completely tight, so the wine still oxidized. The resin thus could not maintain freshness. Yet because it contained antibacterial agents, it at least could delay spoilage.

Since harvest came only once a year, and since people presumably wanted to drink wine for as long as possible afterward, odds seem good that they added a fair amount of resin to the wines they made. The insides of their jars seem to have been coated heavily with it. Those wines, then, would have been thick and sticky. That they contained tree resin may make them seem superficially like contemporary Greek Retsina. But the residue on the pottery shards is reddish, suggesting that these ancient wines were dark in color. That seems logical since making red wine is simpler than making white, there being no need to separate the juice from the skins before fermentation. The best guess, then, is that Neolithic wine was fairly dark—initially purple but quickly becoming brown—and quite viscous in texture, with a sharp tang from all the resin. It probably didn't taste anything like Retsina, which at its best is bracingly crisp. Unless one drank it right after the harvest, one would have tasted little fruit, as the wine's flavor would have resembled old tree sap more than grapes.

To today's palates, a great many ancient wines likely would taste quite unpleasant. The practice of adding boiled tree resin (often called pitch) to fermenting grape juice persisted across the millennia and across many cultures. The Anatolians, Egyptians, and Phoenicians all used resin, as did the Greeks and then the Romans. Pliny the Elder, writing in the first century CE, devoted several chapters of his *Natural History* to "preparing wine," or the practice of adding pitch or fresh resin to it so as to delay souring. "It is a peculiarity of wine among liquids to go moldy or else to turn into vinegar," he wrote, and he approved of anything that might defer this inevitability. Of course, resin also added flavor, thus masking the sour taste of oxidized wines. That new flavor does not seem appealing today, but people in many ancient cultures apparently liked it.

Pliny himself was one of them. A connoisseur of resin even more than grapes, he catalogued a host of different types coming from different trees grown in different places, the choice of additive apparently being much more important to him than the choice of fruit. Resin from Cyprus, described as "the color of honey . . . [with] a fleshy consistency," was his favorite. Hardened pieces of it evidently would swim in the wine, and then "stick to the teeth with an agreeably tart taste."

Ancient winemakers used other additives as well. These included gypsum, lead, lime, lye-ash, marble dust, myrrh, and more, all put into wine so as to enable it to remain drinkable. In addition to resin, lead was perhaps the most noteworthy, less because of the somewhat sweet taste it imparted than because of its potentially toxic effects. Yet no matter the character of the supposed preservative, any batch of wine would sour eventually. One might think that the proof would be on the drinker's palate, but given how sharp and biting these concoctions must have been, it's not surprising that Pliny suggested something else. "It is a proof that wine is beginning to go bad," he declared, "if a sheet of lead when dipped in it turns a different color."

Ancient vintners adulterated their wines with honey and salt, pepper and spice, all sorts of herbs and oils—anything to make the potion taste of something other than acrid juice. Sometimes the winemakers actually encouraged oxidization, aging their wines in the open air and using raisins rather than fresh grapes, leaving the harvested fruit to dry and shrivel in the sun. This sounds something like the process used today to make Amarone in Italy, except these grapes frequently would be left to dry for so long that the resulting wines, often boiled, turned thick and viscous. They were sweeter, more concentrated (hence headier), and more durable than wines made with fresh grapes. Their resiliency made them especially desirable—a situation that persisted for thousands of years. When ready to be consumed, these dried-grape specialties then would be cut or diluted—sometimes with honey, sometimes with crushed dates or figs, and almost always with water, even salt water.

The Greeks, who were fond of using seawater, particularly prized the saltiness of wines from the Aegean Islands, especially Kos. Pliny liked salt water too, though he warned wisely that one should obtain it a long way from shore.

No matter whether fresh or salty, the proportions of water to wine tended to be weighted heavily toward the former. Plutarch recommended as a general rule using two or three parts water for one part wine, a proportion that relieves "the harsh and irregular motions of the soul and secures deep peace for it." His rationale had less to do with enhancing the wine than with improving the water. Seawater by itself could cause nausea, while so-called freshwater, especially in towns and cities, often carried the risk of dysentery or worse. As the Roman military writer Flavius Vegetius Renatus warned, "Bad water is a kind of poison." Adding even sour wine could kill bacteria and thus make the water safe, or at least safer, to drink. And in many places, there would have been few other drinks available, since any fruit juice would have fermented naturally. Wine, full of additives, was added to water to sanitize it and so provide basic sustenance. It would continue to be consumed as such for many thousands of years.

Dark, sticky pitch, salt water, lead, lye, or ash—as a flavoring, none of these sounds very appetizing. But the unadulterated wine, inevitably teetering on the edge of vinegar, doesn't sound like it would have tasted very good either. In fact, the descriptions of most ancient wines make them seem unattractive if not downright dreadful. To contemporary tastes, they probably would be virtually unpalatable. As fermented grape juice, ancient wine was certainly the same basic substance as modern wine. In every other respect, however, the two have little else in common. They quite clearly were used for different cultural purposes, and so were conceived of and consumed in different ways. And were one somehow able to sample them side by side, they most likely would not taste at all alike. Some historians like to posit a continuum from antiquity to modernity, suggesting that wine culture as we know it began in Homeric Greece, or the pharaohs' Egypt, or Neolithic Transcaucasia. Little evidence supports that claim. Ancient wine, the drink itself as well as its role in society, serves as modern wine's precursor, not its progenitor.

Little is known about daily life in Neolithic Transcaucasia. Archeological evidence confirms this society's existence, but that evidence is too fragmented (often literally so) to reveal much about its customs, traditions, beliefs, or practices regarding wine. For example, excavations at a site in northwestern Iran have unearthed the remnants of a village dating from roughly 5000 BCE. Pottery, most of it in shards, was found in what probably was a kitchen, and chemical analyses indicate that at least six clay jars contained wine. Even older are the remnants of a stone vat found in a complex of graves in southern Armenia. This vat would have held about fifteen gallons, so winemaking there probably took place on a fairly large scale. But who drank this wine? And when? Was consumption in this society confined to religious leaders? Was it reserved for specific occasions or ceremonies? Or was it widespread throughout the community, a regular part of life there? No one knows. No written texts, and few artifacts, exist to serve as guides. For instance, a wine jar excavated in Georgia and dated to the sixth millennium BCE has decorations in a sort of relief on it. These have faded badly, and so are difficult to decipher. Small indentations look like grape clusters, and stick figures with what seem to be raised arms appear beneath them. But what are those figures doing? Dancing? Celebrating? Praying? Again, no one can say for certain. Only with the emergence of Bronze Age civilizations does enough evidence begin to accumulate to present a fairly clear picture of what wine was used for and why it was appreciated. And while the specifics differ significantly, depending on the particulars of time and place, wine in these cultures is represented over and over again not as the secular, social beverage we know today, but rather as one with a complex religious role to play. What seems clear, then, is that it was valued more for its power than for its taste.

We might think of that power primarily as wine's alcohol, a percentage of the whole, with all of alcohol's predictable results—a feeling of relaxation when consumed moderately, an aching hangover otherwise. In ancient cultures, however, no one divided wine into subsets of different elements, and no one knew anything about alcohol as such. Instead, wine was itself a single entity, and those effects provided ample evidence that this entity possessed an inherently sacred because an unworldly energy. Few people today would claim that inebriation is a spiritual state (though some do contend just that with certain hallucinatory drugs), but that is precisely how the ancients viewed it. Thus from Babylon to Assyria, and Egypt to Rome, intoxication rituals were part of many religious practices. To be under wine's influence was to be in a state of spiritual communion with the gods. Of course, drinking wine allowed people at the same time to escape, if only temporarily, the toil and trouble of their earthly existence. But besotted flight was in no sense incompatible with ecstatic transcendence, since the drinker was escaping to (not just through) the power of the wine itself.

Bronze Age Mesopotamia, sometimes dubbed the "cradle of civilization," was more a beer- than a wine-drinking culture. Though the inhabitants of Sumer, Akkad, and Babylon grew grapes, their vineyards produced raisins, valued for their sugar. Yet some people there did occasionally drink wine. They imported it—from farther north and west, in and beyond the hills and mountains that stretch from southern Turkey to Syria and the Mediterranean. The wine was shipped south via raft and boat, the Tigris and Euphrates ferrying the first recorded evidence of a commercial wine trade. This was a time-consuming and evidently very expensive enterprise, so not surprisingly the wine was reserved for the upper classes, particularly the royalty. But it was not a luxury commodity in a modern sense. Mesopotamian kings and queens served as representatives or agents of gods. When they hosted banquets, some of which included thousands of feasters, they displayed divine as well as regal beneficence. So if they poured their guests wine, they were offering something blessed or holy.

That rarified status helps explain why wine also was poured regularly in Mesopotamian temples. There, it was presented to individual gods (or their statues) as a form of offering or prayer. The statues obviously didn't drink it, but the priests who served as the gods' representatives or servants did. Wine occupied a similar symbolic space even in cultures where its production was more widespread—for example, in Anatolia and Assyria, which is where much of the wine imported to Mesopotamia evidently was made. In the Hittite culture of the second millennium BCE, wine appears to have been fairly common. Yet while many Hittite texts mention it, they rarely refer to it simply as a beverage. Instead, they almost always point to its ritualistic use, most notably in religious or political ceremonies. The Hittites apparently believed in wine's purifying quality, both for the body (hence its use in medicine) and for the soul. "When a man drinks it," reads a fragmented cuneiform text, "from him all ill vanishes, from you gods in the same way."

Even as late as the early centuries of the first millennium BCE, wine remained less a popular Transcaucasian drink than an emblem of royal and hence godly authority. A wall relief (now in the British Museum) from King Ashurbanipal's palace in Nineveh depicts this well. In it, the monarch reclines on a raised couch, holding a cup of wine to his lips. His wife sits beneath him, also with a cup of wine, but nobody else has one. As a harpist plays to one side, the head of Ashurbanipal's defeated enemy hangs from a tree branch, with birds poised to peck out its eyes. The meaning seems clear: woe to anyone who dares defy this royal couple, as they alone may drink the gods' wine.

Wine served similarly as a mark of privilege in ancient Egypt, where it initially was imported for royal use. But the privilege there was attained less in the here and now than in the hereafter. The most striking archeological evidence comes from the unearthed tomb of a predynastic king in the holy city of Abydos, located near what is now Luxor, midway between Egypt's ancient borders. This multichambered edifice held not only the royal remains, but also various regal effects and objects—wooden boxes filled with clothing, ivory tags with some of the earliest hieroglyphics, various jars, jewelry, furniture, and more—all evidently put there to accompany the monarch into eternity. Over three hundred intact clay jars were found in one part of the tomb. Chemical analysis of the residue in them demonstrates that they had held wine, which like the much older Transcaucasian jars contained terebinth resin. This discovery at first perplexed the archeologists who conducted the Abydos dig. The tomb dates from approximately 3200 BCE, centuries before any vineyards are known to have been cultivated near the Nile. Where had this wine come from? The answer came when scientific analysis revealed that the jars had been made with clay from Palestine, not Egypt. Apparently this monarch, known as King Scorpion, had imported wine specifically to be placed in his tomb. In doing so, he had gone to considerable trouble. The trek from, say, Gaza to Abydos would have taken a merchant or trader hundreds of miles across the Sinai and down the Nile. King Scorpion certainly may have drunk some of this wine during his lifetime, but no evidence proves as much. All we know for certain is that he wanted to take it with him into the afterlife, where he presumably hoped to share it with the gods.

When grape growing came to Egypt, sometime in the third millennium BCE, it supplied the society's elite with something they deemed necessary for a good afterlife. According to one Old Kingdom pyramid hieroglyphic text, wine is what one drinks after death, as grapes for it grow "in the garden of the god." Particularly during the subsequent New Kingdom period (1550 to 1070 BCE), the era of the famed pharaohs, the Egyptians developed sophisticated systems for classifying and categorizing their wines. They stored vintages in jars that sported inscriptions designating not only the year of harvest but also the name of the winemaker and commentary regarding the wine's quality. The famous tomb of Tutankhamen in the Valley of the Kings held twenty-six such jars, each inscribed in detail. One reads, "Year Four. Wine of very good quality of the House-of-Aton of the Western River. Chief vintner Khay." Another says, "Sweet wine of the House-of-Aton—Life, Prosperity, Health!—of the Western River. Chief vintner Aperershop." Such inscriptions appear to constitute the first wine labels, and they certainly suggest a sophisticated level of wine appreciation. This does not mean, however, that ancient Egyptian connoisseurship resembled our own, for even more remarkable than what these inscriptions say is where they say it—on sealed jars that were stored in graves! Clearly wine played a very different role in this civilization than it does in ours today.

The Egyptian vineyards did not supply wine only to the dead. Once viticulture came to the Nile, the living drank it as well, primarily at festivals and ceremonies. One of the largest came at the beginning of their new year, when the star Sothis or Sirius reappeared in the night sky, and the Nile flooded, ensuring the prospect of fertile land and viable crops in the months ahead. Called the Wag-festival, this holiday honored the god Osiris—who according to myth had been murdered by his brother but had been resurrected so that he could father a son, whom the living pharaoh then represented on earth. Osiris was also the Egyptian god of wine, his rebirth being linked with the vine's, and during the Wag-festival his followers honored him by drinking a good deal of it. But not all of them did so. Wine drinking in dynastic Egypt was confined largely to the society's elite, and only priests or nobles owned vineyards. Wall paintings depicting banquet scenes indicate that it was not saved exclusively for religious occasions, but this does not mean that it ever had a wholly secular function. In ancient Egypt, the nobility enjoyed special status because the gods had decreed it so. Thus noble men and women drank wine at feasts and festivals in order to honor Osiris and the other gods as well as to please themselves. At other times, and much like the rest of the population, they drank barley beer or fermented date palm juice, neither of which they imbued with important cultural or symbolic significance.

The most important Egyptian contribution to wine's history was the amphora, a long clay or ceramic carrier with a pointed tip that allowed it to be partially buried in sand. Because the opening in which the wine was poured was small in comparison to the size of the container, the ratio of air to liquid was also small. Amphorae thus could keep wine in decent shape far longer than any sort of container used previously. Their distinctive shape also allowed them to be transported easily—especially on sea voyages, as a ship's hold would be filled with a layer of sand into which the amphorae would be sunk. On land, they tended to be stored on their sides so as to keep the stoppers from drying out and possibly shrinking or cracking. These stoppers were first made of clay, but since the fit was never all that tight, ingenious vintners worked to come up with better because more secure seals. In Egypt, they stuffed reeds and leaves, sometimes along with a circular bit of pottery, into the opening, and then covered the whole thing with wet clay. Later in Greece and then Rome they used rags, wax, even cork, all coated thickly with pitch or resin. Yet whatever the method of closure, the advent of amphorae played a crucial role in preserving wine, enabling it to be something that could be consumed well after it was made. These containers proved especially important in cultures that associated wine with fertility and rebirth, as the wine stored in them could survive winter's death.

This symbolic association was in no sense confined to Egypt. The Sumerians made a similar connection, as did the Bronze Age inhabitants of Palestine, Syria, and the rest of the ancient Levant, as well as peoples in Anatolia and Crete. But why? Grapevines are not the only domesticated perennial plants, not even the only ones to bear fruit whose juice can survive for a long time. The answer, again, appears to come from what happens to this particular fruit—the mysterious or magical process of fermentation and its equally magical result. Beer, mead, and other fermented fruit juices also contained alcohol, so drinking them produced effects similar to wine's. They, however, always were considered human, not divine, creations.

Wine helped people in many different ancient cultures feel happy, almost unworldly so. It thus could bring them closer to heaven. Of course, it also could make people feel bad, especially come the inevitable morning after. Not surprisingly, warnings against excessive consumption could be found in many cultures. An Egyptian sage advised, "Do not get drunk often, lest you go mad." In Babylon, the Code of Hammurabi strictly regulated who could sell wine and to whom. And in the Hebrew Bible, the Book of Proverbs declared that wine "bites like a snake and poisons like a viper."

In what would become the Holy Land, vines were cultivated, and wine was presumably made, for hundreds if not thousands of years before the biblical books were written, but historians and archeologists know very little about who grew what there, let alone who might have drunk what. The Bible, however, is filled with references suggesting that wine enjoyed a special cultural status in ancient Israel. For one, a vine or vineyard was itself often used as a symbol of the Promised Land. In the Book of Psalms, the poet sings to the Lord: "You brought a vine out of Egypt; / you drove out the nations and planted it. / You cleared the ground for it, / and it took root and filled the land." Similar imagery is used both to praise Israel as a well-tended vineyard and to condemn it as a riotous one. In Jeremiah, the prophet quotes the Lord: "I had planted you like a choice vine of sound and reliable stock. How then did you turn against me into a corrupt, wild vine?"

This emphasis on careful cultivation corresponds with another set of biblical references—the repeated insistence on abstinence save for when participating in specific rituals or offerings. God tells Aaron in Leviticus "not to drink wine whenever you go into the Tent of Meeting," just as God tells Moses in Numbers that if a man wants to make a special vow to the Lord, "he must abstain from wine." But why should one refrain from drinking wine if the vine represents home and homeland? Because, much as in other ancient cultures, wine's inexplicable origins and properties render it sacred—something to be venerated as God's gift, so definitely not part of ordinary social life. Israel's enemies repeatedly are represented as excessive wine drinkers, their consumption marking them as heathens or infidels. According to the Book of Psalms, "In the hand of the Lord is a cup of foaming wine mixed with spices; he pours it out, and all the wicked of the earth drink it down to its very dregs." For the faithful Jew, wine was an essential part of communal identity. But precisely because it was so important, it never could be permitted to be abused. In this context, abuse certainly meant drinking to excess, but more crucially separating wine from its rightful place—in a word, secularizing it. "Woe to those . . . who stay up late at night till they are inflamed with wine," warns the prophet Isaiah. The Book of Daniel is even more explicit when it chastises the sinner: "[Thou] hast lifted up thyself against the Lord of heaven . . . They have brought the vessels of his house before thee . . . [and thou hast] drunk wine in them."

—⁂—

Wine certainly retained sacred significance in classical Greece, but in the polis it became more common fare, for the first time no longer the exclusive province of the blessed or the elite. Moreover, Greek traders and settlers took it with them on their journeys—through the Bosporus to the Black Sea, south to Africa, and west to Italy, France, and beyond. They civilized the places they settled in much the same way they had become civilized themselves, since, as Thucydides allegedly remarked, people "began to emerge from barbarism when they learned to cultivate the olive and the vine." By the fourth century BCE, wine had become part of daily life in virtually all of Greek society. Its inclusive cultural role came in large measure from the fact that vines flourished effortlessly and could be cultivated easily throughout Greece—more easily, certainly, than in the deserts of the Near East. Much as would prove true later in Rome, viticulture then became a significant agricultural enterprise, and winemaking an important commercial one. Wine still was regarded as a blessing from heaven, only now the blessing had been bestowed much more broadly. Since the gods' gift had been conferred not simply on the king or the priest but on the populace at large, it belonged not just in the temple or palace but in the entire city or state. That is why Euripides has the *Bacchae* chorus declare that Dionysus gives the pleasure of wine "to the rich . . . [and] to the poor," so that all may enjoy its "sweet spell against sorrow."

No one knows when or where the domesticated vine first came to Greece. It may have journeyed there from a number of places—Egypt to the south, Anatolia to the east, perhaps Thrace and Macedonia to the north. Though it remains unclear which route was traveled first, archeological digs indicate that vineyards were being cultivated on both the mainland and the Greek islands during the third millennium BCE. Seeds from cultivated grapes have been found in sites on Crete, on the Cycladic islands, as well as in the Peloponnese, suggesting that both the Minoan and Mycenaean civilizations were at least occasional wine-drinking ones. Yet wine was never a very common beverage in these early Aegean cultures. Instead, barley beer appears to have been consumed much more widely. One of the earliest evidences of wine in Greece is as part of what archeologist Patrick McGovern has dubbed "Greek grog," a sweet blend containing fermented grape juice, beer, and honey drunk by the Minoans on Crete. This seems to be like the brew served in Nestor's massive gold cup in Homer's *Iliad*, described there as a blend of wine, barley meal, and honey, topped with—of all things—cheese. Residue of something similar also was found in the seventh-century-BCE tomb of King Midas near Ankara in Turkey. At this point, wine by itself still seems to have been reserved for the upper classes, and so still to have been a mark of privilege.

It was not until the Greek classical period of the mid to late first millennium BCE that wine became more widely distributed and consumed. Economic developments provide part of the explanation. Vineyards, like wheat fields and olive groves, became profitable commercial ventures with the rise of cities, since urban inhabitants needed to buy rather than grow what they ate and drank. So in Athens and Sparta, as in Rome and Pompeii later, wine became part of urban life. The desire for increased profit then provided an impetus for producers and merchants to expand the market, both abroad through trade and at home by encouraging new drinkers. Equally important, though, was the shifting cultural perception of wine. Still special, still something privileged, in classical Greece it no longer belonged only to the powerful and mighty. Instead, it became understood as a blessing on the citizenry, consumed in private at home as well as in ritualistic, public celebrations. Wine now was a medicine—Hippocrates advises using it to cure many ills—in addition to an offering. It was a libation that, according to Socrates, "moistens and tempers the spirits, and lulls the cares of the mind to rest."

In turn, wine became the Greek city-state's gift to the rest of the world. When Greek sailors set sail, they inevitably took wine (and then vines) with them, and they certainly sailed far and wide—not just to the seacoasts, like explorers before them, but inland, up to the Crimea and into the Danube, then to both sides of the Italian boot, to southern France and up the Rhône and Saône Rivers. The Greeks were not always the first Mediterranean travelers to arrive in an area, but they often were the ones who introduced wine to places from which it has never left. The Romans later would expand viticulture and wine production wherever possible in their empire, and under Roman dominance wine came to such now renowned regions as Bordeaux in France and the Mosel Valley in Germany. Most of their vines, however, were Greek in origin, and even at the height of their power, many Roman wine traders and merchants came from Greece.

History would prove the Italian settlements the most important of all the Greek wine colonies. The Etruscans had grown grapes and made wine in Italy long before the Greeks arrived, but their more exclusionary wine culture did not survive. That may be because wine played a more limited role in Etruscan society than it did in Greece, but no matter the reason, the new Greek colonies were where Italian wine and wine culture took deepest root. Those colonies served initially as outposts for different Greek city-states. For example, Syracuse in Sicily was originally Corinthian, just as Naples was founded by settlers from Rhodes. The entire foot of the peninsula, dotted with Greek settlements, came to be known as "Magna Graecia," greater Greece, or alternately "Oenotria," the land of staked vines.

In time, the Romans too began exporting wine and vines, particularly when their empire started to extend beyond Italy. In places where vineyards already were being cultivated, they simply expanded them. After all, they needed to supply the legions and garrisons stationed there with palatable wine. So they grew grapes and made wine in southern France, in Spain and Portugal, in North Africa, Turkey, and along much of the coast of the Black Sea. But the Romans also brought viticulture and winemaking to wholly new places. They planted grapes in Germania, in Belgica (today's southern Belgium and Luxembourg), even in Britannia. But Gaul was the part of the empire in which the Romans' pioneering viticulture had the longest-lasting import. Following Caesar's conquest, settlements sprang up along the Rhône River, in the Midi, along the Loire, and in what we now know as Burgundy and Champagne. Midway through the first century, a Roman legion established a port city named Burdigala on the Gironde estuary. Today it goes under a different name—Bordeaux. The Romans planted vineyards in all of these places. They also began using new storage containers, wooden barrels, since amphorae proved impractical for overland transport. In terms of wine quality, barrels were not nearly as effective. Wood, unlike clay, is porous. Any liquid stored in it is subject to evaporation, and as the amount of air in a barrel increases, so too does the rate of spoilage. Yet the soldiers in Gaul, unlike the patricians back in Rome, did not demand special wines very often. They simply needed their daily ration, both to sate their thirst and to honor their gods, and the new imperial vineyards supplied just that.

Though plenty of poor-quality wine was made in Greece and Rome, some wines were in a different class—as were the people who drank them. These wealthy and usually noble citizens became the first people to appreciate and assess wine in anything remotely resembling a modern sense, valuing (and paying more for) specific wines from specific regions and made in specific ways. In classical Greece, the Aegean Islands usually were thought to produce the finest wines, with the islands of Chios, Kos, Lesbos, and Thasos home to especially renowned ones. Thrace on the northern mainland also became famous for viticulture, and like the islands, it gave its name to its wines. But that is as precise as Greek wine appreciation got. Poets praised the wines from one place while disparaging wines from elsewhere, but they rarely singled out individual producers, vineyards, or estates. A general area, not a specific locale, was all that merited distinction.

In terms of taste, the best ancient Greek wines were extolled for being sweet or honeyed, while ostensibly poor examples were belittled for being so sour that they seemed to "bite." Partially or wholly raisined grapes tended to be used for the most prized wines, and many sweet ones became even denser and more concentrated by being boiled. To increase alcohol, and hence promote longevity, some vintners added sugar in the form of honey, dates, or other fruit during fermentation. The resulting wines became thick and heavy. When stored in amphorae, these wines could last for many years, and people who could afford them valued older vintages. Less esteemed wines, though, tasted much thinner and tarter and were consumed as young as possible. These spoiled quickly, especially since they would succumb to oxidation as soon as a large jar or amphora began to be emptied. Greek winemakers added all sorts of spices and other ingredients to mask deteriorating flavors, and these cheaper and more common wines invariably were cut with a great deal of water when they were consumed. For them, the place of origin hardly mattered.

In Rome, wines from the south of Italy always were valued more highly than those from the north. But by the dawn of the empire, at least some palates had become more discriminating. The imperial Roman patrician preferred not just southern wine, but wines from vineyards near the Bay of Naples in Campania or, just to the north, the hills of Latium. Within those more narrowly defined regions, he (the Roman aficionado inevitably was male) differentiated between subregions such as Caecubum, Caulinum, Trebellicanum, and most famous of all, Falernum. Falernian wine, made mainly from a grape variety called Amineum, was celebrated especially for the legendary "Opimian" vintage of 121 BCE. "No other wine," wrote Pliny the Elder, "has a higher rank." He particularly esteemed Falernian from the estate of Faustus—not so much because of that locale's specific properties, but "in consequence of the care taken in its cultivation." By the first century CE, Roman wine appreciation clearly had attained a new level of sophistication.

That appreciation, however, was still far removed from modern wine connoisseurship. Indeed, the wine itself was very different. While Falernian likely was valued at least in part for its taste, that taste was not at all akin to what people appreciate today. Since Amineum vines have long since mutated or been grafted to other varieties, no one can say for sure what the base juice tasted like. We know, though, that the wine started out white but then darkened, and that it came in two styles—one somewhat sweet, the other very sweet. Frequent mention of its strength suggests a high level of alcohol, and descriptions of its color (deep brown) suggest severe oxidation, most likely the result not simply of the wine's having been exposed to air, but also of the grapes' having been left out in the sun. This makes it sound something like Madeira, and Falernian wine may well have had a caramelized flavor. But as a dried-grape wine that most likely had been boiled following fermentation, it seems to have been quite dense and unctuous, almost oily—something like old, sticky syrup.

The technique of intentionally drying grapes, whether on the vine before harvest or on mats afterward, came to Rome from Greece, and it was used in both cultures for nearly all special wines. Since the grapes had turned into virtual raisins, the finished wines became especially concentrated. Sweeter, stronger, and more durable than those made with freshly picked fruit, dried-grape wines were valued in large measure because they did not spoil as quickly and so could survive sea voyages. They remained popular for many centuries, as similar techniques produced prized wines during the Middle Ages and Renaissance. Until the invention of cork stoppers and glass bottles, these were the only wines that did not rapidly sour and spoil. They may have been thick and sticky, but at least they did not smell and taste of vinegar.

The Romans especially esteemed Falernian and other dried-grape wines after decades of aging, when evaporation concentrated them almost to the consistency of goo. Pliny observed approvingly that Falernian "is the only wine that takes light when a flame is applied to it," a comment that certainly doesn't make one's mouth water today. That concentration, however, suggests another reason why the Roman elite so valued this wine. Its strength, coupled with its ability to endure the passage of time, intimated immortality. Put another way, it was the most godly of all wines. So the poet Catullus extolled its virtues, writing, "Waiter, Falernian! That fine old wine, boy pour me another bowl . . . go elsewhere, water . . . Up Bacchus, undiluted." Unlike other wines, Falernian proved too powerful and majestic to be cut with water. Drinking it meant drinking the gods in their purest form. So as divinity incarnate, it had to be consumed neat.

When and where would a Roman sophisticate have drunk Falernian? Unless he was exceedingly rich and powerful, certainly not every day—and even then, not throughout the day. The wine that functioned in the Greco-Roman world as a dietary staple was something else entirely, a diluted, mouth-puckering drink that is hard to imagine anyone prizing anywhere. Certainly one reason why it became so widely consumed was that, unlike city water, it was (relatively) safe. The diluted wine that Greeks and Romans drank for breakfast, served to their children as well as to their servants and slaves, sipped with their food, and rationed to their armies might give them something of a buzz, but at least it would not make them sick. If consumed by itself, this sort of wine would have varied in quality—to today's tastes, it likely would have ranged from barely palatable to putrid—because it invariably was virtual vinegar. But when mixed with two, three, or four times as much water, it slackened thirst. Hence it was drunk often. In Rome, the most common everyday beverage was known as *posca*, a mixture of sour, acidic wine and water. It was consumed by free men as well as slaves; the Justinian Code prescribed it as part of military rations, and according to the Bible, the Roman soldiers on the Hill of Calvary dipped their sponge into *posca* and lifted it up to Christ on the cross. By contrast, Falernian, like the other esteemed ancient wines, was a concentrated drink of seemingly divine strength and power, and so something to be poured only at certain times, with certain companions, and in certain circumstances.

The most important such circumstance was the convivium, Rome's version of the earlier Greek symposium. Not so much a drinking party as a ritualized banquet, a convivium functioned as a formal occasion that united individuals and promoted cordiality. Designed for everything from philosophical discussion to celebration, it existed to promote friendship and prevent strife. Whatever the occasion, wine was a necessary, indeed *the* necessary ingredient. Without it, there could be no convivium because there would be so little conviviality. Drinking during such an occasion was not simply comforting. More essentially, it proved liberating, as it freed the individual from mundane duties and returned him or her to a primeval state of spiritual solace.

Though extravagant behavior seems to have been more prevalent at Roman banquets than at Greek ones, a convivium and a symposium followed much the same form. Both were ritualized, communal events—"a sharing of earnest and jest" according to Plutarch, a "communion of life" according to Cicero. The emphasis inevitably was on conversation, no matter whether serious or lighthearted, and on fellowship—in a word, on community. These banquets brought men together to share their ideas and experiences, their memories and expectations. Nothing represented this idea of convivial sharing so clearly as wine. Usually served from a common bowl called a "krater," wine at a Greco-Roman banquet was consumed more after the meal than during it. Having eaten, the participants would recline on couches to drink, talk, and be entertained, sometimes long into the next morning. Intoxication was likely, but preferably in its spiritual rather than its riotous form. Sharing the wine became emblematic of the event itself, as the occasion existed to cement friendships and strengthen social bonds. At a symposium or convivium, everyone enjoyed equal status, and everyone partook of the wine. "The wine must be common to all," insisted Plutarch, just as "the conversation must be one in which all will share." If the participants in a symposium were to break into small groups, or to start discussing separate, vested interests rather than common, public ones, the evening would be judged a failure. "Gone then is the aim and end of the good fellowship of the party, and Dionysus is outraged." That's because such "good fellowship" was for the Greeks and Romans not just a social nicety but an ethical necessity or moral goal. As such, it came with and from the wine they shared.

The most famous examples of symposia are the learned ones depicted by Plato and Xenophon, both of whom present a symposium as an occasion for a philosophical dialogue with Socrates. But the conversations at Greek and Roman banquets did not always, or even usually, concern weighty, abstruse matters. Once the communal wine bowl was filled and the cups poured, discussions on any of a host of topics would begin. Perhaps the conversation concerned a wedding or birthday being celebrated that day, a deceased friend whose funeral had taken place recently, a god honored at a sacrifice, or a victory achieved—the occasions for symposia and convivia were many. Because these proceedings lasted for many hours, the participants might become noisy or even riotous and disrupt the banquet. Sometimes, too, especially in the later Roman Empire, the events turned into excuses for sexual excess, Caligulan orgies. More often, however, participants became only mildly inebriated, a state regarded as beneficial because wine loosened tongues and so helped promote the best conversations.

Both the Greeks and the Romans frowned on excessive drinking, regarding it as a vulgar practice. Overt drunkenness carried with it the uncivilized suggestion that wine could play a secular in addition to a sacred cultural role. Until the rise of a new religion that insisted on distinguishing Caesar's property from the Lord's, any such view would have been considered barbaric. At the same time, though, neither the Greeks nor the Romans valued abstinence. When consumed at a proper pace and in a proper way, wine was almost universally considered a social good. It promoted friendship, fellowship, even love; it brought pleasure; it spurred wit. Drinking it pleased its maker—not the vintner, but Dionysus and the other gods responsible for it. Wine made a symposium or convivium function properly because it was itself a blessing from the heavens, a blessing that had been bestowed communally rather than individually. So while wine consumption was more widespread in Greece and Rome than in other ancient cultures, the fact that more people drank it more often in no sense detracted from its privileged, even sacred status. It was still something very, very special, and a symposium or convivium invariably both began and ended with a prayer to the god who made it possible. Thus at the very start of Plato's *Symposium*, before anyone begins to discuss philosophy, the participants pour "a libation to the god" and follow "the whole ritual." There can be no doubt who this god is and what this ritual concerns. "Dionysus," says the evening's host, "will soon enough be the judge of our claims to wisdom."

While formal, ritualized banquets such as those depicted in the *Symposium* were attended only by the upper classes in the Greco-Roman world, they served as models for celebratory occasions for members of the lower classes—who also reclined for conversation during and following special meals, and who drank less exalted wines to fuel and foster their dialogues. These people did not have slaves or servants to fill their cups, but they too used wine to help define themselves—that is, to define themselves as members of a group or groups, inhabitants of everything from their empire to their city to their neighborhood. This was true even for people who belonged to marginalized groups. Wine, for example, occupied a privileged place at Jewish festival banquets, and it played a central role in Christian communities, where it eventually moved from the dining table to the altar. The biblical Jesus, however, did not venerate wine as something set apart so much as use it in the communal Greco-Roman tradition. His first miracle came at a wedding feast, where he turned water into wine, thus ensuring that the event would continue long into the night. Similarly, Mark's Gospel depicts him inviting everyone to a symposium-like, wine-filled banquet, thus extending the Greek ideal of equality and fellowship. And of course at the Last Supper, he associates wine with his own blood. For early Christians in the Roman Empire, then, wine provided spiritual solace because, much as it had done for so many different peoples in different places before them, it was imbued with the mystery and the glory of the god they worshipped.

Those early Christians, assembling together to partake of their version of the Roman convivium, formed a sort of cult or club. But in this, they were no different from many other Greeks or Romans. Both cultures were filled with voluntary groups or associations, some wholly religious in nature, others (trade guilds, for example) only partially so. These associations would meet regularly for their own versions of the convivium, what the theologian Dennis Smith has dubbed "the club banquet." No matter the nature of the club, wine flowed freely at these meetings. Indeed, being able to drink wine in the company of one's fellows, whether fellow believers or fellow workers, constituted one of the primary reasons for gathering.

In one cult or club, however, wine was even more central, being emblematic not only of why one came together in a certain place at a certain time but also of why one existed in time and space at all. This was the cult of the wine god himself, and significantly enough, it was the one such association that spanned the two cultures. In Greece, it was called the cult of Dionysus; in Rome, the cult of Bacchus. But in both, people joined in order to be able to drink the god—not simply for intoxication, though that certainly happened, but for communion. Here the communion was less with one's fellows than with the earth—specifically, with nature and nature's fertile power, a power literally felt in the heat of the wine one drank, a power far greater than anything fabricated by human beings. Not surprisingly, the political authorities often feared Bacchus and tried to ban his cult. Not surprisingly, too, they failed.

—⁓—

Bacchus, né Dionysus, was not simply the Greco-Roman god of wine. He also was the god in wine, and so assumed an immediacy or material presence that other ancient gods did not. To drink wine was to partake of him, if only momentarily, and so to share in his power. That power was double and, at least to some extent, conflicting. On the one hand, Bacchus represented raw nature, sexual energy, violence, and excess. On the other, he represented pastoral peace, relaxation, and the good life—a life that might extend beyond one's mortal years, since he also often was associated with the afterlife. In both forms, Bacchus embodied the contradictory but essential powers of nature—violent and peaceful, bestial and benign, wild and mild. While many modern commentators emphasize the more tragic side of this god's character, it seems clear that the Greeks and Romans valued both aspects. Dionysus, opined the Greek-Sicilian historian Diodorus Siculus, in the first century BCE, is "dual in form," old and young, sane and mad, filled with joy and terror. The followers of Bacchus thus worshipped a god of paradox. They did so in many ways—through dancing and feasting, through contemplation and relaxation, through festivals and theatrical performances, comedy as well as tragedy. But most notably, they did so with and through wine.

Though one of the most famous Greek deities, Dionysus was not part of the Homeric pantheon on Mount Olympus. Homer's epic poems, composed in the eighth century BCE, depict a still earlier time, the Mycenaean age, when heroes and gods supposedly strode the earth together. Wine flows through the *Iliad* and *Odyssey*, but Dionysus merits only a few passing comments. In fact, Dionysian worship did not become widespread in Greece until the sixth century BCE. As a new or variant religion, it was viewed initially by many as a threat to the established social order. That is significant because this is precisely the same period that saw wine emerge as a common beverage, something no longer reserved for a society's blessed elite. It also is the same period that saw the rise of city-states in which trade in wine functioned as a significant economic force. Dionysus, as the wine god, was simultaneously indigenous and foreign there. He was in the wine that the inhabitants of these cities drank, but he came from elsewhere—from the hinterland, from the vine, from nature. That nature—not the cultivated nature of the vintner or merchant, but the untamed nature of the vine itself, the nature of "spontaneous wines"—was something that the city dweller both revered and feared. Dionysus served as its eternal because divine embodiment.

Different myths and legends tell the story of how Dionysus came to Greece. The best known is the story Euripides employs in his *Bacchae*, a story the poet surely assumed his audience knew before entering the theater. In it, Dionysus is the reborn son of Zeus and Semele, herself the daughter of the king of Thebes. One version has Hera jealously conspiring to have the pregnant Semele killed, whereupon Zeus rescues the seemingly dead fetus and nurtures it (in his thigh) until the infant is ready to be born. Another depicts Dionysus as the aborted offspring of Zeus and Persephone, saved by the god and implanted in Semele's womb. Both versions emphasize his double birth—initial life followed by apparent death, followed by new life—corresponding neatly with the life cycle of the grapevine. In both, the infant Dionysus is then taken by Zeus to the eastern mountains of Nysa, where he is raised by nymphs, satyrs, and other fabled creatures of nature. There he learns about wine, a lesson that, once he has grown, he will travel the world to teach to human beings.

It is in this role that Dionysus goes to Greece. Euripides depicts him arriving specifically at his mother's home in Thebes. Here is how the play opens, with Dionysus speaking:

The son of Zeus is back in Thebes . . .
changed, of course, a god made man . . .
I festooned [this place] with green,

Clustered it with vines . . . [and] established
My sacraments and dances,
To make my godhead manifest to mortals.

But the Thebans, especially the current king, do not recognize Dionysus as a god. They shun his gifts and distrust his followers, the maenads, or frenzied dancing women, who have accompanied him. As the drama unfolds, Dionysus enacts revenge on these ungracious disbelievers, until at the end the maenads kill the king. "I speak to you as no mortal man," declares the unmasked god at the close: "[It is] too late to know me now; you did not when you should."

The *Bacchae* enacts all of Dionysus's conflicts and paradoxes—joy and horror, insight and madness, innocent gaiety and dark cruelty. But the theme of the play, that the human spirit demands Dionysiac experience, and that denying such experience leads to disaster, seems clear. When that demand is met responsibly, Dionysus's gift brings humanity joy and peace. When it is perverted, the result becomes pain and destruction. More is at issue than the contemporary platitude of wine's being a blessing when consumed in moderation and a curse when consumed in excess. The great mistake made by the king of Thebes comes when he rejects Dionysus as a god and instead treats him as just another mortal man, his gift as something ordinary or mundane. The full theme, then, concerns the folly of trying to tame or control nature's divine powers—the sap in the tree, the blood in the veins, the fire in the wine. These all are things that mortal men and women can neither control nor comprehend fully. They need to be accepted, and respected, for the divine mysteries they are.

The worship of Dionysus in Greece and then Bacchus in Rome took many forms. Some certainly were raucous. In Greece, the wine god was honored at festivals filled with boisterous drinking and revelry. These included the Haloa, when the vines were pruned; the Anthesteria, or festival of spring fertility; and in Athens, the City Dionysia, replete with dancing in the streets and plays performed in the theaters. More riotous still was the biannual procession at Delphi, when hundreds of women climbed Mount Parnassus and, like the maenads, danced and cavorted all night long, their exuberant, erotic ritual culminating with the slaughter of a wild animal that they then ate raw. In Rome, this sort of excess expanded to include both sexes in a celebration actually called the Bacchanalia. The festival became so unruly that, in 186 BCE, the Roman Senate outlawed it, along with all public worship of this particular god. The historian Livy explains why: "From the time that the rites were performed in common, men mingling with women and the freedom of darkness added, no form of crime, no sort of wrongdoing, was left untried." But the cult of Bacchus did not die. Instead, it flourished in secret, until Julius Caesar rescinded the order and Bacchic worship, including the riotous public festivals, returned, more popular than ever.

Frenzied behavior, however, represented only one face of the wine god's cult. The other was much more peaceful, reflective, and sedentary. In both Greece and Rome, societies or clubs devoted to him flourished, and members in them did not practice any kind of debauchery. Instead, they came together to worship in yet another version of the symposium or convivium. They paid homage to the god not only through their prayers and invocations but also through their membership in what after all was a form of congregation.

One such Dionysian society was the Iobakchoi in Athens during the third and second centuries BCE. Its rules and statutes have survived remarkably intact, and they shed light on what happened when members of this sort of a club gathered together. Far from being an occasion for wantonness, the society's gatherings appear to have been subdued and restrained. In part business meetings replete with treasurer reports, in part prayer meetings marked by ritualistic ceremonies, and in part formal banquets, these assemblies were extremely ordered affairs. The regulations were explicit about what sorts of behavior would and would not be permitted. "No one is allowed to sing, cheer, or applaud," they declare emphatically, since members "shall speak and act their allotted parts under the direction of the priest." If a member became disorderly, he would be fined; if he got into a fight, he would be expelled; if he wanted to address his fellows, he needed to request permission. The conversation following the banquet was expected to be proper, and it needed to concern appropriate topics. While the meetings included ceremonial dances, they were anything but frenzied, being marked by "good order and quietness." Meetings of the Iobakchoi society were just as Dionysian as the wild public festivals. In fact, they arguably were more so since no one joined such a society as an excuse for anything, whereas some revelers at the festivals probably cared less about the god than about their own pleasure. Clearly, this more subdued form of worship was just that—worship.

Whether raucous or restrained, veneration of the wine god was particularly widespread in Greco-Roman cities. This is not surprising since the power he embodied was in large measure located outside a city's walls. Urbanization had separated people from nature. The cult of Dionysus or Bacchus was a means of returning to it, if only temporarily. Both riotous public festivals and sedate private clubs represented ways in which the city could renew its link with the countryside. In this regard, the god's connection with the grapevine, his presence within the wine bowl, remained his dominant trait. In imperial Rome, he also became linked with the hereafter, just as he was associated with the theater and maenadism in classical Greece. Yet these and other aspects of his influence remained secondary. He was first and foremost the god of wine—only, again, wine was understood to be not just a drink, but a mysterious liquid that, when consumed wisely, could bring one closer to heavenly truth. To imbibe was to invite the god's spirit into one's self. That spirit certainly could be angry or vengeful at times, but it more often was relaxed and peaceful, a divine illustration of nature's pastoral power. As such, it offered mortal men and women temporary respite from the burdens and demands of urban life.

While there can be no doubt that the cult of Bacchus influenced early Christianity, the extent of that influence long has been a subject of debate. Several parallels, however, seem striking. Both Jesus and Bacchus are born from a mortal woman but fathered by a god; both return from the dead; both give wine to their followers to drink. For worshippers of Bacchus as for early worshippers of Christ, a filled cup of wine contained within it the divine spirit of their god, a deity that was said to live within the believer (as opposed to in the heavens or atop a mountain). Much like the followers of Bacchus, Christians in Rome were tolerated, persecuted, and then accepted. And their central ritual, the Eucharist, followed from the convivium—specifically, from those convivia devoted to the worship of Bacchus. It too was a formal occasion devoted to fellowship, and centered on a mystery—in this case, the mystery of bread and, of course, wine.

For the Greeks and Romans, as for peoples in even more ancient cultures before them, wine was something sacred. That it also became part of daily life did not secularize it. Nor did the fact that trade in it became an extremely important commercial activity. Yes, grapes proved a lucrative crop, being able to be grown without irrigation on a range of terrains, including soils inhospitable to just about anything else. Yes, wine in Greek and Roman cities was valued because, with so much polluted water there, it promoted health. Yes, it found a willing and lucrative international market. These factors help explain how a culture of wine and the vine became widespread, but they do not explain why it did so, for they do not account for what wine was perceived to be. To understand that, one has to return to the gods. Wine in Greece and Rome functioned as an aphrodisiac for lovers and an inspiration for poets, as a source of solace for the bereaved and of joy for the hopeful, as a medium for the mystic and a salve for the sick. But it did all these things because of what was believed to be within it. That spirit or essence, evident in the very act of fermentation, remained beyond human comprehension and control.

The presence of god or gods, made manifest through the mysterious process by which juice turned into wine, explains why, though its production certainly was aided by human beings, wine continued for so long to be conceived of as a holy bequest. To our contemporary tastes, almost all ancient wine would have been barely palatable. But taste is not the crucial factor that separates it from what we drink today. The bigger difference is psychological, even ideological. It involves radically divergent conceptions of where wine comes from and what it is, a divine as opposed to a human creation.

The ancient conception, though alien to wine drinkers today, held sway for roughly six thousand years, from the Neolithic era in Transcaucasia all the way to imperial Rome. But as that empire fell, so too did this understanding of wine's cultural place. Ironically, it was challenged by the rise of a new faith—one that increasingly distinguished between the sacred and the secular, and so between wine in a church and wine outside it. Medieval Christians venerated holy wine, but they did not consider the wine that they drank daily to be sacred. So they in effect secularized it. Moreover, the church fathers, as well as the Christian laity, promoted secular wine's production and consumption, thus rendering the different forms of the one substance two very different things.

Paradoxically, the Islamic world, where all wine became contraband, was the one place in which it always retained its status or property as god's gift. To the followers of Mohammed, wine needed to be outlawed on earth because it had to be reserved for the heavens. In the here and now, where men and women were thought too weak to resist the temptation of excess, wine always brought the possibility of drunkenness and disorder. But in the paradise of the hereafter, wine was believed to bring only joy. The Koran repeatedly represents that paradise as a garden or gardens, filled with streams or fountains of wine. The righteous are promised "rivers of wine" from which they may drink their fill without any unpleasant or dangerous consequences. In heaven, wine "will neither dull their senses nor befuddle them." Instead, "the true servants of God shall be well provided for":

> They shall be served with goblets filled at a gushing
> Fountain, white and delicious to those who drink it.

> They shall recline on jewelled couches face to face,
> and there shalt wait on them immortal youths with bowls
> and ewers and a cup of purest wine.

> The righteous will surely dwell in bliss. Reclining
> upon soft couches they will gaze around them: and in
> their faces you shall mark the glow of joy. They shall
> be given a pure wine to drink, securely sealed, whose
> very dregs are musk.

As the centuries passed, not all Muslims obeyed the injunction against wine, and in fact believers in certain places at certain times (in Persia during the Middle Ages, for example) made wine part of courtly life. But whether conceived literally or figuratively, free-flowing wine as heavenly reward always remained part of the Islamic faith. In the Muslim world, wine was (and is) still very much a divine gift—such a special one, in fact, that it stays reserved for eternal life in paradise.

The story unfolded very differently in the West. Though not its original home, Europe, particularly northern Europe, was where wine slowly acquired a secular and eventually a modern character—both in terms of the ways in which the people who drank it perceived it and in terms of how and why they valued it. In turn, that more modern understanding eventually would be transported all across the globe—as liquid but also as knowledge. Wine is being made today, and vineyards are being cultivated, throughout the world. Their story, with its many twists and turns, plots and subplots, occupies the rest of this book.

Before getting on with that story, however, it makes sense to pause for just a moment to remember where wine first came from—ancient lands that in large measure have now been emptied of it. Yes, wine, sometimes very good wine, is being made today in parts of the Middle East—in Israel, for example, and in Lebanon's Bekaa Valley. And a wine culture certainly continues to thrive in the non-Muslim parts of Transcaucasia. Particularly in Georgia, vintners often use ancient methods, fermenting their wines in huge jars that are buried under ground, and making wines with apparently antique grape varieties such as Matrassa, Rkatsiteli, and Saperavi. Yet granting these exceptions, wine largely has left its earliest homelands, those places where, ironically enough, it first was understood to be a godly good. And it has left because many people living there continue to believe that it is too special for mortal human beings to enjoy. So, sadly, wine's absence from the Islamic Middle East, and its presence in the Judeo-Christian West, serves as but another mark of a great cultural divide that torments the world today.

WORLDLY GOODS
Wine through the Middle Ages

A medieval *hemina*, slightly more than half a quart, was the measure of wine that Saint Benedict of Nursia prescribed as daily fare for some-one living in a strict Christian community. Though this constituted an admittedly modest ration, he freely allowed the leaders of such com-munities to authorize larger amounts "if either the needs of the place, or labor, or the heat of summer, require more." Born to old Roman nobil-ity, Benedict was the founder of western monasticism. He composed his "rule" around 530, treating wine primarily as a secular rather than a spiritual need. To his way of thinking, even people living an abstemi-ous life required wine, regularly mixed with a good deal of water (so resulting in much more than half a quart of drink). Of course, so too did all the many people who lived and worked outside the confines of religious communities, many of whom definitely downed more than a single *hemina* each day. Because water drunk by itself carried the risk of disease, and because wine provided warmth and calories, everyday con-sumption was vital wherever vines were cultivated. So in grape-growing Europe during the Middle Ages, much as in ancient Greece and Rome, men and women of all social classes treated wine as something neces-sary for their existence. The critical difference, and a crucial step in the long journey toward wine as we know it today, came in their no longer always considering it necessary for eternal life. Instead, most wine now satisfied people's earthly needs, its secularized status being something newly invented in a new culture.

These wines definitely did not smell or taste much like twenty-first-century wines. Nonetheless, the medieval secularization of wine marks the beginning of its modernization. As detailed in the previous chapter, faith in wine as god or gods made manifest had persisted for thousands of years. Only following the rise of Christianity, which had become imperial Rome's official faith following Emperor Constantine's fourth-century conversion, did a significant number of people start to conceive of their daily drink as a worldly rather than a sacred good. Yet wine's secularization did not occur because vintners understood winemaking, including the baffling process of fermentation, better than their ancestors did. Instead, wine came to play a new worldly role because its old sanctified one became prescribed much more precisely and much more narrowly. Christians looked beyond earthly nature for salvation. They separated things belonging to God from those belonging to Caesar, and so thought of wine consumed within a church as fundamentally different from wine consumed anywhere else.

This distinction between sacred and secular wines had nothing to do with how the two beverages tasted or how they were made, and everything to do with how they were understood—that is, with the separate roles they played in early medieval society. In the Christian church, consecrated ecclesiastical wine was still very much considered a divine entity. The doctrine of transubstantiation held that it literally was transformed into the Lord's blood during the Mass. As Saint Ambrose of Milan wrote in the fourth century, sacred wine was "what the blessing consecrated," not "what nature formed." To Ambrose, as to most other faithful medieval thinkers, earthly nature was not inherently holy. Thus he could write to the faithful, "There is greater force in a blessing than in nature, because by a blessing even nature itself is changed . . . [Christ] Himself speaks of his blood. Before consecration it is spoken of as something else, after consecration it is named 'blood.'" Because the sacrament possessed a power greater than nature's, sacred wine definitely shared mystery, even magic, with its pre-Christian antecedents. By contrast, all other wines occupied a secular place in the home, the tavern, the banquet hall, even the rectory and convent. Within a Benedictine monastery, for example, wine as a foodstuff held no mysterious power. Being simply "what nature formed," it was neither more nor less blessed than anything else one might eat or drink.

In other contexts, medieval Christians did not differentiate very clearly between the sacred and the secular. Yet with wine, they separated the two, and their doing so set them apart from Greek or Roman wine drinkers (including many early Christians in Rome). In terms of production, medieval wine, being less stable and hence probably less palatable to our contemporary tastes, arguably took a step backward from the better ancient wines. But the best ancient wines, Roman Falernian or an Egyptian pharaoh's prized vintage, always were believed to be sacred. To anyone worshipping Bacchus or the other ancient wine gods, all wine was imbued with divinity. To the medieval Christian worshipper, however, only consecrated wine taken as a sacrament could be considered a divine gift.

Once people began to think of these two types of wine as fundamentally different substances, the Christian church started to restrict the use of sacred wine, rendering it more and more distinct from wines consumed elsewhere. For the medieval laity, the Eucharist became a special event, something often taken only once a year, typically at Easter. Even then, those partaking in it usually received bread, not wine. That's because the chalice increasingly became reserved for the priest, who as Christ's representative would drink its contents on behalf of the congregation. (This practice became formalized in 1215, when the fourth Lateran Council excluded everyone else from receiving communion wine.) Moreover, ecclesiastical wine existed to atone for sin, not to attain union with a deity. Yes, as the Lord's blood it was holy, but since that blood was believed to have been sacrificed because of human failing, drinking it brought forgiveness rather than transcendence. The priest consumed sacred wine both to remember the congregation's sins and to anticipate the possibility of salvation. He did not drink it to become united with his god. But all the while, wine that had nothing to do with anything sacred or holy continued to be made and consumed widely. This wine was a daily staple, a necessary part of millions of people's lives. It provided worldly, not heavenly solace.

While we can trace our modern understanding of wine as an earthly good back to the early Middle Ages, it is important to recognize that wine then was still very different from wine today. Any pleasure it might bring, whether sensory or cerebral, had to be understood as a bonus or boon. That's because the most important function of secular medieval wine was to provide nourishment. It did so by quenching thirst and providing calories. And in an age marked by plague and disease, it was the rare foodstuff that usually could be assumed safe. Yet safe does not mean enjoyable. Even to the palates of the day, a great deal of medieval wine tasted nasty. No matter, people drank it—and a great deal of it—because they frequently had no trustworthy alternatives.

Of course, people also drank it to escape, if only for a while, the difficulties of their daily lives. In his *History of the Franks*, Gregory of Tours describes life in early medieval Europe as a brutal Hobbesian world of pain and cruelty. Yet while the late Renaissance society famously characterized by Thomas Hobbes as "nasty, brutish, and short" offered drinkers choices, Gregory's early medieval one seems to have been lubricated almost exclusively by wine. He mentions wine over and over again, and while he at one point praises the taste of certain wines coming from Burgundy, he for the most part eschews any talk of pleasure. Instead, he depicts wine simply as a source of sustenance. As such, its abundance brings comfort, and its absence sorrow.

As paradoxical as it may seem, the Christian church, considered as an institution rather than a faith or ideology, played a crucial role in inventing secular wine. Priests, monks, friars, and nuns, all of whom cultivated and planted vineyards, helped make wine an everyday drink in places where it had never been before. They also expanded production in places where vineyards already were established. For almost a thousand years, from the fall of Rome to the Renaissance, wine's place in European culture, especially northern and western European culture, depended to a considerable degree on their work. They possessed the land, the expertise, and the requisite patience. Moreover, in a world in which pillage, looting, and warfare proved all too prevalent, a church's possessions, including its vineyards and cellars, were relatively secure havens. As the centuries passed, more and more laypeople became involved with wine, sometimes working for or with clerics, sometimes on their own. Lords and nobles owned many vineyards, as did municipalities, so it would be a mistake to assume that the church alone promulgated wine and winemaking. Yet since those same lords often bequeathed vineyard land to religious orders in hopes of winning heavenly favor, the significance of the clergy to the history of medieval wine can hardly be overstated.

What can be overstated, or misrepresented, is the reason why the church became so committed to wine. Yes, the requirements of the Mass necessitated that wine be available wherever Christian communities were established. Yes, too, wine figured prominently in art and symbolism within those communities. But the Christian church promoted grape growing and wine drinking for broad cultural purposes rather than for narrow religious ones. In places where vines were not native, or where vineyards had not been planted by pagan predecessors, priests easily could have imported small lots of wine for ecclesiastical use. Its presence on their altars then would have seemed even more special, so even more blessed, in the eyes of a laity for whom it otherwise would have been completely foreign. But that is not what happened. Instead, the medieval church established new vineyards and made new wines wherever possible, going to the very geographical limits of viable viticulture. Clerics brought grapes to previously unplanted parts of northern France, Germany, and the Low Countries, even to England and, experimentally, Ireland. They planted vines and made wines in eastern Europe, most notably in Hungary and the northern Balkans, but also in what are now Austria, the Czech Republic, Poland, and Slovakia. Farther south, they established new vineyards in North Africa and Palestine. Some wines from these places apparently were exported far afield. (Gregory of Tours reports a sixth-century knight in central France asking for "a stoup of stronger drink" hailing from, of all places, Gaza.) Clearly these clerics made more wine than they needed for sacramental use. Clearly, too, the vast majority of what they made was secular—that is, wine used not to honor god but to satisfy men and women, each of whom, according to Saint Benedict's rule, needed at the barest minimum half a quart every day.

So while the church used very little wine for the Eucharist, its clergy nonetheless played a leading role in the propagation of medieval viticulture and winemaking. Some commentators go so far as to suggest that monks and priests in effect saved wine following the fall of Rome. Yet the various tribes that migrated west into what had been the empire never really threatened wine. Instead, they rapidly developed a taste for it. And that taste was satisfied in large measure by the church. The clergy worked to convert these peoples, an activity that involved introducing them not only to sacred doctrine but also to secular culture. Wine was a central part of that culture. Thus as Christianity spread, so too did viticulture. Particularly in northern Europe, monks, priest, nuns, and the laypeople working with them all expanded the land devoted to vineyards. In the sixth and seventh centuries, for example, they cleared the forests in both Burgundy and the Île-de-France in order to plant grapes, and brought a wine culture to much of Germany.

Early medieval kings, princes, and feudal lords certainly owned and managed vineyards, just like bishops and friars. Once they supplied the needs of their households or courts, however, they often donated excess vineyard land to monasteries and bishoprics, whose holdings kept expanding. The motivation for such gifts was often mixed, with everything from guilt to diplomacy playing a role. Yet regardless of intent, a great deal of land first owned and cultivated by laymen became church property. Emperor Charlemagne, for instance, gave many vineyards (including most famously what would become Corton-Charlemagne in Burgundy) to the church. By that time, the late eighth century, wine had become so pervasive in northern Europe that the historian Pierre Riché can describe the period as one "obsessed with wine." And no one seems to have been more obsessed than the monks and priests, abbots and clerics, who kept growing vines and making, serving, selling, and drinking wine.

The German-speaking lands east of the Rhine provide a good illustration of how clerical and lay winemaking intersected in the early Middle Ages, with the church playing a leading role in wine's propagation, and the populace at large drinking it as a secular staple. The Romans had brought viticulture to western Germany, but their wine culture never really crossed the Rhine. Only after the migrations of the fifth and sixth centuries did grape growing and winemaking spread east (and north, Europe being warmer then than it is now). It was brought there by monks and missionaries, including Saint Columban in Bavaria and Saint Kilian in Franconia. Lords and nobles soon planted their own vines, but by Charlemagne's time, when grape growing had been established throughout the German interior, monasteries, abbeys, and churches, almost all with vineyards, were flourishing in the region. The clerics living there owned many of the largest wine properties. The Abbey of Saint Nazarius at Lorsch, near Heidelberg in Württemberg, for example, was founded in 764. Within decades, its vineyard holdings had expanded in virtually all directions, largely as a result of gifts from local lords. The monks tended many of the vines themselves, but they also employed tenant farmers. These men and women paid rent in wine, enabling the abbey to sell a significant volume. Of course, the peasantry also kept, and drank, a fair amount. Before long, Württemberg, much like Hessen and Thuringia, found itself transformed into a wine-drinking region. Moreover, wine began to alter the local economy. Barrels filled with it soon were being shipped down the Neckar River to the Rhine, and then in later centuries both north to the Baltic and south to Bavaria, Switzerland, and beyond. So the abbey's vineyards served cultural and economic ends more than ideological or religious ones. As in so many parts of Europe, the church's efforts enabled grapes grown there to become a principal crop, and in turn the wine made from those grapes a worldly good.

—⁀∾⁀—

What was it like, this new because no longer sacred beverage that people drank to quench thirst, receive at least some nourishment, and escape, if only momentarily, the toil of medieval life? For the most part, horrible. The clichéd view of the Middle Ages as a cultural and gastronomic wasteland may not always be accurate, but wine quality definitely proved very poor in most places. This was especially true of dry wine, which, much as in earlier epochs, spoiled quickly. In this regard, even the better wines of the era were probably in worse shape than the best wines of antiquity—or at least those made in ancient Egypt, Greece, and Rome. Except in some parts of the eastern Mediterranean, amphorae had disappeared, and once those regions fell under sober Islamic rule, there was little chance of their reemerging. Were we today somehow able to try the ancient wines stored in amphorae, we probably would find them extremely odd, being sticky with resin and other additives. Yet even though those wines likely tasted somewhat vinegary, they would not have become significantly more so over time. After all, an amphora, if properly sealed, was virtually airtight. Not so a wooden barrel or cask, and all supposedly good medieval wines were kept in casks. Unless carefully monitored, with new wine added so as to replace the lost share (as is standard practice today), wine left in a wooden barrel will turn sour. And that apparently is what happened with a great deal of medieval wine, even allegedly good wine. It may well have tasted fine when it was first put in casks, but once there, it soon spoiled.

Because casks and barrels often were exposed to the elements outdoors, the wines in them frequently became infected with bacteria. To avoid this, vintners rushed their new wines to market. These had dead yeasts floating in the liquid, so were cloudy, even opaque. No one much cared. Medieval men and women tended to drink from metal cups or beakers, not glasses, so how a wine looked was irrelevant compared with how it tasted. And freshly fermented wine, hazy and perhaps still somewhat fizzy, was just about the only wine that did not taste unpleasantly shrill. Consequently, winemakers sold their wine in autumn, immediately following harvest, for significantly more money than in spring. Everyone knew that spring wine, sometimes called "rec" or "reck" owing to its having been racked from the dead yeast or lees, simply did not taste as good. Then come summer, when that same wine almost always had just about turned into vinegar, vintners and drinkers alike would look longingly ahead to the next harvest. Yet since heat made it especially imperative to quench thirst in summer, the absence of fresh wine proved quite painful. Given how rapidly wine's flavors degenerated with the seasons, it is not surprising that medieval men and women celebrated the grape harvest with feasts and festivals. The peasantry especially rejoiced in autumn. It was the one time of year when they could drink decent-tasting wine.

As bad as barrel-stored wine surely was, plenty of medieval wine must have tasted even worse. Following fermentation, a great deal of it, the sort customarily consumed by serfs and laborers, never saw a cask or barrel. It was stored instead in animal hides. These imparted flavors of their own, which, while they might mask vinegary ones, would seem extremely undesirable to our contemporary tastes. Moreover, since the hides often were dirty, they could infect the wine with even more bacteria. Wine's value as a staple came in large measure from its being safe to drink. Unsanitary storage conditions posed a significant and recurring problem. Yet not until the Renaissance would people begin to have viable alternatives.

As in earlier epochs, medieval wine usually was diluted with water. Since people drank it all day long, this was done as much with the goal of sanitizing the water as doing anything to improve the wine. A person then could drink a substantial amount without getting roaring drunk. Still, men and women living in towns and cities, where clean water proved scarce, were probably at least slightly inebriated pretty much all of the time. After all, wine, even badly stored wine, often was just about the only beverage available to them. Many poor people, though, did not even have wine. They instead had to make do with *piquette*, a thin, acerbic drink made by adding water to pomace—the mass of skins, stems, seeds, and pulp left after grapes have been crushed. Even though this must have tasted dreadful, they drank it from morning to night.

The abundance of bad medieval wine explains why so much commentary concerned efforts to prevent it from souring or, if it already had turned, to restore it. This, after all, was the age of alchemy, and just as people fantasized about magically acquiring gold, they dreamed of drinking wine that could stay forever fresh. They employed all sorts of methods to preserve it, including adding burnt salt, boiled wheat, eggshells, cardamom, holly leaves, sand, or lead to their casks or hides. One supposed solution was to plunge a torch dipped in pitch into the cask; another was to boil the wine; still another, to expose it to frost. Here is a Parisian "cure" for "sick," meaning cloudy and vinegary, wine:

> Take a dishful of wheat, soak it in water, throw away the water, boil it in other water until it is just ready to burst, and remove it. If there are grains that have burst, toss them out, and throw all the rest hot into the cask. If the wine doesn't come clear with this, take a basketful of sand well washed in the Seine [and] throw it into the cask.

But just as lead never turned to gold in the Middle Ages, vinegar never reverted to fresh wine. Indeed, palates had to be pretty tough to endure the stuff. Certainly one reason why people kept drinking it was that they often had little choice. Another was that doctors and healers promoted wine's health benefits. Yet as the cultural historian Rod Phillips notes, physicians often considered diseases to be the work of demons or devils, so they deliberately made wines that tasted horrible, the theory being that these would drive any evil spirit away. As a medicine, medieval wine actually needed to smell and taste bad.

All in all, then, whether served to the healthy or to the sick, a great deal of medieval wine must have been terrible. Not surprisingly, the ancient practice of adding flavorings remained quite common. Wines were adulterated with honey, herbs, spices, and other aromatics—all in an effort to make them more palatable. So too were beers, which usually were homemade and which, without additives, tended to taste disagreeably bitter. Spiced ale proved popular, though it did spoil quickly. But when either beer or wine started to go bad, people simply poured in more flavorings. In fact, they added cinnamon, garlic, ginger, mustard, nutmeg, and more to all their different drinks. They also sometimes combined them. *Bochet*, a French concoction, blended beer, honey, various spices, wine, and water. Its English equivalent, called "braket," included a good deal of pepper, and Anglo-Saxon oxymel was made by combining vinegar and honey. Even mead, fermented honey and water, was often adulterated through the addition of herbs and spices.

People in all levels of medieval society drank spiced wines, sometimes called "piments" (after the *pigmentarii*, apothecaries who specialized in herbs). Spices not only would disguise a wine beginning to turn bad but also could make an otherwise dry wine taste somewhat sweet. And medieval men and women craved sweets. They used cloves, cinnamon, honey, and the like to season and sweeten everything from salted fish to dried meat. One of the most fashionable piments was called Ipocras or Hippocras, an allusion to Hippocrates's sleeve, a cloth strainer allegedly invented by the ancient physician. This potion supposedly had medicinal properties, and as the following English recipe indicates, it definitely needed to be strained: "To make Ypocrasse for lords [use] gynger, synamon, and graynes sugour, and turefoll: and for comyn pepull ginger, canell, longe peper, and claryffyed hony . . . Fyrst do in to a basen a gallon of redwyne . . . then put in your pouders." Clearly the choice of additive and audience for this concoction was deemed more important than the choice of grape or wine. Whether heated or served cool, spiced, sweetened potions like Hippocras proved very popular. After all, if enough additives had been included, they hardly tasted like the invariably sour wines at their base. Even in the Renaissance, when better non-spiced wines became available, men and women of means continued to drink piments.

During the early medieval era, the roughly six-hundred-year span from the fall of Rome to the first millennium, viticulture and winemaking remained primarily local, regional activities. While there certainly was some trade in wine, there was no large-scale commerce similar to what would emerge in later centuries, when fleets of ships ferried wine north and south, east and west, all throughout the then-known world. Because business was limited, winemakers faced little competition, and so had little encouragement or incentive to alter practices or try to improve their work. Grapes were grapes and wine was wine—grown and made in whatever way they had been for generations. Those ways did differ by locale. In southern, Mediterranean Europe, the old estates that had supplied Rome and other cities with Bacchus in material form had long since disappeared, replaced by a system of subsistence farming, with peasants growing vines alongside olives and wheat. These poor people would have to give some of their crop to their feudal masters, but they otherwise grew only as much as they needed. In the north, however, properties tended to be larger. Peasants and serfs worked the land, keeping wine for their own needs, but making more—some for the owners and some for people living in nearby towns or villages. Many northern towns or cities owned their own vineyards, the wines from which supplied the local citizenry.

Medieval vineyards usually were planted with vine cuttings set extremely close to one another in ploughed furrows, since experience showed that not all of the plants would take root and grow. In the north, where rain fell frequently, planting was especially dense; in the more arid south, it tended to be a bit sparser. Yet vineyards everywhere seem to have been awash in vines. The renowned wine writer

Hugh Johnson estimates that northern fields contained up to twenty thousand vines per hectare (or roughly eight thousand per acre), which is approximately two and a half times as many as are planted in what would be considered a dense pattern today. The vines grew, however, alongside or interspersed with other crops, and the available grape varieties depended wholly on local tradition. Many vineyards were planted with both red- and white-bearing vines, all of which would be picked at the same time and often used to make the same wine. Though some grapes might be ripe, others almost always were under-ripe. Farmers, fearing the possible loss of their crop owing to rain, rot, or predators, tended to harvest when the fruit had just begun to sweeten. As a result, many wines tasted extremely green and vegetal. They were shrill and sour even before they began to spoil.

Vineyards at the time tended to be planted with all sorts of grape varieties growing beside each other randomly. To our contemporary palates, the choice of grape makes a tremendous difference in the taste of the wine, but there is little evidence that early medieval vintners paid much attention to varietal differences. Especially in northern Europe, they surely cared whether their crop would ripen sufficiently before winter's freeze (and whether their vines would flower after the last frost in spring), so they may well have preferred one type of vine to another. But since their wines were blends, they did not bother to distinguish between the tastes of the wines coming from these different plants. To the medieval palate, only one distinction mattered—did the wine taste fresh or sour, or more to the point, did it taste slightly sour or very sour?

Just as varietal differences were for the most part unknown to early medieval winemakers, distinguishing between particular plots of land in terms of the taste of the wines coming from them was considered unimportant, if even considered at all. All that mattered was harvesting a crop. Some places produced larger harvests than others, just as some produced generally healthier fruit. These were deemed the best sites. By contrast, no one valued land in which smaller crops might yield more concentrated-tasting grapes, and hence potentially finer wines, as quality-minded growers do today. Medieval winemaking was a crude, rushed process that eliminated most distinctions having to do with flavor. After all, once picked, the grapes were foot-trodden in open tanks and then left to ferment in vats or buckets. Since the carbon dioxide produced during fermentation could prove deadly in closed quarters, these containers usually were left outdoors, meaning that the fermenting juice was exposed to all sorts of weather as well as to insects and vermin. If the grapes were white, that juice would be separated from the skins before fermentation started; if red, it would be left with them (and with the stalks and stems). Yet the technology was primitive, so most red wines were actually quite pale, and most whites tinged green or gray. In northern Europe, cool growing seasons led to low alcohol levels, probably well under 10 percent, the result of large crops of low-sugared fruit. In Mediterranean vineyards, where hotter temperatures yielded sweeter grapes, the wines often were headier. As such, they were prized.

Alcohol, though not yet identified, was valued in wine for two reasons. First, because alcohol is a natural preservative, a wine with a high percentage could survive without souring for a longer period than a wine with a low amount. (Levels below 10 percent have little preservative effect, which helps explain why so many northern European wines turned bad so quickly.) Second, alcohol can help a wine taste stronger and sweeter. So even if the inevitable process of oxidation and souring had begun, a wine with a relatively high alcohol content would convey the illusion of freshness. Not surprisingly, early medieval commentary tended to praise "strong" wine. Not surprisingly, too, that commentary frequently alluded to its potentially intoxicating effect.

The Middle Ages was an often drunken era, with wine providing the most common vehicle for excess. For much of the population, the inevitable periods of privation that accompanied the seasons produced intervals in which people would eat and drink as if there were no tomorrow. Though gluttony was condemned by the church as a deadly sin, men and women invariably gorged themselves whenever possible, their motivation being not only their present pleasure but also their well-founded knowledge of future hardships. They feasted especially voraciously during harvest. And wherever grapes were cultivated, wine was an essential part of their revelry. But if it functioned as a staple in times of celebration and communal sociability, it was considered equally necessary in harsher times of need and want. Wine always remained essential to one's diet, no matter whether lavish or meager.

While both civil and religious authorities sometimes frowned on excessive drinking, they were largely powerless to do anything about it. Medieval folklore often distinguished between stages of drunkenness, based on the animals they made people resemble—sheep, lion, ape, or sow. Though some lords or kings (Charlemagne, for example) became known for their moderate consumption, others became just as famous for their drunkenness. So too with clerics. The church fathers tried to penalize monks, priests, and nuns who overindulged, and medieval penance handbooks repeatedly prescribed strict sanctions for members of the clergy who got drunk in public. Still, plenty of them drank plenty of wine. Gregory of Tours records many examples, including a Breton hermit named Winnoch who became so drunk that he insisted he was possessed by devils, and Cautinus, a bishop, who became "so completely fuddled with wine that it [required] four men to carry him from the table." Moreover, while ecclesiastical authorities warned against excess, they often used wine to bring people together, pouring it liberally for their congregations on feast or saint days as a means of social bonding. Offering wine to the poor became recognized widely as an act of charity, regardless of whether the donation came from a cleric or a layperson. And church-sanctioned guilds emerged in which people drank wine to commemorate their community's dead. In short, wine flowed freely in all strata of early medieval society, noble and peasant, clergy and lay. It might not have tasted good, but drinking it, sometimes to stupor, was considered a normal and quite common social activity.

—⚭—

Because dry wine turned sour so quickly, it is hardly surprising that people long hungered for something else, a wine they actually could enjoy drinking. For centuries, the only known examples were strong, sweet potions made with dried grapes in parts of the Eastern Roman Empire, where autumn rain and frost posed little threat. The old practice of letting grapes shrivel in the sun, thus concentrating their sugars, persisted in Crete and Cyprus, the Ionian Islands, Palestine, and the Levant. It resulted in heady, sweet libations that, owing to their high levels of extract and alcohol, proved more stable than lighter wines made with fresh grapes. Fashioned with what were essentially raisins— either late-harvested grapes left to dry on mats, or grapes dried on the vine itself, their stems twisted to cut off the flow of sap—these were the successors to the old patrician favorites of imperial Rome, and so often were called Romneys. Yet once the eastern Mediterranean fell under Islamic control, with most trade routes cut off, hardly anyone in the courts and castles of western Europe could get them. Then in the eleventh and twelfth centuries, the crusaders discovered these wines during their time in the Holy Land. Returning home, they tried to make their own versions. But those same knights and lords, or the serfs and peasants laboring under them, could not produce anything comparable in northern Europe, where cool temperatures kept alcohol levels low, and autumn rains promoted rot rather than raising. Since they let it be known that they were willing to pay handsomely to satisfy their new desire, enterprising Mediterranean merchants soon devised new ways to bring Romneys north. Italian traders started to ship them through passes in the Alps and then, with the late-thirteenth-century opening of the Strait of Gibraltar to Christian commerce, up the Atlantic coast. These exotic potions then became late medieval Europe's most sought-after wines. As relics of a truly ancient tradition, they were in no sense modern. Yet the demand for them initiated the modern wine trade, as they were the first wines widely thought worth importing and consuming instead of, or in addition to, local or regional ones.

Genoese and especially Venetian merchants popularized dried-grape wines. In 1178, Venice took control of the Brenner Pass through the Alps. Twenty-six years later, Venetian soldiers and sailors, having already seized a number of locations on the eastern shores of the Adriatic, conquered Crete, long a stronghold of the raisined-wine tradition. The Venetians both exploited already established vineyards there and encouraged the cultivation of new ones closer to home. They planted grapes in Dalmatia and Istria, as well as in the Veneto, much as the Genoese did on the other side of the Italian boot in Liguria. Over the next two centuries, dried-grape winemaking spread throughout Italy.

The principal market, however, was never local, as these wines always were made primarily for export.

In most of Italy, vines snaked up the trunks of trees and grew in fertile lowland soil so as to yield large crops. They produced what was called "Latin wine," the everyday sour drink of the masses. The new specialized, pricey nectars were of an entirely different sort. Like Romneys from the east, wines such as Tuscan Moscadello and Ligurian Vernaccia were made only with sun-dried, heavily sugared grapes. Vernaccia enjoyed a long vogue as a favorite of lords and kings, bishops and popes, one of whom, Martin IV, became immortalized in Dante's *Purgatorio*. According to the poet, this pope would drown Bolsena eels in sweet Vernaccia, whereupon he would eat plateful after plateful of them, accompanied by cup after cup of the sweet, heady drink.

Wines like these clearly were luxuries, available solely to a privileged class. "I want only," sang the Sienese poet Cecco Angiolieri in the thirteenth century:

> . . . only Greek and Vernaccia
> for Latin wine is more distasteful
> than my woman, when she nags me.

As this verse indicates, wealthy Italian consumers coveted both imported and domestic dried-grape wines. The Greek one that Angiolieri yearns for probably was Malvasia or Malmsey, named for the Peloponnese port of Monemvasia from which it likely was shipped. Yet this wine would not necessarily have been made in one specific place, as the phrase "Greek wine" designated a style more than a single source. Like medieval Vernaccia, and quite unlike today's dry, light Vernaccia di San Gimignano, it tasted strong as well as sugary. Its high alcohol content helped preserve it, which explains why it didn't sour or "nag" so much.

Whether coming from Italy, Crete, or lands farther east, raisined wines like this were expensive extravagances. Initially drunk only by the rich and powerful, they were considered especially luxurious in northern Europe because they tasted so radically unlike the local dry wines made there. Those wines were lighter, drier, and much more sour. In

1224 a Norman poet, Henri d'Andeli, wrote about a contest organized by the king of France, pitting the light wines of the north against the headier wines from the south. In addition to French wines, the northerners included Germans from the Mosel, while the smaller southern contingent came from throughout the Mediterranean. In the poem, "La bataille des vins," an English priest serves as the judge. While he spends many lines describing the French wines (presumably for political reasons), the winner comes from Cyprus. Sweet and strong, it is said to gleam like a star.

During the High Middle Ages, when the northern European wine market expanded rapidly, Mediterranean wines made in this strong dried-grape style became even more popular. Many factors, including an increase in international commerce and an expanding population base, led to the increase in demand. No factor, however, was more important than the emergence of a new, fledgling social class. Composed of merchants and tradesmen, as well as their socially conscious wives, this was the beginning of the modern bourgeoisie. Most of its members lived in walled communities called "boroughs" or "burghs," those terms coming from the German *burg* and the old French *bourg*, words that originally denoted a populace large enough to sustain a market. As that etymology presages, this social class would grow into a powerful economic and political force in cities and towns. Its members valued dried-grape wines not only for their sweet, durable flavors, but also for the sense of urbane refinement that purchasing and then drinking them conveyed. In turn, these wines initiated something that still holds true today: people buying certain special wines both for their inherent quality and for the status conveyed by their consumption.

The forerunner of modern middle-class consumers, these medieval men and women constituted less than 1 percent of the population. Nonetheless, their presence helped to begin undermining belief in the *scala naturae*, or "great chain of being," the previously unquestioned system in which all of life, including society, was structured in a divinely ordained hierarchy. Medieval feudalism separated mankind into three classes or "estates"—the clergy, responsible for society's spiritual welfare; the nobility or aristocracy, in charge of its military well-being; and the common people, responsible for the production of its material goods. The third of these was by far the largest, and within it, various subdivisions further distinguished people by station—serfs, for example, who had to be servile to their lords, as opposed to freemen, who could have holdings of their own. But the new townsmen belonged to no preestablished rank. They were subjects of a king or duke, but because they lived in a city or walled town, they were not subjects of a feudal lord. Thus they became "citizens." Still commoners, they nonetheless wielded significant muscle, as the economic lifeblood of the community often depended disproportionately on their work. Some became so wealthy that it proved difficult to distinguish them publicly from nobles of the second estate, and by the late Middle Ages, sumptuary laws dictating how each social rank should dress were enacted in many places so as to avoid mistakes. No laws, however, regulated what one could drink, and these urban citizens definitely admired dried-grape wines.

Members of this new social class clearly considered these imported specialties to be potential emblems of standing. They could afford something different from what their peasant ancestors drank, and they much preferred sweet imported wine to sour local wine. They saw it as an acquired and hence displayed taste, much like fine cloth, art, and the foods they liked to eat. Unlike the urban poor, who often had to make do with coarse brown bread and salt fish, they ate whitened bread, soups or stews laden with meat, eggs, fresh fish, and imported fruits (Seville oranges, for example). They seasoned these foods with exotic spices. And they drank foreign dried-grape wine whenever they could afford it. Doing so helped set them apart. Wine clearly was something that could make these medieval men and women both feel and appear different. But not all wine. Not, for example, diluted Latin wine or the vinegary stuff made by farmers living nearby. No, the merchants, bankers, and officials who eventually would destroy medieval feudalism wanted, and would pay for, fine wines—meaning special wines, expensive, imported dried-grape wines.

The Goodman, or Ménagier, of Paris provides a fine example of this new taste. An anonymous merchant or official (some scholars believe he was Guy de Montigny, an aide to the Duke of Berry), he wrote a book of instructions for his young wife in 1393. He was in his sixties, she in her twenties. The book is a moral as well as a practical guide designed to help the woman live well after his death. It has two main sections. In the first, the Ménagier advises his wife on religious and social responsibilities, while in the second he turns his attention to more domestic concerns like gardening, caring for horses, overseeing servants, cooking, and dining. He clearly consumed a good deal of wine, as references to it are sprinkled throughout his manuscript. And he drank many types— local wines from vineyards near Paris, lots of Hippocras, and on certain, special occasions, sweet, imported, dried-grape wines. One such occasion, described in considerable detail, was a banquet he hosted. At it, guests ate fruits, followed by a sort of capon pudding decorated with pomegranate seeds and sugar-coated aniseed, a roast, stews, aspics, cheeses, sweetmeats, pastries, and more. With these they drank various wines, with two singled out by name, Vernaccia and Malvasia. Whether or not these were the Ménagier's personal favorites, they were the ones in which he took the most pride. Serving them allowed him to make a not-so-subtle statement about his social place.

Though the Ménagier does not detail what he paid, sweet wines like these cost considerably more than other wines. As such, they served as emblems of status. Drinking them, or serving them to guests, marked one as a certain kind of person—not just a wine drinker, but as important, a sophisticated wine drinker with taste. Such taste was both physical, the literal sensation of the wine in one's mouth, and mental, for it was part and parcel of an explicitly socially conscious conception of this type of wine's value. So long as these sweet, dried-grape wines were rare and costly, they would continue to be marks of secular standing and sophistication.

Some wines are made with dried grapes today, and must taste something like their medieval antecedents. While contemporary examples, such as Vin Santo and Recioto della Valpolicella from Italy, and Vin de Paille from the Jura in France, are cleaner, they still display raisined flavors. Yet in many places once home to dried-grape winemaking— southern Spain, for example, and the Midi in France—this type of wine has largely disappeared, having been replaced by still headier and more stable wines fortified with spirits. (Fortified wines were not invented until the propagation of distillation for drink in the seventeenth century.) But what has not disappeared is their audience. As with all special wines before them, late medieval Romneys and Vernaccias certainly were consumed by the nobility. But they also were consumed by the nascent bourgeoisie. These dried-grape wines thus provide links to wine's future as well as its past. They represent vestiges of an ancient tradition of production, one necessitated for thousands of years by the difficulties inherent in wine's preservation. But they also represent the first signs of a modern tradition of consumption, one in which high-quality or premium-priced wines become the province of the middle even more than the upper class.

It would take many centuries for this bourgeois tradition to become established widely. Not until the 1800s did large numbers of middle-class men and women come to possess sufficient economic and cultural power to claim special wines as their own. Yet behind the walls of medieval cities, where people like the Ménagier and his wife first displayed a taste for these unusual dried-grape specialties, something new was definitely happening. No longer were allegedly superior aromas and flavors the exclusive property of those privileged by birth. They instead could be enjoyed by people willing (and able) to pay for them. And while the Ménagier's doing just that certainly compelled him to imitate those above him in social rank, there can be little doubt that the satisfaction he took in drinking and serving these wines was very much his own.

Dried-grape wines stopped being such obvious emblems of social privilege once they became more widely available, and hence both less expensive and less exclusive. This happened during the Renaissance, when a new source emerged, one located closer to the thirsty cities of northern Europe. Winemaking in Spain, long outlawed, became a legal and lucrative enterprise with the overthrow of Moorish rule. Most Spaniards, like other southern Europeans, had to make do with acrid, fresh-grape wines, but the well-to-do wanted something else. So vintners in the warmest areas of the kingdom, particularly Andalucía, began to specialize in strong, sweet wines in a raisined style. Much as had happened in Italy some 250 years earlier, they made these for the nobility and clergy, and then for export markets. The rest of the local populace rarely drank them.

The Spanish authorities promoted the sale of these new dried-grape wines actively. In 1491, for example, the Duke of Sanlúcar abolished taxes on wine for export and extended special commercial privileges to English and Dutch merchants. The wine that these traders purchased and transported north was known by various names—Rumney, Sherris, Sack, and others. As the first of these suggests, it was made much like heady Romneys from the eastern side of the Mediterranean. The word "Sherris" is an anglicization of "Jerez," but these wines were not Sherries in a modern sense. Unfortified, their relatively high alcohol levels came from the grapes having been picked after months of baking under the blazing Spanish sun. These grapes were harvested late in autumn, the growing season having been extended or drawn out, the word for which in old Spanish was *sacar*, which may explain the origin of the name "Sack." Though probably made in part with Palomino Fino and Pedro Ximénez grapes, as are more modern Sherries, Sacks were never aged for long. Instead, like all wines at the time, they were sent to market quickly. To reduce costs, winemakers often blended some cheap dry wine with their sweeter, more potent raisined wines. And because the voyage north from Andalucía was shorter and safer than that from Crete, Cyprus, or even Venice, transport was relatively cheap. No wonder Sack became all the rage in Tudor England. Shakespeare's Falstaff, who seems always to be drinking it, says that it has a "twofold operation," as it both produces "excellent wit" and "warms the blood." He credits it for Prince Harry's becoming valiant, and declares, "If I had a thousand sons, the first humane principle I would teach them would be, to forswear thin potations and to addict themselves to Sack."

Like its exotic dried-grape medieval predecessors, Sack's great appeal came in its being so different from fresh-grape wines, virtually all of which were very thin potations indeed. The name denoted a type even more than a particular place of origin. Though the finest and hence most expensive examples came from Jerez, Sack also was made in other parts of southern Spain (notably Málaga), as well as in the Spanish- and Portuguese-controlled Atlantic islands. While it certainly remained something of a luxury, it was much more available to bourgeois consumers than earlier wines made in a comparable style had been—meaning that in the Renaissance, unlike the Middle Ages, non-sour wine could become a fairly common drink of fellowship. Sack remained popular in England even when that Protestant country went to war with Catholic Spain. As part of those hostilities, Francis Drake attacked Cádiz in 1587, destroying some thirty Spanish ships moored in the harbor. Before heading home, he filled the holds of his fleet with cask after cask of Sack. Back in London, "Cádiz wine" became the height of English patriotic fashion, *the* drink with which to celebrate the defeat of Spain's armada the following year.

—⁂—

By the late Middle Ages, commercial trade in wine was not restricted to dried-grape specialties. Demand for more common dry wine was growing ever stronger, fueled in large measure by the growth of northern Europe's urban population. That demand cut across virtually all social classes, as everyone except the very poor and destitute wanted wine. England and then Holland, two countries in which very few people grew grapes and made wine, dominated the international trade. English and Dutch merchants certainly bought, shipped, and sold plenty of sweet, strong southern Sacks and eastern Romneys, but their bigger business was in less costly drier wines. This was not because dry wines now tasted any better than they had before, but because, being significantly less expensive than the sweet Mediterranean ones, they could attract more consumers and thus generate larger profits. So while wines made with fresh grapes still tasted sour, and certainly still proved perishable, international commerce helped them become a staple part of many people's diets even in places where grapes did not constitute a local crop.

The advent of long-distance trade had a profound effect on European culture. As affordable imported goods became more widely available, the old feudal system built around the self-contained manor or castle began to break down. Market fairs became important events on the calendar, and active trade routes developed both inland and at sea. Wine was only one of many goods being shipped by ship or cart, but the demand for it corresponded with the Continent's shifting demographics. New markets for imported wine emerged in places like Flanders, Holland, and northern Germany, as well as in already thirsty cities, including London, where the total population grew from roughly ten thousand at the millennium to some two hundred thousand by

1600. Moreover, beginning in the 1300s, Europe entered a roughly five-hundred-year period of sometimes severe cold known as its "little ice age." The climate in places that previously supported viticulture proved too variable for it, so winemaking had to become more specialized. Yet men and women living in those places—most notably, in England and northern France—wanted wine. Europe's population did decline during the fourteenth and fifteenth centuries (owing to plague and famine), but the people who could afford wine still demanded it on their tables.

Why didn't they drink beer, a beverage that could be produced almost anywhere? Many people, especially the third-estate poor, certainly did, but two factors long prevented beer from challenging wine as an object of cultural desire. The first was taste. Most medieval beers were extremely bitter and spoiled quickly, having a shelf life of less than a week. People in England and Ireland, northern Germany, Scandinavia, and much of eastern Europe all drank grain-based beer—which they often spiced to disguise its flavor—but there is little evidence that they or anyone else valued it as anything remotely special. In fact, travelers regularly disparaged the beer drinkers living in these places. The French poet Eustache Deschamps famously depicted Bohemia as a place filled with "fleas, stink, pigs, mold," where twenty people drink "from one bowl / A bitter drink—it's beer." Like wine, beer was a staple, but since it turned sour even faster than wine did, there was no real trade in it. Most medieval beer was made as part of a regular routine of preparing food beside the hearth. Save for the local innkeeper, no one thought to sell it.

The second factor working against beer is that people widely considered it an inferior product, something worth drinking only if one could not afford wine. This was true not only for the clergy, the nobility, and the emerging bourgeoisie, but also for just about anyone with even a few coins to spend on drink. In grape-growing Europe, which before the little ice age had included parts of northern France, as well as much of western Germany and the Low Countries, beer thus was a drink only for the very poor. Or for the self-deprived—Wazo of Liège, for instance, a pious eleventh-century bishop who during Lent forbade himself wine and drank beer in its place in an act of penance and sacrifice. Comparisons between beer and wine almost always favored wine. According to one twelfth-century Goliardic poem, for example, wine makes the old young, gives light to the eyes, and takes care from the heart, while beer simply gets one drunk. In a similar vein, Aldobrandino of Siena, who catalogued medieval foodstuffs in his *Regimen Corpus*, declared that beer harms the head and stomach, causes bad breath, rots teeth, and results in angry drunkenness. By contrast, wine gives one "good blood, good color, and good flavor." Drinking it "will strengthen all bodily virtues and make a man happy, good-natured, and well-spoken."

Beer's cultural value did begin to increase in the thirteenth century when German brewers started to use hops in its production. These made it both less bitter and more durable. Before then, people had tried to combat beer's inherent bitterness not only by adding spices to the finished product but also by using aromatic herbs during fermentation, most notably bog myrtle in a concoction called "gruit." Nothing worked as well as hops, which imparted a sweet flavor while also acting as an antibacterial preservative. Yet since the taste of these new beers was an acquired one, it took a long time for them to become a viable commodity of trade. When they did, though, hopped beer became the first alternative beverage to threaten wine's cultural dominance. Northern Germany, especially the port of Hamburg, then emerged as the most important center of commercial brewing, and barrels filled with beer were shipped from there all across the North and Baltic Seas.

The commercialization of brewing enabled beer to become a viable substitute for wine. Yet old habits die slowly, and for a long time commercial beer, much like its domestic antecedent, remained primarily a drink of the lower classes. Though the changed climate meant that the wine production border had shifted south, many people living at or above that boundary still wanted wine. They certainly would drink beer if wine prices rose too high, or if war rendered wine supplies scarce, or if a particular cask of wine had turned too sour. But if they could afford it, they preferred wine. By the early Renaissance, merchants were ferrying both beers and wines to cities and towns in the Baltic and Scandinavian countries, England, Poland, even Russia. They sold them in Bergen and Königsberg, Lübeck and Visby, London and Hull. And in all of these places, the nobility and the urban middle class bought the wines, while the poor had to be satisfied with the beers.

German wine was the first dry wine imported throughout northern Europe. As early as 1157, Henry II of England granted the merchants of Cologne the exclusive right to supply wine to his court, a privilege enlarged upon a century later when merchants from Westphalia and the western Baltic joined them to form a single monopoly that would dominate the sale of German wines in England for some three centuries. In addition to supplying the king and his many dependents, they sold wine to English barons, knights, and other landowners. Equally important, they set up shop at large city fairs that were held at regular intervals throughout the country, where the urban populace at large could buy "Rhenish." That term referred to any wine shipped on the Rhine River, whatever its origin. Regardless if made from grapes grown in Alsace in the west or Franconia to the east, the Mosel Valley in the north or Württemberg in the south, and regardless if red or white, it all was Rhenish. This sort of general identification, with the name of a wine reflecting a river or a port rather than a vineyard or grape-growing region, was quite common. Consumers tended to identify wines neither by grape variety nor by grape-growing locale, but rather by their place of transport. During the fourteenth and fifteenth centuries, French wines surpassed German wines in popularity in most northern markets. But they too were identified in terms of where they were shipped—specifically, the names of the Atlantic ports at which the merchants filled their ships, notably La Rochelle and Bordeaux.

The commerce in these French wines was controlled initially not by foreign traders but by local merchants. Some were vintners themselves, but more were buyers holding stocks of wine from many different grape growers and winemakers. The forerunners of today's *négociants*, they purchased and blended wines and then brought these to market. Of course, they did this quickly, since consumers wanted their wines to be as young and fresh as possible. England was the wealthiest market, so these merchants sailed up the Atlantic coast each autumn, bringing that vintage's wines with them. There was no aging or cellaring of the wines, the goal always being to sell, and drink, them as quickly as possible. The merchants sold their wares at fairs in places like Boston and Winchester, huge markets at which people bought all sorts of goods to last through the impending winter. Many enterprising merchants also traveled throughout the country, bringing wine to anyone and everyone who could pay for it.

Before the English started drinking wine from Bordeaux, the region had been an obscure backwater. The Romans had planted vineyards there, and Roman galleys were the first ships to bring southwestern French wines north, but the market had disappeared once the empire fell. Though local viticulture survived, trade in wine did not. By the eleventh century, even the port was in decline, having been eclipsed by its new, thriving rival to the north, La Rochelle. That younger city, founded only a hundred years earlier, attracted commerce from all over Europe. Merchants and traders came there for salt, a precious commodity collected from the lagoons on both the coast and the nearby islands of Ré and Oléron. Yet since salt and wine were staples, it only made sense to load ships with both products. Thus during the twelfth century the flat fields stretching east of La Rochelle in what today is the Charente-Maritime *département* became filled with vineyards. At that point, La Rochelle, not Bordeaux, was the commercial center of the Atlantic wine trade.

War and politics, not wine quality, soon conspired to have Bordeaux surpass its rival and become what it remains today, the world's preeminent wine capital. Both ports were part of the independent Duchy of Aquitaine. But in 1151, when Eleanor of Aquitaine married Henry Plantagenet, the future king of England, the stage was set for the duchy to pass into English hands. (For fifteen years, Aquitaine had been French, as Eleanor originally had married Louis VII of France, separating from him in one of history's more dubious royal annulments.) Even though all Aquitaine wine enjoyed an exemption from English custom taxes, Eleanor and Henry's son, John, ordered wine from Bordeaux for his court as an expression of thanks for that city's having successfully resisted Spanish attack. Not surprisingly, the Bordeaux merchants soon had a much easier time selling their wine to the king's subjects than did their rivals from La Rochelle. Then in 1224, when a French army invaded Aquitaine, Bordeaux's citizenry resisted the assault while La Rochelle's capitulated. From that point forward, boatloads of wine flowed north to England from Bordeaux.

A special relationship began to develop between wine shipped from

Bordeaux and the English marketplace. Despite interruptions due to politics and war, it has remained vital ever since. The relationship's significance comes not only from English drinkers' having consumed a great deal of Bordeaux wine for a long time, but also from their having influenced the wine's style and character, changing and eventually improving it to such an extent that the very best examples came to be considered the finest wines in all the world. Those examples eventually would become objects of both veneration and emulation, so much so that they set a truly international standard of excellence. This did not happen, however, during the Middle Ages or even the Renaissance. It was instead a later, more modern phenomenon, one that began with a handful of late-seventeenth- and eighteenth-century wines that came mostly from the Médoc—a region close to the city that before then was largely forest and swamp, and so unfit for viticulture. By contrast, most medieval and Renaissance wines shipped from Bordeaux came from vineyards much farther afield. They were ferried downriver, loaded aboard boats, and then sent north. The city's initial renown thus was due less to the prestige of its wines than to its status as a bustling port. Bordeaux wines became common fare throughout England and other northern European countries precisely because their transit proved inexpensive. None were at all like today's prized collectibles. Instead, as with virtually all fresh-grape wines of the period, they were pale and perishable. Proof that they deteriorated quickly can be found in the fact that tavern owners would automatically discount and then discard old wine whenever new wines arrived in the market.

By the early fourteenth century, the Bordeaux merchants were exporting nearly twenty-two million gallons of wine annually. That's equivalent to more than 110 million bottles today. Grapes grew all over the greater Bordeaux region. Vineyards came right up to the city walls; just about everyone, rich and poor, clergy and lay, grew vines, and the sale of the resulting wine became the city's dominant business. While nearby regions, including Graves to the south and Entre-Deux-Mers to the north, supplied a great deal of wine, still more came from the *haut pays* farther inland, particularly vineyards in Bergerac, Cahors, Gaillac, and Quercy. Even though these wines were somewhat more expensive than those made from grapes grown closer to the city, the higher price reflecting the greater cost of transport and local taxes, consumers wanted them and so were willing to pay. That's because these wines tended to be slightly stronger and longer lasting, climate conditions inland being less variable than those in places closer to the Atlantic coast. Each September, the wines from these regions would journey downriver to Bordeaux, where they would be transferred into large casks holding about 250 gallons apiece. Called "tuns," these would be loaded on ships whose capacity was measured by the number of casks they could carry safely. Then, in a matter of weeks, they would be unloaded in England and other northern European countries, where they immediately were offered for sale.

As demand for these wines increased, the trade in them gradually shifted from exporters to importers. Northern consumers viewed the Bordeaux merchants as aliens, and with wine now a domestic staple, as it had been for centuries in warmer Mediterranean climes, they wanted to buy it from their own countrymen. In England, native traders began to dominate the island country's wine business. By the 1330s, London importers were selling almost as much wine in that one city as the Bordelais sold throughout the entire country. English merchants now sailed to Bordeaux, where they purchased wine, and then returned home to sell it. They sold it to the Crown, to the butlers who supplied noble and ecclesiastical households, and to taverns (which functioned as retail outlets as well as places in which to eat and drink). As importers, these Englishmen came to exert more and more influence on the Bordeaux négociants. After all, they had the money and so could insist on certain wines at certain prices.

Some of these wines were white, others red, and still others pink. The pink ones were called "Clairet," and were made by co-fermenting dark- and light-skinned grapes. That name eventually turned into "Claret," and by the eighteenth and nineteenth centuries it was being used to refer to deeply colored red wines with a firm tannic structure that allowed for aging—the forerunners of today's classified-growth Bordeaux, as well as all the wines made on that model elsewhere in the world. Thirteenth- and fourteenth-century Clairets, however, were nothing like today's wines. They were made from apparently now-lost grape varieties that, while perhaps the ancestors of the modern Cabernets, Merlots, and Sauvignons that dominate contemporary Bordeaux blends, were treated very differently. For one, the grapes were picked earlier. For another, they were macerated and fermented for a much shorter period of time. Some modern commentators have speculated that medieval Clairet may have tasted something like today's Beaujolais Nouveau, but that comparison does not really seem apt. These grapes were most likely more tannic and less aromatic than Gamay, the variety that yields Beaujolais. Moreover, the wines lived in porous casks, not corked bottles. As a result, they must have lost the effervescent charm of youth quite quickly. By the time they arrived in England, Flanders, or Holland, any such allure had to have largely evaporated, replaced by flavors that would become shriller by the day.

Yet during the late fourteenth century, northern Europe's thirst for Clairet became so strong that the Bordeaux wine fleet sailed twice a year—first in the fall, when the ships were filled with as much of the new harvest's wine as they could carry, and then again in the spring, when they transported what was left. This second shipment, the "reck," consisted of wine that had been racked and transferred to clean barrels, so while not fresh it was at least tastier than what remained for sale. By the end of summer, though, virtually all of the wine in the northern cities was turning very sour, so it was time for the fleet to set sail once again. And this indeed was a fleet. England's King Edward III, fearing French or pirate attack, had commanded that the wine ships bound for his country sail in convoy, some two hundred or so at a time. And while the Bordelais did sell their wine to other countries, England received roughly 80 percent of their exports.

In England and elsewhere, the sale of this and indeed all wine was highly regulated, with prices set by act or edict. Those prices indicate that Bordeaux wine was always common fare, the everyday drink of people up and down the social ladder (though never the very poor, who were stuck with beer, most of it homemade). While the specifics changed frequently, depending on the size, though not the quality, of the particular vintage, this wine invariably came cheap. The law would set a maximum price that a merchant could charge. In 1330, for example, the price in London was fixed at four shillings for a gallon of dry Bordeaux wine, while Rhenish sold for six. This pattern, with German wine costing roughly a third more than Clairet, remained fairly constant. Prices rose later in the century when England went to war with France, but if wine from Bordeaux sold for eight shillings, wine from the Rhine inevitably cost at least twelve. Other wines, however, were much more expensive than either of these two. What were these luxuries, the more exclusive wines reserved for those who could pay? Not surprisingly, they were the sweet, strong, dried-grape wines that could last longer without spoiling—Vernaccia from Italy (thirty-two shillings a gallon in April 1362), Malvasia from Greece (twenty shillings), and Romneys from farther east (sixteen shillings). Centuries later, dry red wine from Bordeaux would become the most expensive and most coveted wine in London and in fact the whole world. Not so in the late Middle Ages and early Renaissance. Bordeaux's popularity at that point came from its great volume coupled with its always low price.

The laws that set prices also regulated sales. The 1330 London act not only decreed "a reasonable price" for various wines, but also commanded "that all taverners of the City shall keep the doors of their taverns and cellars open." The rationale behind this at first odd-sounding order was simple—"so that the buyers of their wines may be able to see where their wines are drawn." As that explanation suggests, fear of fraud was widespread. All wine was stored and hence sold from casks, and many an unscrupulous merchant or tavern owner would try to pass a cheap wine off as a more expensive one. The fourteenth- and fifteenth-century statutes are filled with warnings against such deception. All wines found to be corrupt were to be dumped out and their casks broken. Later edicts promised imprisonment for anyone trying to sell false wine. The sheer number of such warnings, however, suggests that hoaxes were not uncommon. In an age in which most wine tasted sour, and in which no wine came in a labeled bottle, the old admonition *caveat emptor* must have carried great weight.

Though sales reached their peak during the early decades of hostility, the Hundred Years' War between England and France marked the decline of the medieval Bordeaux wine trade. The fighting rendered the sea voyage more perilous and the supply of wine less steady, so English merchants soon sought other sources, particularly in Spain and Portugal. Then in 1453, when the French army captured Bordeaux, all shipments ceased. Two decades later, the Treaty of Picquigny restored commercial trade between the two countries, but by then wine exports were only a fraction of what they had been the century before.

The Bordeaux trade would remain in something of a slumber for the next two hundred years. Grapes were still grown there and wine was still shipped north, but in nowhere near the volume as during the medieval boom years. Part of the problem was political, as all of Europe soon found itself fighting a long series of bitter religious wars. Part also was economic, as new wines from new places, including Sack, had become available in northern European markets. But part, too, involved quality. Clairet had made many fortunes back in the thirteenth and fourteenth centuries, but it always had been a bulk wine. With Bordeaux now in French hands, it enjoyed no special cachet, so wines from other places took its place. As the Renaissance unfolded, English and Dutch traders supplied northern Europe with all sorts of different wines—cheap ones from the Iberian countries as well as western France, and expensive ones from the Mediterranean. They also brought wine to and from their colonies. But they cared little about Clairet, the market for it having largely disappeared.

During the Renaissance and Reformation, when much of Europe was in a seemingly constant state of warfare, importing and exporting a fragile commodity like wine proved difficult. Nonetheless, the range of wines available to consumers, particularly bourgeois consumers, slowly increased. A Dutch burgher in Delft or Leyden, much like an English trader in London, could choose from among wines made in Germany, France, Italy, Portugal, Spain, even Greece and the Levant. Save for the headier, sweeter southern wines, most still quite expensive and all still very much prized, these wines would have tasted similarly sour. Yet there sometimes were subtle differences between them. And as drinkers gradually began to learn to recognize these differences, they also began to think of these wines in less generic and so more particular terms.

When both noble and bourgeois consumers became more discriminating, they began to seek out wines that tasted distinctive or particular. Their doing so went hand in hand with equally subtle changes in the conditions of at least some wines' production. Ever so slowly, a vineyard's exact location began to matter, as did the grape varieties planted there. During the early Middle Ages, viticulture had been widespread throughout Europe, but consumption had been primarily local. By the Renaissance, when grape growing became more specialized, consumption became more wide-ranging. Particular places then came to be known not simply as sources of wine, but more precisely as sources of wines of a specific style, type, or quality. In turn, this association of both style and quality with the particularities of place signaled a significant second step in wine's slow march toward becoming the beverage we drink today. But the first step already had been taken. Men and women, no matter common or noble, religious or lay, now had a nearly thousand-year history of thinking of wine as something secular, its worth or value reflecting its new cultural status as a worldly rather than a spiritual good.

PARTICULAR TASTES
New Wines and New Challenges

People continued to drink plenty of wine during Europe's three centuries of Renaissance and Reformation, but for the first time in history some chafed at having to do so. "Take your Money for your (Stuff call'd) wine, / Which from this time I utterly decline," wrote the Grub Street wit Richard Ames in a seventeenth-century poem titled "A Farewell to Wine." Ames was complaining specifically about the Portuguese and Spanish wines then flooding the English market. "They [go] off more quick," he wrote, and so are "poys'nous Drink." Thus he concluded his verse by declaring that he would rather "leap into the Thames or Severn, / Than Venture on the Wine in any Tavern." Of course, drinkers for thousands of years had never had many, if any, options. Especially in cities, with water disease-ridden and fresh milk or juice usually unavailable, nasty-tasting wine often was the only beverage available to them. But in this age of discovery and exploration, many people began to thirst for alternatives. They found the first one in beer, newly improved owing to the commercialization of brewing that had made it more durable. Then wholly new drinks—alcohols like whiskey and brandy, as well as non-alcohols such as tea and coffee—began to attract interest. These quickly drew so many appreciative consumers that some people started to question why they needed to bother with wine at all, especially since so much of it turned bad so quickly. If more reliable drinks also could satisfy the need to relieve thirst and provide nourishment, why put up with vinegary wine? That question heralded the first real challenge to wine's place in European culture. In the increasingly competitive marketplace of the fifteenth, sixteenth, and seventeenth centuries, dry wine, no longer an unquestioned staple, became less a necessity and more a choice. And when people started thinking of it as such, they needed to find new reasons to buy and drink it. Despite the era's fascination with antiquity, those reasons could not stem from a belief in anything supernatural or divine. Instead, new rationales for drinking wine had to come from what actually was in the cup or cask.

Any such rationale required that people reconsider why they valued wine to begin with. Gradually but inevitably, those with money to spend started to think of it as a sensory pleasure that they might choose to enjoy rather than as a spiritual or secular necessity. Beginning in the late Middle Ages and extending through the Renaissance, these drinkers purchased not only imported Romneys and other sweet wines but also specialized northern European ones that displayed particularly appealing (though still fleeting) aromas and flavors. Made with fresh grapes and fermented dry, these wines acquired a newfound cultural cachet as products worth valuing and choosing for themselves. Primarily because of the care that vintners devoted to their production, they tasted significantly better than other dry northern wines. And owing to their scarcity, they fetched steep prices. The fortunate few who experienced them—at first only the wealthy—then began to differentiate more precisely between quality wine and regular wine, what in France later came to be called *vin fin* and *vin ordinaire*. The gap between these two types grew cavernous, as did the social distinctions between who drank which, as well as when and where they did so. In the process, the very idea of quality became reinvented, and wine began to play a new cultural role, becoming in Richard Ames's words, something that should (but he thought too rarely did) confer "Notes of Pleasure, Love, and Wit."

The arrival of these new specialized wines did not signal the end of the old-fashioned, sour sort of stuff that people had been drinking for thousands of years. Indeed, from the Middle Ages through the Renaissance and Enlightenment, and even well into the modern, industrial worlds of the nineteenth and twentieth centuries, millions of men and women continued to consume vin ordinaire for much the same reasons as their ancestors. It provided them with a relatively cheap source of calories as well as a ready means of inebriated escape. But people chose to drink vin fin for different reasons. The progenitor of wine esteemed today, it was made with special grapes grown in special places, and so tasted individual rather than generic. As a result, it satisfied intellectual and emotional desires in addition to physical ones.

The new conception of quality based on gustatory pleasure required that people identify the specific sources of such pleasure, concentrating on the individual characteristics of the wines they drank. They clearly valued many of the same qualities that contemporary drinkers do. A first-class wine obviously could not taste sour or spoiled, but the mere absence of defects was not good enough. As important, the wine had to evidence positive properties, particularly the crucial threesome of balance, depth, and length. Then as now, for a wine to be judged superior, it needed to have body and substance; lingering, even evolving flavors; with no single element, neither acidity nor tannin nor fruit, overpowering the others. Contemporary connoisseurs believe that these features signal quality. So too did people in the Renaissance and Reformation. After all, they were the first drinkers to prize and pay more for wines with attributes much like those esteemed today.

At first, very few fresh-grape wines displayed any of these characteristics. Instead, most tasted thin and watery, with little concentration. Typically fashioned with under-ripe and therefore vegetal-tasting fruit, their harsh acids invariably left them unbalanced. And the few flavors that lingered on drinkers' palates tended to be undesirable ones coming from bacterial spoilage or oxidation. Romneys and other dried-grape wines, especially those that had been heated, evidenced oxidation too, the sort of taste still recognizable in Italian Vin Santo and French Vin de Paille, but their relatively high levels of alcohol and overt sweetness tended to conceal their other flaws. By contrast, dry, fresh-grape wines remained unmasked. In order to become valued for themselves, they needed to taste deeper, longer, and be better balanced, with distinctive flavors that could set them apart—both from other wines, and from the hopped beers and other beverages beginning to offer consumers new options. Otherwise drinkers, especially middle-class ones like Richard Ames, might well be tempted to bid wine in general a not-so-fond farewell.

Some superior dry wines did exist at the start of the Renaissance, but only a small handful ever came to market. Over the next three hundred years an awareness of these wines developed slowly. They would not become valued broadly in Europe until the 1800s, when new technologies and new scientific knowledge allowed vintners to produce a far wider range. Radical changes then transformed wine's production as well as its consumption, enabling it to become newly respected as an object of cultural connoisseurship. Yet the seeds of change had been planted much earlier—initially in the swales and slopes of viticultural Burgundy, then on the steep hillsides along the Rhine and Mosel Rivers in Germany, and finally in gravelly vineyards near the city of Bordeaux. These were the three areas in which a special or fine wine's identity first became linked with the particularities of place, and in which people began to understand the complex interplay of soil, climate, and culture, which constitute what contemporary enthusiasts call a wine's terroir.

Terroir is itself a modern term. Derived from the Latin *terratorium*, it entered the French lexicon during the Renaissance, but at that point it simply meant "territory." During the nineteenth century it acquired a second meaning as an area of land valued specifically for agricultural properties, but still rarely was employed in connection with wine. Only in the 1900s did it come to be used specifically to designate a vineyard's natural environment, including geology, soil type, topography, climate, and more. Then it also began to signify a particular feature of wines made with the grapes grown in that environment. The presence of this feature, sensed physically but recognized intellectually, explains why discerning drinkers today claim to be able to taste it in fine wines coming from particularly fine vineyards.

As something smelled and tasted, terroir has a mental as well as a physical aspect. When applied to wine, the word means more than just locale. It designates the human recognition of locale and so indicates both what may make a wine from one place taste unlike a wine from another place, and what helps that first wine taste like itself. Put another way, vin fin, unlike vin ordinaire, needs to be self-referential. That is, it has to taste as previous renditions indicate it should taste, meaning above all that it must be true to its origins. A taste, or *goût de terroir*, thus invariably recognizes particularity as a necessary aspect of quality, one understood to be a property of the wine itself.

The first wines to be prized for their ability to display such individualized aromas and flavors were made in Burgundy by white-habited Cistercian monks in the late Middle Ages. Though these devout clerics did not use the word "terroir," they clearly thought of their vineyards and their wines in this new way. Of course the notion that grapes from one place can produce better wine than grapes from another was not new. As the inscriptions on the amphorae in the pharaohs' tombs demonstrated, the ancient Egyptians recognized as much. So did the Greeks, who repeatedly expressed a preference for wines from certain Aegean Islands, as well as the Romans who venerated Falernian and other dried-grape wines from Campania. In antiquity, however, distinguishing between wines simply meant recognizing general merit. There was as yet no sense of a wine's individuality. The Burgundian monks also differentiated between wines in terms of merit or class, but their understanding of their work involved something else as well—identity. When they singled out particular parcels of land for special recognition, they did not necessarily judge the wines from one to be better than the wines from another. They simply contended that those wines tasted different, with particular characteristics that repeated themselves vintage after vintage. Thus they insisted that both the wines and the vineyards needed to be identified as distinct entities. And by doing so, they invented what over the following centuries became a crucial part of our modern concept of high-quality, or fine, wine, a concept that ultimately enabled wine in general to overcome the many challenges that it soon would have to face.

—⁂—

The Cistercian order, founded in 1098, was a dissenting and especially devout monastic society. Its most celebrated member, Bernard de Clairvaux, publicly attacked other religious communities for profaning monasticism's original "rule." He indicted the Benedictine monks living in the large abbey at Cluny for their bellies filled with fat, their beds covered with furs, and their minds awash with sin, and he adapted this basic message to apply to anyone, lay and clergy alike, whose love of earthly things diverted attention from God's work. Bernard attracted scores of followers to the Cistercian movement. By his death in 1153, the order could claim nearly three hundred abbeys or houses, all modeled on the original "new monastery" built south of the city of Dijon in a swampy spot called Cîteaux. Food, architecture, even worship were kept very plain in all of them. Neither carvings nor stained glass adorned these churches; candlesticks were made of iron rather than gold or silver; the monks ate only the simplest meals, and they did so in silence. The Cistercians, sometimes later called Bernardines, wore coarse white wool habits. They fasted frequently, and they drank only the *hemina*, or half quart of wine that Saint Benedict initially prescribed.

It may seem surprising that over the course of the next few centuries such a severe religious order would go on to excel at grape growing and winemaking. Part of the Cistercian revival of Benedict's dictates, however, entailed a renewed emphasis on manual labor—viewed not just as a good in itself but also as a reflection of prayer. By working "under cross and plow," as their motto had it, the monks put their devotion into action. Because they deliberately built their houses in isolated areas, away from towns and hence possible distractions or temptations, their major work came in the fields. All through northern Europe, they drained swamps and cleared woodlands, raised sheep and cattle, planted orchards, and cultivated vineyards.

The Cistercians tended their vines with near-fanatical zeal, and the renown their wines came to enjoy surely owed as much to the care the monks devoted to their work as to the terroirs they discovered. Unlike growers in other regions, who cultivated vines interspersed with different crops, theirs was a monoculture. At the time, most farmers raised grapes alongside other fruits, vegetables, and cereal crops. But the newly plowed swaths of land on the well-drained hills above Cîteaux contained only vines. The monks meticulously recorded which plots produced healthy grapes and which produced sickly ones. They noted where bud break came early and where late, as well as where the fruit matured evenly and where ripening proved irregular. Somewhat surprisingly, they found that significant differences in such matters could come in short measure, with only a few paces sometimes separating an excellent grape-growing spot from a merely good one. When the monks were certain—and it took a great many vintages to become certain—they then marked each separate locale. No matter that vines might be growing in an unbroken swath all the way up a hill, they would distinguish between what they understood to be individual plots on that hill. At times, especially when they prized a specific spot, they would build stone walls around it and create a *clos*—a cloistered or enclosed vineyard. Though most of those walls long since have fallen down, the boundaries between many of the sites that the Cistercians first delineated remain in place today, solidified not by stone but by the rules of the modern French appellation system, as those same borders identify many of contemporary Burgundy's most famous crus.

In Burgundy today, the word "cru" designates both a wine and a vineyard, a celebrated wine from a celebrated vineyard. The Cistercians certainly made celebrated wines, but their significance in the history of wine comes much more from their vineyards. That's because their winemaking techniques were just as rudimentary as those anywhere else. Grapes typically were foot-trodden. With whites, the liquid would be strained into open casks, where it would be left to ferment; with reds, the treading would take place in deep vats, so that the juice and skins could stay mingled together during fermentation. Sometimes, especially in large communities, presses were used, yielding potentially brighter whites and fuller reds. But, regardless of the method, speed always was of the essence. Though no one knew why, everyone understood that excessive exposure to air hastened a wine's souring. Thus all wine was fermented quickly and rushed into barrels as swiftly as possible. As a result, medieval and Renaissance Burgundies were lighter in body, with less alcohol and, in the case of reds, less color, than Burgundies today. The Cistercians made the most invigorating ones, wines that tasted not only unlike other wines but also subtly unlike one another. The monks distinguished them as crus, with names like Chambolle, Corton, Pommard, and Volnay, because they thought those more nuanced differences reflected different terroirs.

Once the Cistercian message of austerity had been heard by northern Europe's rich and powerful—particularly by those who feared that their affection for worldly wealth could endanger their immortal souls— the order received many gifts of land. Some of these either contained vineyards or were suitable to be planted with vineyards. Before long, wine grapes were being cultivated in the Loire and Rhône river valleys, as well as throughout the Duchy of Burgundy. Sometimes the monks actually purchased land, as for instance at Pontigny on the Serein River. They planted white grapes there and created the forerunner of what we know as Chablis. On the east-facing hillsides stretching south from Dijon, an area known today as the Côte d'Or, the Cistercians tended the Cent Vignes vineyard in Beaune, Perrières in Meursault, and Clos Blanc in Pommard—all premier crus now. They also grew grapes in some of today's grand crus such as Les Musigny and Les Bonnes Mares, while Cistercian or Bernardine nuns planted Clos de Tart. But the most celebrated of all Cistercian vineyards, Vougeot, was across the valley and up the hillside from the original monastery at Cîteaux.

This vineyard was (and is) large, some 125 enclosed acres. The monks clearly considered it special, and so used it as a laboratory of sorts to perfect their viticulture. They studied individual vines, grafted cuttings from especially good ones onto weaker-performing ones, and gradually came to grow only two varieties, one for red wine and the other for white. The choice of grape, they realized, was as important as the choice of locale, and the red wines from this particular place benefited from their planting only Pinot Noir, which they called "Noiren." (The white variety was probably a related family member, a precursor of today's Pinot Gris.) Though they initially divided the vineyard in thirds, and then later subdivided it into some fifteen plots, they never marked any of these as separate crus. Again, qualitative differences are not the same as distinctions based on terroir, and the walls at Vougeot demonstrate that the monks tasted something in the wines they made there that compelled them to identify the vineyard as a single entity.

Vougeot and the other Cistercian crus changed perceptions of Burgundy wine. The Benedictines at Cluny certainly owned vineyards, many in places that would become famous later (Gevrey, for instance, and Vosne-Romanée), but their wines always remained largely local fare. Because the Côte d'Or is not on a navigable waterway, wines made there had to be transported to market by horse-drawn cart. Farther west, near the cathedral town of Auxerre, wine could be shipped to Paris on the Yonne River, a fact that explains why thin, tart *vin d'Auxerre* had been the best-known wine from Burgundy until the emergence of the Cistercian crus. In no sense distinctive-tasting, it was easy to ship. But the wines made by the Cistercians tasted sufficiently different to be worth the trouble and expense of overland transport. Often called Beaune wines, after the nearby market town from which they were sold, they were the first unadulterated dry, fresh-grape wines (as opposed to Romneys made with raisins, or medieval piments filled with honey, herbs, and spices) to become widely admired and desired. So they were carted north to Brussels and Ghent, west to Paris, and east to the Saône River, where they would be transferred to barges that sailed south to cities like Lyon, Avignon, and Marseille. By the early Renaissance, Beaune wines were being drunk in Paris at the court of the king and queen of France, by lords and ladies in Flanders, Picardy, and Lorraine, and in the chapter houses of bishops in places like Amiens, Cologne, and Liège. These special dry wines even became the favorites of the papal court, then in residence in Avignon. In 1366, when the poet Petrarch implored Urban V to return to Rome, he had to admit that wines like these could not be found there. The wine-loving pope stayed put.

The Cistercian focus on the particularities of grape and place marked a significant advance in the history of wine. While these monks certainly were not the first people to care about their vineyards or their wines, they were the first to care about their terroirs. Not surprisingly, ambitious lay farmers who saw the prices that these wines fetched began before long to employ equally meticulous viticultural practices. Not only in the Côte d'Or but also in select locales in the Loire and Rhône Valleys, as well as in Alsace and, most notably, in Germany, they labored long and hard to produce vin fin rather than vin ordinaire. Much as with the monks cloistered behind the walls of Vougeot, their goal was to capture an admittedly short-lived taste of individuality.

Proof that such individuality was valued by at least some wine drinkers living outside monastic communities can be found in the supposed exile of Gamay grapes from the Côte d'Or by Philip the Bold, Burgundy's first Valois duke. Easy to cultivate and vigorous, this vine grew alongside the much more finicky Pinot Noir. Because Philip thought that wines made with it displayed "natural bitterness" and tasted "quite foul," he wanted all farmers in the region to follow Cîteaux's example and use only Pinot. So in 1395 he ordered that all Gamay vines be cut down or uprooted, setting a deadline of the following Easter for their removal. Gamay, he proclaimed publicly, is "a very bad and very disloyal plant."

Loyalty from one's subjects makes sense, but fidelity from fruit? Gamay was no novelty in Burgundy. Local farmers cultivated it because it proved hardy and high-yielding. In warm, sunny harvests, they would blend it with later-ripening, less prolific Pinot Noir, while in rainy or frost-plagued years they would use only Gamay and so salvage the vintage. Without it, they feared financial ruin. To whom or what, then, could this grape have been disloyal? The answer is not Philip as a duke, but rather the vineyards of the Côte d'Or as a place—a specific place capable of producing specific wines. Whether fashioned by the Cistercians at Cîteaux or by farmers nearby, all of Philip's favorite red wines were made with Pinot Noir. (Unlike the vast majority of the local citizenry, he could afford them.) So he associated red Burgundy, or Beaune wine, with the variety's distinctive taste. When he drank a wine grown in the same place but made with a different grape, he condemned it as disloyal to its terroir.

Because Gamay was easy to grow and Pinot quite difficult, many farmers ignored Philip's edict. (His grandson tried again to ban Gamay forty years later, with no more success.) In fact, Pinot Noir did not become the sole red grape cultivated in the Côte d'Or's crus until the mid-twentieth century. The wines made with it fetched high prices and enjoyed considerable renown, but few people drank them regularly. For many centuries, most Pinot vineyards were owned by either religious orders or aristocratic families, so not much wine was sold commercially. Nonetheless, the transformation of the Côte d'Or from an obscure backwater to a region producing esteemed terroir-driven wines was an early example of the development of specialized, site-specific grape growing and winemaking, a fundamental change of mind and approach that eventually would include many more wines in many more places.

Ever so gradually, specific regions, and then vineyards and properties within regions, became recognized for specific styles or types of high-quality wine.

Such recognition resulted in large part from the discovery that there are natural affinities between certain grapes and certain places, a discovery that marked a significant advance over the earlier realization that some locations grow fruit more reliably than others. But it also came from farmers in certain places paying more attention to the particularities of their properties—where the soil profile might change within a vineyard, for example, or where a slight shift in contour brought more sunlight to the vines. Yet for a long time, few vintners could afford to devote this sort of attention to grape growing. Until new techniques and instruments for winemaking and wine storage were invented, virtually all dry wines lasted at best a year or so before turning undrinkably sour. Even the famed Côte d'Or crus never retained their appeal for long. No matter how fastidious the winemaker, air inevitably would seep through the staves of his casks, liquid would evaporate, and bacteria multiply, leading the remaining wine to begin its inexorable decline.

During the Renaissance, only one place produced dry wines that retained even a semblance of vigor. In Germany—owing in part to the arrival of a special grape, and in part to the construction of particular casks for storage—some select wines were able to remain lively for a relatively long time. Like the Côte d'Or crus, these Mosel wines and Hocks (after the village of Hochheim on the Rhine) displayed true distinction and expressed their terroirs. But unlike virtually all other dry wines, they stayed fresh-tasting past the vintage. Old German wine, meaning wine from one or at most two harvests past, then became something that people actually wanted to drink—so much so that a seventeenth-century playwright could have a character praise "the best old Hock" as an especially good "drink in a morning."

Wine-laden barges had journeyed down the Rhine for centuries, but most German wines remained relatively common fare, much as Rhenish had been in the Middle Ages. Primarily white, these wines tasted tart, and like all northern European wine, they proved extremely perishable. As in Burgundy, the first people to try to make something better were Cistercian monks. In 1136, a group of brothers founded what would become a large monastery, Kloster Eberbach, in the Rheingau. Like their compatriots did at Vougeot, though more rapidly since the entire property had been a single bequest, they cleared the forest, planted grapes, and, after numerous trials and errors, enclosed a vineyard—the sixty-two-acre Steinberg. For a while, they used the same grapes as in Burgundy, but before long they discovered that this was an entirely different place. Red varieties did not ripen as well, and the resulting wines tasted much shriller than those from Cîteaux. So gradually they converted the vineyard to white grapes—the Burgundian imports initially, then hardier local varieties like Elbling. Kloster Eberbach came to control more than two hundred Cistercian houses along the Rhine, most of which had vineyards of their own. The monks shipped the wine downriver, to markets in Flanders, Holland, and across the sea to England and Scandinavia.

During the late fifteenth and early sixteenth centuries, German wine experienced a surge in popularity, in large measure because of a series of freakishly warm vintages. Yet most growers still pursued quantity at the expense of quality. Since their wines invariably had a short life, they wanted to make and sell as much as possible. Then in the 1500s, some farmers began planting a new grape called Riesling. No one knows exactly where this variety came from or who first promoted it, but quality-minded vintners, religious and lay alike, quickly recognized that it yielded superior wines. This superiority involved flavor, but even more longevity. Wines made with Riesling sported very high levels of acidity, which not only enabled them to taste refreshing but also acted as a preservative, especially if the wines were stored in big casks, or tuns, that could be topped off regularly in cold cellars.

Enthusiasm for this new grape and wine was interrupted by religious and political warfare, but it revived in the 1600s. The revival proved most notable at wealthy estates or abbeys, particularly those in the Rheingau and on the Mosel and its tributaries—at Saint Maximin in Trier, for example, and at the war-ravaged Benedictine abbey at Johannisberg (later rebuilt as a castle, or *schloss*). The wines made at these properties were stored in massive wooden tuns, some of which could hold over thirty-five thousand gallons and which only very wealthy proprietors could afford to have built. These had the distinct advantage of allowing only a very small percentage of the wine stored within them to come into contact with air. Since new wine was added whenever older wine was taken out, the contents could stay bright and lively longer than other fresh-grape wines.

With the passage of time, these new wines tasted ever more distinctive, the result in large measure of their uncanny ability to maintain vitality while acquiring new, nuanced flavors. Such flavors, mineral-rich and stony, proved very alluring. Before long, people began to identify subtle distinctions between wines coming from separate vineyards. Those distinctions became more pronounced the longer the wines stayed in their tuns, and could be traced to nothing except the differences in terroirs.

Of course, as soon as any wine was removed from its cask, it began the inescapable process of spoiling. Unless transported in completely full barrels, exported German wines did not have a significantly longer life than other dry wines. Much as happened with the Burgundy crus, an appreciation for fine German wines thus remained the province of a select few—primarily the aristocratic or religious owners of the properties where they continued to taste special. Like the Cistercian vineyards, these also were cloistered places. Most German growers cultivated more prolific grape varieties and made more generic-tasting wines. Only a select few, working largely in seclusion, could afford to devote the care and the resources to producing fine, because specialized, wines.

This sort of specialization involved making specific types of wine in specific locales and in specific ways. So even in areas known primarily as sources of bulk wine, some vintners in particular subregions began to specialize in wines that were anything but ordinary. That's exactly what occurred in Bordeaux, though not on a wide scale until the 1700s. Before then, no one paid much attention to the exact origin of a Bordeaux wine. Customers cared more about the merchant selling it, and contracts specified simply that the wine should not taste of rot or vinegar, rather than that it come from a particular place. Yet the initial phase of Bordeaux's specialization belongs in this chapter of wine's history. It came a century earlier, and brought to what would become the modern world's most famous wine region the first awareness of its own terroirs.

Specialization in Bordeaux began with one man—Arnaud III de Pontac, a leading nobleman and the first president of the regional parliament—who insisted that the red wine from his family's estate was something distinct and different. That estate, located south of Bordeaux in the dry, gravelly subregion of Pessac, had been in the Pontac family for many years. Arnaud's father, like his father before him, had grown grapes and made wine there. As was true with all the commercial grape growers in the region, the Pontacs sold their wine every year to négociants, who then blended it with other wines, giving them a sufficient stock to take to market. Arnaud, however, was determined to do something else. He thought of his wine as unique, and he wanted to offer it to customers as such. Yet because he sold it in casks, there was little he could do to prevent whoever purchased it from using it as part of a merchant's large blend—except, he thought, charge more for it. His reasoning was that if his wine cost twice as much as other Bordeaux wines, no one would sacrifice it to a generic mélange. So he did just that. Starting in 1660, he demanded a premium price for a wine with a name that no one beyond Bordeaux knew—"Haut-Brion," his family estate. Three years later, the author Samuel Pepys tried it at the Royal Oak Tavern in London. Writing in his diary, he described the experience: "Drank a sort of French wine, called Ho Bryan, that hath a good and most particular taste that I ever met with."

Because no records indicate that this wine was made with special grapes, or that special viticultural or oenological practices were employed at Haut-Brion, most commentators have concluded that Arnaud III de Pontac's talent came more as a marketer than as a vintner. After all, he sent his son to London five years later to open a tavern, where his wines were sold exclusively and at quite steep prices. (Named Pontack's Head, it remained in business for more than a century.) Yet before Arnaud could market his wine, he must have sensed that there was something special about it other than its name. His estate was a distinct block of land, and simply by insisting that the wine from that block not be blended with other wines, he indicated that he viewed the wine as distinctive, or "most particular." Where could that distinction or particularity have come from, except from the place itself? Arnaud clearly took exceptional pride in his property, his vineyard, his terroir. That's why he spoke of his wine, sold it, and marketed it as an individual entity coming from an individual place. As Samuel Pepys's description indicates, this was in no sense false advertising. As soon as the then-thirty-year-old Englishman took a sip, he recognized that "Ho Bryan" simply did not taste like the other wines being poured at the Royal Oak Tavern. It may or may not have been better, but it clearly seemed different.

No one today knows exactly what this wine tasted like, winemaking and grape growing having changed too much over the centuries. Yet plenty of evidence suggests that it was special, and that its distinctive taste could be traced to the vineyard. The philosopher John Locke visited Haut-Brion in 1677 and described it in terms that definitely anticipate the modern notion of terroir: "The vine de Pontac . . . grows on a rising open to the west, in a white sand mixed with a little gravel, which one would think would bear nothing; but there is such a particularity in the soil, that at Mr. Pontac's, near Bordeaux, the merchants assured me that the wine growing in the very next vineyards, where there was only a ditch between . . . was by no means so good." Those same geological and topographical features contribute to flavors that some contemporary connoisseurs claim to taste in current wines from Château Haut-Brion, and there is no reason to think that comparable flavors could not have been discerned 350 years ago as well. Today, wines made at nearby properties, even neighboring Château La Mission Haut-Brion, display somewhat different profiles. The British critic Clive Coates calls it "fascinating" that, despite their proximity, today's Haut-Brion and La Mission "remain two entirely distinctive wines." La Mission, he writes, is "the more minerally, the more austere, the more apparently tannic," while Haut-Brion is marked by "warm brick, aromatic flavors, roundness and spice." Such distinctions may sound subtle, but they help account for particularity—not just the one wine tasting unlike the other, but also each wine tasting like itself. No doubt, the seventeenth-century wine was quite different from the twenty-first-century one. Nonetheless, as Coates concludes, "terroir will out!"

Arnaud de Pontac's Haut-Brion model did not become widely followed right away in or around Bordeaux, but by the end of the seventeenth century a flurry of planting began to transform the region from a source of fairly cheap bulk wine to one of the world's most important sources of fine wine. The new improved wines came from estates with now fabled names, such as Lafite, Latour, and Margaux, properties whose boundaries also were based on the idea of terroir. These estates were located in what before had been unplanted land—the Médoc, a low-lying swath stretching northwest from the city of Bordeaux. Previously forest, marsh, and swamp, this area recently had been drained by Dutch engineers, exposing gravelly soil well suited for vines. The new, ambitious owners purchased the stoniest, best drained spots available. Like the Pontac family, they too tried to sell their wines under their own names. At first only those who had selected the top sites succeeded, and all the rest had to sell their wines to négociants who used them in the blends that continued to make up the great majority of Bordeaux's production. Yet by the dawn of the eighteenth century, more people, many living far away from Bordeaux, wanted something different—the "most particular" new dry Clarets.

Much as happened with the early crus in Burgundy, at first only the rich could afford these new and special Bordeaux wines. They became especially fashionable in Restoration and Georgian England. John Hervey, the first Earl of Bristol, kept an expense book in which he recorded his wine purchases for fifty-four years. He began in 1688, but until he purchased four casks of Haut-Brion in 1702, he identified all his wines with generic regional names such as Rhenish and Sack. From that point on, however, he bought many Clarets identified by estate—Haut-Brion again in 1705, 1707, 1709, and 1714; Margaux six times; "La Tour Claret" once; and "La Fittee Claret" twice. Owing to prohibitions against French imports, these had to be smuggled into England. Middle-class tavern-goers could not get them, but such subterfuge only added to their allure among the aristocracy.

Unlike the crus from Burgundy's Côte d'Or and the long-lasting German Rieslings, the new Bordeaux wines were made with an assemblage of different grapes. These included Cabernet Franc and Carmenère, along with other varieties no longer grown today. (Cabernet Sauvignon, a chance offspring of Cabernet Franc and Sauvignon Blanc, appeared later in the eighteenth century, while Merlot arrived in the nineteenth.) This does not mean, however, that they expressed the

particularity of place any less than the Burgundians. The taste of terroir does not depend on a single grape. Rather, it requires choosing the
varieties that grow especially well in the specific site, and then cultivating them with extreme care—regulating yield, for example, so that
wines made from them can taste distinctive. That is precisely what the
proprietors of the new Bordeaux estates did. Rather than have peasant
families work as sharecroppers, they hired specialized workers to tend
their vineyards. They also began to propagate superior vines, using the
best-performing ones from their own properties as the source of new
plant material. And they started to harvest different grape varieties at
different times, rather than picking everything all at once. In the cellars,
they experimented with racking wines off the dead yeasts instead of
leaving them in barrels to become infected by bacteria and acquire dirty
flavors, as well as with fining them with egg whites to render them clear
rather than hazy. Much as with the Cistercians in Burgundy centuries
before, their improvements were based on trial and error, not scientific
knowledge. Yet like the monks, the new Bordeaux vintners succeeded in
making a new type of wine. And eventually that new type would serve
as a stylistic model for winemakers all across the globe.

—m—

During the Renaissance and Reformation, production of the new
terroir-driven wines always remained small. Thus an appreciation for
particularity linked to place developed slowly. For a long time very few
wines demonstrated anything of the sort, so very few consumers had
the opportunity to experience it. Those who did invariably lived in or
near cities, as the markets for these special wines were always primarily
urban. The iconic image of a farmer drinking the unspoiled fruit of the
earth in his own vineyard has a certain pastoral appeal, but it is largely a
romantic fantasy. Hardly any individual grape growers had the knowledge or the financial means to make vin fin. And even those few who did
possess the necessary resources characteristically found an audience for
their wines in the city (or at court), not in the country. Thus the paradox
of terroir-driven wines: their distinctive taste originates in nature, but
the human recognition and appreciation of that taste always have come
more in man-made, usually urban settings.

Not only did few people have an opportunity to try this era's better wines, most consumers did not even know they existed. Their distinctive flavors represented the advance guard of wine's modernization, but until the 1700s the vast majority of drinkers continued to consume the same sort of wines as their forebears—thin, sour ones much of the time, and fuller-bodied, sweeter ones only if or when they could afford better. Flavored piments continued to be popular, as did sweet wines in any form. Whether made with dried grapes or adulterated with honey and spice, syrupy wine remained a Renaissance favorite. This was in part because, much as had been true in the Middle Ages, palates of the day preferred sweet flavors. But it also stemmed from the fact that so much dry wine continued to taste so bad.

Because vintage variation proved much more extreme than it is today, overall wine quality during the fifteenth, sixteenth, and seventeenth centuries was notoriously inconsistent. In years marked by spring frost, harvest rain, or cool weather that prevented ripening, the resulting wines could taste dreadful. Rhenish from cold years like 1529, for example, was so tart that Lutheran and other mainstream Protestant drinkers pejoratively dubbed it "Anabaptist," and called for it to be discarded or destroyed. The wines of west-central France, often still referred to as "Rochelle" after the city from which they were shipped, were made with grapes that frequently struggled to ripen. In cold years, they tasted so green that they were known as "hedge wines." Many vintners continued the old practice of masking such flavors by adding other ingredients. In addition to honey and spice, they adulterated their wines with such diverse things as lead, molasses, wood shavings, powdered lime, citrus peel, beetroot, and sloe berries. In an unintentional nod toward ancient practices, they even sometimes added pine sap.

Cultural history often focuses on the social elite, if only because the upper classes have provided us with fuller records of their lives. With Renaissance wine, we know much more about what the nobility drank than about what was available to the rest of society. Yet it seems clear that fine wines were priced out of reach of most people, and that even common wines, especially when imported, cost more than either the rural peasant or the urban laborer often could afford. In Elizabethan London, for example, a gallon of Claret cost roughly half a working-man's daily salary, and a gallon of Rhenish half again as much. Prices may have been somewhat lower in the Mediterranean wine-producing countries, but no evidence suggests that the lower classes in Florence or Barcelona ever drank wine that displayed anything remotely resembling "most particular" flavors. But they did drink wine, often diluted, and often made out of rotting grapes deemed unacceptable for higher-quality lots, or *cuvées*. They needed it because for a long time little else was available to them. Especially in towns and cities, sanitation continued to be a constant problem. Human waste ran through the streets, cesspits leaked into wells, and infection could become epidemic. Bad wine always proved preferable to contaminated water.

The working poor sometimes received wine as a condition of their employment. Domestic servants, for example, drank it with meals provided by their masters. Soldiers and sailors, often conscripted against their will, were given daily rations, as were members of North Atlantic fishing crews. And in Venice, the state-owned Arsenale, a combination shipyard, armory, and warehouse, employed some 2,500 laborers, all of whom were supplied with over two quarts of diluted wine to drink at work each day. There can be little doubt that this wine was of ordinary if not downright poor quality. But there also can be no question that the Venetian authorities, much like the workers themselves, thought of it as something necessary for productive labor.

Though Calvinists and other Protestant reformers frequently condemned excessive drinking, this era was no less inebriated than the Middle Ages had been. Men and women continued to drink, and drink copiously, because they both needed and wanted to do so. Life remained hard, and alcohol provided respite as well as nourishment. Northern Europeans, especially the Protestant Dutch, English, and Germans, were famed for their abundant consumption. These people drank wine, but they also consumed a great deal of beer. Commercial brewers had learned how to produce a consistent, reliable product, and so not only satisfied an existing demand but also created many new markets. As a result, commercially produced hopped beer became popular in many places (northern France, for example) in which the populace previously had drunk mostly wine.

Beer consumption in Europe reached its highest historic level around

1600, with many new beer drinkers being people who once had consumed wine regularly, as surely had their forefathers. Because it could be produced year-round, beer generally cost less than all but the very worst wines. In the city of Ghent, for example, a late-sixteenth-century laborer could buy a quart or so of beer for less than a third of the money he would have to spend on a comparable amount of wine. Low prices encouraged consumption, and with quality high, few people still thought beer inherently inferior to wine. Brewing also took place in Europe's newly established colonies. The Spanish in Bolivia and Peru learned from the Incas how to brew *chicha*, or corn beer, and both English and French settlers in North America planted barley specifically to make beer. Later colonists, dissatisfied with the quality of what they were brewing, began to import heavily hopped beer, including English Porter and what would become India Pale Ale.

Wine was produced in the various colonies too. In warm climes the colonists tried to make raisined, Romney-like wine to ship back home, while in cooler ones they concentrated on more common, dry wines for their own consumption. The Spanish came first, both as an empire and as a global wine-producing power. They planted vines in the Canary Islands off the coast of Morocco in the 1490s, and sweet Canary wines, often made with sun-dried Malvasia grapes, became very popular in the sixteenth and seventeenth centuries. Available in both white and red versions, Canaries fetched premium prices not only back home in Spain but also in northern Europe. Demand for them became so intense that grapes soon replaced most other crops on the islands, and the people living there even had to import grain for bread. Much the same thing happened on the Portuguese island of Madeira. Wine sales there benefited from the close political ties between Portugal and England, and English merchants oversaw the production of sweet, raisined wines made much like late medieval Sack.

Virtually any dry wine transported across the oceans in the sixteenth and seventeenth centuries would have arrived at its final destination in poor shape, the long voyage having sloshed it around in often leaky casks, some wine evaporating, the rest oxidizing. People living in Europe's many colonies thus did not import much wine. They instead tried to make their own. Cortés, who had brought wine with him (and watched it turn to vinegar) when he led the Spanish invasion of Mexico in 1519, decreed five years later that anyone settling in what later would become Mexico City had to plant a vineyard. At much the same time, Giovanni da Verrazano, exploring the Atlantic coast of North America, was delighted to find grapes growing wild there. They reminded him of his native Italy because the vines snaked up the trunks and out along the branches of trees. If they could be "dressed in good order," he predicted, "without all doubt they would yield excellent wine."

North American settlers made wine from these native grapes as well as from imported European ones. In Virginia's Jamestown, English officials required each household to cultivate a vineyard. In South Africa, where vines were not indigenous, Dutch colonists planted French grapes, both to sustain themselves and to supply the ships that stopped there for provisions on the way to Java and the East Indies. Across the ocean to the west, Portuguese settlers cultivated vineyards in the São Paulo state of Brazil, much as their countrymen did to the east, near Goa in India. In short, wherever Europeans for whom wine was a regular part of life explored and settled, they brought wine and vines with them.

Yet the wines that these colonial settlers made do not play a significant role in this history. They apparently tasted neither good nor distinctive, and so did little to contribute to the emergence of modern wine. One reason was that winemaking conditions tended to be quite primitive. Colonial vintners encountered all the difficulties faced earlier by Europeans, so their wines frequently were unstable, spoiled quickly, and tasted vinegary. Another reason was that the new lands contained new pests and new diseases, often making viticulture difficult if not impossible. And in North America, contrary to Verrazano's prediction, the native grapes that grew so abundantly yielded wines that tasted terrible. They reeked of something resembling animal musk, and the common pejorative used to describe them was (and still is) "foxy." No one knows exactly where this term originated, but by 1705 Robert Beverley's *History and Present State of Virginia* condemned both their "rank Taste when ripe" and their bouquet, which he said resembled "the smell of a Fox."

The poor quality of most colonial wines helps explain why so many settlers turned to other forms of alcohol when they became available—

to rum in Africa and India, to brandy in South America, and to corn or rye whiskey in North America. Though wine continued to be consumed in virtually all the colonies, it rarely took center stage. With one notable exception, and not until the late 1700s, no New World wines were considered to be of high quality. But even then, that exceptional wine had little to do with terroir, a notion that would not gain any credence in non-European vineyards until the late twentieth century. Instead, it was a throwback, the last wine made in an old-fashioned Romney style with dried, raisined grapes to attract a wide, enthusiastic audience.

That wine was called Constantia. Coming from an estate of the same name near Cape Town in South Africa, it tasted heady and sweet, and became coveted by European connoisseurs. Part of its allure was its scarcity, as there never was very much to go around. But part too was its by-then exotic character. Constantia came in dark and light versions, both made primarily with dried Muscat grapes. Most important, owing in large measure to the use of modern methods, including bottles and corks, it could age for a long time without turning sour. Kings and queens, lords and ladies, clamored for it. Drinking Constantia allegedly helped people overcome discontent or forget defeat. Napoleon sipped it on Saint Helena, and a character in Jane Austen's *Sense and Sensibility* extolled "its healing powers on a disappointed heart."

Though old-fashioned and raisined, Constantia did have one thing in common with the new terroir-based Clarets, the best German Rieslings, or the crus from the Côte d'Or, as it was consumed primarily by the social elite. So long as all these special fine wines were produced in small volume, they could not reach a big enough audience to affect how the population at large thought about wine in general. And beginning in the 1600s, some people began to think that they neither wanted nor needed wine, particularly coarse, vinegary dry wine. Other drinks— first the new, superior hopped beers, and then whole sets of completely new beverages—were starting to challenge wine's age-old cultural monopoly. As a result, wine started to be viewed, especially by all those who had never tasted vin fin, as something antiquated, even archaic, the drink of generations past but not of the increasingly enlightened present. Put another way, forward-thinking minds wanted something new, and wine seemed old.

—⁊⁊—

By the close of the Renaissance, a bevy of new drinks had arrived in European markets to present wine with its first great cultural challenge. Initially, distilled spirits became popular. They were full of fire and warmth, and most important, they proved stable and so traveled safely. Soon afterward, a completely new set of nonalcoholic beverages started to become fashionable. Made with boiled water, they proved both safe and alluring. Alongside spirits like gin and brandy, hot sipping beverages such as tea, coffee, and chocolate changed the common perception of drink in general. Expanding the range of consumer choice, they soon started competing with one another, and with wine, for public favor. Previously, the only differences in what people drank came from class or rank. Ancient priests and kings consumed wine as commoners drank barley beer. Roman patricians downed Falernian while plebeians had *posca*. And in the Middle Ages, both lords and newly rich burghers enjoyed sweet Romneys when serfs had only sour, local *piquette* to provide them with a modicum of nourishment. But by the seventeenth century, for the first time in history, people of various social ranks could opt for different beverages at different times in different places. Only the very poor in the Mediterranean grape-growing countries remained stuck with vinegary wine. Everyone else had choices, and often desirable ones at that.

Spirits definitely constituted an extremely exciting new option. Though distillation had been practiced in ancient Babylon, the first vessels specifically designed for it, the forerunners of modern pot stills, had not been constructed until the second or third century CE. Alchemists such as Maria Prophetissa in Alexandria used them, not to manufacture drink but to make medicines and perfumes. Distillation is a method of separating liquid mixtures based on differences in volatility, and it can produce a wide variety of products. Early practitioners, particularly in North Africa and the Near East, distilled flowers and herbs to get what they sometimes called "perfumed waters." Paradoxically, abstemious Muslims then brought the practice (along with the word *"al-koh'l"*) to Europe, where in the thirteenth century the alchemist and physician Arnaldus de Villanova made something he called *aqua vitae*, meaning water of life, even though the heat required to make it could burn and kill. De Villanova thought of the fiery liquid as a medicine, and most Europeans until the 1600s considered distillation to be part of an apothecary's craft.

Distillation specifically for the purpose of making drink seems to have first taken place in fourteenth- and fifteenth-century Germany, though the practice does not appear to have been very widespread. The equipment likely was crude, but then the process was (and is) quite simple. Since alcohol vaporizes at a lower temperature than water, the distiller simply needs to collect the vapor from a boiling compound and then let it cool back into a "spirituous" liquid. The Germans called their distillates "burned" or "hot" water, and they made them by boiling soaked grain. Since they also soaked grain to make beer, they likely distilled beer, and perhaps some wine, as well. Yet what they made was still considered primarily medicinal. Alcoholic spirits, often prescribed as preventatives for plague and other illnesses, were not yet widely drunk for either sustenance or sensory pleasure. That began to happen only in the sixteenth and seventeenth centuries, with Dutch rather than German entrepreneurs taking the lead. They deliberately promoted these new, forceful drinks as an alternative to weak, sour wines. From that point on, distilled alcohol's cultural role changed forever. There simply was no going back to wine as the sole or even primary staple.

The Dutch merchants who had sailed to La Rochelle in western France for many years to buy salt also had purchased wine there. But because Renaissance long-distance trade offered northern European consumers increased choices, the thin, vegetal wines of the region had become difficult to sell. So the Dutch thought up a new use for them: distilling the wines into clear brandy. At first, they shipped this young *brandewijn* home to Holland, but they soon realized that they could make more money by having the farmers distill it in France. (A cask held the same volume of liquid, whether brandy or wine, but the more potent brandy would sell for a much higher price.) So beginning in the 1600s, in cities and towns like Saintes and Cognac along the Charente River, the winter air each year became heady with the scent of distillation as more and more of the area's wine went into stills. The Dutch drank and sold the brandy clear and young. Because it tasted harsh, they often flavored it with flowers, herbs, sweets, and spices, much as vintners did with wine. Not until late in the century did another market emerge that wanted brandy, and would pay for it, after it had turned brown and mellow from being aged in barrels. That market was English (and to some extent Irish), and British merchants during the early eighteenth century were the first to specialize in aged, smooth "Coniack brandy."

Brandy is not the only drink that seventeenth-century distillers made. Sugar cane from the West Indies served as the base for rum; grain was used to make whiskey and gin; potatoes, to make vodka. And the Dutch were not the only producers. Distilling spirits soon became big business in Ireland and Scotland, Scandinavia, eastern Europe, Russia, North America, and to a lesser extent wine-producing countries, including France, Italy, and Spain. Spirits had one great advantage over wines. Not their potency, even though drunkenness remained very common. No, the advantage lay in their stability. Unlike wines, spirits simply didn't spoil. They could be exposed to air, to heat, to cold—it didn't matter. So they could be shipped and transported easily, and neither merchants nor consumers needed to worry about their condition. Spirits certainly tasted harsher and headier than wines, but they easily could be diluted or cut with water, with the added benefit of making the water safer to drink. Given the poor quality of so many Renaissance-era wines, it's surprising that these new alcoholic drinks didn't totally eclipse wine in the marketplace. Yet while wine never disappeared, its popularity certainly waned. It once had been virtually everywhere. Now, it was something to choose from among a crowded field.

By the dawn of the eighteenth century, spirits were being consumed ever more widely and ever more often. The middle and upper classes drank them, but so too did the urban poor. Cheap liquors quickly established themselves as an ordinary, though sometimes dangerous, part of social life in cities in Europe and in all of Europe's many colonies. Not surprisingly, alcoholism then became a serious social problem. Particularly for the poor and destitute, hard spirits being a source of calories and stimulation brought sometimes vicious consequences.

Whether gin in England, vodka in Russia, brandy in France, or rum in Spain, distilled spirits nonetheless remained extremely popular. Since the growth of Europe's urban populace meant that families often found themselves living in cramped rooms, imbibing was a communal activity. The public audience for liquor remained largely male, and men tended to drink copiously all through the day. Not surprisingly, drunkenness proved rampant. In one English town, according to Dr. Samuel Johnson, "all the decent people . . . got drunk every night." They were not, he hastened to add, "the worse thought of." This lust for inebriation crossed all national boundaries. Firm figures do not exist with which to trace the sales of spirits as compared to wines, but the new alcohols definitely disrupted the wine trade. So did the arrival of that other new set of stimulating beverages—chocolate, coffee, and tea. These started to be imported in volume in the seventeenth century, and then became truly fashionable in the eighteenth. They too contested wine's place in the commercial market and so in consumers' minds.

These non-alcohols were made with new ingredients that had to be imported from new worlds. Coffee was introduced to Europe in the sixteenth century by Venetian merchants who purchased beans (and learned how to roast them) from Ottoman traders. Some one hundred years later, the Dutch, English, Portuguese, and Spanish were planting trees and harvesting beans in their colonies in the East and West Indies, Brazil, and Central America. Similarly, tea first came to Europe when Portugal established a trading company in Macao. Then both the Dutch and the British East India Companies imported it in volume and popularized its consumption. And by the mid-1600s, the Spanish, who had introduced chocolate to Europe's courts in the previous century, were using African slave labor to grow cacao plants on their Central American plantations. (The French would follow suit in West Africa.) Served as a drink and flavored with two other imports, cane sugar and vanilla, chocolate was initially a coveted luxury item. Much like coffee and tea, it became widely available only after the European powers came to control its production. All three, then, can be considered imperial drinks.

People today tend to distinguish sharply between alcoholic and non-alcoholic beverages, but few drew that distinction before the 1700s. After all, water was the only widely available nonalcoholic drink, and it frequently was unsanitary. But the arrival of tea, chocolate, and especially coffee significantly changed how people conceived of drink in general. These beverages also could alter one's mood, but they did so differently from those containing alcohol. Chocolate became all the rage first, then coffee and tea. All three, though, occupied much the same cultural place. They were truly new—that is, they had been unknown to the ancients—and since they stimulated clear thinking (due to the presence of caffeine), they seemed to embody the emerging Enlightenment ideals of reason and progress. Jules Michelet, an eighteenth-century French writer, called coffee "the sober liquor, powerfully cerebral," and noted that "unlike alcohol, [it] increases clarity and lucidity." He could have been talking about chocolate or tea as well, especially since all three beverages were commonly served in the same place, a coffeehouse as opposed to a tavern.

Europe's first coffeehouse opened in Venice in 1645. Before long, similar businesses began operating in other large cities. London's first, in Cornhill, opened in 1652. Twenty years later, one of its owners, a man named Pasqua Rosée, crossed the English Channel and started one in Paris. And in 1683, following the Battle of Vienna, the first coffeehouse opened in that city, using spoils collected from the defeat of the Turkish army. By the dawn of the eighteenth century, such establishments had become ubiquitous throughout urban Europe. They were not just places where one drank. As important, they were places in which one reasoned—not loudly or irrationally, but, as befit the era, logically and sensibly. People frequented coffeehouses to learn the latest news, exchange information, conduct business, discuss politics and philosophy, all accompanied by copious cups of hot, caffeine-laced drink. Centers of intellectual exchange, coffeehouses were where the Age of Reason did much of its work. (Adam Smith wrote a good deal of his *Wealth of Nations* in one in Edinburgh, much as Denis Diderot and Chevalier Louis de Jaucourt compiled their *Encyclopédie* in one in Paris.) Like the beverages served in them, they were wholly new institutions, a far cry from old-fashioned taverns, where wine, beer, and spirits were served, and where conversation invariably proved less intellectual. Most important, no one ever staggered around drunk or flew into an inebriated rage in a coffeehouse.

Much the same was true of another new type of establishment that would emerge in the next century. This one also took its name from what it served—here something called a *restaurant*, a word that in the parlance of France's *ancien régime* designated a soothing light soup or bouillon. Made with long-cooked meat or fowl, *restaurants* were clear nonalcoholic liquids that served as light meals. Thought to be very healthy, they were particularly prized by people who felt themselves in need of physical restoration (hence their name). Businesses serving them began opening in Paris in the 1760s. As *L'Avantcoureur*, a popular journal, put it when announcing a new one, "Those who suffer from weak and delicate chests . . . will be delighted to find a public place" in which to restore themselves. Because this *salle de restaurateur* also made available "the many new periodicals that appear every month in the capital," it offered its patrons "both solace for the body, and distraction for the soul."

A half century of revolution and empire would pass before the modern restaurant, a place where one goes to enjoy a meal, replete with wine, would emerge. The mid-eighteenth-century restaurant was by contrast a place where one neither ate much food nor drank much, if any, wine. It did, however, introduce a new social convention—that of drinking (and later eating) in public as if in private, with individual rather than communal tables. As *L'Avantcoureur* explained, patrons of a public restaurant could consume "without offending their sense of delicacy." Wine later would become an integral part of the restaurant experience. Yet when these establishments first opened for business, wine did not belong in them. That's because they served healthy restoratives for various excesses, including the excessive consumption of alcohol.

The advent of both the new alcohols and the new non-alcohols issued a severe challenge to wine's place in European culture. Wine increasingly seemed antiquated. It often even tasted so. Vintners badly needed to improve it. What remained unknown, however, was how to do so. Winemaking had not changed significantly for thousands of years, and even the era's best wines spoiled much too rapidly. What could raise quality and make more wines both more stable and more distinctive? Put another way, what would make them objects of choice and desire? Enlightenment learning provided important answers to these questions, in the process allowing the number of fine wines to increase exponentially, and more and more people to experience them. Yet new knowledge could not by itself transform sour swill into something estimable.

Before any new winemaking methods or tools could be employed, there had to be something worth preserving. That is, there needed to be wines that already tasted specialized or particular, and that at least some people chose for gustatory pleasure. So while science and technology would enable vintners to make more vins fins in more styles, the very idea of particularity predates wine's technical (and technological) modernization. It first had emerged in late medieval Burgundy, and by 1700 it was being expressed in select places with other wines—with the new Clarets, for example, and the estate German Rieslings, as well as the Côte d'Or crus.

Those crus remained, however, what they had been three centuries earlier—islands of particularity within a sea of indistinct, low-priced generic wine. Gamay grapes still formed the base of most red Burgundies. For whites, Aligoté was widely planted, with some vintners using Pinot Blanc. Only in specialized sites did growers cultivate Chardonnay. Before the French Revolution, virtually all such places, whether owned by religious orders or by members of the aristocracy, were still isolated, as few of the wines made with grapes from these vines found their way into the marketplace. During the eighteenth century, some merchants and officials from Dijon and Beaune did purchase vineyards in the Côte d'Or. Like the Cistercian monks many generations earlier, they made wines identified by cru and clos, one small plot here, another tiny parcel there. Each site within each commune was said to be distinct, each wine different. There never was much fine wine made, the Côte being small, its prime spots even smaller. But what little was produced was famous, though often by virtue of reputation rather than actual experience. And more than any other wine made anywhere else, its fame rested on the perception or sense of terroir. The English writer Arthur Young, who visited Burgundy near the end of the century, did not have that word to use when talking about wine, but he understood the concept well. Young wanted to learn specifically about the vineyards that were "so famous in France, and indeed in all Europe," so he went to Vougeot. He found it "walled in, [still] belonging to a convent of [Cistercian] monks." And he clearly thought it remarkable. "When are we to find these fellows choosing badly," he asked rhetorically. "The spots they appropriate show what a righteous attention they give to things of the spirit."

BATTLING AIR AND
BOTTLING STARS
Inventing Early Modern Wines

Like their ancient forebears, vintners during Europe's philosophical and scientific Enlightenment understood neither how wine came into being nor why it turned sour so quickly. Yet unlike all those who had toiled in vineyards and cellars before them, they knew that its short life threatened their livelihoods. The competition wine now faced opened many eyes to what long had been its persistent failing, an infuriating inability to remain stable. Thus when people crowded into the era's cabarets, inns, and taverns, they often chose more durable forms of alcoholic drink. In England, gin became all the rage among the working classes, much as vodka did in Poland and Russia and rum did in the various American colonies. Beer remained a mainstay in northern and eastern Europe, while people with more money to spend bought aged brandies and whiskies. The popularity of coffee, tea, and chocolate had done little to restrain the public's thirst for intoxication, and the fact that wine did not fall even more out of favor was due largely to the simple fact that it contained alcohol. In southern France and Italy, farmers on average drank close to a gallon a day, while their urban counterparts imbibed only slightly less. Public drunkenness, whether brought on by distilled or fermented drink, proved extremely common, especially since conventional wisdom held that consuming a substantial amount in either form was good for one's health. The German writer Johann Wolfgang von Goethe made sure to down half a gallon each day when he took the cure at a Carlsbad spa. Similarly, the French gourmand Jean Anthelme Brillat-Savarin recommended that his readers drink multiple bottles as a prerequisite for living a long life, recounting with evident admiration the case of an army officer who knocked back eight bottles "every morning at breakfast, without turning a hair."

The desire for alcohol explains why a good deal of eighteenth-century wine, which otherwise would have spoiled and become unpalatable, went into mixed drinks like punch. These could be served either hot or cold and were commonly poured in taverns and inns. Much like a bouillon, or *restaurant*, punch supposedly helped settle stomachs, though accounts of how much people drank suggests that it more frequently may have been the cause of distress. Unlike Hippocras and the other spiced wines that had been so fashionable in the Middle Ages and Renaissance, punches were not primarily wine-based. Instead, the punch maker used wine as one of at least five ingredients, the others usually being fruit, sugar in some form, a sweet spice such as nutmeg, and most important, rum or another hard spirit. Reflecting how it tasted on its own, the wine often was called "the sour." The New Englander Samuel Mather, writing in verse in 1757, urged using specifically Portuguese wines for punch, noting that "some [people] any sours they get contented use / But men of taste do that from Tagus choose." Given the long sea voyage from Lisbon to Boston, wines from that Tagus port city must have tasted very sour indeed.

Even some of the era's better-tasting wines often were viewed simply as vehicles for drunkenness. The "three bottle men" who allegedly consumed that amount regularly in London, like the Parisians who gathered daily in the city's taverns to drink pitcher after pitcher, thought of wine as such. In these and other cities, the enlarged income of the growing bourgeoisie provided people with all sorts of opportunities to indulge. And indulge they did, from morning well into night. Wine in this regard served much the same function as any sort of spirit, the one important difference being that, unlike a spirit, it invariably turned vinegary. Hence when compared with more stable (and more potent) drinks like gin and whiskey, it continued to seem tired and old-fashioned.

It took roughly a century for minds to change, and change fundamentally. By the mid-1800s, vintners were fashioning wines that could stay fresh-tasting much longer than before. Some of their dry wines even improved with the passage of time, something inconceivable earlier. Over the same period, equally far-reaching social and cultural changes brought these wines to the attention of new consumers. And as more men and women started to value their individualistic aromas and flavors, wine as a whole began to be esteemed anew, becoming in many ways the drink (or drinks) consumed today. No one then complained that wine seemed out of date. Instead, a taste for it began to signal cultural sophistication and *savoir-faire*. Though this new form of appreciation would be severely disrupted by a series of late-nineteenth- and twentieth-century crises, it presaged wine's more inclusive contemporary golden age.

The Enlightenment, when men and women began to see themselves as elevated by reason and united by social contract, constitutes the era in which wine, like so much else in European culture, became modern. Distinctive forms and styles emerged that remain recognizable, as did new ways of understanding both what wine is chemically and why it might be valued culturally. In many places, the techniques of grape growing improved markedly, as did practices in cellars and wineries. Vintners became more selective when choosing which varieties to grow, as well as more fastidious when deciding how to train and trellis their vines. They also paid more attention to the harvest in determining both when to pick their fruit and how to care for it afterward. Similarly, cellars became cleaner, and more winemakers started keeping their casks or barrels as full as possible so as to delay souring. Most important, the advent of bottles and corks allowed wines to taste good for surprising lengths of time.

Wine's modernization resulted from veritable revolutions in both its production and its consumption. Those revolutions started in the eighteenth century, reached a climax of sorts in the nineteenth, and then accelerated anew in the second half of the twentieth. For vintners, new techniques and tools, coupled with a new comprehension of wine's chemistry, resulted in cleaner, more stable, and by all accounts generally superior wines than what their forefathers had been able to make.

For consumers, the decision to purchase, drink, and even cellar these wines gave wine in general, and fine wine in particular, a new cultural standing as something to be valued aesthetically. These two revolutions went hand in hand. But revolutions only occur because of some perceived injustice or inadequacy, and this one came in large part because the quality of most premodern wines remained so poor for so long. Not until many more distinctive-tasting ones came onto the market could significant numbers of people begin to develop an appreciation for them. Then at long last, wine conceived of as "the sour" would stop defining all that it could, or should, be.

—∞—

Many of the most important advances in winemaking originated in the analysis of wine's chemical composition. Scientists started studying wine seriously in the mid-eighteenth century, and their work reached an initial climax roughly one hundred years later. Researchers provided new knowledge that enabled vintners to begin making more attractive, longer-lasting products. In turn, the era's new wines turned something previously desired largely for its effect into something now chosen for itself. Proceeding slowly and systematically, scientists examined wine's makeup, trying to give winemakers greater control over their craft. Their collective efforts culminated in 1860, when Louis Pasteur finally solved wine's most baffling age-old mystery. This French scientist, already world famous at age thirty-seven, explained for the first time what happens during the course of fermentation. After eight thousand years, people finally could understand what wine is. As a result of his research, Pasteur often is considered the father of modern wine. Yet his conclusions were sometimes incomplete or even erroneous, and later scientists had to correct them so as to reveal the complexity of wine's biochemistry. It thus is more accurate to think of Pasteur as a transitional figure, straddling eras, bringing the initial stage of wine's modernization to a close while preparing the way for a more inclusive second act. Wine science after him became very different from what it was before. So while a more complete analysis of wine's composition would not emerge until the mid-twentieth century, Pasteur's discoveries mark a crucial turning point in the history of wine. They stand as the culmination of a series of earlier scientific advances, all of which played a critical role in saving wine from what had appeared not all that long before to be possible obsolescence.

Antoine Lavoisier had been the first important wine scientist. An *ancien régime* nobleman (he would meet his fate at the guillotine), Lavoisier is sometimes called the inventor of modern chemistry. He gave that science new precision by, for example, discovering the nature of both combustion and respiration, showing that air, far from being a single entity, contains different gases, and solving the long-standing problem of the composition of water. He drew up the first table of chemical elements, identifying thirty-three, including hydrogen and oxygen, both of which he named. Lavoisier also spent considerable time studying fermentation, something he called "one of the most striking and extraordinary [operations] of all those that chemistry presents to us." His eighteenth-century discoveries paved the way for Pasteur's nineteenth-century ones, for Lavoisier was the first person to explain wine's chemistry with any degree of accuracy.

According to Lavoisier, grape juice turns into wine through a chemical reaction in which an exchange of oxygen divides its sugar into alcohol and carbon dioxide. That reaction constitutes fermentation. After carefully measuring the carbon dioxide and the alcohol, he was able to assert that the total mass of the final product is equal to that of the original one. "If it were possible to recombine these two substances," he declared, "sugar would [again] result." In a series of tables, he demonstrated that this reaction entails a change in form rather than a loss of matter. (Later scientific experiments, using more precise instruments, showed that this is not exactly true, since a small percentage of the sugar does become consumed during the reaction.) In the process, Lavoisier formulated the law of the conservation of mass, which states that the mass of a closed system of substances remains constant, regardless of the processes taking place inside the system. His analysis was clear and simple, and it solved fully half of wine's mystery. Far from being a magical or miraculous event, fermentation was predictable and rationally comprehensible.

Lavoisier, however, did not specify any basis or cause for fermentation. An Italian scientist, Adamo Fabroni, did that in 1785, winning a prize from the Academy of Florence for demonstrating that yeasts, which he likened to gluten in wheat, initiate it. Then, twenty years later, two French chemists, Louis Jacques Thénard and Joseph Louis Gay-Lussac, went a step further. They proved that the yeasts remain in contact with the sugar all through fermentation, making it an ongoing process rather than a momentary phenomenon. Yet because they could see only spent or dead yeasts in the wine's lees, they and other scientists tended to conclude that these organisms caused fermentation through putrefaction. In this theory, yeast was irrelevant to the process except as a dying or dead substance, its decomposition being what initiated the chemical reaction. A few researchers did suggest that living yeasts might play a role, but their so-called vital theories were dismissed broadly. As late as the 1840s, the learned German chemist Justus von Liebig scoffed at any suggestion that fermentation might be a biological as well as a chemical process. Arguing that such an idea confused cause and effect, he compared anyone proposing it to "a child who would explain the rapidity of the Rhine current by attributing it to the violent movement of the many millwheels at Mainz." Liebig's reasoning followed the beliefs of the majority of authoritative scientists, who insisted that fermentation as a closed chemical reaction had to be something that was generated spontaneously.

Pasteur debunked the very notion of spontaneous generation. He established that wine is produced through a chemical reaction that is not only caused by, but actually becomes part of, a biological process. His experiments demonstrated, first, that living yeasts serve as catalysts for juice's conversion into wine, and second, that this transformation cannot continue without the ongoing engagement of those same yeasts. Put another way, though often invisible to the naked eye, life is necessary to engender new life, and microorganisms live everywhere—even in the air.

By introducing live yeasts into a liquid containing only sugar and mineral salts, Pasteur revealed that, far from dying, yeasts in fact multiply as sugar ferments. The production of both alcohol and carbon dioxide depends on their life, not their death. It then did not take him long to discover that different but also previously unrecognized life-forms also account for wine's souring. He spent much of the decade of the

1860s proving that just as fermentation depends on active yeasts, wine turns bad when it is exposed to too much air, encouraging the growth of active bacteria. The souring occurs faster in proportion to the amount of bacteria present in the wine, and the bacteria multiply faster in proportion to the amount of oxygen available to them. Thus a half-filled beaker of wine spoils rapidly; a half-filled bottle closed with a stopper does so slowly; and the wine in a completely full and well-sealed bottle may remain healthy for years. Looking through his microscope, Pasteur saw the bacteria. He catalogued different sorts and became so adept at recognizing them that he could identify a particular problem in a wine by observing it microscopically. Pasteur's great discovery, then, was that living agents serve as the causes of wine's effects—its initial emergence, its eventual souring, and many of the possible stages between.

Pasteur investigated much more than wine during his long and distinguished career. Regardless of the particular subject he studied, however, his research kept revealing that live organisms are integral to different chemistries. Thus he proved that reactions such as fermentation are in fact living, vital processes, not closed chemical ones. His writings are filled with expressions of surprise at the range of his discoveries. As the distinguished microbiologist René Dubos evocatively put it, they "leave the impression of a child running to and fro in a forest, overwhelmed with a sense of wonder at the signs of unknown life . . . intoxicated at discovering the diversity of the Creation."

Scientists today know that alcoholic fermentation is not as simple a process as Pasteur thought, for the yeasts that initiate it produce enzymes that also can alter a wine's chemistry. Similarly, oxygen is not always a detrimental influence on a wine's development, and bacteria are not always a destructive force. Nonetheless, as the influential twentieth-century oenologist, or wine scientist, Émile Peynaud acknowledged, Pasteur's research proved fundamental since his "principles [retain] their full import." That's because his discoveries, much like those of the men who labored before him, allowed people to do more than comprehend wine abstractly. Vintners used the new scientific knowledge to produce more consistent and hence more reliable wines. Pasteur himself owned a vineyard near the town of Arbois in the Jura region of eastern France, and the wine made from the grapes grown there certainly benefited from his research. (That vineyard, now owned by the Henri-Maire company, still produces a wine from the "Clos de Pasteur," a small-production blend of the different grape varieties he cultivated in his vineyard.) With the promulgation of new knowledge and technology, vinification methods and techniques changed wherever vintners aimed for something more than cheap, sour wine. In turn those changes enabled wines, especially quality dry wines, to improve markedly. And because some of those wines, just a select few at first, not only maintained flavor but actually became more nuanced over time, wine began to acquire a new cultural status, serving for the first time as an object of an aesthetically conceived connoisseurship.

Connoisseurship, however, was always a consequence, not a cause, of wine's initial modernization. No one ever would have thought to collect, cellar, or covet any wines until at least some had shown the ability to become stable—or to put it the other way around, until virtually all dry wine was not always teetering on the edge of vinegar. Pasteur's discoveries provided vintners with the necessary understanding and rationale, but the scientific movement toward more durable wines had started well before he first trained his microscope on the yeasts and bacteria in his laboratory's jars and beakers. People now knew that a dry wine's appealing because particular character did not have to be exasperatingly fleeting. And when more wines started to retain freshness and vigor, more consumers embraced them. Thus it is no exaggeration to say that science rescued wine by stabilizing it.

Well before Pasteur solved the mystery of fermentation, winemakers had searched for better ways to preserve their wines. They added many ingredients to their casks so as to disguise vinegary flavors. Some, like lead, proved dangerous; others, such as ash and dye, simply were odd-tasting. Two, however, proved revolutionary. Sulfur and sugar enhanced rather than altered the taste of wine, and became a regular part of the modern vintner's craft. Sulfur, first identified as a distinct chemical element by Lavoisier in the 1770s, had been used sporadically by winemakers since antiquity—first as a cleaning agent and later as a preservative. In Renaissance Germany, where cellars were cold and the high-acid wines had a potentially long life (if they could be kept away from oxygen), using it became common practice. Vintners would burn powdered sulfur mixed with wood shavings and dried herbs in barrels before filling them with wine. While they did not understand the science, they recognized that casks treated in this way yielded fresher, longer-lasting wines than those left untreated. Later generations would burn sulfur candles or wicks in barrels both when filling them and when moving or racking wine from one to another. So long as they kept the barrels full, the wines could last for up to two or even three years.

Modern science explains that sulfur dioxide, the colorless gas produced when elemental sulfur burns, kills microbes and protects wine from potentially harmful exposure to air. While large amounts can cause an adverse reaction in someone suffering from asthma or certain allergies, sulfur dioxide is completely harmless for the vast majority of people. Many centuries passed before scientists understood how and why it works as it does, but advances in chemistry in the 1600s enabled them to promote the idea of adding salts containing sulfur to newly fermented wines. These salts were the first agents that could safely stabilize wine to any significant degree without significantly changing its flavor. Because they helped prevent souring, they also permitted otherwise fragile dry wines to travel longer. As one oceangoing commentator observed, unsulfured wine "could not keep on the sea, but it would spoil."

The one disadvantage of sulfur dioxide in winemaking comes from its aroma, which resembles the acrid smell of a freshly struck match and can be detected at even low concentrations. Vintners had to learn to be judicious with it, and even today oenologists debate the proper amount to use. Yet when compared with the far worse smell (and taste) of vinegar, a whiff of sulfur in an early-modern wine surely would not have been thought such a bad thing. Using it offered winemakers the advantage of cleaner fermentations, something that in turn reduced the risk that their wines would be contaminated by bacteria. In short, its addition made their wines taste fresher.

The addition of sugar, either during fermentation or after a wine started to sour, served a similar function. It raised alcohol levels, making wines headier and longer-lasting, in addition to helping them become better balanced. Though grape growers since antiquity had recognized that they should pick their fruit at its ripest and sweetest, the identification of that sweetness as a form of sugar was yet another Enlightenment discovery. It came only after cane sugar became widely available, and that happened only after cane had been planted, harvested, and then shipped in volume to Europe—something that began in the seventeenth century and then became big business in the eighteenth.

Native to the Far East, sugar cane first came to Europe in the Middle Ages. Expensive and rare, it was for a long time a luxury unavailable to all but a privileged few. Europeans then planted it in their Caribbean colonies, but not until the early 1700s did the plantations there become sufficiently productive (in large measure owing to the massive amount of slave labor used on islands like Cuba, Haiti, and Jamaica) to provide enough supply for sugar to become a culinary staple rather than a prized extravagance. Before long, scientists had identified sucrose in ripe fruit, and so had established a link between cane and grapes. Following Lavoisier, they knew that fermentation involved the transformation of sugar into alcohol, so they soon deduced that the addition of non-grape sugar could increase the amount of alcohol in a finished wine. In an age that craved alcohol, this undoubtedly was an exciting discovery, and winemakers quickly began to experiment by adding cane sugar to grape juice. Then, led by the German chemist Andreas Marggraf, scientists also discovered sugar in beetroot, a plant native to Europe. For winemakers, it did not much matter whether sugar, as an additive, came from cane or beets. Both gave yeasts more material from which to produce more alcohol without altering the inherent flavor of the grapes. Thus both made thin wines fuller and tart wines richer, and gave vinegary wines (temporary) new life.

Adding sugar to fermenting wine is known today as "chaptalization," after the chemist and Napoleonic minister Jean-Antoine-Claude Chaptal, whose writing on wine, particularly his *Traité sur la vigne*, first published in 1801 and subsequently translated into many languages and reprinted multiple times, remains the most influential winemaking guide ever written. But Chaptal did not invent (or ever claim to have invented) chaptalization. The practice had been described as early as 1765 in the secular Enlightenment bible, the *Encyclopédie*, in which Chevalier Louis de Jaucourt complained that Parisian merchants were adding all sorts of sweets, including syrup and cider, to their wines. (Cane and beet sugar work better precisely because they do not disguise the taste of the grapes.) In fact, no single person can be said to be the originator of chaptalization. It became an obvious remedy for both feeble and sour wines once scientists learned and then publicized the connection between sugar and ripe grapes. Thus by the dawn of the nineteenth century chaptalization had become a standard part of winemaking, particularly in places where the climate sometimes prevented the fruit from ripening fully. In 1819, when Chaptal published a new edition of his book, the practice of adding sugar to fermenting wine had become so common that he could claim it had brought a "felicitous revolution" to the winegrowing countries of Europe.

Chaptal's *Traité* examined, evaluated, and commented on winemaking from a modern because a decidedly scientific point of view. He had been Lavoisier's student, and like his teacher, he insisted that scientists could improve wine by better comprehending its chemistry. As important as any specific technique (even sugaring) was his general outlook, a way of understanding wine and indeed the world that marked a radical change from centuries past. As he explained in his book's preface, "It is for chemistry to make known the laws of fermentation; to unscramble the different effects of soil, climate, situation, and cultivation; to discover the reasons why wines change; in a word, to direct and master all the operations of oenology." This emphasis on comprehending reasons and deciphering laws marked the book as distinctly modern, as did the claim that vintners indeed could control winemaking. More than anything else, that sense of control, manifest in techniques and procedures such as sulfuring and chaptalizing, led to the emergence of significantly more durable and hence more desirable wines.

As important as these scientific advances, and yet further evidence of human control, were advances in technology—most notably, the development of a container and then a closure that could preserve wine better than anything used previously. The first of these was the glass bottle, and the second the cork with which to plug that bottle shut. Both also helped modernize wine, further stabilizing it so that an entirely new practice emerged—that of aging wine so as to allow it not just to keep but actually to evolve and improve over time.

Glass had been blown since antiquity, but most of it was thin and fragile, so not well suited for wine service. During the Renaissance, glazed stoneware bottles, as well as some made with tin or pewter, had been fashionable, but these were used principally to bring wine to tavern tables. The wine itself remained stored in a cask—perhaps the same one in which it had been shipped from its place of origin, perhaps a new one into which a merchant had transferred it. The obvious problem came once the cask began to be emptied. As air displaced liquid, the remaining wine started to spoil, with the result that a great deal of wine, even if in good shape when the cask was first opened, soured quickly. The solution began literally to take shape in the seventeenth century, when glassmakers started experimenting with coal-fired furnaces. Because these generated more heat, they could produce stronger bottles.

In 1615, Sir Robert Mansell, a retired vice admiral who had won fame at the English court for routing Algerian pirates, applied for a royal patent or monopoly to open a glassworks using coal rather than wood for fuel. King James I granted it, though he wondered aloud why "Robert Mansell, being a seaman, whereby he got so much honor, should fall from water to tamper with fire." But Mansell was a shrewd entrepreneur who recognized that this new enterprise could yield big profits. Imported Italian glass had become fashionable in Stuart England, so he went to Italy to entice master glassblowers to come north and work for him. They ran his new factory, where they made, among other things, wine bottles. The intense heat rendered these bottles green or brown, rather than white as with the finest Venetian glass, but they were certainly sturdy. Even sturdier were the bottles blown a decade or so later in a glassworks owned by Sir Kenelm Digby, a genuine English eccentric who coincidentally also had been a seaman (in his case a privateer), and who improved on Mansell's procedure by using a blower to make the furnace even hotter. A Royalist and a Catholic, Digby was exiled and then imprisoned during the English Civil War, when others claimed his technique as their own. But in 1662, Parliament recognized him as the inventor of a new sort of glass-making furnace that produced a new sort of wine bottle.

These English bottles, as they came to be called, were dark, strong, and heavy. Globular in shape, they sometimes had collars or rings around their necks, around which one could tie string so as to secure stoppers. The bottoms were fairly flat, with an indentation or "punt" that helped them stand up safely. Digby had experimented with a mixture containing more sand than usual, something that helped strengthen the glass. Over the next fifty years, other glassmakers melted more sand at even higher temperatures, making ever darker, thicker bottles. Gradually the shape changed, the bottles becoming less round and more elongated. By 1700, enterprising manufacturers were making strong bottles in Holland and France as well as England, and during the eighteenth century, glassworks specializing in them opened in many European countries. The shape of the bottles continued to evolve, with the height increasing, the bottom diameter becoming smaller, and the neck shortening. Then in the nineteenth and twentieth centuries, particular shapes began to be used for particular wines—thin ones for Rhenish, for example, and ones with rounded rather than sloping shoulders for Bordeaux. The modern wine bottle had arrived.

These early bottles were not used by winemakers. For the most part, bottling at the estate or domaine, or even in the region, where a wine was made did not become common practice until the mid-twentieth century. Before then, merchants did most of the bottling, having first purchased and transported the wines in casks. Most early bottles were blown by hand, meaning that they came in many different sizes. The differences led to laws requiring that wines be sold in standard volume or measure—a liter or gallon, say, rather than a bottle or jug. Wealthy clients had their own bottles marked with their initials or family crests. So too did many commercial customers such as taverns, inns, clubs, and eventually restaurants. The merchants sometimes came to their clients, and consumers sometimes went to the merchants, but regardless of who filled what and where, the advent of the glass bottle revolutionized the wine trade. Here at long last was a consumer-friendly container that, when full, virtually guaranteed stability.

That guarantee only worked if the bottle was well sealed. Cork had been used off and on as a closure ever since the Romans first coated pieces of it with pitch to seal their amphorae. In the Middle Ages, however, when no wine was bottled, barrels or casks used for storage tended to be closed with cloth, leather, or wood. Cork was largely unavailable then because Portugal and Spain, home to the cork oak tree, were under abstemious Moorish control. By the Renaissance, with both Iberian countries again in wine-drinking hands, rough-cut pieces of cork began to be used as stoppers for earthenware bottles, especially in taverns. But since these bottles were employed just for service, the stoppers never needed to be all that secure. A slice of cork would be jammed into a bottle that a customer had not finished, and then pulled out when the next customer placed an order. This surely is what Shakespeare's Rosalind is thinking of when she tells Celia in *As You Like It*, "Take thy cork out of thy mouth, that I may drink thy tidings."

Only with the arrival of glass bottles did corks begin to be used as more than temporary stoppers. Yet because those initial bottles were hand blown, the diameter of their necks proved irregular. Since a piece of cork that might fit snuggly in one would be loose in another, cork was not the first popular bottle closure. Individually made, ground glass stoppers worked better, as each one was fashioned to fit securely in a specific bottle. Though expensive, these stayed with the bottles, often literally so, as they were tied on with string. Beginning in the 1740s, however, glassblowers started to work with molds that enabled them to produce bottles in a more uniform size and shape. The merchants who purchased those bottles then began to use corks to seal them shut. They did so, though, only after the wines had been shipped to them in casks, at least some portion of the contents having evaporated. So while bottles and corks greatly relieved the age-old problem of spoilage, they did not eliminate it.

At first, corks were not pressed all the way into the bottles. After all, they soon had to be pulled out. They did, however, sometimes get stuck, a situation that led to the invention of what initially was called a "bottlescrew." An early reference to such a device, "a steel worm used for the drawing of corks out of bottles," comes from the 1680s, but the implement did not become a common tool until the middle of the next century. By then it was called a corkscrew, and by then corks were at least sometimes being inserted completely into bottles. For by that time bottles, by virtue of the widespread use of molds, had become consistently cylindrical, and so could be stored on their sides, keeping the corks moist. Since dry corks can crumble, this was important if one wanted to age the wine in the bottles. And by the mid-eighteenth century, some people wanted to do just that.

Cork closures, along with thick, sturdy glass, were the technical innovations that permitted wine to shift from being simply served in bottles to being stored and matured in them. Equally important, though, was the emerging desire on the part of a select segment of the wine-drinking public to age wine. For over a thousand years, anyone who drank any sort of dry wine had wanted to consume it as quickly as possible, so as to enjoy it before it spoiled. This was true even with sweet Mediterranean wines, which lasted longer than low-alcohol northern European ones but were still always in danger of turning sour. Of course, the ancient Greeks and Romans had aged some wines. But they had made those wines with raisined grapes, added all sorts of other ingredients, and stored the resulting potions in pitch-coated amphorae. As a result, their wines were distinguished as much by the taste of additives as by any natural grape flavors. By contrast, the wines in the new glass bottles with the new corks did not contain herbs or spices, oils or resins, and were made for the most part with fresh, ripe grapes. Moreover, the goal of aging was not to accentuate any single ingredient but rather to soften and mellow the whole. In fact, softening wine so as to allow nuanced, subtle flavors to emerge was the very point of binning and cellaring it—something that was discovered gradually, even accidentally, during the eighteenth century.

Aged dry wine was appreciated first in Georgian England. Its taste must have seemed strange initially, but then fashion's tides never shift on the basis of taste alone. Because bottled wine cost more than cask wine, aged wine came from only the most prestigious places. Priced out of reach of the majority of the populace, it initially was unavailable to most wine drinkers, as one needed both money to invest in it and a place to store it. Buying, storing, and finally drinking aged wine thus first functioned as signs of aristocratic exclusivity. By the mid-eighteenth century, the size of a lord's wine cellar was fast becoming as much a mark of standing as the size of his estate.

It did not take long, however, for the taste of aged wine to become appreciated by more than the established elite. Despite its somewhat stiff sense of decorum, eighteenth-century English society was very mobile. As novels from *Pamela* to *Tom Jones* make clear, the age held many opportunities for social advancement, more certainly than what existed in countries across the English Channel. While the landed gentry owned the most extensive cellars (Sir Horace Walpole's was especially renowned), ambitious men and women of more middle-class means soon also started to buy and bin bottled wines. By the early 1760s, the London publisher Robert Dodsley was offering for sale a cellar-record book, replete with sections for the different types of wine that a respectable household would likely have. Within it, one could record both one's purchases and one's consumption. The simple fact that this book found a ready market demonstrates that the audience for aged wine was expanding.

It may seem surprising that England, a country whose climate precluded significant viticulture, would play such an important role in the development of modern wine. But English consumers influenced wine styles and wine quality almost as much as winemakers on the Continent. The format of Dodsley's cellar-record book intimates why. It included sections for Burgundy, Champagne, Claret, Madeira, Port, Rhenish, and Sack, all of which a gentleman presumably would be expected to stock in his cellar. By contrast, in wine-producing countries, people drank native wines almost exclusively. This was true even for the nobility, the members of which certainly could afford whatever they wanted. The French court at Versailles, for example, consumed copious quantities of wine, but virtually all of it was French (and most from northern France at that). By contrast, precisely because domestic wines were virtually nonexistent, a London wine lover, no matter whether a lord or a tradesman, had no patriotic pride when it came to deciding what to buy and drink. As a result, English tastes became extremely wide-ranging. And given the country's wealth, coupled with its expanding middle-class population, it's not surprising that virtually all of winemaking Europe vied for the English market's attention. This was a classic case of demand shaping supply. The English palate wanted new wines in new styles. Winemakers in France, Germany, Portugal, and Spain (and to a lesser degree Italy, the Middle East, and even some of the colonies) were more than happy to oblige.

Not all of the wine coming to England from these places was crafted in styles that benefited from extended aging, but as the eighteenth century progressed, more people began to prize the mellow taste of mature wines. Because that taste came only from wines that had been cellared, and because cellars tended to be in private houses rather than public establishments, more wine began to be consumed at home. Only a generation earlier, few people, whatever their social class, kept much wine in their houses. The reason was simple. A cask stored in a private home had the same problems as a cask in an inn or tavern. Once the bung or stopper had been removed and some wine drawn off, the remaining contents would start to spoil. And the contents of a cask or barrel usually lasted longer at home than in a tavern, giving the bacteria in the air even more time to turn the wine even sourer. With the advent of glass bottles and secure corks, however, there was less need to worry about spoilage. So beginning in aristocratic Georgian mansions, people constructed wine storage bins in their cellars. The common practice was to contract for the wine one wanted with a merchant, who then would bring the barrel to the house, where he or his assistants would bottle and bin the wines. Since some wines aged better than others, these came to be in particular demand. "I love everything that's old—old friends, old times, old manners, old books, old wine," declares a character in Oliver Goldsmith's 1773 play, *She Stoops to Conquer.* In terms of wine, that sentiment never would have been expressed before the advent of bottles and corks, sulfur and sugar—Enlightenment science in the service of an emerging modern connoisseurship.

In addition to the scientific advances and technological developments that helped improve existing wines, the eighteenth and early nineteenth centuries saw the invention of new wines in new styles. These sometimes reflected specific terroirs, but even more significantly they represented new visions and ideas—ideas of how certain wines might taste, and so how they might be enjoyed. The ideas evolved over time, as did the wines themselves. These wines certainly benefited from the same technical developments that made aged dry ones fashionable. Sparkling Champagne, for example, required sturdy cork-finished bottles, since the bubbles would dissipate were it stored in casks. Similarly,

Port needed to age in cool cellars in order to transform itself from an inexpensive, fiery tavern drink into a prized, mellow collectible. Champagnes and Ports, as well as Sherries, other wines fortified with a dash of spirit, and sweet dessert elixirs like Sauternes and Tokaji, also profited from new scientific knowledge. That knowledge in turn further modernized wine, demonstrating that human involvement matters just as much as natural conditions in the fashioning of quality. Before long, drinkers began to think and talk about wines rather than just wine, different types satisfying different markets and desires. These helped wine as a whole become more culturally desirable. Savvy consumers sought them out. By 1800, fizzy Champagnes, fortified wines such as Port and Madeira, and sweet dessert wines fashioned from fresh rather than raisined grapes were offering drinkers wholly new experiences. As a result, many people began to think of wine less as one product among others than as a set of different products, each in its own way valuable, and each enhancing the value of the whole.

Perhaps the most notable new type of wine was the one that fizzed and bubbled. Though sparkling wine was first produced slightly earlier in Limoux in southwestern France, eighteenth-century effervescent Champagnes were the wines that made bubbles fashionable. And fashionable they certainly were—so much so that in less than a century they became what they remain today, the world's favorite wines for celebration and romance, and one of the first modern luxuries, expensive to be sure, but highly desired.

Wines had been made in the region of Champagne for over a thousand years, but none sparkled for long until the late seventeenth century. Instead, Champagnes, red as well as white (or more accurately, grayish pink), came in still form. These quite acidic wines could be shipped easily by barge or riverboat to Paris, where aristocratic lords and ladies regarded any bubbles in them as a flaw. Yet bubbles there sometimes were. Owing to the harsh winters in northern France, the wines often stopped fermenting in the cold, only to begin again come warmer weather. By then they would have been shipped in barrels, the wooden bungs from which would fly off because of the pressure of the carbon dioxide within, as the frothy wine spilled out. After a day or so, though, the remaining wine would have settled down and become what all wines from Champagne were supposed to be—tart and still. Dom Pierre Pérignon, a Benedictine monk who served as the treasurer of the Abbey of Hautvillers, was this wine's most ardent champion. Though legend has it that he invented sparkling Champagne, supposedly declaring, "I am drinking stars," the historical record indicates the opposite. Dom Pérignon actually spent his forty-seven years at Hautvillers trying to modernize the production of still wine. He racked his cuvées repeatedly, purchased strong, English-style glass, and always worked assiduously to prevent the wine from becoming fizzy. Yet it was during his lifetime that still Champagne fell out of fashion, only to be replaced with something he likely regarded as frivolous—a wine deliberately made with bubbles.

Sparkling Champagne first became all the rage in Restoration London. Wine from the region had been introduced there in the 1660s by the Marquis de St-Evremond, a French *bon vivant* who exiled himself after writing a satiric public letter about King Louis XIV's powerful minister, Cardinal Mazarin. St-Evremond took a few casks of Champagne with him when he fled to London, and the wine quickly became popular at court. He then arranged to import more. It was shipped soon after harvest, and bottled on arrival, using sturdy new English glass. Unlike Champagnes in France that finished fermenting in casks and then turned flat once the bungs were removed, these finished their fermentation in bottles, with the result that they emerged fizzy. People loved them. The playwright George Etherege referred specifically to "sparkling Champagne" in his comedy *The Man of Mode*. There this new type of wine is said to be what "quickly recovers / Poor languishing lovers," since drinking it "makes us frolic and gay, and drowns all sorrow."

Sparkling Champagne came a bit later to Paris and Versailles. With relatively few strong bottles available, the common practice on the Continent continued to be to ship and sell wine in casks. Even if some frothy wine spilled out, the remaining contents would turn still. But by the time of Dom Pérignon's death in 1715, enterprising merchants and vintners (including his successors at Hautvillers) had learned how to trap the bubbles in bottles. Their wines became the height of fashion during the regency of Philippe, Duc d'Orléans. Philippe was an atheist who openly read works by Rabelais instead of his catechism during Mass, a liberal who made education at the Sorbonne free and opened the Royal Library to the public, and an unabashed hedonist whose debauchery became legendary. He drank copious amounts of fizzy Champagne, often at great banquets that he dubbed his "orgies." Though his regency lasted only eight years, and the subsequent reign of Louis XV proved more publicly decorous, Philippe's court at the Palais Royal is where the ongoing association of sparkling Champagne with luxury and sensual pleasure was first established.

As the eighteenth century progressed, the effervescent swell of fashion swept more and more still Champagnes off the runway. Consumers, particularly wealthy ones, wanted bubbles, and since they could pay handsomely, their new demand led to a reorganization of the Champagne trade. Because individual growers rarely had the resources to finance export operations, companies emerged that would purchase wine, bottle it, and then market and sell it. In Epernay, Claude Möet had started selling wine, most of it without bubbles, to Parisians in 1716; fifty years later, his son, Claude-Louis Nicolas, was handling primarily bottled, sparkling wine. And in Reims, Nicolas Ruinart, who had dealt almost only in cask wine through the 1730s, was shipping some thirty thousand bottles per year three decades later. These went all over Europe. His son, who took over the company in 1769, kept careful records, which indicated that he sold Ruinart Champagne to clients in cities and courts in Germany, Holland, Sweden, Denmark, and England. Others courted other markets, including ones in Austria, Russia, and even North America.

These eighteenth-century wines were not full-formed Champagnes in a contemporary sense, since the development of the complete *méthode champenoise* had to wait for later inventions. One of the first involved riddling, or *remuage*, the practice of dislodging the spent yeast cells in a bottle of sparkling wine by inverting it and shaking the sediment down into the neck. The widow (or *veuve*) Nicole-Barbe Clicquot's cellar master, Antoine de Müller, devised the procedure around 1815. By the mid-1820s, virtually everyone making sparkling wine in Champagne was riddling bottles, and the volume of wine being produced began to rise exponentially. Even then, however, the bubbles in sparkling Champagne came from a continuation of the initial fermentation, not from an induced second one as happens today. This inevitably involved a good deal of chance, since the amount of yeast living in the wine varied wildly. A winemaker would add sugar to the wine, but if most of the yeasts already had died, there would be few bubbles. (On the other hand, if the yeasts were very active, there would be millions of bubbles, and likely a broken bottle.) As late as 1860, the influential writer Cyrus Redding complained that "the effervescence of the Champagne wine, considered in all its bearings, is most uncertain and changeable." Ten years later, no such criticism could have been made. Following the publication of Pasteur's discoveries regarding yeast and bacteria, vintners began adding both sugar and yeast at the time of bottling so as to guarantee a controlled second fermentation. Champagne then became much more consistent, the wine in one bottle virtually identical to the wine in another.

The final technological step in the evolution of the *méthode champenoise* involved devising a way to get rid of the spent yeast so as to leave the wine clear and bright. When done by hand, this was a very slow and laborious process that invariably included spilling a great deal of wine. But a Belgian inventor came up with a much faster procedure. He put the necks of the inverted bottles in a bath of icy brine, thus freezing the sediment so that it could be expelled easily without more wine escaping. Coupled with riddling and the controlled use of sugar and yeast, this process of disgorgement transformed Champagne production from an artisanal operation to an industrial one. The numbers tell the story. At the end of the eighteenth century, fewer than three hundred thousand bottles of sparkling wine were being made annually in the region. By 1900, production had increased to thirty million.

Sparkling Champagne would become a wine appreciated by an ever-expanding bourgeois audience all during the 1800s. At the start of the century, however, it had been the near-exclusive province of the aristocracy, a drink enjoyed by tsars and emperors, but rarely by middle-class consumers, no matter their level of connoisseurship. There simply was not enough wine to go around. Not surprisingly, what little was available came at a high price. This wine tasted undeniably modern, meaning unlike anything made before, and the people who purchased it invariably were very rich.

The people who first drank another new Enlightenment wine were not. Port initially was made to satisfy the English tavern market when French wines were banned because of war. Coarse and cheap, it served as a substitute for Claret—not the exclusive wines being made by Arnaud de Pontac and the other ambitious vineyard owners in Bordeaux, but rather the old-fashioned sour tavern staple. Only gradually did Port become bottled, enabling it then to be cellared and aged. Only gradually too did its method of production evolve, brandy being added to the fermenting must, giving it sweetness and potency as a wholly new type of drink—a fortified wine. Port began the eighteenth century as a harsh table wine sometimes known as "black-strap." It entered the next one as a mellow because a matured fortified wine, something very different and very modern.

The Methuen Treaty of 1703 allowed Portuguese wine to be imported to England at a third less duty than would be placed on other wines (this in exchange for English textiles gaining favorable access to Portugal). So all during the eighteenth century, Portuguese wines flooded the English market. They were for the most part quite cheap. Some, from the north, tasted light and acidic, so initially something like today's Vinho Verde. Tart even when fresh, they soured quickly, and barely survived the sea voyage. Others were sappy and sweet— Osey, for example, made near Lisbon from what may have been Muscat grapes, and the unfortunately named Bastard, a blend of wine and honey. The demand for red wines proved particularly strong. Not surprisingly, a number of foreign merchants, looking to cut costs by going to the wine's source, set up shop in Portugal. In Minho in the north of the country, they found red wines that tasted thin and astringent. Farther south, near the capital, they discovered shrill ones that they simply called "Lisbon wine." But in Porto at the mouth of the Douro River, they purchased fuller-bodied reds that were made inland and shipped in *barcos rabelos*, ancient-looking open galleys equipped with massive oars and broad sails. The upper Douro was forbidding country, fabled to be filled with demons and devils. Hardly anyone from the coast went there. But this wine was strong, dry, and tannic. Though often dirty, in large part due to its being transported in moldy barrels or animal hides, it found an audience in English taverns, for it came very cheap.

Consumer demand for better Portuguese wine helps explain why a few bold English merchants began to travel up the Douro themselves. The wine there was far superior to what they could buy in Porto, as it wasn't dirty and hadn't begun to sour. Most of what they shipped home was dry table wine, but before long some became fortified with brandy. The spirit made the wine not only heady but also more stable than it would be otherwise, thus ensuring a safe voyage. This wine, however, was not yet Port in a full modern sense, as the brandy was put in the casks after the fermentation had finished. Adding the fortifying spirit during fermentation did not become standard practice until the early 1800s, which was when aged Port began to be venerated. The difference in technique proved crucial. Adding spirit to fully fermented wine increases the level of alcohol, but it does little to change the wine's flavor. Introducing spirit during fermentation, however, alters, or rather preserves, otherwise fleeting flavor. That's because the spirit kills the yeasts whose very existence occasions fermentation, and so leaves the now heady wine with plenty of unfermented, residual sugar. Hence modern Port's delicious paradox—a strapping wine that also tastes delicately sweet.

Port's transformation from something cheap and coarse to something refined and sophisticated came gradually, but two factors proved critical. The first was the organization of the trade, the second the discovery of the advantages provided by aging the wines. The Portuguese king's chief minister, Sebastião de Carvalho, later Marques de Pombal, established the Douro Wine Company in 1756, in effect giving the government control of the Port business. Lisbon had been devastated by an earthquake the year before, and Carvalho used this new monopolistic company to help finance rebuilding the city. He fixed prices, and in the first official classification system anywhere in the world, he distinguished between vineyards of first and second rank. Before long, exports started to increase, the prices that merchants could charge began to rise, and Port acquired a more distinguished reputation. Enhancing that reputation was the discovery that this wine improved notably when aged. The spirit needed time to become integrated with the red wine in order for Port to taste smooth and supple rather than rough and fiery. Once the market back home began to express an interest in Port as something more than coarse "black-strap," the English merchants in Porto built lodges across the river in Vila Nova de Gaia, where they aged their best wines in barrels. After a few years, they would ship the barrels home, where the wines would be bottled. Consumers began to observe that some of these wines in bottles improved notably with time, acquiring unexpected nuances of aroma and flavor. This proved particularly true with wines from certain years. It is difficult to know precisely when the first vintage Port was made and identified as such, but this sort of wine quickly became prized. It would be "sipped at leisure . . . talked about and enjoyed over the mahogany with the dessert, while reminiscences flowed and candles burned brightly into the night." Those words belong to the writer André Simon, whose *Bottlescrew Days* documents in detail the increase in both quality and quantity that led to this new wine becoming so fashionable. As Simon puts it, by the first decades of the nineteenth century "the superiority of Port over all other wines had become part and parcel of the creed of every true-born and true-hearted Englishman."

Port wasn't the only fortified wine to introduce new tastes and so entice new drinkers as part of wine's modernization. The practice of adding distilled spirit to young wine began in the early eighteenth century as a method of making some otherwise disagreeable wines more palatable. This happened most notably in northwestern Italy, where a dash of clear spirit and an array of herbs would be added to tart young wine to produce a new beverage called Vermouth. For the most part, it and other early fortified wines came cheap. In select places, however, fortification evolved into a process used to impart a distinct character to specific wines, giving them individuality. Much depended on when the spirit was added. In western France, where making brandy had become big business, and the still wines often tasted sour, winemakers took to adding some young spirit to grape juice before fermentation. The result was a heady *vin de liqueur* such as Pineau des Charentes. In Mediterranean France, some vintners added the spirit later, arresting the fermentation and producing a *vin doux naturel*. The best known of these at the time came from Frontignan in the Languedoc. Made from Muscat grapes, it for some reason became a favorite of two eminent Enlightenment philosophers, Voltaire and John Locke. Elsewhere, vintners or merchants simply added the spirit to finished wines, much as the early Port producers had done. That is what an English merchant named John Woodhouse did in 1773 in Sicily. To each 105-gallon cask of wine he purchased, he added eight and a half gallons of young brandy. He then shipped the barrels home to England, having invented a wine he named after the Sicilian town in which he was living, Marsala.

Madeira and Sherry were two other popular fortified wines. Madeira came first. The Portuguese-controlled island of that name sits right in the middle of the Atlantic trade routes, where ships bound to and from Africa, Asia, and the Americas sailed regularly. When those ships docked to provision, they invariably stocked up on the local wine, which, as detailed earlier, was made with dried grapes and often classified with wines from other Atlantic islands as a "Canary." While the sailors certainly appreciated its alcohol, they recognized that it had to be drunk quickly, as it would deteriorate rapidly in the heat of a ship's hold. So to cater to a larger export market, vintners on the island began to add spirit (probably first made from sugar cane) to their wines when those wines began to oxidize. By the late seventeenth century, fortified Madeira was showing up in Europe and in the European seafaring powers' colonies. But the fortifying spirit did more than preserve the wine. It enabled Madeiras to soften in texture and deepen in flavor. Moreover, in large measure because of their piquant acidity, these wines displayed an uncanny ability to age no matter how they were transported or stored. Nothing bothered them. In fact, heat actually seemed to help them mature. Before long, and as odd as it may sound, connoisseurs decided that they wanted to buy Madeira that had crossed the equator. Wines from well-traveled casks had a following in London and Lisbon, but they were especially popular in England's colonies—in India, in the West Indies, and in North America.

Just as Madeira evolved from being a raisined Canary, fortified Sherry developed from Sack, the Andalusian wine made at least partially from dried grapes that Falstaff had so enjoyed on Shakespeare's stage. That Elizabethan favorite was never Sherry in the modern sense, as it had not been aged in a *solera*, a cask to which new wine is added when old wine is taken out. Only in the early nineteenth century did vintners in Jerez begin deliberately aging their wines in a blending system. They made some in a sweet style, others in a dry one, and both became extremely popular, particularly with English enthusiasts, who continued to exert tremendous influence on wine styles worldwide. By mid-century, an astonishing 40 percent of British wine imports consisted of Sherries. Today, these wines often are thought of as aperitifs, but back then they were just as commonly drunk with food. The novelist Thomas Love Peacock recounted drinking a full bottle with a cold saddle of mutton, and a popular Victorian etiquette guide noted that whenever one is entertaining guests, "small decanters of Sherry should be placed at intervals at the dinner-table."

Late-harvested, botrytis-infected wines were yet another eighteenth-century invention. Of course, sweet wines were nothing new. The Greeks and Romans had prized them, as had nobles and burghers in the Middle Ages and Renaissance. Yet Falernian, Vernaccia, and Romney all had been made with raisined grapes and deliberately exposed to air. They tasted oxidized, and represented a very different style than the fresh sweet wines that began to emerge during the Enlightenment.

These new wines were invented at roughly the same time in three places: southwestern France, the German Rhineland, and northeastern Hungary. In each of these locales, farmers would try to pick their grapes, or at least some of their grapes, late in the harvest, when sugar levels were high, because they knew that many of their customers preferred sweet flavors over dry ones. The potential problem was rot. The riper the grapes became, the more likely the possibility that the fruit would become infected with mold, seemingly rendering them useless. Only gradually did vintners discover that not all molds are the same. While most types do make the fruit inedible, one sort actually improves it (at least for winemaking). *Botrytis cinerea* attacks grapes, particularly those grown in low-lying, foggy or humid areas, as they finish ripening. Instead of destroying them, however, it effectively sucks water from each berry, thus concentrating the sugar and acids that remain, and in the process imparting a distinctive, honey-like flavor. The resulting wines taste very sweet but also very fresh, the result of both sugar and acid levels being high. When properly sealed and stored, these wines also can be very long-lived. That's why botrytis is popularly known as "noble rot."

No one knows when and where winemakers discovered that this particular sort of moldy grape can be transformed into exceptional wine. While ancient winemakers may well have experimented with it, the very sight of a botrytis-infected cluster probably deterred most of them. It also is difficult to know when botrytis-infected wines began to be made deliberately. Though winemakers in Tokaji in Hungary were the first to confess to the practice, it seems likely that their compatriots in France and Germany did not follow far behind. What is clear, though, is that when consumers tasted these new sumptuous elixirs, they fell in love with them.

Because Hungary was controlled by the Islamic Ottoman Empire in the seventeenth century, most wine there had to be made surreptitiously. Though the occupying Turks tended to ignore a cultural practice that they knew was ongoing, they never publicly condoned it—which explains why in 1650 a winemaking priest on the Rákóczi family estate in Tokaji, having heard that a Turkish regiment was about to invade the province, delayed the harvest. The army never came, and according to legend, when the priest finally picked the grapes, he found them infected with botrytis. Whether true or not, the story's date seems about right, for thirty years later, when the Turks were being routed from what would become part of the Hapsburg Empire, sweet Tokaji wines were definitely being made. The best came from that same Rákóczi property, the owner of which sent some to Louis XIV at Versailles in an effort to enlist French aid in a doomed rebellion against Hapsburg rule. The king didn't send any cannons or soldiers, but he liked the wine, as did other monarchs in other courts throughout Europe. Once Ferenc Rákóczi's uprising failed, the Hapsburg emperor confiscated much of his land, including the choicest vineyards, and during the eighteenth century Imperial Tokaji became a royal favorite in Vienna, Saint Petersburg, Warsaw, Prague, and the rest of eastern Europe. The little that found its way west, to Brussels and Paris and London, was snatched up by connoisseurs with cellars. No one had ever tasted anything quite like it.

Eighteenth-century Tokaji occupied a stylistic middle ground between old-fashioned, oxidized Romneys and the other new botrytis-infected wines. Vintners used noble-rot grapes, but they aged the wines

in small barrels in which they allowed evaporation and hence oxidation to occur. And in dry harvests, when only small parts of their vineyards would be infected with botrytis, they harvested grapes with a
distinctly raisined character. By contrast, German winemakers tended
to be obsessive when it came to picking healthy fresh grapes and keeping their large tuns filled to the top with wine. No one knows when the
first intentionally botrytized German wine was produced, but by 1676
the mold had been identified in the Rhineland. By the middle of the
next century, reports of casks of special wines made from special grapes
were circulating fairly frequently. (One of the more famous came from
the old Cistercian Steinberg vineyard.) The first full vintage of botrytis-
infected wine came in 1775 at Johannisberg, where rot infiltrated the
vineyard after the command to begin harvesting was delayed in transit.
The estate manager, one Johann Engert, expected disaster but discovered nirvana. Everyone who tried the wines had the same reaction. As
Engert explained, "[The] wines in the seigneurial cellar receive such
extraordinary approval from all manner of true connoisseurs, that you
often hear nothing else said at tastings than, 'I've never had such a wine
in my mouth before!'" The first official regulations delineating when
grapes for sweet wines could be picked came thirteen years later. They
were issued in Mainz, where the grapes and wines were called Spätlese,
meaning "late harvest."

The reluctance to admit picking rotten grapes seems to have been
more pronounced in France, particularly in and around Sauternes,
home today to the world's most famous botrytis-infected wines. Some
accounts date the origin of Sauternes as a sweet, nobly rotted wine to
the mid-nineteenth century, when a German winemaker working at an
estate there allegedly brought with him the requisite knowledge of how
to make it, but other reports suggest that wines in this style had been
produced in the region for a hundred years before his arrival. Records
indicate that wines capable of aging for many years were being crafted
in the 1750s, and that in order to pick just the right grapes for them,
growers had to work at intervals, passing through the vineyards multiple times (presumably waiting for the botrytis, which can infect even
individual clusters unevenly, to arrive). Thirty years later, when Thomas
Jefferson visited the region, he delighted in Sauternes, particularly the

wines from a property called Yquem, which he described as "most excellent." And perhaps most tantalizing of all is the hint in a 1786 document that the distinctive character of the region's wines results from a mystery or secret that is of "benefit to those who are determined to keep it." So while no one confessed to using rotten grapes, some vintners likely were doing just that. Yet even if modern Sauternes was being made regularly and intentionally, it had not yet acquired more than local fame. The only eighteenth-century botrytis-infected wine then being ranked among the world's finest wines was Tokaji, which also was the only one about which growers and vintners did not keep any secrets. Much like their counterparts with sparkling Champagne and vintage Port, they were proud of its being so distinct and different, so enlightened and so modern.

These new age-worthy and collectible wines appealed initially only to a small minority of consumers—those who had developed a taste for them and, as important, those who could afford them. If that minority's influence on the wine trade exceeds its numbers, the reason is not difficult to grasp. The English gentleman who purchased Port to lay down, much like the French nobleman who toasted his king at Versailles with Champagne, and the Russian lord who imported Tokaji from Hungary, was willing to spend a premium to gratify his taste. By contrast, the laborer who drank sour wine daily paid very little for his ration. Though hard liquor had replaced it in many diets, plenty of poor people still had to seek sustenance and solace in wine. And by all accounts, the quality of what they consumed remained as dreadful as it had for centuries. This sort of wine invariably tasted vinegary, as it often had begun to turn even before it left the farm. It existed not to be collected or celebrated, appreciated or esteemed, but simply to serve as a cheap source of nourishment and inebriated escape. In this, it was much like bread—though for the comparison to be truly apt, the loaf of bread needs to be imagined old, hard, and moldy.

A huge chasm thus developed in the eighteenth and nineteenth centuries between the new fine wines and the old-fashioned wines drunk by the poor. The former resemble wines we know today; the latter definitely do not. That's because the contents of a gentleman's cellar and the swill poured at many a working man's tavern would have tasted so different as to seem entirely different products. The markets for both sorts of wine were wholly separate, as the example of Paris at the end of the *ancien régime* illustrates. That city's poor drank very cheap, thin, sour wine, often in taverns known as *guinguettes*. (These were located just outside the city gates so as to avoid a tax levied on wine brought into Paris.) This wine invariably came from vineyards located nearby, since its low price depended on low transportation costs. Some sixty thousand acres of high-yielding vineyards ringed the city. The largest were in what today is the suburb of Argenteuil, and the wine quality was by all accounts horrible. By contrast, the Parisian aristocracy prized sparkling Champagne and lively Beaune wines, both reds and whites. Though these were much more expensive than the local wines, the people who drank them could afford whatever they wished.

But what of Paris's merchants and shopkeepers, its tradesmen and bookkeepers, all those in the city's middle class? Though the ranks of the French bourgeoisie would grow much larger following the revolution, these people already were exerting economic influence. And while they rarely could afford the costliest wines, they did not want to purchase the cheapest ones. A shopkeeper might be able to drink Champagne only on special occasions, but his sense of pride and place wouldn't let him touch the swill from Argenteuil. So he bought second-tier wines from Burgundy, as well as new wines coming into the city from the Loire and Rhône Valleys. These were not as prestigious as the more aristocratic wines, but they were far superior to common wine. Much the same was true across the English Channel. In Georgian England, the new breed of middle-class connoisseurs would not be satisfied with anything they considered pedestrian. So they called specifically for quality Claret, aged Port, and before long, Sherry. These drinkers had begun to conceive of wine less as a generic beverage than as a category containing different drinks for different circumstances. And before long, the various wines they purchased were being treated with sulfur, chaptalized, and sold in bottles, much like their costlier cousins. The era's technological and scientific advancements did not affect very cheap wine, which remained as horrid as ever, but they made a significant difference in the quality of bourgeois wines.

By the start of the nineteenth century, more new wines were emerging to satisfy the expanding market. Some came from already established and already renowned regions—from upstart estates in the Médoc, for instance, and from vineyards just outside the long-tended crus in Burgundy. Others, however, came from new places, or places in which winemakers only recently had raised their ambitions. For example, vintners working in Austria's Burgenland, and on the shores of Hungary's Lake Balaton, and in Switzerland's Vaud and Valais cantons, began making higher-quality wines to satisfy the thirsts of people living in the nearby cities of Vienna, Budapest, and Geneva, respectively. Though these particular wines did not travel much beyond those cities, other wines were taken farther afield. In Beaujolais, for instance, top examples of the local wine began to be exported—not just to nearby Lyons, but to Paris, Brussels, and beyond. And in the Rhône Valley, enterprising growers with vineyards on the hill of Hermitage sold their wine, made with the local Syrah grape, for prices that rivaled fine red Bordeaux. Native-born négociants then shipped it to Paris and other markets. This pattern would continue throughout the century, with countries and regions previously thought of only as sources of cheap common wine becoming home to some prized quality wines. That category now included a much wider range of products, many with an elevated status, than ever before.

The most elevated were differentiated not only by place but also by time—specifically, by vintage. With the advent of bottles, corks, and cellars, people began to pay more attention to the differences between harvests. There were many years in which bad weather ruined crops. The 1816 vintage, for example, proved disastrous. Sometimes called "the year without a summer," it brought frosts in June, July, and August all through the Northern Hemisphere. (Meteorologists now attribute the freakish climate to the eruption of an Indonesian volcano, Mount Tambora, the previous spring.) But there also were years in which everything seemed to go right, and that produced wines that connoisseurs cherished even decades later.

One of the first, and still one of the most famous of these vintage years was 1811, sometimes called "the year of the comet." A long hot summer and a dry warm autumn that year meant an abundant harvest of fully ripe grapes in most European vineyards. Some people attributed the remarkable weather to an astonishing astronomical event—the presence of a comet in the night sky that burned so brightly in September and October, right when wine grapes were being picked, that it was visible to the naked eye. Many vintners took this to be a sign or blessing on the harvest, which yielded such superlative wines that more than one commentator writing later dubbed 1811 *the* first true vintage year. That judgment was reinforced in 1926, when the proprietors of Château Lafite-Rothschild in Bordeaux opened some of the last bottles of their 1811 vintage for a group of selected guests. Maurice Healy, one of the lucky attendees, declared that "at its age of 115 years it still drank graciously, with not more than a suspicion of fading. I think it must have been the greatest Claret ever made."

Wine's new appeal also involved how and why people drank it, since an appreciation for fine wine was gradually coming to be considered a sign of sophistication and urbanity. That last is especially important, for this taste almost always could be gratified more easily in cities than in the countryside. In order for such gratification to become widespread, however, the idea of taste itself had to change, evolving from a wholly physical sense to one that, while still bodily, had an intellectual component as well. Taste in this new guise was yet another eighteenth-century idea that became popularized during the nineteenth, and that continues to be important today (though less and less under that particular heading). It too helped modernize and elevate wine—or at least certain fine wines—to a realm apart from, and often thought to be above, other foodstuffs. Wine's mid-nineteenth-century golden age, which saw dry wine become for the first time an object of broad consumer appreciation, thus resulted from altered perceptions of its value as well as from its own clearly enhanced quality. Whether with already esteemed wines like Champagnes, Clarets, fine Burgundies, and sweet German Rieslings, or newer wines like Italian Barolos and Spanish Riojas, more and more people in more and more places now believed that they indeed could drink stars—wines that tasted truly special and so were worth choosing and even celebrating.

NEW TASTES AND TRADITIONS
Wine's First Golden Age

During the nineteenth century, record numbers of people began to appreciate, and hence to acquire, high-quality wines. Modern wine production expanded significantly, as did the ranks of an already swelling social class that wanted to drink good wine and, as important, could afford it. Considered together, these two developments resulted in a short-lived period of triumph for fine wine. Led by red Bordeaux, it attained unprecedented cultural prestige, being viewed by many consumers as an object of aesthetic even more than physical desire. Ever since the fall of Rome, people had valued wine as a means to the twin ends of calories and escape. Now at least some considered certain wines to be veritable *objets d'art*, so worthwhile in themselves. Commentators and historians often mythologize this era as an idyllic "golden age." Yet much as with the fabled ancient Greek golden age, when according to the poet Hesiod men and women "lived like gods without sorrow of heart," doing so depicts nostalgic longing more than historical fact. For in truth, this triumphant moment was simply that—a moment, brief and limited, with only select wines from select areas displaying glory. Moreover, the seeds of crisis that soon would plunge all wine into a near century of decline already were beginning to take root. Before long, devastating vine diseases would send not only Bordeaux but all of viticultural Europe into economic freefall. Then came a series of social and cultural catastrophes—a cataclysmic war fought in or near some of the world's greatest vineyards, an increasingly powerful prohibitionist movement, global financial collapse, and finally yet another world war. By the middle of the twentieth century, spirit-based cocktails, not vintage crus, were all the rage, and many people once again viewed wine as something old-fashioned if not outdated. Not until the 1970s and 1980s would it regain its lost luster.

Though short-lived, wine's nineteenth-century age of triumph was nonetheless quite real in certain places and with certain wines. Those perceived to have distinguished pedigrees acquired unparalleled cultural standing, something reflected both in the prices they fetched and in the audience they attracted. As Hugh Johnson colorfully puts it, "Bankers were ready to pay any money for famous properties, [and] vintage-time in the Médoc was a Champs Elysées of flounces and flirting." But all this fuss and fury came only because fine wine had become fashionable for many of those bankers' bourgeois clients. Unlike their fathers or grandfathers, most of whom had tended to treat all wine as something to consume quickly, these middle-class wine drinkers cellared, collected, and celebrated with it—in private homes, in clubs, and in another important modern invention, restaurants serving food.

Bourgeois consumers wanted not only new wines but also new places in which to enjoy them, and restaurants came to serve just that function. Defined as places in which one orders food and drink from a menu that offers choices, restaurants began to assume modern form following the French Revolution. They had started as *ancien régime* soup shops, but with the collapse of the culinary guild system in which separate purveyors supplied separate items for the table, savvy entrepreneurs offered their customers more varied fare. One of the first modern restaurants, La Grande Taverne de Londres in the arcades of the Palais Royal in Paris, was owned by Antoine de Beauvilliers, who had been a chef in the employ of Louis XVI's brother. As the name suggests, Beauvilliers modeled it in part on an English tavern. Yet unlike a tavern, where food was served communally, he followed the earlier restaurateurs in seating his patrons individually. And Beauvilliers offered them much more than bouillons. His menu featured soups, meats, fish, desserts, and more, including a variety of wines. Patrons were enticed by this tantalizing array of choices.

Born during revolution, restaurants soon came to represent a form of cultural democratization. This was not because, as legend sometimes has it, they were all owned by the former cooks of aristocrats. In truth, only a handful of chefs like Beauvilliers opened restaurants, the rest preferring to conceal rather than exploit their past employment. (With the guillotine busy at work, few considered a history of close contact with the aristocracy to be much of a job recommendation.) Instead, a restaurant functioned as an inherently democratic institution because it made available to anyone with sufficient money to spend an experience previously reserved for an exclusive social class. As Brillat-Savarin put it in his 1825 *Physiology of Taste*, "Whoever, having fifteen or twenty pistols at his disposal, sits down to the table of a first-class restaurateur, that man eats as well as and even better than if he were at the table of a prince." Since no one dining in an aristocratic household ordered from a menu, this social leveling did not necessarily pertain to the specifics of the cuisine. It definitely did apply, however, to wine. As the nineteenth century unfolded, restaurants often offered their customers wines otherwise unavailable to them—either because the wines were produced in limited volume or because they were sold exclusively there. Restaurants also often featured wines previously reserved largely for the aristocracy. And the very organization of these establishments, with private tables grouped together in a public space, allowed a customer to enjoy the wine individually while being observed communally. In this regard, restaurants represented a triumph of the emerging bourgeois sensibility, and they soon became popular with middle-class consumers throughout the Western world.

Restaurants served another important function when it came to wine. The very fact that their proprietors made wine part of their menus, eventually giving it a menu of its own, helped cement its association with dining in people's minds. We today may think that the link between wine and food is of long standing, but in truth it is only about two hundred years old. For many millennia before then, people drank wine all through the day, regardless of whether they were eating or not. Only in the nineteenth century, when other beverages had become widely available, did people begin to think of wine not just as a choice, but more specifically as a choice to be made when dining. By mid-century, when restaurants had opened in just about every European country (and in most current or former colonies), consumers were able to distinguish firmly between wines and other beverages in large measure because of where and when they would drink what. One ordered beer in an alehouse or pub, gin or whiskey in a bar or tavern, coffee or tea in a coffeehouse or café, but one drank wine in a restaurant. And the specific wine one ordered depended on a variety of factors—the content of one's purse to be sure, but also who might be watching, and what one was going to eat. Wine and cuisine went hand in hand. In fact, by the early nineteenth century, wine was fast becoming part of cuisine.

Just as restaurants separated foods from their sources, transforming them into works of art by concealing the steam and smoke of the kitchen behind a theatrical façade of formal presentation, they helped turn wine into an object of aesthetic desire. A bottle of fine Bordeaux or Champagne became something to covet. Its presence on the starched linen of a grand restaurant table, much as at an exclusive gentlemen's club, bespoke sophistication. Restaurant customers never witnessed the preparation of dishes, and they never knew wine as anything but a finished product. As a result, wine appreciation, which had been confined to grand aristocratic mansions during much of the eighteenth century, expanded exponentially during the nineteenth.

Consumers willingly paid high prices for wine, and by doing so further elevated its cultural standing. Yet the simple fact that more people spent more money tells only half the story. Equally important was their desire to purchase and possess something they believed had aesthetic worth. Unlike other beverages, wines—or more precisely, fine wines—became widely thought of as such. To appreciate them, people needed to develop discernment. Doing so involved altering both personal attitudes and cultural habits, and gradually a taste for vin fin became widely shared among the urban bourgeoisie. More than the production of any new cuvée, the development of this new taste constituted the true triumph of the golden age. Cultivating it applied to many different things. Yet whether with wine or with music, art, literature, or cuisine, acquiring taste became a shared cultural goal that cut across all differences of politics or nationality. Whether a Whig or a Tory, a monarchist or a republican, and whether living in London or Paris, Vienna or Rome, a nineteenth-century *bourgeois gentilhomme* wanted to be—and as important, wanted to be seen as being—a discriminating man of taste.

Becoming such a person required education and training. In terms of the arts, people had to learn not simply to read poetry or listen to music or view painting, but more profoundly how to do these things. Much the same was true with wine. The acquisition of taste involved learning to detect differences and draw distinctions, to recognize subtleties and so to appreciate nuances. It had little to do with feeding one's appetite, and everything to do with bettering one's self. Consequently it also involved manners and etiquette. After all, the sensibility represented by a cultured sense of taste was always social and communal, not just personal. Changes in how middle-class consumers perceived both food and wine thus were linked closely with changes in how they viewed themselves. And by the middle of the century, wine had become the most aesthetically conceived of all foods and drinks. Learned authors wrote eruditely about it, and it served as an object of cultural criticism—the form of thought defined by the English writer Matthew Arnold as "a disinterested endeavor to learn and propagate the best that is thought and known in the world." Whether enjoyed in public or private, wine provided many thousands of consumers with the opportunity for both cultivating and displaying their newly refined taste, an experience that a great many of them found deliciously alluring.

—⁓—

Taste in this sense had been yet another Enlightenment invention. When Voltaire defined it in the *Encyclopédie* as a "capacity for discriminating," he was referring not to the physical sensation, but to that sensation as embodied in an idea, even an ideology, and a distinctly modern one at that. Human beings obviously long had preferred some foods and drinks to others. Taste as a purely physical sense is a basic part of human life, its source being anatomy, the receptors on a man or a woman's tongue. But taste as a concept, an idea, even a value, one that begins with the physical sense but then expands to include aesthetic and social dimensions, is not. It instead comes from culture, and in the

Western world, from modern culture. Scholars do not agree as to when the word first acquired this meaning. The seventeenth-century Spanish Jesuit writer Baltasar Gracián actively promoted it when he advocated taste as a mark of civilized accomplishment, but the phrase "good taste," meaning something akin to "good understanding," had entered various lexicons almost two centuries earlier. (The Italian humanist Leon Battista Alberti had employed *gusto* to mean "judgment" as early as the mid-1400s.) Yet no matter the specific language or locale, "taste" did not begin to be used widely to denote differentiation and discernment until the Enlightenment. Its new meaning then quickly became ubiquitous. "In all known languages," wrote Voltaire, "this sense, this capacity for discriminating between different foods, has given rise to . . . the word 'taste' [being used] to designate the discernment of beauty and flaws in all the arts. It discriminates as quickly as the tongue and the palate, and like physical taste it anticipates thought."

Eighteenth-century thinkers were obsessed with taste. Burke and Hume in England; Dubos, Montesquieu, and Voltaire in France; Kant in Germany; Gerard in Scotland—these and other leading *philosophes* considered it a fundamental problem. Perched as they were (and as they often understood themselves to be) between old and new, inherited wisdom and modern understanding, they grappled with the question of whether the pleasure one experiences when listening to music, or reading verse, or viewing a painting—or for that matter, when eating a dish or drinking a wine—is a function of the object itself, or of the sensibility that experiences that object. This became such a central concern that a new field of philosophy, aesthetics, emerged to deal with it. That name, coming from the ancient Greek *aestheta*, meaning "things perceived," was coined by the German philosopher Alexander Baumgarten in the 1730s, when he and other theorists began to link artistic beauty explicitly with expressions of taste. That association brought the beautiful into intimate contact with the individual human subject. Men and women, regardless of the contents of their purse or their social standing, then began to think of themselves as aesthetic creatures, capable of developing a sensibility that would enable them to discriminate successfully between a variety of potentially pleasing objects. And since taste was not confined by class or wealth, its invention, which so privileged the individual, went hand in hand with the emerging ideologies of capitalism and democracy.

According to some accounts of aesthetic history, physical taste merely provided a convenient metaphor for discussions of art and beauty. In this view, the philosophers were not really concerned with eating or drinking, but only borrowed language used to describe these activities so as to talk about more important subjects. Yet many eighteenth-century thinkers were preoccupied not just with appreciating art but also with appreciating food and wine. Moreover, the metaphor worked both ways, as the sensibility one cultivated to understand poetry or drawing could be applied equally well to cuisine. "One has a taste for music and painting, just as for ragouts," observed Jaucourt, also in the *Encyclopédie*. And as Dr. Johnson famously explained: "Some people have a foolish way of not minding, or pretending not to mind, what they eat. For my part, I mind my belly very studiously, and very carefully; for I look upon it, that he who does not mind his belly will hardly mind anything else."

With food, discussions of taste invariably focused on choice—for a chef, the choice of ingredients and techniques; for a diner, the choice of dishes. Just as wine changed during the eighteenth century, becoming more durable and hence more desirable, approaches to food underwent a revolutionary shift—in part because of the introduction of new ingredients (many coming from the New World), but even more because of the emergence of a new way of thinking about what constituted quality. Beginning in France but then spreading quickly throughout Europe, and eventually making its way to Europe's colonies, modern gastronomy broke with long-standing traditions. Instead of working to transform natural ingredients into artificial concoctions, chefs began to think of their craft as an attempt to preserve the purity of nature. Of course, the ideals of simplicity and naturalness were not confined to the eighteenth-century kitchen. Valuing the authenticity of the natural became a central theme in an emerging critique of mannered artifice in the arts and even in politics. That critique climaxed with political revolution and artistic Romanticism, and by the dawn of the nineteenth century, food increasingly was valued when it tasted of itself, something that led before long to the invention of both national and regional culinary traditions.

This was the original *nouvelle cuisine*. That phrase, first coined in the 1740s, described an approach that used seasonings to complement and help express, rather than to disguise or obscure, the flavor and aroma of the principal ingredients in a dish. Much the same thing happened with wine. The growing consumer appreciation of fresh-grape wines had much to do with advances in both their production and their storage, but it also reflected a shift in taste—away from flavored or adulterated wines toward natural or authentic ones, and away from raisined flavors toward drier, subtler ones. As detailed earlier, this shift began in fits and starts in the late Middle Ages and Renaissance, with select wines made in select places. Until the eighteenth and nineteenth centuries, however, very few people had the opportunity to experience these wines, which were reserved either for the extremely wealthy or the proprietors of the estates at which they were produced. But when increased production made them more available, people found that they liked them and wanted to taste more of them. As a result, broad cultural perceptions of what constituted high-quality wine shifted as well—away from a simple absence of defects to the presence of particularity and provenance.

Considered together, the era's new foods and wines marked yet another front in the ongoing battle between the ancients and the moderns. The change in what people ate and drank (and in how they thought about what they ate and drank) proved particularly profound for the middle class. This portion of the population grew faster in some places than in others, but by the early decades of the nineteenth century it was flexing its economic muscle just about everywhere. Its influence was felt most forcefully in the countries or regions then becoming industrialized—England to be sure, but before long most of northern Europe as well. Men and women bought things as never before, acquiring not just necessities but also comforts. When tea, for example, became a part of domestic life, items such as cups, pots, sugar bowls, and the like started to adorn the tea table that any proper woman set. Much as happened with fine wine, the aristocratic rich led the way in the acquisition of such consumer goods. But they soon were followed by what at the time was called the "middling class," the members of which, if they could not afford exactly what a lord or lady might purchase, definitely now had the means to acquire quality merchandise. Manufacturers like Josiah Wedgwood in England met this new demand with new products, manufactured in new ways, which in turn became objects of ardent consumer desire.

Even when widely shared (Wedgwood made a fortune selling literally tons of china), such desire always remained rooted in individual choice. The choice may well have been illusory, but whether reality or chimera, the idea of it was essential in order for this new consumer culture to flourish. The decision to buy one item rather than another, while certainly influenced by external factors—everything from advertising to fashion to peer pressure and snobbery—simply had to be believed to be of one's own volition. Otherwise, since the objects in question were not essential to survival, one might choose not to purchase anything at all. Thus people came to believe that consumption was a form of personal expression. The books one read, like the clothes one wore or the silverware on one's table, announced who one was. In this regard, no consumer purchases were so clearly personal as food and drink. After all, there was nothing remotely metaphoric about taste when what one consumed was taken into one's mouth.

With the object of perception literally brought into one's body, taste became the private property of the taster. But how then could it be subject to standards, rules, or principles? So Kant had worried when he complained, "I try [a] dish with *my own* tongue and palate, and I pass judgment according to their verdict (not according to universal principles)." This problem long vexed aesthetic theorists when they transferred the language of taste from the dining table to the concert hall or library. But it also occupied the attention of people who thought seriously about food and wine. They too wanted to set standards for enlightened appreciation. After all, since tastes both change and can be acquired, it was obvious that one's "own tongue and palate" could be trained to learn and then propagate "the best."

So it seemed to all the late-eighteenth- and early-nineteenth-century gourmands who made it their business to do the training. These were the men, and to a lesser extent the women, who spoke and wrote publicly about food and wine in regency London, postrevolutionary Paris, Hapsburg Vienna, and eventually all of cosmopolitan Europe. They proclaimed principles and published rules, not so much about cooking and winemaking, as about understanding and appreciating cuisine and wine. They spoke, that is, to consumers rather than to producers, thus providing the ever-enlarging middle class with a degree of *savoir-faire* that even noble lords and ladies had not enjoyed a century before. Accessibility certainly distinguished the new "art" of gastronomy, as fine dining was becoming available to more and more people all the time, both in private homes and in the era's new fashionable restaurants. But discernment proved ultimately to be even more important. As food and wine became objects of intellectual as well as bodily desire, what most distinguished the new gastronomy was a level of appreciation and understanding largely unknown in centuries past.

When developing a taste for certain wines or foods, the mind helped train or teach the body. William Kitchiner suggested as much in his 1817 *Cook's Oracle*. He insisted that reasoned, informed judgment functioned as a check on animal appetite, so that a "rational epicure" constituted the best sort of gastronomic consumer. Such a person needed to be moderate in his or her consumption, always focusing on quality, not quantity. Like so many of the early-nineteenth-century food writers, Kitchiner distinguished between a gourmand and a glutton, the former with an aesthetic sense of taste, the latter with mere appetite. An English physician, he spent much of his career trying to educate his countrymen about the aesthetics of cuisine. He declared writing about gastronomy to be "an occupation neither unbecoming nor unworthy [of] philosophers of the highest class." To Kitchiner, whose books were bestsellers, "The perfection of all enjoyment depend[s] on the perfection of the faculties of the Mind and Body," the tongue's sense of taste as informed by the brain's.

Kitchiner was following along a path first trod by Alexandre Balthazar Laurent Grimod de la Reynière, a Parisian whose *Almanach des Gourmands*, published in eight volumes between 1803 and 1812, initiated this new genre of gastronomic literature—writing centered on reflection instead of recipe. Grimod wrote eloquently and at length about taste. His many subjects included not simply foodstuffs but also behaviors, all the practices and principles that composed what he called "gastronomic etiquette." That etiquette had become more refined due to the changes brought by the *nouvelle cuisine*, but more important still was the progress in consumer attitudes. "Hosts have come to consider the dining table a serious matter," he insisted, and "guests have become more refined in their taste." Moreover, that table had become "the lynchpin of political, literary, financial and commercial matters," as more and more people cared about, and so took the time to appreciate, what they ate and drank. Grimod's own writing certainly helped spur this change. He convened a tasting panel to help him judge the merits of various meals (including wines). He then reported the results to an eager public. His *Almanach*, a gastronomic etiquette guide for an increasingly democratic world, became very popular. It was adapted, and parts of it translated, into other languages, and Grimod himself became something of a celebrity, the proof being that other writers soon took to satirizing him. Eccentric to be sure, he made for an easy target. But Grimod was not a snob. He did not try to hold onto something privileged and set himself above his readers, but rather worked to disseminate—in short, to teach—what he knew and loved. So too did the many gastronomic writers who followed him—Kitchiner in England, Brillat-Savarin and Alexandre Dumas in France, and a host of others elsewhere in the decades to come.

"The best meal without wine," wrote Grimod, "is like a ball without an orchestra." Despite that enthusiasm, specific wines were never a major focus of attention for him or the other pioneers of gastronomic literature. Unlike later writers, they waxed rhapsodic about croquettes and custards, not crus or cuvées. The reason is not difficult to discern. There simply weren't enough high-quality wines available in the marketplace for significant numbers of their largely bourgeois readers to be able to experience them. Commercially available vin fin (as opposed to vin ordinaire) remained a limited category at the start of the 1800s. But over the course of the nineteenth century, many more high-quality wines became available to many more people, and the contrast with sour, common wine became increasingly apparent. An appreciation for these new objects of consumer desire then spread rapidly through the middle class. Much as happened with cuisine, that appreciation was fueled by writers who took it upon themselves to educate their readers—in this case, to learn about and then propagate knowledge about fine wines. Not surprisingly, these authors shared the early food writers' conviction that taste, conceived of as an aesthetic as well as a physical sense, could be trained and improved. Alongside the vintners responsible for the new fine wines, they led the revolution that brought quality wine to the dining tables of thousands of new consumers.

André Jullien was one of the first and one of the most influential of these writers. Born in Burgundy, Jullien had moved to Paris to sell wine during Napoleon's reign, when the newly empowered French bourgeoisie, like the English middling class a half century earlier, began to exercise significant economic power. Jullien encouraged his countrymen's new consumer desires by writing a groundbreaking book for them. His 1816 *Topographie de tous les vignobles connus* (translated into English eight years later as *Topography of All the Known Vineyards*) did for the literature of wine much what Grimod's *Almanach* did for gastronomic writing— initiate a new tradition by concentrating on consumption rather than production. Since he focused on how to appreciate wine, not how to make it, his audience was less grape growers and winemakers than enthusiasts and connoisseurs, all of whom he inspired by helping to educate their tastes.

Before Jullien, virtually all books or treatises on wine were concerned primarily with the specifics of viticulture and oenology, Chaptal's *Traité* being the most notable example. Jullien's *Topographie* certainly explained how wines were produced, but he was much more interested in describing what makes one wine better than another, and so with detailing where the best wines came from and what a consumer might expect to experience when drinking them. He distinguished first between vins fins and vins ordinaires, and while he occasionally mentioned the latter, his attention was focused primarily on what he called "those wines which are in the greatest vogue and estimation." Within this group, he offered a system of classification, with wines divided into up to five categories or classes based on merit. In addition to identifying the best crus from Bordeaux, Burgundy, and Champagne, Jullien tried to provide informed opinions on the defining characteristics of wines made all over the world. He insisted on discriminating between them, ranking and classifying them in terms of their distinctive features. As he explained in his introduction, "We possess several good volumes on the culture of the vine and on the best procedures to follow in winemaking; but none, to my knowledge, deals with the characteristics which distinguish between them the wines of different vineyards, and still less with the nuance of quality which is often noticed in the produce of adjacent crus." Then, making his rationale for writing clear, he added, "I have tried to fill this gap."

When considered historically, what seems most notable about Jullien's *Topographie* is not the specifics of his classifications (especially since he apparently never actually tasted much of what he catalogued), but rather the assumptions that inform them. Specifically, he took for granted that taste in wine, like taste in art, can be developed. The sagacious taster does not simply discover a preexisting hierarchy of quality, but actually defines that hierarchy through his or her refined sense. In this regard, Jullien surely agreed with Grimod, who defined the "first principle" of an enlightened sense of taste as "an exceptionally delicate palate, developed through extensive experience." Jullien may well have possessed such a palate, but significantly enough, he did not rely on his individual sense alone when proclaiming this or that wine superior. He insisted in addition on collaboration—evidence from the marketplace as well as a record of informed judgment. Like so many other eighteenth- and nineteenth-century aesthetic thinkers, he resisted relying solely on private, subjective opinion.

Jullien was on solid ground with wines identified by cru or estate, but he was essentially on his own with all the rest. And his *Topographie* detailed all sorts of other wines—not only French ones, but also wines from Italy and Spain, eastern Europe, Africa, the Levant, the Americas, India, even China, all places where his knowledge was, at best, partial, and his experience extremely limited. Yet despite his evident lack of familiarity, and his admitted reliance on "statements from books and travelers," he still placed these wines in different categories. In the process, he defined a superior wine as one that tastes *delicat*—translated best as harmonious. Such a wine can be "neither harsh nor sharp," he wrote. It "may have spirit, body, and even *du grain* [noticeable tannin]; but it is necessary that these should be well combined, and that none predominate."

But since this definition applied to all fine wines, what separated one wine from another? And what enabled Jullien to distinguish between his different classes of wine? The answer was not a momentary sip, but rather a history or tradition of taste. To be appreciated fully, a superior wine, whether French or foreign, had to have a sufficient record of quality so as to be self-referential. That is, it needed to taste like itself—all its past vintages, the total of which could be said to provide it with its own identity.

With established crus, the market reflected when a particular wine became valued for such a harmonious character, since demand for it and hence the price charged for it rose accordingly. Very few wines were in that sort of demand, when Jullien published the first edition of his *Topographie*. By 1900, however, the category of *delicat* wine had grown to contain much more than he ever experienced. It included non-French wines, such as Rioja from Spain and Barolo from Italy, both of which belonged to new traditions, as well as many new French crus—some coming from already recognized regions, others from newly developed ones. But then, Jullien had presaged as much. He was one of the first people to grasp, if only intuitively, that tradition could solve the dilemma of taste's subjectivity. Fine wines required models against which their present incarnations could be measured, and there could be no better model than a wine's own past. Put another way, they needed legacies of their own. As the English edition of his book explained, a modern consumer needed to know "what qualities each wine ought to have." Without such knowledge, "he can only pronounce [a wine] agreeable or disagreeable, in respect to his own palate." And such a pronouncement never can have much cultural value, "as tastes differ even to a proverb."

—⁂—

No one embraced the idea of tradition as a sign of quality more fervently than vintners in Bordeaux. And during the nineteenth century, no wines came to enjoy greater international prestige than châteaux-designated Bordeaux crus, some white and sweet, but many more red and dry. These became the most glamorous wines of this first golden age. They served as standards or benchmarks for ambitious vintners elsewhere because, more clearly than any others, they embodied vin

fin's new aesthetic status. In Bordeaux itself, this status became both certified through classification and strengthened through title. Crus there
were very different from those in Burgundy, where the word continued
to refer to specific vineyard plots, often with multiple owners. By contrast, in Bordeaux, crus represented single properties. The grapes could
come from one part of the estate or from several different parts, from a
single plot one year and another the next, from a certain blend of grape
varieties in one vintage and a different blend in another, all so long
as the estate name remained constant. The wine certainly reflected its
origin, but as properties kept expanding and contracting, dividing and
enlarging, it reflected something more, an idea of tradition in addition
to terroir.

In Bordeaux, that idea was expressed by a new use of the term "château," which carried the suggestion of heritage or legacy. Derived from
chastel, the word referred originally to a fortified citadel. Then during the
Renaissance, it came to identify a noble or royal palace. After the French
Revolution, when a château might be owned by a banker or an industrialist, the term still often designated a historical residence, the once heredi-
tary home of a noble if not royal family. But not so in grape-growing
Bordeaux, where very few nineteenth-century estates included old palaces or castles. There the word acquired a new and quite peculiar meaning. It referred less to a building than to both a grape-growing estate and
the wine coming from it. Though many wine-producing properties in
Bordeaux do contain mansions today, the vast majority of these are not
truly historic. Instead, all were constructed in the 1800s as part of Bordeaux's deliberately marketing itself as a source of aesthetically valuable
wines. They exemplify the then newly established traditions that made
the region the world's most important home of fine wine.

Château Pichon-Longueville provides one of the most striking illustrations of Bordeaux's new traditions. In 1850, its owner, the Baron
Raoul de Pichon-Longueville commissioned the architect Charles Burguet to design a home for him on his winemaking estate in the Médoc
commune of Pauillac. Since the baron already had a comfortable house
there, his desire for a new dwelling was not utilitarian. Instead, he
wanted to make a statement—about himself, but even more about his
wine. So he commanded Burguet, already well known for ornate archi-

tecture, to design an extravagant faux Renaissance palace. It was (and is) huge, with massive stone walls, a steeply arched roof, and a set of conical turrets perched atop tall circular towers. Calculatingly planned to look old—or more precisely, to look like an idealized and so sanitized version of something old—it towered over the nearby vineyards like a flamboyant, fairy-tale fantasy. Much the same was true of other grand buildings in the region, including the first designed to make such a statement, the Palladian-styled Margaux (completed in 1816). Some looked eccentric as well as impressive, most notably the pseudo-Oriental Cos d'Estournel, a building that the novelist Stendhal wryly described as "very amusing." And soon there would be more—Palmer, also designed by Charles Burguet, with twin turrets resembling witches' hats, Phélan-Ségur with its columned courtyard, and the ersatz-Elizabethan Cantenac-Brown, to name but a few. All of these were called châteaux. They appeared historic as well as opulent because, while new, they sported a façade of age.

The suggestion that the grandeur of a wine estate was born of tradition rather than just money could prove very useful to its owner. Raoul de Pichon-Longueville's new but historic-looking home intimated that the wine coming from his property could claim a heritage of quality. It might taste distinctive at present, but even more significant was the insinuation that it had done so in the past, and so likely would continue to do so in the future. This was especially important to him in 1850 because he and his sister had jointly inherited the family vineyard. French law dictated that it be divided between them, and the siblings were fast becoming commercial rivals. While the quality of the wines each produced might be judged equal, his château announced that his was the more venerable.

Five years after construction began at Pichon-Longueville, a joint committee of the Bordeaux chamber of commerce and the city's syndicate of wine brokers issued a report in which they ranked the region's top wines. Nothing like this public classification existed anywhere else at the time. It served as a formal validation of distinction, both for individual wines and for the region at large, since it codified what in actuality were still emerging traditions. Though no dry whites made the grade, twenty-six late-harvest ones were listed in three levels, with only

A reconstructed Neolithic wine jar dating from 5000 to 5500 BCE. It was found in an excavated dwelling in Hajji Firuz Tepe in what today is northwestern Iran. *(The University of Pennsylvania Museum of Archeology and Anthropology, image #151075)*

A wall painting depicting a symposium, or convivium, dating from about 470 BCE. It was discovered in a tomb in the Greco-Roman city of Paestum in Campania. *(akg-images / Andrea Baguzzi)*

A Roman amphora, most likely used for transporting wine over long distances. When well sealed, amphorae kept air away from the wines stored in them, allowing those wines to remain drinkable well after the harvest. *(The University of Pennsylvania Museum of Archeology and Anthropology, image #152896)*

A Greek wine bowl, with a painting of Dionysus on the inside, so visible only after the wine was drunk. The god is sailing, perhaps to Thebes, in a ship with a massive grape vine climbing up its mast. *(The Bridgeman Art Library)*

Treading grapes and making wine in the Middle Ages. Though this illustration comes from a twelfth-century prayer book, the wine most likely satisfied secular, not specifically religious, needs. (*The Bridgeman Art Library*)

Drunkenness proved common among all social classes or estates during the Middle Ages, including the clergy. This illustration comes from an illuminated manuscript depicting, but not always condemning, various vices. (*The Bridgeman Art Library*)

A statue of Bernard de Clairvaux holding a replica of the church at Citeaux, the original home of the Cistercian monastic order. The Cistercians made some of the first specialized dry wines, emphasizing the importance of terroir in giving each wine a distinct identity. *(Gianni Dagli Orti / The Art Archive at Art Resource, NY)*

Arnaud III de Pontac, owner of a grape-growing estate named Haut-Brion, was one of the first people to insist on the potential of a specific terroir in Bordeaux. *(Used by permission of Domaine Clarence Dillon)*

By identifying what happens chemically during fermentation, the Enlightenment scientist Antoine de Lavoisier helped give winemakers a greater understanding of their craft. *(The Bridgeman Art Library)*

The nineteenth-century scientist Louis Pasteur solved the mysteries of fermentation and bacterial spoilage, bringing 150 years of scientific research to a triumphant close and initiating the modern study of oenology. *(The Granger Collection, New York)*

Two English wine bottles, made around 1700. The advent of sturdy bottles and securely plugged corks gave wine significantly greater durability, enabling it to age and even improve over time. *(The Bridgeman Art Library)*

Sparkling Champagne, an Enlightenment invention, was from the start a wine associated with celebration, romance, and *joie de vivre*. (*Marc Chamet / The Art Archive at Art Resource, NY*)

Botrytis, or "noble rot," shrivels grapes, leaving a high concentration of sugar that results in opulently sweet, seductive wines such as late harvest Riesling, Sauternes, and Tokay, all of which were first crafted in the eighteenth century. (*Cephas Picture Library / Mick Rock*)

An early-nineteenth-century English restaurant scene. Wine already was very much a part of the dining experience, even if decorum apparently was not. (*The Bridgeman Art Library*)

Alexandre Balthazar Laurent de la Reynière with his tasting panel in 1805. He championed the art of dining, giving physical taste an aesthetic dimension. (*akg-images*)

Château Pichon Longueville Baron in Pauillac, a striking example of how the new nineteenth-century Bordeaux architecture was designed to look old. *(Cephas Picture Library / Nigel Blythe)*

A merchant tasting German Riesling, the only still wine to rival classified-growth Bordeaux in prestige during wine's nineteenth-century golden age. *(ullstein bild / The Granger Collection, New York)*

A nineteenth-century Port drinker. Originally a cheap tavern drink, Port became a refined English passion once people discovered the benefits of aging it. *(The Granger Collection, New York)*

Giulia Vittorina, Marchesa di Barolo, improved her estate's wines by hiring a French winemaker to import Bordeaux-inspired methods of grape growing and winemaking to Italy. (*Used by permission of Opera Barolo*)

The Marques de Murrieta, inspired by the French vins fins he drank in London, brought modern winemaking to Rioja in Spain. (*Used by permission of Marqués de Murrieta*)

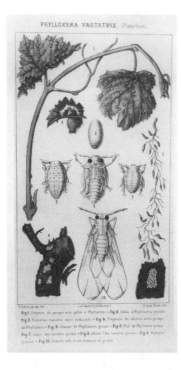

Phylloxera, a tiny insect that feeds on the roots of grape-vines, devastated Europe's vineyards starting in the 1860s, ushering in a cata-strophic century for wine in general. *(The Bridgeman Art Library)*

Antialcohol campaigns exerted political influence in many countries, but none was more powerful than the American Prohibitionist movement. It treated wine as cheap booze. *(Imagno - ullstein bild / The Granger Collection)*

The First World War issued a serious challenge to both wine production and wine consumption. The fighting especially devastated the region of Champagne, as this photograph of the Reims Cathedral in 1919 illustrates. *(The Bridgeman Art Library)*

During the first half of the twentieth century, drinking cocktails rather than wines became a sign of sophistication and urbanity. This illustration appeared in a French fashion magazine in 1927. *(The Bridgeman Art Library)*

Baron Pierre Le Roy de Boiseaumarié in Châteauneuf-
du-Pape insisted on strict
grape-growing and wine-
making rules of the sort that
eventually led to the implementation of the French
appellation system. *(Used by
permission of Château Fortia)*

Two French legislators, Joseph Capus (left) and Edouard Barthe, played crucial
roles in the improvement of wine quality throughout the country. Capus, who
more than anyone else was responsible for the creation of Appellations d'Origine
Contrôlée, insisted that geographical designations were meaningless without
some form of quality control. Barthe, who cared little about vin fin, fought tirelessly for farmer's rights and government regulation of the vin ordinaire market.
(Bibliothhéque de l'Assenblée nationale)

Emile Peynaud's philosophy of control in both the vineyard and the winery helped change the stylistic profile of Bordeaux wines and their many imitators worldwide. *(Copyright Magnum Photos)*

The most important technological innovation since bottles and corks, temperature-controlled tanks enabled vintners in warm growing areas to make fresh-tasting wines. These are at the Aveleda winery in Portugal. *(Marguerite Thomas)*

Max Schubert, holding
a large bottle of Grange,
the wine that opened the
world's eyes to Australia's
winemaking potential. *(Copyright Penfolds)*

Maynard Amerine, working
alongside his colleague and mentor, Alfred Winkler, at the University of California at Davis,
insisted that making quality wine
must begin with growing the
right grapes in the right places.
(Wine Institute of California)

Nicolas Catena revolutionized Argentinean wine by modeling his estate-grown Malbec on Robert Mondavi's
Cabernet Sauvignon, which in turn was
modeled on classified-growth Bordeaux.
(Used by permission of Bodega Catena Zapata)

The 1982 vintage in Bordeaux, with its expansive fruit-forward flavors, offered a new stylistic model for winemakers, one promoted by critics like Robert Parker and pursued by consumers just about everywhere. *(Marguerite Thomas)*

The widespread use of oak barrels has been a crucial element in wine's globalization. The vanilla-tinged taste and smell of toasted wood is part of today's popular flamboyant style of wine. *(Marguerite Thomas)*

Biodnynamic viticulture may sound strange, but the resulting wines are almost always excellent. The tools used by its practitioners include cow horns (to bury manure and other treatments) and crystals (to spur the growth of nutrients in the soil). *(Paul Dolan, Dark Horse Vineyard)*

Specialization goes hand in hand with globalization in the contemporary world of wine. Here are six specialized southern European wines, each made with indigenous native grape varieties rather than international ones. *(Marguerite Thomas)*

one, Yquem, at the top. Most famously, the committee categorized fifty-eight red wines in a list that still holds sway today. These were assigned to separate tiers: four premier crus, or first growths, at the top; twelve second growths; fourteen third growths; eleven fourth growths; and seventeen fifth growths.

In deciding where to rank wines, this committee focused much more on history than on the present moment. Its members studied old sales records, reviewing the prices that individual wines fetched in the marketplace, looking above all for consistency and reliability. They did not care about onetime price spikes or falls, just as they paid scant attention to properties that might just be beginning to attract attention. They wanted to provide a classification that would both represent and propagate legacies, so they included only estates for which the market could affirm high quality over time. As their report stated, they realized "how delicate a thing this classification is," and so took pains to submit "a work which has drawn its elements from the best sources." Thus in 1855, the two Pichon properties were not even recognized as separate entities. Since neither had sufficient history to be evaluated alone, they were listed simply as one cru. Today, when enough time has passed for each to display its own identity, Château Pichon-Longueville and Château Pichon Comtesse de Lalande are listed separately. Both, however, remain second growths, as they were then.

The 1855 classification became a self-fulfilling prophecy, since it helped make fledgling traditions permanent. It was made public, and many of the wines were exhibited, at the Paris world fair, or Exposition Universelle, later that year. Then seven years later, when Bordeaux city officials received an invitation to exhibit wines at another grand fair, this one in London, they sent the same list, along with a statement asserting that the wines on it were ranked according to their merit. This apparently applied even within the individual classes, so Lafite was first among the firsts, and Mouton led the seconds, just as Kirwan topped the thirds, Saint-Pierre the fourths, and Canet (Pontet-Canet today) the fifths. Despite the fact that many estates have changed owners and a few have been divided or gone out of business, only two official changes have been made to the classification in the more than 150 years since it was published. The first represented an afterthought or correction, as

Cantemerle became the final fifth growth late in 1855, while the second came 118 years later, when Mouton (by then Mouton-Rothschild) officially was promoted from a second to a first growth.

With the exception of Haut-Brion, a wine whose history as well as reputation meant that it simply could not be left out, the 1855 classification included only wines from the Médoc. This was not, as sometimes has been alleged, because Bordeaux's chamber of commerce privileged the wines marketed by city merchants (as opposed to those in the town of Libourne, where most wines from St-Émilion, Pomerol, and other communes on the right bank of the Dordogne River were sold). Instead, the vineyards in the Médoc simply had longer histories as independent estates. They were the only ones with identifiable traditions. While the twenty-first-century Bordeaux trade reserves some of its highest prices for wines from other areas, the nineteenth-century market judged only red wines from the Médoc to be of *cru classé* quality. They alone had a suitably extended record of distinction. The Bordeaux committee did send wines from St-Émilion and Pomerol to Paris in 1855. Yet, as if to prove that only wines from the Médoc merited classification, they did not send any from individual properties. Instead, they exhibited what most wine from Bordeaux had been for centuries, regional blends.

The committee's emphasis on heritage and lineage, on a wine today tasting like a wine from vintages past (and with luck, vintages to come), helps explain why the château concept became so deeply rooted in Bordeaux, and then was imitated elsewhere. It first marked the ambition (and pretension) of certain wealthy owners, those who could afford to hire architects like Charles Burguet and build palaces like Pichon-Longueville. But the term's increased use in the second half of the nineteenth century, when red Bordeaux became the most aesthetically valued wine in the world, came to signify the entire region's identity. The stress on tradition also explains why every commentary both before and after the introduction of the 1855 classification listed the same four wines as Bordeaux's best. Haut-Brion, Lafite, Latour, and Margaux first had produced individually identified wines over a century earlier. They were the first growths in large measure because they were the oldest vins fins in the region.

Consumers considered these wines aesthetically superior because they tasted good vintage after vintage. In turn, their consistent high quality resulted from continuity in the wineries as well as the vineyards. And continuity in both places required capital—money spent on barrels, cellars, replanting, and more, the proprietors willingly sacrificing immediate profit for long-term gain. The 1855 list ensured such continuity, for it in effect guaranteed that the wines on it could remain strong. People worldwide trusted it, and so used it to guide their purchases. To many minds, it almost had the force of law. Moreover, and perhaps not surprisingly, it soon turned all the listed wines into "châteaux." In 1855, only five of the fifty-eight classified red crus had been called by that name. By 1900, all claimed the château mantel. Much the same thing happened both off the exclusive list and beyond the Médoc. In the entire Bordeaux region, forty-eight properties were identified as châteaux in 1850. But nearly seven hundred employed the designation in 1870, and then almost fifteen hundred in 1900. Few of these were graced with grandiose mansions. All, however, used the word to designate tradition—either, as with the classified growths, a tradition they could claim or, as with newer properties, one to which they aspired.

The best of these wines could be cellared for a long time, and being distinct, they were both gustatorily and culturally recognizable. So an appreciation for them represented discernment and sophistication. The British connoisseur H. Warner Allen, writing in the next century, described "the Golden Age of Modern Vintage Wines" (which he saw beginning with the comet year of 1811) as the first one in which modern wines might "possibly surpass the finest classical wines of Greece and Rome." Like many chroniclers, Allen had a misguided because a romanticized understanding of ancient wine. Yet his sense of the superiority of these modern wines seems to have been on the mark. No comparative tastings can prove the point today, but there can be little doubt that these were the finest—meaning the most stable, most reliable, most compelling and age-worthy—wines made to date anywhere. Scientific and technological advances in viticulture and oenology, a more competitive marketplace, and an increasingly discriminating clientele all combined to make them so. But so too did the sense of heritage that the château designation evoked. Consumers, their palates developed to value certain tastes, found these wines superior precisely because they could recognize them so readily. Their appeal came from their consistency. It was inseparable from tradition. That's why as the century progressed, ambitious vintners elsewhere tried to claim a tradition for themselves, even if in many cases they had to invent it.

The idea of inventing tradition may seem strange, but many people in nineteenth-century Europe tried to link their rapidly changing modern world to a seemingly stable past. In an age abuzz with industry and innovation, they longed for continuity. As historians have noted, this longing often led them to romanticize, distort, and even fabricate cultural legacies. Specific conventions that developed during the century, such as wearing Highland tartans in Scotland and venerating the druidic Gorsedd stones in Wales, appeared to be old but in actuality were quite new. The popularity of neo-Gothic architecture and the revival of medievalism in England, much like the emergence of an idealized concept of "the folk" in Germany, linked the present with the past, even if that past might be largely fictitious. Christmas carols, the fairy tales of the brothers Grimm, and the "restorations" of the architect Eugène Emmanuel Viollet-le-Duc are all examples of new artifacts whose popularity stemmed from their being disguised as something historic. Though logic dictates that something new can never be truly old, it hardly mattered that this history was itself constructed. Invented traditions worked precisely because they implied stability.

So too with wine. In the nineteenth century, only a handful of the world's wines could claim true traditions, and at least in terms of style and quality, few of these traditions were very old. Even within grape-growing Bordeaux, only a small percentage of wines were true vins fins. Plenty of Claret still came to market as a coarse blend, and most wines from individual estates were sold to négociants at such low prices that the owners could not afford the investment necessary to realize the sort of consistency that defined the classified growths. Nonetheless, the classified wines, joined at century's end by a select group of others (including both Château Ausone and Château Cheval Blanc from St-Émilion, but nothing yet from Pomerol), were universally recognized as being the world's finest because the most aesthetically pleasing wines.

The Bordeaux châteaux certainly had rivals in the late-nineteenth-century marketplace. First, of course, came the top Burgundies, crus sporting more tradition than any other fine wines. But the division of estates in the Côte d'Or—due initially to church properties being sold piecemeal during the French Revolution, and then to inheritance laws subdividing the already small estates—meant that no owner ever had all that much wine to sell. In France, improved wines also came from the Rhône Valley, especially vineyards on the hill of Hermitage. Though these were often used in blends, some made quite far away, determined vintners crafted their own crus, with the example of the Bordeaux growths firmly in mind. Their wines appealed to a discriminating but growing clientele, as did Champagne, which was becoming more fashionable seemingly every year.

Elsewhere in Europe, new wines soon started to court much the same market as the classified-growth châteaux. Many came from old wine-growing regions where ambitious winemakers began working with new aspirations. These included Piedmont and Tuscany in Italy, Rioja in Spain, and the Rhine and Mosel Valleys in Germany. And much as in Bordeaux, the vintners responsible for many of those wines invented traditions to present them as something important, wines worth buying because they were worth savoring.

The cultural practice of savoring wine, as opposed to just drinking it, helped define the connoisseurship that emerged with wine's initial modernization—the advent of corks, bottles, cellars, scientific oenology, and the rest. When wine first became stable and consistent, it also became the object of a new consumer desire, with at least some wines being valued aesthetically. Certain wines definitely had been prized highly before then, Roman Falernian, for example, and Cistercian Vougeot, but no evidence exists to suggest that these were consumed differently from other wines. They may have been better, or have been perceived as better, but since they possessed no special aesthetic status, they tended to be gulped down and tossed back just as all wines were. Savoring wine was something new. Because it required education and effort, it was a mark of cultural refinement, particularly for self-conscious members of the bourgeoisie. A sophisticated nineteenth-century gentleman, especially if living in a city, was simply expected to know something about wine. And while some enthusiasts tried to link this new practice with ancient wine drinking, it soon became clear to anyone who studied the subject that modern connoisseurship was just that—a new practice made possible by new wines. Many of these wines became advertised, marketed, and valued as traditional, but their tastes, and the public's taste for them, were in reality quite new.

—⚹—

After André Jullien, the most important nineteenth-century wine authority was an Englishman, Cyrus Redding, whose *History and Description of Modern Wines*, first published in 1833 and then revised and reissued numerous times until his death in 1870, was the most informed book on wine yet written. Redding recognized that the new wines then being purchased and cellared were indeed new, and that a romantic veneration of classical wines made little sense. "There is no doubt," he wrote, that "the wines of the moderns . . . are much more perfect than those of the ancients." How could he be so certain? The best modern wines are "pure" and "natural," while ancient wines were invariably "mixed and adulterated." Like Jullien, Redding surveyed the wide world of wine (unlike Jullien, actually traveling through much of it). In the process, he was more than willing to expose practices that he considered irresponsible if not fraudulent. So he decried many old-fashioned methods of farming and winemaking, reserving his severest scorn for all those vintners whose "wines have stood still and remained without improvement" despite the many modern advances in oenology and viticulture.

Redding was especially critical of the wines he tasted in Italy. The modernizations that had so changed other wines were barely known there. Very few vintners used bottles or corks, sulfur or sugar, and they sent little wine abroad to compete internationally. Since the local populace remained thirsty, plenty of wines continued to be made, but these had little in common with the new French, German, and Portuguese ones that were beginning to acquire international fame. They were traditional, but to Redding, whose taste had been honed on Bordeaux crus, bottled Champagnes, vintage Ports, and the like, they also were at best ordinaire. In central Italy, whites sporting what remain familiar names such as Orvieto and Frascati were fermented with the grape skins and finished slightly sweet. Invariably oxidized and shrill, they tasted off-putting. Farther north, red wine was more prevalent, but it tended to be both sappy and tannic. And virtually all wine in the hot south was sour, since storage conditions there proved poor. Redding acknowledged that Italy's raw materials were potentially very good, but he insisted that unhygienic winemaking and slovenly farming practices were far too pervasive. "Ripe and unripe, sound and unsound [grapes] are commonly intermingled, and flung into vats that remain uncleaned from last year's vintage," he wrote. So too, "the vines producing every quality of wine grow together, without assortment of any kind." Rarely pruned or trained, they grow "in wild luxuriance, and waste their vitality." The lack of export markets hampered any Italian vintner with fine-wine ambitions. Realizing such ambitions depended on experiencing wines produced elsewhere via the new international traditions then becoming fashionable. So in Italy, much as would prove true in Spain, Mediterranean France, still undeveloped parts of Germany, Austria, and much of eastern Europe, imported, invented traditions had to replace old, outmoded ones.

That's precisely what happened in Piedmont, where Nebbiolo-based Barolo, sometimes called the king of wines and the wine of kings, emerged as Italy's first high-quality fine wine. Though a written mention of a grape with that name dates from the thirteenth century, this wine's modern invention began in 1843, when the Marchesa di Barolo hired a French winemaker with the express purpose of trying to produce wines that would taste something like those she had enjoyed when she was young in France. A remarkably accomplished woman who devoted much of her life to improving conditions for the area's poor, the marchesa had grown up near Paris and never liked the local Piedmontese wine. It tasted sugary, sharp, and somewhat fizzy, so completely unlike the new-styled dry wines gaining international renown. The winemaker she hired, Louis Oudart, came from Champagne, but his models were the top Bordeaux crus. Oudart saw that the combination of dirty equipment and cold winter temperatures could halt fermentation, leaving the wines sweet and unstable. So he cleaned and heated the estate's cellar, made sure that the grapes were picked when truly ripe, and produced the prototype of a wine that shared certain basic characteristics with fine Bordeaux—dark color, full flavor, and the ability to age—but at the same time tasted true to its terroir and hence to itself. The marchesa sent some to King Charles Albert of Savoy and then later to Victor Emmanuel, the first king of unified Italy. Both liked it so much that they ordered vineyards of their own to be planted nearby. The reputation of Barolo as a regal wine persists today.

Other vintners in the area soon began making wines in a similar style, and the success of their wines led to raised ambitions elsewhere in Piedmont. In terms of acknowledged quality, the region became the leading wine producer in Italy. Two institutes of oenology, their curriculums promoting Louis Pasteur's science of grapes and wines, opened their doors in the 1870s, and vintners throughout the region adopted the new techniques that the professors there advocated. In Barbaresco and Gattinara, vintners used Nebbiolo to make power-laden wines that tasted similar to Barolo, while different winemakers elsewhere started treating different grapes, notably Barbera and Dolcetto, with new-found respect. And near the town of Asti, the one old grape variety that had long been in demand, Muscat ("Moscato" in Italian), began to be used to make an entirely new style of wine—not a heady one from dried grapes as in centuries past, but a light frothy one, redolent of peaches and spring flowers. By the close of the century, seemingly everything in the region had been reinvented. The new traditions were fast becoming entrenched.

Winemaking and grape growing did not change as radically or as rapidly in the rest of Italy, but here and there new traditions began to replace old ones. Though most southern regions remained winemaking backwaters, Sicily's Duke of Salaparuta made a dry white from local grapes. Radically different from the island's heavy, sugary wines, it gained considerable renown. In the northeast, long home to sweet wines fashioned from dried grapes, some vintners began experimenting with more modern ones made with fresh, ripe fruit, which they fermented to true dryness. And in Tuscany, Chianti was (temporarily) reinvented.

The first recorded mention of a wine with that name dates all the way back to the late fourteenth century. White at first, it changed color over the following centuries, as records reveal "red Florence" being exported to northern Europe during the Renaissance. Yet the subsequent improvements in other wines caused that market to disappear. Then, starting in the 1840s, Baron Bettino Ricasoli, a prominent landowner in the region, began working to modernize and improve Chianti—or more precisely, to improve the red wine from his estate, the Castello di Brolio. He did this in part because, much like the Marchesa di Barolo, his discerning palate recognized the superiority of fine French wines, but also in part because his ancestral property was mortgaged severely. He hoped to inaugurate a new, profitable Tuscan tradition with a new wine.

Ricasoli was an austere visionary known as "the Iron Baron" who soon found an even more important calling as a political reformer. He played a leading role in the unification of Italy, serving as the country's second prime minister, but even when managing affairs of state in Rome, he always supervised agricultural and winemaking experiments at Brolio. He tested different grape varieties, blending them in different percentages, and by 1872 had arrived at a formula for success. It involved utilizing Pasteur's principles in the winery, and growing only select varieties in the vineyard, the start of a tradition that eventually would be sanctified by law. "Chianti wine draws most of its bouquet (which is what I aim for) from Sangiovese [grapes]," he wrote, going on to advocate the addition of a small amount of red Canaiolo for wines meant to be aged. Before his experiments, no one would have thought to cellar any Tuscan wine, for no one would have thought of it as being in the same league as fine Bordeaux—or for that matter, as Barolo. But connoisseurs who tasted this new Chianti could tell that it was superior, and Brolio was fully disencumbered of debt by the time the baron died in 1880.

Unfortunately, few growers in Tuscany followed Ricasoli's lead. Most found Sangiovese difficult to cultivate, and being unaccustomed to truly dry wines, they thought the wine made with it tasted odd because it was tart. They preferred Canaiolo, from which they made *frizzante* wines, as well as Trebbiano, a high-yielding white variety that they added to the otherwise red blend. Since the vast majority of Tuscan red wine still was drunk well before the next harvest, they paid little attention to a formula designed to help wines age. After Ricasoli's death, his tenants returned to their old methods, and both Brolio and Chianti fell back into disrepute. The wine once again was cheap, simple, and often acrid. According to legend, it was at this point that the baron's ghost, accompanied by a white horse, began wandering forlornly across the Tuscan hills.

At least one other person in Tuscany wanted a wine to savor. When Ferruccio Biondi-Santi returned to his family farm near the town of Montalcino following the Italian war for unification, he planted cuttings taken from a Sangiovese vineyard that his grandfather had tended. In this particular terroir, the vines produced unusually small berries, and he guessed rightly that the resulting wines would be concentrated and age-worthy. Starting in the 1880s, he began producing a dry wine from them. It tasted richer, more tannic, and definitely more intense than other Tuscan wines. Biondi-Santi stored the wine in large oak casks for up to four years before bottling it, and he priced it significantly above other wines from the region. Many of his neighbors joked that it was better suited to chewing than drinking, but their jibes faded away when the wine revealed an extraordinary capability to improve in the bottle. The 1888 vintage in particular became famous. Whether due to the soils, the climate, the altitude, or the grape alone, this was the first Tuscan wine that could be cellared like classified-growth Bordeaux.

Ferruccio Biondi-Santi called this unusual strain of Sangiovese "Brunello," and Brunello di Montalcino has since become one of Italy's most famous, prestigious, and yes, traditional-tasting wines. Yet until the second half of the twentieth century, Brunello remained very much a one-man band, with only Biondi-Santi (followed by his son and grandson) making wines in anything resembling this style or quality. Much as with Chianti, most other winemakers and grape growers simply did not follow the visionary vintner's lead. So with the exception of Barolo and the other quality Piedmontese wines, Italian production as a whole remained stuck in the same rut that Cyrus Redding had complained about. Winemakers and grape growers alike followed old customs and practices, producing wines that tasted quite unpleasant to discerning palates. As Redding bluntly put it, "The wines of Italy have not obtained that high character which might be expected, if the excellence of the grape, and the congeniality of the climate to the culture of the vine, be duly considered."

Across the Mediterranean in Spain, the situation proved only marginally better. With the exception of vintners in Jerez, where Sherry already was established as one of the world's most distinctive wines, general quality proved extremely poor. Here too, farmers tended to follow inherited traditions blindly instead of consciously adopting new methods and techniques designed to increase quality and promote distinction. But, much as happened in Italy, a number of independent producers worked largely in isolation over the course of the nineteenth century to invent traditions of quality. And again, the example of classified-growth châteaux wines from Bordeaux served as their inspiration.

Any visionary nineteenth-century Spanish vintner had to swim against the country's cultural current to attempt to make something that the new audience for fine wine would consider palatable. As in Italy, one big problem involved hygiene, both when making wine and when storing and transporting it. Few farmers knew anything about modern science, and their wines often were dirty and unstable. Moreover, the Spanish custom was to store and transport wines for the domestic market in animal hides—usually those from butchered hogs—rather than wooden casks. Cyrus Redding, for one, thought these wines disgusting, going so far as to declare, "[They] are often found so defiled, even in the tavern, with the pitchy taste, and the filth of the uncleansed skin, to say nothing of the deposit owing to the coarse conduct of the vintage, that they cannot be drunk by a foreigner at all." He acknowledged, however, that the quality of the grapes in Spain was every bit as high, if not sometimes higher, than those in France. "France ranks before Spain in its wines," he wrote, only because "science has led the way to excellence there."

Other contemporary connoisseurs shared similar opinions. Some lived in Spain but had developed a taste for fine French wines when they were abroad. That was the case with Luciano Francisco Ramón de Murrieta, who, with the example of Bordeaux fixed firmly in his mind, was one of the first to try to realize a Spanish region's untapped potential. Raised in England, he had developed an appreciation for fine wine as a young man in London, where he served as an aide-de-camp to the exiled royalist General Baldomero Espartero. In 1844, following the coronation of Queen Elizabeth II, Espartero returned to his home near Logroño in Rioja, where Murrieta found the local wine very different from what he had enjoyed in gentlemen's clubs and restaurants in London. Coarse and crude, tasting of pitch and pig, it was putrid stuff. "It saddened us," Murrieta wrote years later in his *Memoirs*, "to see a potential treasure being wasted."

Murrieta recognized that there was nothing wrong with the grapes growing in Rioja's vineyards. "The only problem was that [the wine] was not being produced correctly." So he decided to do something about it—in part, he said, so as to "do a good deed for the region that adopted me as its son," but surely also in part to have something better to drink. Determined "to obtain sufficient knowledge on winemaking" to make a decent modern wine, he went to Bordeaux, where he studied both grape growing and winemaking techniques. Four years later, he began producing wine in Rioja using local grapes, mostly Grenache ("Garnacha" in Spanish) and Tempranillo, the 1852 vintage being the first of what today is considered traditional or "classic" Rioja—a red aged in oak casks, marked by the taste of both fruit and wood, and possessing the potential for extended cellaring.

Luciano de Murrieta was not alone. Another exile, Camilo Hurtado de Amézaga, Marqués de Riscal, had been living in France during the Spanish wars of succession. When he returned to Rioja after peace was restored, he came via Bordeaux, bringing with him both barrels and vines. He then built a winery, modeled on the ones he had visited in the Médoc. His first vintage appeared in 1860, and it found favor quickly—not so much with the locals, who after all had no experience with the new foreign wines or traditions, as with connoisseurs in Madrid and in Spain's colonies. The Marqués de Riscal's estate soon included a new building built by an architect whom he sent to Bordeaux to study winery design. Though he called his property a bodega rather than a château, there was little doubt as to his inspiration. So too with Luciano de Murrieta, who eventually also became titled as a marqués, and who built his own bodega at Ygay, replete with a restored castle.

By 1880, Rioja was enjoying an economic boom, with new money financing new construction, a new railway providing easy transport, and new bodegas putting all sorts of new ideas into practice. Many were owned at least in part by French businessmen, and while the top Rioja wines certainly had a distinct style, being made mostly with different grapes and coming from different terroirs, they always paid homage to Bordeaux. This was most evident in their characteristic smell and taste of oak, for Murrieta and Riscal had discovered the basic idea of barrel aging when in the Médoc. During the boom years, winemakers in Rioja started to keep their top wines in wood for even longer than châteaux vintners in Bordeaux—so long, in fact, that flavors imparted by the barrels rather than the grapes became a recognizable part of Rioja's signature.

The invention of tradition elsewhere in Spain was not nearly as encompassing. In La Mancha and regions to the south, wine typically was made in dirty earthenware vessels called *tinaja* and then stored in skins. Its availability placated the lower classes in Madrid, but pleased no one else. In the north, some vintners started to make better wine in casks, but they shipped a great deal of it to France to be blended with French wine. Here and there, however, individual Spanish entrepreneurs did go against the grain. The most famous was Don Eloy Lecanda y Chaves, who in 1864 built a winery in a remote corner of Old Castile, near the Douro River. Like his counterparts in Rioja, he was motivated by the example of Bordeaux, and so planted some eighteen thousand vines of Cabernet Sauvignon, Carmenère, Malbec, and Merlot that he had purchased there. (He also planted some Pinot Noir, though how that variety got to a nursery in Bordeaux is anyone's guess.) Lecanda y Chaves kept some of the wine made at his Vega Sicilia estate, but he sold most of it to merchants in Rioja, who presumably passed it off as the local product. After he sold the property, however, the new owner, Domingo Garramiola Txomin, decided to make only estate-grown wine. By the early decades of the twentieth century, Vega Sicilia had become Spain's single most famous wine. Like Ferruccio Biondi-Santi's Brunello di Montalcino, it improved remarkably with time in bottles.

The one other Spanish wine-producing region that enjoyed a nineteenth-century boom was Catalonia. The successful wine there had nothing to do with red Bordeaux, but it did have a French model—in this case, Champagne. José Raventós came from a Catalan winemaking family that sold wine locally, but like so many other vintners, a trip to France was what led him to raise his ambitions. He was especially taken by the taste and feel of Champagne—bright, lively, and frothy, without any of the oxidized character so typical of Spanish white wines. He visited cellars in Reims and Epernay, where he asked plenty of questions and learned about the still-evolving *méthode champenoise*, knowledge that he put to good use when he returned to his family winery, Codorniu, in the town of San Sadurni de Noya. Raventós used a trio of local grapes—Macabeo, Parallada, and Xarel-lo—rather than imported French ones, but he called his wine *champaña*. First released commercially in 1872, it proved so popular with consumers in nearby Barcelona that, thirteen years later, his son, Manuel, who now was running the business, decided to convert all of Codorniu's production to sparkling wine. It won medals at international exhibitions, and by 1895 production had grown to some one hundred thousand bottles, many of which were being exported. The family then built a new, larger winery, and even with local competitors, output continued to expand, so much so that by the turn of the century Codorniu was selling fully half of all the sparkling wine in Spain.

Of course, vintners in Champagne itself had invented their own traditions earlier in the century, resulting in the wine that so excited José Raventós and that continues to delight people today. Some were technical, but others were cultural. As production grew in the region, the managers in charge of the various Champagne houses deliberately promoted an image for their still fairly new product as the traditional wine of celebration, the social elixir necessary for true *joie de vivre*. Marketing masters, they advertised their wines boldly, and even made different cuvées for different markets, thus inaugurating separate traditions for separate groups of consumers. Producers elsewhere followed their lead, and before long sparkling wine of all sorts became associated with gaiety and sophisticated merriment.

Until the mid-nineteenth century, virtually all sparkling wine was sweet. The Russian and Scandinavian markets preferred the most sugary versions, but the Germans and even the French were not all that far behind. American and British consumers liked their bubbly drier, though no one sold a truly dry or brut cuvée until 1848, when an English merchant convinced the Champagne house of Perrier-Jouët to bottle some wine without adding sugar. Attractive at first as a curiosity, this style gradually became popular with consumers who wanted to collect, cellar, and so savor the wine. As the literary critic George Saintsbury observed when he looked back over a lifetime of discriminating connoisseurship in his 1920 *Notes on a Cellar-Book*, Champagne then became "everybody's wine." It never was priced so as to be something drunk by the poor, but it also never cost so much as to be out of reach of the middle class. Dry Champagnes were, as Saintsbury put it, *"winy* wines," not frivolous ones, the proof being that they so evidently improved with age.

The various tricks of sparkling-wine production could not stay bottled up in one region for long, and over the century vintners in many other places made their own versions. Though new, these too were promoted as traditional wines of celebration. Elsewhere in France, Burgundies, both red and white, fizzed, as did wines from the Loire, the Rhône, and Bordeaux. (There even was bubbly Sauternes.) In other countries, much as happened with José Raventós in Spain, enterprising vintners visited Champagne and then returned home determined to craft their own renditions. A Russian bubbly, made with grapes grown in Crimea, had been produced as early as the 1790s. A Slovakian one was offered for sale in 1825, an Austrian in 1842. Sparkling sweet Moscato d'Asti, invented by Carlo Gancia, who spent two years apprenticing at Piper Heidsieck in Reims, dates from the 1860s; twenty years later, József Törley, who also had worked in Reims (at Louis Roederer), set up a "Champagne factory" on the outskirts of Budapest. But Germany was the country outside of France with the biggest sparkling-wine production. While some fizzy wines had been made, probably accidentally, on the Rhine back in the late 1700s, German bubbly in a Champagne style was first fashioned deliberately in the 1820s. Georg Kessler had worked for the widowed Madame Clicquot, and in fact had partnered with her in purchasing a wine estate in Württemberg. When they separated, he started his own firm there. By 1850, more than forty other producers were selling German bubbly, and twenty years later, production had risen to nearly four million bottles.

One reason for the success of German sparkling wine is the simple fact that the country's vineyards lie so far north. The grapes grown there tend to have high acidity but relatively low sugar content, just what bubbly needs to taste refreshing rather than cloying. Those same attributes also enable both still and sparkling wines to age well, for the acidity prevents them from turning fat and flabby. As Cyrus Redding observed, "Wines grown so far to the north" possess "extraordinary durability." Unlike stronger southern wines, which "deteriorate sensibly" after a year or two in a bottle, they "seem possessed of inextinguishable vitality." It thus is not surprising that age-worthy white wines constituted Germany's greatest contribution to Europe's mid-nineteenth-century golden age of invented traditions.

As noted earlier, German winemakers during the Renaissance were among the first to use sulfur, and then to top their casks and tuns regularly with new wine. The technical advances of the eighteenth and nineteenth centuries further assisted them. Adding sugar helped yield decent wines in difficult because overly cold vintages, while using bottles helped keep those wines stable when out of cask. Then in 1834, the Zollverein, or customs union, opened trade between the various German states, giving the best wines a new and larger audience. The widespread availability of quality modern wine quickly chased a great deal of old-fashioned swill from the market. Vineyards in marginal areas such as those near Berlin and Dresden fell into disrepair once people living there were able to purchase wines from the Rhine, Mosel, and Pfalz. And by that point, the top wines from the most respected producers in the best regions were almost all being made with Riesling, which Redding described as "a small white species, harsh in taste, but in hot seasons furnishing a remarkably good wine, having a fine bouquet." The later the harvest, the less harsh the resulting wine tasted, and the more alluring its bouquet became. Thus while sparkling wines were quite popular, people self-conscious about their sense of taste coveted wines made with late-harvested, botrytis-infected Riesling grapes even more. As the nineteenth century unfolded, the selections for these wines became ever more severe, resulting in the German system for identifying them as Ausleses, Beerenausleses, and Trockenbeerenausleses. Drinkers all across the globe came to consider these the country's most renowned because most traditional wines, and by 1900, bottles of botrytized Hock and Moselle regularly fetched prices that matched and sometimes surpassed those for the classified-growth Bordeaux châteaux. They improved notably with time in bottles or casks, displaying remarkably complex and opulent flavors, and so became connoisseurs' darlings.

—⁓—

By the closing decades of the nineteenth century, many of what today are considered Europe's finest wines had assumed recognizable form. From Barolo to Bordeaux, the Rhinegau to Rioja, these wines were displaying modern yet paradoxically traditional temperaments. This does not mean that were one somehow able to taste them today, one would find them identical to contemporary renditions. In some places, different grape varieties were being grown, and in all places, the technology that would further revolutionize wine in the second half of the twentieth century had not yet been invented. Red wines made for aging tended to be more tannic than comparable wines do now, and whites often were darker and nuttier-tasting, having been exposed to a considerable amount of air following fermentation. Vintage variation certainly proved much more extreme, and the potential for spoilage remained far greater. Most wine was not bottled where it was made, and a great deal never saw bottles at all. Oxidation, though nowhere near the level tolerated in previous centuries, still proved more a rule than an exception. Moreover, many other places recognized today as sources of truly fine wine had not yet proved their worth. Whether in the Old World or New, they had few traditions to call their own.

The Cape vineyards in South Africa were the only ones outside of Europe with anything resembling a fine-wine heritage. Yet the inaugurator of that heritage, Constantia, had become a shadow of its former self. European connoisseurs treasured what George Saintsbury called "the old original," not the current pretender, as recent vintages bore little resemblance to the elixir that had so captivated drinkers a century before. South Africa's wine farms, initially profitable because of the availability of slave labor, fell on harder and harder times following the passage of England's Slavery Abolition Act in 1833. Then London imposed tariffs, effectively isolating the Cape vintners. (Cyrus Redding noted that "no method recommended by European science or experience" was practiced there.) Wine would continue to be produced, but for nearly 150 years no one beyond the Cape much cared.

No one cared all that much about Latin American wine either. The most widely planted wine grape there was a prolific, dark-skinned one called País (in Chile), Criolla Chica (in Argentina), and Negra Corriente (in Peru). It made decent though undistinguished wine, a great deal of which ended up being distilled into brandy. Peruvian brandy, transported either by boat or overland by llama, became consumed widely throughout the Americas. In nineteenth-century Peru, wine certainly was drunk domestically, but brandy was sent all over the world. Called Pisco (after the port from which much of it was shipped), it tasted strong and heady. Then in the 1880s, after vine diseases devastated the Peruvian vineyards, production moved south to Chile, where in the next century Pisco gained new popularity as a cocktail mixer. Today, with production reestablished in Peru, the governments of these two neighboring countries squabble about the brandy's true home. The Peruvians cite history, the Chileans market share.

Nineteenth-century Chilean winemakers worked to quench the local market's thirst. Given the difficulty of importing something as perishable as wine around Cape Horn, European wines were not commonly drunk there. Nonetheless, the aristocratic gentry knew the top crus, as they invariably took grand Continental tours, during which they came to appreciate fine wines and new traditions. Not surprisingly, some of them aspired to replicate the experience at home. In 1851, Don Silvestre Ochagavía Echazarreta brought both Bordeaux vines and a Bordeaux winemaker to his Vina Ochagavía estate south of Santiago. He planted Cabernet Franc, Cabernet Sauvignon, Carminère, Malbec, Sémillon, and Sauvignon Blanc there, and from that point on, the top Chilean wines almost always were fashioned on a Bordeaux model. He also generously supplied cuttings to other wealthy would-be vintners—including Matias Cousiño, who founded a winery at Macul in the Maipo Valley five years later; the brothers Bonifacio and José Gregorio Correa Albano, who brought viticulture to the Curicó Valley at their San Pedro estate; Don Maximiano Errázuriz, who founded his eponymous winery in the Aconcagua Valley; and both Domingo Fernández Concha and Don Melchor Concha y Toro, who planted the Santa Rita and Concha y Toro properties, respectively. Large, almost feudal estates like these dominated the quality Chilean wine industry for the next hundred years. Plenty of less ambitious wines still were made with País, but a Bordeaux-inspired tradition definitely had taken root. For much of the twentieth century, political instability, coupled with geographic isolation and high taxes, tempered growth, so the world beyond the Andes knew little or nothing about it. But on the estates themselves, as in exclusive, private clubs in Santiago, these wines found an appreciative audience.

In Argentina, wine, not brandy, was always the principal product. Though vines had been planted in the western part of the colony as early as the 1550s, viticulture and winemaking remained fairly provincial enterprises for three centuries. But an initial rush of immigrants following independence in 1816 led settlers to homestead in the foothills of the Andes, where some planted vineyards. Their market, however, was quite local. Since bottled European wines were by now fairly stable, imports from Bordeaux and Champagne often would arrive in Buenos Aires in better shape than domestic ones that had to be transported some six or seven hundred miles by horse or mule cart. Moreover, wealthy city-dwelling Argentineans often preferred imported wines, as drinking these connoted privilege. Not until 1885, with the opening of a railroad linking Buenos Aires with the western city of Mendoza, did quality Argentinean wine begin to be made in any significant volume. Tiburcio Benegas, who imported vines as well as barrels from Bordeaux for use at his El Trapiche estate, was its champion. The governor of the Mendoza province, he built dams and dug irrigation ditches so as to expand the area suitable for viticulture. He also sent his son to France to study oenology, and then installed him as the head winemaker at El Trapiche. Yet Argentina did not become an international player in the world of fine wine until the late twentieth century. That's because the domestic market, having discovered decent Argentinean wine, demanded more and more of it. Great waves of immigration washed across the country in the early 1900s, increasing the country's population from four million in 1895 to almost fifteen million thirty years later. Most of these new immigrants came from places with established wine cultures, notably

Italy and Spain. The majority of them lived and worked in or near the eastern cities, and they drank a great deal of wine. Argentinean vintners had to work overtime to keep them supplied.

These late-nineteenth-century Bordeaux-inspired South American wines, whether Chilean or Argentinean (and eventually Uruguayan), paved the way for what, a century later, would become a booming international business. More open markets and foreign investments would be needed to get that business going, but wines from estates like El Trapiche and Vina Ochagavía led the way. The situation was quite different across the Pacific, where except for inaugurating a tradition of fortified wines, Australia's nineteenth-century wines barely influenced today's Down Under wine culture. Then as now, the small size of Australia's population meant that its vintners had a limited domestic market. And few nineteenth-century Aussie drinkers cared for dry, table wines. Instead, they preferred something stronger, often made with cane or grain, but if coming from grapes, usually baked brown and bolstered with a heady dose of coarse spirit.

Winemaking started in Australia in the late 1700s, when New South Wales, home to the continent's original colony, was a penal settlement. The first vines came from Brazil and South Africa, and settlers were encouraged to make wine as an alternative to the rums and other spirits that the convicts as well as their jailers guzzled. Yet the climate in Sydney, the initial settlement, did not prove very conducive to viticulture, and production did not begin to flourish until the 1830s, when a Scotsman named James Busby planted a vineyard some hundred miles to the north, in the Hunter Valley. Busby is sometimes called "the father" of Australian wine. He purchased nearly 600 different vines in Europe to bring back to Australia, 362 of which reached New South Wales alive and "for the most part, healthy." Busby's rationale was less a connoisseur's than a reformer's campaigning against strong spirits. But despite his efforts, dry wine with a modest level of alcohol barely penetrated the market in Sydney, which by mid-century had become a rowdy port city of thirty thousand inhabitants, almost all of whom seemed perpetually thirsty for the most alcoholic drink they could find.

Grapes and wine came to the other Australian colonies as soon as they were settled—to Tasmania, for example, as early as the 1820s, to

Western Australia around 1830, and to Queensland in the 1860s. The most substantial plantings were in Victoria and South Australia, where European immigrants tried to replicate wines they knew from home. In the 1840s and 1850s, many vineyards in Victoria's Yarra Valley, north of Melbourne, were planted by French and Swiss settlers, including one ambitious colonist who imported vine cuttings from Château Lafite. At much the same time, German immigrants fleeing religious persecution began settling in South Australia's Barossa Valley. In 1847, Johann Gramp planted vines at Jacob's Creek, to be followed closely by Johann Henschke and Joseph Seppelt, whose Seppeltsfield winery would become that colony's largest. Its growth, however, was fueled mainly by the production of Aussie "ports" and "sherries," fortified wines that satisfied the more prevalent thirst for strong stuff. Lower-alcohol Rhine-styled Rieslings and other table wines were popular within the German community, but did not sell well elsewhere. In Australia's major cities, the ruling gentry of British descent looked down their noses at these and other colonial wines. The only category that found a receptive audience continued to be fortified wine, a situation that continued for a full century more. As late as the 1960s, some 80 percent of the country's wine production consisted of "sherry," "port," and other fortifieds. While many were cheaply made and coarse-tasting, a legacy of quality did develop. Today, sampling luscious Muscats from Rutherglen in Victoria or velvety "ports" from the Barossa is really the only way to taste anything that might resemble an Australian wine tradition. All the ripe, fruit-forward Chardonnays, Shirazes, and other varietal dinner wines that have become so popular represent much more recent inventions.

Grapes would be grown and wines made across the Tasman Sea in New Zealand beginning in the 1840s, but a true Kiwi wine industry did not start to develop until the late 1970s. Dalmatian immigrants arriving at the end of the nineteenth century planted vineyards near Auckland in the North Island, but that region's subtropical climate hardly proved conducive to quality winemaking. The soils proved too rich, the rainfall too frequent, and before long the wine they made came to be known as "Dally plonk." As late as 1960, the entire country, South and North Island, had fewer than one thousand acres under vine, the majority being planted with non–*Vitis vinifera* grape varieties. As in so many New

World colonies and countries, the traditions that then rapidly developed in New Zealand, in this case involving a series of wines marked by rivetingly direct, pure flavors, were wholly new inventions.

High-quality New World wines would radically transform the international wine market in the second half of the twentieth century. Yet many of the stylistic models for those wines already existed a hundred years earlier, both in Europe (particularly Bordeaux) and occasionally abroad. Fine wine in the various forms we enjoy today clearly existed by the late 1800s, consumption as well as production having been modernized over the course of the previous two centuries. Yet two things starkly separated wine then from wine now. The first was the chasm that divided aesthetically conceived wine from vin ordinaire; the second, the fraud that pervaded all wine's trade and commerce. The emergence of superior, modern wines had only increased the opportunities for unscrupulous merchants to deceive consumers. In large measure because so few wines were bottled where they were made, even fairly knowledgeable connoisseurs could not be absolutely certain that what they were buying was what had been advertised. Unscrupulous vendors were more than happy to pass a cheap wine off as a prestigious cuvée, so plenty of Gamay still pretended to be fine Burgundy, just as heavily sugared whites masqueraded as late-harvest Ausleses, and bulk Portuguese and Spanish reds were adulterated with cider and then sold as Claret. How could consumers know that what was in the bottle or barrel actually was what the merchant claimed it to be? Even more to the point, how could they assess the quality of one estate or cru or négociant's offering as opposed to another? Modernization had brought with it increased choice. Yet with more options came increased opportunities for deception.

The second critical factor separating late-nineteenth-century wine from early-twenty-first-century wine was the qualitative and stylistic disparity that continued to exist between fine modern wine and old-fashioned cheap wine. The difference did not solely or even primarily involve price, though vins ordinaires obviously cost much less than distinctive-tasting vins fins. More important was the role these different wines played in people's lives. For the poor, wine remained a means to the dual ends of calories and intoxication. By contrast, the discriminating middle-class consumer now thought of wine as an end in itself, a valued (and valuable) object of aesthetic appreciation. That new outlook was this brief golden age's great glory, for as much as any technical advance in production, it fueled the exponential increase in the volume of high-quality wine available in the marketplace. New traditions developed as new consumers pursued new experiences. Thus an appreciation for wine's diversity became a hallmark of refined connoisseurship. A snob might drink just one type of wine, preferring to look down his nose at all others. But a man or woman who had developed a sophisticated palate remained ever curious to experience ever more.

Of course, late-nineteenth-century consumers experienced many new things. A bottle of wine was no more significant in itself than a gentleman's cravat or walking stick. What distinguished it, or more precisely what distinguished those who drank it, was the cultural recognition of it as something possessing intrinsic worth. Though that recognition could be manipulated (by advertising, for example), millions of people believed it was very much their own, the expression of their personal taste. Wines from the Bordeaux châteaux, with all their fabricated connotations of tradition or legacy, were very much modern inventions, as were Champagnes and other sparklers, fortified wines such as Port and Sherry, botrytis-infected Rieslings and Sauternes, full-bodied dry Barolos and Riojas, and even Chilean Bordeaux-inspired blends and South Australian Germanic "hocks." But then, so too was the new taste for these wines. In transcending the demands of mere appetite, that sense had completed wine's initial modernization. Thus the London wine merchant Thomas Shaw, writing in 1863, could insist that savoring fine wine was itself an aesthetic experience. "A taste for painting [or] music," he wrote, "may be improved by study and application, till a degree of knowledge and discrimination is acquired . . . Similar reasoning applies to the palate and material taste, for unless the sensations caused by certain kinds of wine are studied and compared with those which others produce, the power of forming opinions, and of acquiring skill founded on experience, cannot be gained."

Different factors thus led to wine's short-lived first golden age. Some involved the liquid in the bottle. Because of advances in science and technology, overall quality had improved immeasurably. But others involved the people who consumed it, what they chose to value, and why they did so. Those consumers, or a growing number of them, came to esteem at least some wines as artifacts that satisfied their sense of taste rather than just their appetite or need. Vintners often presented these wines, though many were of recent origin, as something venerable, and so worth taking the time (and spending the money) to savor. It hardly mattered that when considered historically, both the wines and the appreciation of them were in fact quite new. The final stage in wine's nineteenth-century modernization involved a new conception of what defined or constituted quality. For thousands of years it had been understood simply to mean an absence of defects or flaws. Then it had come to signify the presence of distinction or particularity, even if rare and fleeting. But now it meant something more—a particularity that could be recognized beyond the immediacy of the present moment, a distinction that endured.

Enduring merit or worth eventually would become the hallmark of all high-quality modern wines, whether coming from traditional European wine-producing regions or from new vineyards far away. Unfortunately, that would not happen for another century. Wine's nineteenth-century glory ultimately proved insufficiently inclusive to be able to last. While the range of choices definitely had multiplied, only select wines from select places displayed true particularity. And though more people than ever before had acquired a taste for these sophisticated vins fins, millions more knew only coarse ordinaires. Thus in the decades ahead, when wine experienced a crisis of steady cheapening, consumers all too easily could revert to thinking of it as booze—a mere means to the end of drunkenness. Not until the second half of the twentieth century did the idea of wine as something worth savoring for itself become revived. By that point, however, the quality gap separating the common from the special or fine had narrowed considerably, enabling wine in general to enter its second golden age, one marked by much less "sorrow of heart" than the first.

CRISES AND CATASTROPHES
A Century of Cheapening

The nineteenth century's golden age did not glitter long. During the 1850s, when the demand for fine wine was spreading across all but the lowest social classes, supply began to shrink suddenly and unexpectedly. The cause was a series of vine diseases that eventually forced growers to replant virtually all of Europe's vineyards. The different infestations made a great deal of allegedly fine wine taste old-fashioned because ordinaire. As a result, many people reverted to thinking of wine in general as something cheap and common. Countless late-nineteenth- and early-twentieth-century consumers, particularly middle-class ones, became suspicious of it. Some distrusted its quality and provenance, while others feared its alcohol, and still others simply considered it unexciting when compared with other drinks. Wine in almost any form became widely viewed as *déclassé* and hence no longer very desirable. Then came war and economic depression, followed by still more war, all of which contributed to a full-blown market catastrophe. Even if vineyards and cellars managed to survive unscathed, their owners rarely did. At much the same time, new social developments undermined any lingering association of wine with cultural sophistication. These came from two opposed directions. On one side, social progressives condemned wine for containing alcohol. On the other, legions of *fin de siècle* dilettantes, then jazz-age flappers, Hollywood movie stars, and other celebrities, treated it as something stodgy. With the exception of Champagne, wine no longer represented urbanity and *joie de vivre*. Different drinks, particularly spirit-based cocktails, surpassed it in prestige.

Wine would recover, and recover spectacularly. The story of its revival is the story of the drink that so many people in so many different places enjoy and esteem today. It involves remarkable improvements in overall quality, something that came in large measure from important advances in oenology and viticulture, as well as equally significant changes in consumption. Yet recovery, by definition, follows illness or collapse. A full century of suffering and depreciation would have to pass before wine could assume its current form as a reliable part of what millions of men and women consider a fully satisfying life. The distress had economic, cultural, even political aspects. But it began, quite literally, with disease.

The initial sign of viticultural crisis appeared in the summer of 1845, when an English gardener named Tucker noticed a strange, dusty substance on the leaves of vines he was tending. Confused, he sent a sample of the plant material to a minister well known for an expertise in botany. The Reverend M. J. Berkeley identified the growth as a fungus. Writing in the *Gardeners' Chronicle and Agricultural Gazette*, he paid Tucker the dubious honor of naming it after him—*Oidium tuckeri*. Better known today as powdery mildew, this previously unknown but virulent vine disease soon became a scourge. Within a few years, it had crossed the English Channel and was attacking vineyards throughout winemaking Europe. Its ash-colored spores spread with the wind, covering the vines' stalks and leaves with a cobweb-like growth, killing young shoots, and severely reducing crop yield. Powdery mildew had disastrous effects in the short term (the French harvest of 1854 was the smallest in more than sixty years), but scientists soon discovered that spraying the vines with sulfur dust worked as a preventative treatment. By the early 1860s, this first plague had largely passed. What remained extremely perplexing, however, was its origin. Where had this blight come from? European vintners certainly knew about poor vintages, but a destructive disease like this was unprecedented.

Much worse was to come. Beginning in 1863, in a vineyard in

France's southern Rhône Valley, vines started withering mysteriously. Unlike with oidium, there were no mildew spores or other physical signs of disease. These plants simply began behaving as if they were ill, their leaves drooping, the fruit failing to ripen. Then, two or three years after the first display of sickness, they died. And most curiously of all, when unearthed and examined, the dead vines' roots had withered away to virtually nothing. Even old plants could be pulled out of the ground easily, their root systems, which should have been extensive and unyielding, all but gone. By the late 1860s, entire swaths of vineyards in the region were suffering from this baffling condition. And within two decades, the disease had spread to most of the rest of Europe. Finding a cure proved maddeningly slow. At first, no one understood the malady. Then, once it was identified, hardly anyone believed it could be real.

The first identification came in 1868 when a group of scientists, led by Jules-Émile Planchon from the University of Montpellier, literally uncovered the problem. Working on a hot July day in a vineyard near the old Roman city of Arles, they laboriously dug up a range of vines, from the dead to the infirm to the healthy, to compare the differences. Their historian, George Ordish, describes the scientists as dressed in black, moving systematically through the vineyard, jotting down their observations "in neat, spidery pencil writing, with much mopping of their brows, sweating under their top hats." Planchon was the first to spot tiny gold-colored insects on the roots of the sick vines. There were so many of these creatures, he reported later, that some of the uprooted plants appeared to have been painted or varnished yellow. A magnifying glass revealed that they were some sort of minuscule aphid, and "from that moment," he wrote, "one fact of capital importance was established; namely that an almost invisible insect . . . [was bringing] about the destruction of even the most vigorous of vines."

These minuscule creatures, each no larger than a pinprick, were sucking sap from the roots, in effect forcing the plants to die of starvation. Planchon, awed by both their number and their efficacy, recognized that they resembled recently identified insects, called *Phylloxera quercus*, found on oak leaves. Since these underground ones were much more dangerous, he named the pest *Phylloxera vastatrix*—the destroyer. But his discovery was greeted with widespread skepticism if not outright disbelief. Armed with their microscopes and diplomas, Planchon and his fellow scientists claimed expertise, but people living and working nearby did not trust them. After all, those men had never pulled a plow in a vineyard or fermented grapes in a winery. Moreover, farmers could not accept that something so tiny could cause such destruction. As a result, many growers remained complacent, their underestimation of the threat coming in large measure from its seeming so unreal. And when vintners beyond the Rhône Valley heard about the tiny pests, they easily convinced themselves that streams and rivers would function as natural blockades, preventing any insects from getting into their vineyards. The first signs of infection already had been spotted in greater Bordeaux, but few people there were taking them seriously. In 1870, largely on Planchon's urging, the French government offered a prize for a cure, but it carried only the modest sum of twenty thousand francs.

Four years later the reward had grown to three hundred thousand francs. By then, both the vintners and the authorities were taking the epidemic—and it indeed was an epidemic—very seriously. Whether cause or effect, this destroyer was wreaking unprecedented havoc. All sorts of people began proposing all sorts of ways to eradicate the infestation. Over the next few years, the Montpellier scientists tested over three hundred proposed remedies. These included flooding a vineyard so as to drown the insects, beating the ground with sticks to drive them out, and fumigating with chemicals. Some of the treatments worked. For example, injecting the soil around each vine with carbon bisulfide killed the pests. It also, however, sometimes killed the vines. Similarly, spraying with urine and potassium sulfocarbonate proved somewhat effective in the short term, but could not prevent reinfestation. Moreover, the chemicals were expensive, and some proved flammable or toxic. Not surprisingly, people tried different proposed cures, at least for a season or two. Something called "Mozambique Oil" (a fish oil in which supposedly exotic plants had been steeped) was patented as a cure in 1877. It turned out to be a useless hoax. So too with a powder said to heal the pricks in the roots made by the phylloxera aphids. Other alleged solutions included packing the base of each plant in either ice or coffee grounds, coating the vines with tar, and pouring everything from oil to seawater on them. None of these accomplished anything.

By the mid-1870s, the Montpellier scientists knew that the aphids on the roots were in their "crawler" stage, and that the insects in winged form could travel from vineyard to vineyard, making controlling the epidemic even more difficult. But they still did not know what constituted home base for these destroyers. As Planchon himself asked imploringly, "But what of this insect? From whence did it come?" It was much the same question that had perplexed the researchers who had studied the initial infestation of powdery mildew fifteen years earlier. What constituted the source or origin of the plague?

Though phylloxera was definitely the most destructive nineteenth-century vine disease, it was not the last. In 1878, a new form of oidium appeared. Known today as downy (as opposed to powdery) mildew, it attacked all the green parts of vines and proved especially voracious in regions with warm, humid summers. All through the 1880s, farmers saw it ruin vintages. Then midway through that same decade, yet another fungus arrived. This one went under the frightening name of "black rot," and it attacked leaves, shoots, and individual grape berries, especially in mild weather conditions. By then, vintners were at their proverbial wits' ends. No matter whether the climate turned hot or cold, wet or dry, some insidious blight, unknown just a generation earlier, seemed poised for attack, devastating their crops and destroying their livelihoods. Yes, with sufficient investment they could make wines that by all accounts were superior to those fashioned by their ancestors. But earlier generations had never faced anything like this. Pestilence was following pestilence in near biblical proportions. What had anyone done to occasion such troubles?

The answer turned out to be the same in all cases. North America was the source of every one of these infestations. And what Europeans had done was import American nursery stock. They planted it, often ornamentally, in gardens, orchards, hothouses, and the like. But during an era without agricultural quarantines or certifications, these plants could carry pests and diseases against which European species had never developed any sort of resistance. And the various maladies were more than happy to feast on vulnerable, verdant Old World prey. (Much the same thing happened in Ireland with potato blight—a disease that, though not native to North America, likely crossed the Atlantic in the 1830s and 1840s aboard ships sailing from the United States.) Since substantial commerce had been conducted between North America and Europe for two centuries, it remains unclear why the diseases attacked at this particular time. Some people have credited steamships, which shortened ocean voyages. Yet compared with sail, steam reduced the passage from New York to England or France by only about a week, so both phylloxera and the fungal diseases certainly could have crossed the Atlantic earlier. A more probable explanation can be found in the fact that wide-scale interest in exotic gardening (and American plant material was definitely considered exotic) exploded in Europe during the 1840s, 1850s, and 1860s. For Mr. Tucker in England, or for businessmen and their wives living outside Paris or Berlin or Vienna, being able to plant a garden with unusual imported plants had become yet another fashionable form of bourgeois consumption. Grapevines, particularly new varieties being hybridized in America, ranked among the most popular imported plants. Yet when unloaded in ports such as Southampton, Marseille, and Hamburg, those vines often were infected with disease.

The transplanted American vines, however, were not withering and dying like the European ones. In 1873, Jules-Émile Planchon journeyed to the United States to investigate. He traveled widely, digging up vines wherever he went, in the process observing that phylloxera, though present, did not destroy the roots of many native species there. Back home in Montpellier, he and his associates planted thirty-five different American vines in an experimental vineyard plot so as to test the plant material's resistance. They knew that a grapevine's roots do not dictate the specific character of its leaves or fruit. Thus when one variety is grafted onto the rootstock of another—Chardonnay onto Concord, for example—the plant will produce the new variety's fruit and foliage. Vintners as far back as ancient Rome had grafted vines as a means of breeding specific grape varieties. The issue now was preservation, not propagation, but the same principle applied. The Montpellier scientists speculated that a cutting from a vulnerable European *Vitis vinifera* vine could be grafted onto a resistant non–*V. vinifera* American root, with the result that the plant would produce European grapes, and that vintners could continue to produce their often new traditional-tasting wines.

By 1880, the scientists working on the phylloxera crisis found themselves divided into two camps, those who advocated grafting and those who favored the continued use of chemical treatments. The latter questioned the wisdom of using the very plants that had introduced the plague to Europe, and feared that wines made from grafted vines would taste at least somewhat foxy (like those made from American grapes). But the Montpellier researchers found no evidence of this. Moreover, they knew that the chemicals, which remained both dangerous and costly, had not been all that effective. In 1882, the Montpellier Agricultural School published a small booklet advocating grafting. Written in clear, nontechnical language, it turned the tide. Though some producers continued to disinfect their vineyards, often as a safety measure, grafting gradually became standard practice. That same year also saw the development by scientists in Bordeaux of a spray that could combat both downy mildew and black rot. A blend of copper sulfate and lime, this "Bordeaux mixture" stained the vines (and everything else it touched) bright blue, but it effectively kept the fungal diseases at bay.

Vine grafting and fungicide treatments served as the remedies for a series of calamities that, when considered together, formed one of the greatest agricultural disasters that Europe ever experienced. They could not, however, resolve the crisis immediately. While sprays soon became accepted as the antidote for fungal diseases, many growers, especially those living in poor regions, did not make enough money to be able to use them regularly. Their vines, and wines, inevitably suffered. Similarly, even though grafting became generally recognized as the only viable solution to the phylloxera problem, many farmers could not afford the expense involved. They often had no choice but to watch their vines die and then to abandon viticulture altogether. Moreover, not all of the American roots adapted well to European soils and climates. It would take many years of research and experimentation to find and then propagate a sufficient number that would grow successfully in these conditions. Much of the credit goes to American horticulturalists, including George Husmann and Charles Riley in Missouri, and Thomas Munson in Texas, who worked to isolate and breed different vines for different vineyards. In appreciation, the municipal authorities in Montpellier erected statues honoring the Missourians, and in 1888 the French national government awarded Munson the rank of Chevalier du Mérite. During the next decade, when sufficient supply finally became available, European wine growers imported massive quantities of different American vine varieties for use as rootstock. Yet the arrival of so much foreign plant material meant that both the phylloxera aphid and the various fungal diseases had even more opportunities to spread to previously uninfected places. So they did, prolonging the crisis well into the twentieth century.

At first, when the various American vine infestations came to France, vintners in other countries, notably Italy and Spain, prospered. They began to export wines to England, northern Europe, and the Americas to replace French ones. The Rioja boom of the 1880s, for example, came precisely when Bordeaux's vineyards were under siege, and Barolo's late-nineteenth-century renown resulted at least in part from the decline in the prestige of French crus. Some Italian and Spanish winemakers even sent wine to France, where it was blended with what vintners there could make, and then marketed and sold as being completely French. Before long, however, the vineyards in Spain and Italy too succumbed to disease, as eventually did those just about everywhere that *V. vinifera* vines were cultivated. Vintners in countries or regions where the plagues came late did have the advantage of learning from their French counterparts' experience. So the crisis, though certainly serious, did not prove as calamitous for them. Yet everywhere it hit, it destroyed livelihoods, particularly for growers whose fruit never went into the era's aesthetically valued wines. These farmers simply could not afford the cost of the cures.

The viticultural crisis of the second half of the nineteenth century fundamentally altered Europe's wine-growing map. In marginal or economically depressed regions, farmers now found it difficult to eke out a living cultivating vines. So in various parts of northern and eastern Europe, many simply abandoned their small family vineyards and either moved to cities, where they found work in factories, or emigrated overseas. Even in prestigious winemaking regions, the amount of land devoted to vineyards often shrank. Tokaji in Hungary, for example, which had nearly fifteen thousand acres under vine in 1870, could count fewer than forty-five hundred acres twenty years later. And in Portugal's upper Douro Valley, home today to some of the best grapes for Port, many of the steepest, and so most difficult to tend vineyards (but also potentially the most valuable in terms of wine quality) were simply abandoned. In France, the area devoted to wine growing decreased by roughly 25 percent between 1880 and 1920, by which time virtually all the work of replanting with grafted vines had been completed.

Yet as paradoxical as it might seem, while vineyard acreage declined, overall production volume increased. Farmers in traditional winemaking regions simply needed to grow and sell more grapes to cover the costs associated with grafting and spraying. Production multiplied even in prestigious areas like the Médoc, where vintners started using chemical fertilizers in a misguided effort to improve the vigor of their vines so as to resist disease. Greater productivity per vine, however, resulted in many wines tasting thin and unappealing. Consumers certainly took note. Everyone who drank wine regularly knew about the viticultural crisis. Not surprisingly, people worried about how the different pesticides and treatments might affect them. And they certainly were concerned about how the use of American rootstock might change their favorite wines. It did not take long for the answers to seem unsatisfactorily clear. The wines coming onto the market at the turn of the century were by and large inferior to those that had impelled the golden age a generation earlier. It hardly mattered that the decline in both overall quality and individual particularity actually came less from grafting and spraying than from overproduction. People knew, or at least thought they knew, their own tastes. A generation earlier, such self-knowledge had impelled the aesthetic rise of fine wine. Now it hastened a fall.

In addition to higher volume but reduced quality in established areas, the crisis led to a dramatic increase in viticulture in regions where growing conditions encouraged large-scale production—in Sicily, for example, in Spanish La Mancha, and most notably, in the French colony of Algeria, where labor costs were very cheap and the hot North African sun enabled vintners to grow massive quantities of fruit. Though no one thought of the wines coming from these places as anything special, steamships and railroads easily carried them north to thirsty cities, including Paris, Brussels, and Berlin. The crisis effectively had destroyed grape growing in many regions located closer to these northern, industrial centers—in the Paris basin, for example, and in much of Lorraine—so the amount of land under vine in Algeria went from approximately 26,000 acres in 1865, to nearly 415,000 in 1905. The wines made there filled a void.

Many of these cheap wines were sold as what they were, vins ordinaires from a new source. But many also were used by merchants and shippers to add weight to what barely was wine at all—fermented raisins mixed with water, the late nineteenth century's version of medieval *piquette*. Even more problematic, unscrupulous merchants were passing off a good deal of the era's cheap, undistinguished wine as something more prestigious, and the turn-of-the-century market became dominated by deception. Plenty of alleged crus consisted of concoctions that included little if any wine from the actual estate or vineyard. Numerous barrels of Bordeaux, including some allegedly coming from classified châteaux, were completely bogus, as were many casks of Chambertin, Chassagne, and other Burgundies. Growers in these and other prominent regions felt cheated, but they frequently had to shoulder their share of the blame. The increased yields in their vineyards had resulted in thin, weak wines which they then chaptalized excessively. The addition of sugar gave the liquid alcoholic punch but obliterated any presence of terroir. As a result, their wines tasted less and less distinctive.

The deliberate falsification of a wine's provenance sometimes yielded quick profits, but in the long term it brought substantial losses. The most substantial surely involved consumer attitudes and perceptions. People, already skeptical owing to what they had heard about phylloxera and the various vine diseases, began to view wine in general suspiciously. If they could not be sure that a certain wine was what it (or the person selling it) claimed it to be, why should they buy or drink it at all? The connoisseurship that had made mid-nineteenth-century fine wine so fashionable depended on the perception of authenticity. By 1900, however, the possibility of deception was devaluing even legitimate wines. Consequently, wine in general was falling out of vogue.

The problem of fraud helped alter consumer attitudes toward wine in general and fine wine in particular. This was especially true of people in wine-importing countries. In 1895, the American consul in Le Havre reported to his superiors in Washington that a great deal of what was being shipped as French wine had little or no connection with French grapes. At much the same time, the *London Evening Standard* opined that the abundance of fraudulent Bordeaux in the marketplace meant that Englishmen might as well make their own. Elsewhere, vintners started doing just that. Particular names previously tied to particular places began to be exported and used with abandon abroad. American wine-makers started producing "burgundies," Algerian ones "clarets," and vintners in South America "champagnes." The end result was a slow but steady cheapening of wine—both the actual beverage and consumer perceptions of it.

Things weren't all that much better in wine-producing countries or regions. As early as 1879, Robert Louis Stevenson reported that when traveling in France he heard former grape growers, their vines all gone, declare that "the country was going to the devil." Vintners' incomes kept falling, owing first to the scourges and then to the overproduction that accompanied the cures. The situation became especially dire in south-ern France, where wine prices fell so low in the first decades of the new century that an actual revolt ensued. Led by a grower named Marcelin Albert, a crowd of farmers estimated at over half a million gathered in Montpellier in June 1907, demanding that the government do some-thing to protect their livelihoods. The French prime minister, Georges Clemenceau, responded by arresting Albert and the other ringleaders, and five people died during riots a week later in the city of Narbonne. Though this uprising eventually led to laws and regulations delineating what could and could not be classified as true wine, the more imme-diate consequence was a further depreciation of virtually all wine in consumers' eyes. It now was something cheap, so cheap in fact that the people responsible for it apparently could not make even a meager liv-ing from it.

Equally important, more and more wine now tasted cheap—both because excessively high yields rendered so much of it thin and because all the bad news surrounding it made people leery of it. Even the top crus, their provenance something that often could not be trusted, lost much of their aesthetic appeal. Moreover, the first decades of the twen-tieth century saw a series of poor vintages in Bordeaux, still the interna-tional standard-bearer for fine wine. Quality continued to decline, due in part to bad weather, in part to overfertilization, and in part to the tenor of what remained very panicky times. Wines from the best châteaux seemed to lose much of their particularity. The consumers who kept their taste for fine wines now coveted what they called "pre-phylloxera" cuvées. Whether Burgundies, Champagnes, Clarets, or Ports, these supposedly tasted more distinctive than anything produced during or after the crisis. Of course, since stocks could not be replenished, such wines became ever scarcer (and more expensive) over time. They rarely found their way onto middle-class tables.

For an all-too-brief cultural moment fifty or sixty years earlier, fine wine had been poised to become a bourgeois passion. In the early decades of the twentieth century, however, many middle-class consumers, increasingly suspicious of what was in the glass, began to opt instead for spirits. Though harsher-tasting, these were more reliable, or at least people believed they were. Spirits also were fast becoming newly fashionable, a phenomenon that would only intensify following the First World War, when cocktails became all the rage internationally. Fine wine rapidly fell out of favor in the still extremely influential English market, where sales plummeted, and native pride fueled a newfound appreciation for Scotch whisky. Thus while plenty of cheap vin ordinaire continued to be drunk by laborers and farmers, vin fin hardly enjoyed a privileged status anymore. Even wealthy consumers no longer thought of it in the same terms as had their fathers or grandfathers. Sixty years before, the best wines represented cultured sophistication and refinement. But tastes had shifted. Fewer people now regarded wine, even classified or supposedly traditional fine wine, as something aesthetically desirable. Instead, to many minds it had become suspect.

—m—

At the start of the twentieth century, wine was nowhere more suspect than in the United States. Far from enjoying special aesthetic status, it was widely considered a drink for degenerate drunks, poor men (and they were almost always male) called "winos." That revealing colloquialism, which entered the national vernacular before the First World War, neatly reflects wine's fall into American disrepute. A variety of forces, including the legacy of fundamental Protestantism, a belief in the country's moral destiny, and a powerful populist-progressive political movement, led many Americans to treat it as an especially insidious form of alcohol. In their view, any guise of respectability and refinement that it might display was a sham. By wine's very nature, it was demon drink, and so no different from the cheap whiskey being tossed back in the era's roadhouses and saloons.

These suspicions would not play an important part in wine's global history were it not for America's growing influence within that history. At the start of the twentieth century, having just won a war with Spain, the United States was poised to become a world power, with its customs and mores exerting as much international sway as its military might. As the century unfolded, American movies, books, fashions, and other cultural habits would be both critiqued and imitated widely abroad. Clearly, those habits included attitudes and cultural practices involving wine. A great many American wines produced in the early decades of the century came heavily fortified with coarse spirits, which led much of the population to consider them fraudulent as well as dangerous. Often referred to as "stimulating" wines, these were not refined, age-worthy elixirs like Madeira, Port, and Sherry, but rather cheap, fiery intoxicants whose appeal came solely from their high levels of alcohol. They too were poured in bars and saloons. And because they cost so little, they often ended up being the one type of alcoholic drink that the poor and destitute could afford. Of course, some American vintners also made dry dinner wines, some of which apparently were quite good. Yet these never were accepted widely in American society, or at least not in respectable middle-class society. To many Americans, particularly those living in the country's vast heartland, drinking wine seemed foreign and dangerous. It was a cultural practice that belonged to the two segments of urban society they distrusted most: wealthy aristocrats and poor immigrants. Thus they considered it a threat to the moral good.

Things had not always been so. In the early days of the republic, powerful voices had urged that wine be woven into the fabric of American life. Thomas Jefferson, who both traveled through Europe's vineyards and planted one of his own in Virginia, was wine's most vocal advocate among the founding fathers, but he was far from alone. George Washington tried to grow grapes and make wine, as did fellow

Virginians James Madison and James Monroe. Though John Adams did not plant a vineyard, Massachusetts being too cold, he drank wine regularly. So did Benjamin Franklin, who publicly promoted it to his fellow colonists and then countrymen as something both desirable and beneficial. Writing as Poor Richard in his famous *Almanack*, Franklin offered his "Friendly Reader" explicit directions for crushing grapes and fermenting the juice, all because he thought that "every Man [should] take Advantage of the Blessings of Providence." Or as he put it elsewhere, "God loves to see us happy, and therefore He gave us wine."

These early Americans promoted wine for two separate but related reasons. Many of them, worried about their countrymen's high rate of spirit consumption, valued wine because it was a temperate alternative. The young nation was a notoriously hard-drinking place, with rum, brandy, and whiskey downed in record volume. Not surprisingly, it also was often drunken and violent. Sloth and strife threatened the late-eighteenth- and early-nineteenth-century vision of the new nation as an agrarian state. Indeed, the belief that wine, a natural product like apples and wheat, belonged in that state was the second reason for advocating it. Jefferson, who served as an eloquent spokesman for an agrarian republic, expressed "moral and physical preference [for] the agricultural, over the manufacturing, man," insisting that farming was "the employment of our first parents in Eden, the happiest we can follow, and the most important to our country." Wine, he declared, should be the natural drink of the American yeoman: "Being among the earliest luxuries in which we indulge ourselves, it is desirable it should be made here . . . we have every soil, aspect, and climate of the best of wine countries."

Unfortunately, Jefferson's enthusiasm got the better of him. Just as would happen in Europe two generations later, *V. vinifera* vines planted in America proved susceptible to disease and infestation. Like many people before and after, Jefferson tried to grow imported wine grapes in eastern America, and just like them, he failed. Some people had a little success with native grapes, though the resulting foxy flavors invariably tasted strange to anyone acquainted with European wine. That's why, all through the nineteenth century, American horticulturalists hybridized literally hundreds of new grape varieties, searching for better ones with which to make better-tasting wines. Many of these hybrids could claim at least some *V. vinifera* in their parentage. Almost always hardier than the imports, they sometimes made decent wines. One of the better varieties was Catawba, a white grape that in the hands of Nicholas Longworth in Cincinnati, Ohio, yielded the country's first successful commercial wine during the 1840s. A sparkler made via the Champagne method, it proved quite popular, with the poet Henry Wadsworth Longfellow going so far as to call it "more dulcet, delicious, and dreamy" than Champagne itself. That surely was an exaggeration, but the wine did find favor with consumers. Unfortunately, Longworth's vineyards fell victim to black rot and downy mildew in the 1850s, and by the next decade he was essentially out of business. Catawba's partial *V. vinifera* ancestry, precisely that which made his wine successful, had rendered it vulnerable.

Over the next half century, Americans in virtually every state east of the Rocky Mountains tried to make and sell wine. Though most worked on a small scale, often on family farms, some had grander ambitions. In northern Ohio, commercial vintners used Catawba, Delaware, Isabella, and other hybridized but primarily native grapes to produce wines that sold well locally. Farther west, in Missouri, German immigrants planted a wholly native grape named Norton (after the Virginia doctor who first propagated it). Their winemaking proved so successful that they shipped some of their wines east, and by the 1860s the Show Me State had become the largest wine producer in the Union. In later decades, "New York Champagne" from companies like Great Western and Gold Seal in the Finger Lakes region became America's most popular bubbly. And in the south, "Virginia Dare," made originally from native Scuppernong grapes, became one of the region's best sellers.

Despite these examples of commercial success, eastern wines did not really compete with imported European ones in Boston, Chicago, New York, or other potentially lucrative urban markets. Being made with such different grapes, these wines simply tasted too odd. Moreover, they never enjoyed the cultural prestige displayed by the Champagnes, classified-growth Clarets, and elite crus that attracted a small but well-heeled nineteenth-century American audience. The only domestic wines in any sense comparable to imports came from California. Because phylloxera and the various fungal diseases were not native west of the Rockies, vintners could cultivate European *V. vinifera* vines successfully there. When the Missourian George Husmann first visited the Golden State in 1880, he declared it *"the* great Vineland . . . destined to overshadow all others."* In fact, Husmann was so enthralled that a few months after returning home, he quit his job, packed up his family, and moved to a farm in southern Napa County.

The Spanish priests who had established missions along the Pacific coast in the late eighteenth century had brought vines with them. The grape variety they planted was the one called País or Negra Corriente in Pacific South America. Known in California as Mission, it proved adaptable and hardy. So for nearly a hundred years, Mission vines yielded the grapes for virtually all California wines. Commercial viticulture started in the 1830s and 1840s. Centered in southern California, and led by a Frenchman with the delightfully appropriate name of Vignes, pioneering vintners produced primarily sweet wines. One in particular, a fortified wine known as Angelica (because it came from Los Angeles), became a big seller. Production took off when gold was discovered in the Sierra foothills in 1848, as it quenched the thirst of thousands of speculators arriving at the mines. Angelica's claim to fame came from its alcoholic punch. It was poured liberally alongside both whiskey and California brandy (also made from Mission grapes) in the gold rush camps, thus inaugurating the American practice of especially heady wine drinking. When Jean-Louis Vignes sold his business in 1855, he retired a rich man.

Since Mission made relatively poor dry wine, the hunt soon was on for better grapes. Yet many vines carted overland from the east died en route, as did those imported by ship, the only viable passage being the seemingly endless one around Cape Horn. Nonetheless, Golden State vintners kept at it, and by the late 1850s at least a few were making wines with superior varieties. The most successful ventures were centered in Santa Clara County above Monterey Bay, where a number of immigrants planted vineyards and, even more important, started nurseries. The most celebrated promoter of what were called "foreign vines" was a Hungarian, Agoston Haraszthy, who owned a farm in Sonoma County and traveled to Europe on behalf of the state legislature to select vines to ship home. Overflowing with bluster, his legend outshines his actual achievements, since many if not most of the varieties he imported already were being cultivated in nurseries. Nonetheless, Haraszthy was so loud and flamboyant that his words could not be ignored. "California can produce as noble and generous a wine as any part of Europe," he famously proclaimed, "when it will have the proper varieties of grapes."

By the 1870s, no Californian aiming to make quality wine on the European model could be satisfied anymore with Mission grapes. The bar had been raised. A number of winemakers crossed it during the last decades of the century. Their vineyards were located for the most part in northern California—in Alameda, Livermore, Santa Clara, Sonoma, and most notably, Napa Counties. By 1880, when Robert Louis Stevenson came there on his honeymoon, Napa had approximately eleven thousand acres under vine. Mission grapes were used mostly for brandy, while table wines were being made with all sorts of more recently imported varieties. Many of the vintners were of German descent, and many of their wines reflected that heritage. Riesling, in particular, was quite popular. Stevenson visited Jacob Schram's property near Calistoga and drank the Schramsberg wines, which he described as "bottled poetry." Though the place "was still raw," a "wild spot," and Schram's "Hock" was "no Johannisberg," he marveled at "the stirring sunlight, and the growing vines, and the vats and bottles in the cavern," all of which he thought "made a pleasant music for the mind."

Following the opening of the transcontinental railroad, which made shipping wines east both easy and profitable, Golden State winemaking became big business. The business became so big, in fact, that in 1894 seven of the state's largest wine companies banded together to form a monopolistic trust. During the next two decades, this conglomerate, the California Wine Association, came to control roughly 80 percent of the state's wine. It owned warehouses in all the big eastern cities, where it sold wines under both its own name and the names of various wineries it purchased. Though phylloxera did soon infect vines in California, being brought there on nursery material much as had happened in Europe, growers quickly grafted their vines onto resistant rootstock, and their businesses hardly slowed down. The wine association shipped wine all across the country and even exported some to Europe. With high tariffs inflating imported wine prices, production skyrocketed. California vintners made eighteen million gallons of wine in 1895, thirty-one million in 1905, and over forty-five million in 1915.

Some of these wines were dry, but many others were sweet and fortified. Starting in the 1890s, owing in part to a lowering of the government's tax on brandy and in part to the realities of a changing marketplace, the volume of fortified wines began to rise rapidly. This intoxicant came cheap, and so functioned as the Gilded Age's version of Georgian England's black-strap, its sole perceived virtue being its high level of alcohol. Rarely poured in restaurants or social clubs, this was primarily a saloon or roadhouse drink, increasingly purchased by impoverished drunks and hobos. And they became so popular so quickly that many Americans, particularly those who did not drink any wine at all, began to think that all wines must be like them. Millions of people thus linked wine in general with the even more popular saloon drink, whiskey. To their minds, drinking either form of alcohol led to drunkenness and depravity.

That point of view was in no sense uniquely American. Turn-of-the-century antialcohol reformers fought for their cause on both sides of the Atlantic, arguing that any alleged veneer of sophistication that wine might have was just that—a mask or covering that disguised its true nature. Yet both because no other society quite shared this country's faith in its own moral exceptionalism, and because such a significant proportion of the country's wine was in fact fortified with cheap spirit, the antialcohol movement led to legislation mandating national prohibition in the United States. In the early twentieth century, some Americans did try to distinguish wine from spirits. Among them was Andrea Sbarboro of the Italian Swiss Colony wine company in California. Like so many progressive-minded citizens of the day, he opposed what he called "the evil of drunkenness," a plague that he contended came principally from the consumption of whiskey and other spirits. Much as Thomas Jefferson had done a century earlier, Sbarboro recommended "the use of the healthy beverage of American wine on every American table." Yet subverting the logic of his argument, he refused to distinguish table wines from fortified ones, insisting that anything labeled "wine" should be exempt from the various prohibition statutes then being debated in legislatures across the country. The reason is easy enough to understand. Italian Swiss Colony distilled copious amounts of grape spirit for use in the production of the cheap, heady wines it sold to the saloons, and Sbarboro, his company part of the California Wine Association, needed to keep profits high. So within the American wine industry—and given the dominance of the Wine Association, it indeed had become an industry—even advocates of an old-fashioned vision of table wine as part of the national ethos were being corrupted by the changing marketplace.

In much of the United States, that marketplace was controlled by distillers, who owned both saloons and retail outlets, and so exerted significant economic leverage. Many wine producers had little choice but to become their bedmates. The distillers, however, had increasingly powerful enemies, notably the various prohibitionist associations then attracting more and more political support. These groups had found their populist rallying cry when they began attacking the saloon rather than just the bottle, and the Anti-Saloon League, led by an Ohio attorney, Wayne Wheeler, became America's first truly successful single-issue political lobby. Known as "the dry boss," Wheeler advocated a ban on the manufacture of all beverage alcohol. He portrayed the wine poured in saloons as a social evil just like whiskey. Since some saloons contained curtained "wine rooms" for assignations, and since some saloon-keepers sold sex as well as booze, it was not difficult for Wheeler and his supporters to link wine consumption with perversion and immorality. Reform-minded voters were all too easily persuaded. This was the progressive era, when millions of middle-class Americans believed that their moral principles could solve society's age-old ills. Whether the issue was breaking up industrial monopolies, outlawing child labor, enabling women's suffrage, or prohibiting the sale and production of alcoholic drink, progressive reformers insisted that the law should compel social change. The Anti-Saloon League exerted pressure at every level of government. Beginning in 1906, when Wheeler helped defeat a "wet" governor in Ohio, and culminating on January 16, 1919, when the Nebraska legislature's vote for ratification guaranteed the passage of the Eighteenth Amendment to the Constitution, his support almost always meant political victory, his opposition defeat.

National prohibition, however, proved a dismal failure in the United States. Though reported cases of intoxication and arrests for drunkenness did go down initially, alcoholism rates started rising after only five years, and public intoxication actually became more commonplace. The new law, known as the Volstead Act (after Congressman Andrew Volstead, who had overseen its passage), prohibited "the manufacture, sale, or transportation of intoxicating beverages," not the consumption of them. So whether acquired legally before Prohibition or illicitly afterward, alcohol could be drunk with abandon. And indeed it was. Many people, particularly first-generation immigrants living in the large eastern and midwestern cities, began making wine at home. They either bought grapes shipped by rail from California or used concentrated grape extract to which they added yeast. Particularities of flavor invariably proved less important to them than the presence of alcohol. Much the same was true for people purchasing rather than making the drinks that they consumed. For many of them, the goal of drinking was simply to get as big a jolt from the stuff as possible. Booze was being made in basements and bathrooms all across the country, and then sold illicitly in speakeasies and drugstores. And with every glass of bathtub hooch or home-fermented wine tossed back, disdain for the Volstead Act became more blatant. Otherwise law-abiding citizens broke it openly and regularly.

By the mid-1920s, licensed saloons had been replaced by unlicensed speakeasies, and organized crime had become powerful and brazen. Clearly, the effort to alleviate one social ill had brought multiple new ones. Politicians began to talk about modifying the Volstead Act, and Wayne Wheeler came under increasing attack for his sometimes strong-arm tactics. (He would die in 1927.) The Senate held hearings, and a series of witnesses spoke out against various aspects of the law. Some urged that beer and wine should be exempted from the statute. John Sullivan, president of the New York State Federation of Labor, for example, testified that many working men and women who had never before drunk whiskey, gin, or other hard spirits were doing so regularly now. If legal, he suggested, they would much prefer to purchase beer or wine. When one senator asked him if he thought that outlawing distilled drink but legalizing fermented beverages would in fact assist the cause of moderation and morality, his reply was clear: "Absolutely that is true . . . There is no question about it. That is the unanimous opinion of everybody I have come in contact with." The turning point came with the stock market crash of 1929. With the country falling into depression, organized crime, unemployment, and bread lines all seemed greater social problems than being able to order a drink. More and more people began to advocate complete repeal, and the election of Franklin Roosevelt three years later tolled Prohibition's death knell. Congress quickly passed and the states ratified the Twenty-First Amendment, repealing the Eighteenth—the first (and only) such reversal in American history.

Despite repeal, the most important legacy of the Prohibition era was an entrenchment of the public attitudes that had formed during it. From the 1930s all the way until the 1960s, very few Americans thought of wine as anything remotely special, precisely because so many continued to associate it with hard liquor. This association was encouraged, even promoted, by the many new laws governing the sale of alcohol that went into effect. At first, some states remained dry, or partially dry, while others created either government-run monopolies or complicated bureaucracies to regulate sales. Because the Twenty-First Amendment gave individual states the right to control the distribution of "intoxicating liquors" within their borders, a maze of different rules and regulations emerged throughout the country. These differed from state to state (and within some states, county to county), but most had at least a few features in common. First, they enabled the jurisdiction to raise revenue—either by selling alcohol or by licensing those businesses that could sell it, as well as by taxing it directly. Second, they imposed restrictions on who could buy it, and when and where they could do so. Finally, and ultimately most important, the new laws mandated what came to be called the "three-tier" system. In this scheme, a producer would sell products to a licensed wholesaler or distributor, who in turn would sell them to a retailer, bar, or restaurant. In theory, this prevented brewers and distillers from controlling retail outlets, as had happened with many of the old saloons. In practice, however, it simply transferred power from the producers to the wholesalers. They were the ones now dictating who could purchase what and where. And since wholesalers sold much more liquor than wine, they invariably treated wine as a subset of their main product line—their "book" of whiskeys, gins, and the like.

But more than new laws cemented the identification of wine with liquor in American culture. In the years following repeal, with economic despair ongoing, the memory of one war fresh and the prospect of another looming large, high-alcohol, fortified wine was by far the best-selling type in the country, dominating the market by a ratio of approximately five to one. (Not until 1967 did the production of table wine overtake that of "stimulating" wine.) During the Second World War, when the federal government ordered the country's distillers to convert much of their production to munitions use, the companies started buying vineyards and making wine. By 1945, they owned roughly half of the country's stock. Though the distillers divested themselves of most of it as soon as they again were permitted to manufacture and sell more spirits, the so-called whiskey invasion provided an economic foundation for the widespread perception that wine was just another form of liquor. So in the 1950s, regardless of whether a wine company was owned by a distiller or operated independently, its production tended to be dominated by wines whose only reason for existence was that they gave poor drunks what one vintner unabashedly called "a drink for skid row."

There are probably many reasons why post-Prohibition Americans purchased so much cheap fortified wine. With many vineyards in disrepair, the quality of most commercial table wine proved fairly bad. Fortifieds had the advantage of not spoiling as quickly and, being sweet, not showing their defects as plainly. Moreover, some consumers who had taken to making their own wine during Prohibition continued the practice following repeal. They thus had no need to buy wine of any kind. But the most important explanation, surely, involves taste—in every sense of that word. Prohibition, coupled with Depression-era poverty, had taught Americans to value alcoholic punch in whatever they drank. Fortified wines thus were widely regarded as a poor person's substitute for spirits. People with taste—that is, people with style and discernment—had little use for them. They instead drank cocktails. Imported wines, particularly Champagnes, did attract a small but steadfast American audience, but even during the prosperous postwar years, domestic wines remained almost universally viewed as tawdry and cheap. Not until the late 1960s would that perception begin to change.

—m—

The idea of wine as something cheap was in no sense confined to America. Nor was antialcohol reform. In the first decades of the twentieth century, many laws were passed in European countries regulating pub and tavern service, as well as prohibiting sales to minors. A handful of nations, including Sweden, Russia, and Iceland, even went dry, though for relatively short periods. In wine-producing countries, most reform efforts focused on distilled spirits—for example, on absinthe in France, brandy in Spain, and schnapps in Germany. "The consumption of schnapps is not only rooted in the hopeless condition of the modern proletariat," declared one German labor leader, "[but] it also helps prevent the worker from freeing himself from this hopelessness." As that language suggests, campaigns against specific types of alcohol often were coupled with fights for political and social reform. And wine was not exempt from attack, especially since its perceived quality had declined so precipitously following the phylloxera crisis. Prices for even the finest European wines fell even though production levels did not, and a good deal of wine ended up having to be distilled for industrial use. Both growers and winemakers suffered, with proprietors of even prestigious properties facing hard times. Whether in Oporto or Jerez, Piedmont or the Rhinegau, they ran businesses that relied heavily on export markets, but financial worry, coupled with changing consumer tastes, had reduced demand significantly. In Bordeaux, some classified-growth châteaux had to be sold, as their owners faced bankruptcy, while in Burgundy more and more wine, even some from famous crus, went into cheap generic blends. In Champagne, home to the one wine that retained widespread appeal, the loss of foreign customers was felt especially acutely. The region had been hit late but hard by phylloxera, since American rootstock had difficulty surviving in its chalky soils, and the Champagne houses, the majority still family-run, desperately needed new capital. For the most part they didn't get it.

As the supply of quality wine dwindled, its aesthetic status, precisely that which had distinguished it from other alcoholic beverages during its earlier golden age, began to be questioned. Middle-class drinkers whose fathers or grandfathers may have aspired to connoisseurship developed other interests, with different consumer goods (everything from automobiles to golf clubs) and different drinks satisfying their more contemporary tastes. While they did not necessarily abandon wine, they treated it differently, thinking of it once again primarily as a vehicle for intoxication. They thus often regarded any talk of vintages and crus as fussy and old-fashioned. But when considered simply as a source of alcohol, an increasingly pervasive point of view in the decades following the First World War, wine always had to take a backseat to other drinks. It usually was more expensive than beer, and it always was less potent than spirits.

Spirit consumption had surged in Europe during wine's agricultural crisis. Scotch whisky exploded in popularity in England, as did akvavit in Scandinavia. Unlike the first rush of spirit passion some two hundred years earlier, the audience for these drinks was now largely and comfortably middle class. Even France experienced a bourgeois spirit craze, this one centered primarily on absinthe, the popularity of which skyrocketed in the last decades of the nineteenth century, precisely the period when wine quality often became suspect. In 1875, French absinthe drinkers downed approximately 185,000 gallons of the stuff; by 1910, that figure had increased to an astonishing 9,500,000 gallons. Both celebrated and feared for its allegedly hallucinogenic effects, absinthe was a favorite of artists and aesthetes. But as these numbers suggest, a great many other people drank a great deal of it as well. It was an essential part of Belle Epoque culture, as much if not more so than wine.

The only significant victory for the French antialcohol movement came when absinthe was banned in 1915. Some doctors contended that this particular spirit could cause madness, and with the country at war, the government could not risk sending insane soldiers to the front. Yet as with all the European combatants, the French military authorities did not want those same soldiers to be stone sober. Regardless of prohibitionist movements at home, the different countries' war ministries made sure that alcohol became a staple in the trenches of the First World War, where it bolstered morale by giving men the courage to fight—or at least, not to flee. It also helped comfort the wounded, gave solace to the dying, and could temporarily counteract the effects of gas attacks. As one newspaper noted, drinking copious amounts of alcohol allowed people "for one brief moment [to forget] their pain," and "even the parents of the dead got caught up in it." So no matter whether at or behind the front, soldiers drank a great deal of alcohol during the war years, including plenty of wine. Their doing so, however, only strengthened the growing cultural perception that wine was just another form of booze.

During the First World War, the English army was fortified primarily with rum, the German with schnapps and brandy, the French with cheap wine. Though American doughboys sailing to Europe expected to have to fight dry, General John Pershing commanded that they have access to at least beer and wine. Trench warfare was simply too horrific otherwise. In addition to what was rationed by the armies, soldiers on both sides of the front drank oceans of alcohol at makeshift bars and cafés in villages and towns behind the front lines. They often did so to the point of numbness. For example, English Tommies fighting in northern France drank gallons of the tart local white wine, much of which they adulterated with sugar to help make it palatable. Mispronouncing *vin blanc*, they called it "plonk," and then guzzled it down.

While the armies in the so-called Great War were well supplied with drink, civilians on the various home fronts were not. Since all the wartime governments requisitioned alcohol for munitions and fuel, all sorts of crops, everything from grain to grapes, started to go into industrial stills. Wine production fell everywhere except France, where the government purchased huge amounts to provision the army. But civilian French beer and spirit consumption plummeted, the former dropping by a third, the latter by twice that much. So too in Germany, where beer production fell to 25 percent of prewar levels, and in England, where the government took steps to reduce both the volume that brewers could make and its alcoholic strength. All of the combatant countries raised taxes on alcohol, making what little was available more expensive. (The English duty more than doubled the price of a pint of beer in a pub.) At the same time, most governments enacted new restrictions on both who could drink and where and when he or she could do so. In England, pub hours were cut by two-thirds, while in France public intoxication became a crime for the first time. Sobriety, dreaded in the trenches, turned into a form of patriotism at home.

The wartime rationing of wine actually brought profits to some French vintners, since the government needed to purchase an enormous volume to supply the army. Growers in previously impoverished regions, particularly the still-depressed Languedoc, prospered. For some, the war years constituted the first financially successful vintages since the phylloxera devastation. Yet at the same time, the war kept devaluing wine in important and sometimes long-lasting ways. One of the most significant could be found in France's vineyards themselves, where fully a third of the grapes being grown were hybrid crosses of European and North American ones rather than classic wine varieties grafted onto American rootstock. These first had been planted a generation earlier as possible solutions to the phylloxera crisis. By 1914, however, everyone knew that grafting *V. vinifera* onto resistant roots constituted a much better solution. The hybrid grapes invariably tasted somewhat foxy, and the pure *V. vinifera* varieties definitely made superior wines. Nonetheless, the hybrids proved disease-resistant and vigorous. Growers, especially in regions where the price their grapes fetched barely covered costs, loved them. Varieties such as Baco Blanc and Baco Noir (named for their hybridizer, François Baco), Chambourcin, Plantet, Seibel, and Villard proliferated during the war years. After all, government bookkeepers paid scant attention to matters of quality.

The French army never differentiated between wines in terms of taste. The only distinction the government made involved potency; the higher the level of alcohol, the higher the price it paid. That view, which reduced all wines to their one shared intoxicating component, further cheapened wine, as it had the effect of compelling vintners to overproduce in their vineyards in order to make ends meet. So while some farmers who grew cheap vin ordinaire prospered, those who owned land or worked in regions with traditions of vin fin tended to suffer. The money they received could not cover their expenses, and both higher taxes at home and tariffs abroad combined to shrink their market. Bordeaux vintners complained that the national government was taxing them out of existence. But the bureaucrats in the various ministries in Paris paid scant attention. After all, the army was requisitioning a significant amount of the region's production. Moreover, a great many vineyards were in bad shape. With so many men away in the trenches, women and children often had to tend the vines. Their work was complicated by the fact that chemical sprays, now a necessary part of European viticulture, were in scarce supply, as were healthy farm animals. As a result, the quality of even supposedly superior wine suffered.

No wine, or wine region, suffered more than Champagne. Some of the most horrific fighting of the war crisscrossed its vineyards, the chalky soil of which became stained red with blood. The German army occupied both Reims and Epernay in the first month of the war. Before the soldiers left to fight the First Battle of the Marne, they pillaged the two cities' cellars. The roads they took out of town soon were littered with thousands of empty bottles, many smashed and broken, and with scores of abandoned trucks, their tires torn to shreds by shards of glass. Though the battalions had left, Reims was only beginning to suffer. On September 14, 1914, German artillery, perched in the hills some four miles away, began to shell the city. The bombardment lasted for 1,051 consecutive days. Nearly all of the city's buildings sustained damage. The magnificent Gothic cathedral, where France's kings and queens had been crowned, was reduced to a smoldering ruin. The citizenry, some twenty thousand people, including the mayor, Maurice Pol-Roger, moved underground to the *crayères*, the extensive network of limestone tunnels and caves used by his and the other Champagne houses for storage. There, amid the bottles, the city set up shop—literally, since all sorts of subterranean businesses opened, as did schools and churches. Over the course of four years, babies were born in these dark warrens, and old people died there. Meanwhile, aboveground, the shells kept falling—not only in the city but also in the surrounding vineyards, many of which had been dug up to make the trenches in which the soldiers on both sides lived and died. In Champagne, as was true all along the northern front, the war had turned into a lethal stalemate. No one was winning, no one losing; men were just dying.

Finally, in 1918 the deadly standoff began to end at the Second Battle of the Marne. As the Germans retreated, the French army advanced. In Reims, the soldiers helped themselves to massive amounts of wine from the cellars, much like their enemy had done four years earlier. The managers of the various Champagne houses watched helplessly as their stocks disappeared. By the time the armistice was signed in November, the region was in ruins. It had lost over half of its population, and some 40 percent of its vineyards. Where vines remained, many were barely alive, having been poisoned by gas. Huge swaths of land were designated as dead zones. The cost of rebuilding and replanting promised to be astronomical, but there was little money available. The French franc quickly lost much of its value, and wine exports withered to barely a third of their prewar levels. The situation wasn't that much better elsewhere. Though no other wine-growing region had been hit as hard by the ravages of war, the devastation had taken a severe toll everyplace.

The men who returned home physically unscathed from the battlefields brought with them not only haunting memories but also an appetite for the sort of high-alcohol drink that had helped them endure the horrors of the war. Not surprisingly, the subsequent years were filled with very heavy drinking. The gruesome experience of war had given millions of people, both veterans and civilians, a ravenous thirst for alcohol. So while the volume of wine made in the world rose in the 1920s, the rise was almost exclusively in cheap vin ordinaire. A tidal wave of it flooded the market, and consumption rose just about everywhere vines were cultivated—in South American countries such as Argentina and Chile, in Australia and South Africa, in the United States (even though production there was now illegal), and in the traditional winemaking countries of Europe. In France, per capita consumption increased by roughly a third over prewar levels, which was just about the same percentage as the increase in global production.

Yet while vintners had more wine to sell to more customers, few benefited from the postwar thirst. Throughout Europe, the 1920s was marked by inflation and declining prices. In Spain, Italy, and especially Germany, winemakers frequently could not make enough money to cover their costs. And in France, unlike during the war years when the government paid relatively high and always stable prices for the wines it bought, the new decade turned the market into a veritable rollercoaster. Sales rose, but prices fell. Then at the close of the decade the entire world plunged into economic depression. The collapse of the various financial markets affected growers of cheap vin ordinaire less than it did those who produced vin fin. While the former made only a pittance selling their wines, their market at least remained thirsty. Not so for the owners of Bordeaux châteaux or Burgundy crus, Rhine or Mosel estates, Port lodges or Sherry bodegas. Their rich customers, nearly all of whom had seen much of their wealth diminish if not disappear, cut back on their purchases. As a result, the prices that vintners could charge tumbled. By the mid-1930s, as the world prepared to face yet another horrific war, bottles of the most esteemed wines—vintage Ports and Champagnes, Trockenbeerenauslese Rieslings, first-growth Clarets and grand cru Burgundies—could be purchased at rock-bottom prices.

The only possible silver lining in this dark cloud of financial gloom came in the world's finest wines now being within reach of more people. Hugh Johnson argues that "the woes of the winegrower in the 1910s, 20s, and 30s had one unpredictable result that has since stood him in good stead; the price of the finest wines came down to a level where they could be drunk by a much wider and more inquisitive range of amateurs." Yet while a few people developed a newfound appreciation for wine (the young Ernest Hemingway, for instance, managed to drink a sea of it while living on a frayed shoestring budget in Paris in the early 1920s), many more wanted nothing to do with the stuff. The democratization of high-quality wine did not really occur until the second half of the century—at which point both prices and incomes actually began to rise.

The principal explanation for what may seem like a bafflingly long delay came in the fact that a good many people during the century's first fifty or sixty years shared unfavorable views of wine. Some continued to think of it as a moral evil from which they righteously abstained. Others, however, drank lots of alcohol but cared little about wine. The agricultural crisis had dismayed the generation that came of age at the turn of the century. Distrusting wine, they turned to spirits. Twenty years later, the men who survived the First World War craved booze in whatever form. If they drank wine, they tended to care far more about quantity than quality. Then in the 1920s and 1930s, when people drank to forget a whole new set of troubles, they again found solace in hard liquor. Moreover, through all these decades of upheaval, wine, even distinctive-tasting wine, functioned less and less as a mark of cultural refinement. With even the world's storied quality wines now thought of primarily as forms of alcohol, they had been displaced by more exciting, and more invigorating, potions: cocktails.

That term, originally an Americanism, had entered the lexicon in the early 1800s, initially referring to "stimulating liquor[s], composed of spirits of any kind, sugar, water, and bitters." The recipe soon became less restrictive, and while purists sometimes object, the word evolved to denote any sort of mixed alcoholic drink. Initially, cocktails (as opposed to straight shots of spirit) tended to be morning libations, consumed by drinkers who craved fortification before noon. By the 1840s and 1850s, however, they were more commonly served after dinner. When Charles Dickens toured the United States, he was both fascinated and delighted by "the mysteries of Gin-sling . . . Sangaree, Mint Julep, Sherry-cobbler, Timber Doodle," and other cocktails. He especially enjoyed these drinks served over ice, something unknown in England. At around the same time, an American bartender named Jerry Thomas began mixing new cocktails as a way of attracting new customers. Thomas worked in many cities but eventually settled in New York, where his theatrical performances behind the bar became quite famous. His signature drink (and trick) was the Blue Blazer, which combined whiskey, simple syrup, boiling water, and lemon peel, and which he prepared by lighting the whiskey afire and passing it back and forth between two glasses, one held high and the other low, thus creating an impressive arc of flame. In 1862, "Professor Thomas," as he came to be known, published *The Bar-Tender's Guide* (also known as *How to Mix Drinks*), which set down in print what previously had been only oral recipes, many of his own devising. These include the Fizz, the Flip, and the Sour. Later editions added still more, drinks like the Martinez (a precursor of the Martini) and the Tom Collins. At his death in 1885, the *New York Times* noted in its obituary that Thomas was very well known "to club men and men about town," and "very popular among all classes."

Cocktails remained primarily bar drinks, and so male fare, until the 1920s, when they became fashionable choices for both sexes. Many women at the time were taking new and sometimes daring social steps (everything from voting to smoking), and had started to drink alcohol in public. Some ordered straight spirits, but cocktails tended to be the smarter choice. These were not fruity long drinks sipped slowly, but rather short, potent ones tossed back fast and furiously, a *carpe diem* response by a generation that had come of age during the ravages of war. As the legendary barman Harry Craddock advised when asked how best to drink a cocktail, do so "quickly, while it's laughing at you."

In America, cocktails were ordered in speakeasies, while abroad they were poured in bars and clubs. They rapidly became chic all across the globe—in London and Paris, Buenos Aires and Singapore, on the Riviera and in Hollywood. If the gusto with which they were gulped down waned during the economic depression and then the war years that followed, their popularity did not suffer. Well past mid-century, cocktails remained chic and stylish, often at the expense of wine. They also came home. Starting in the 1930s, cocktail parties became popular forms of entertainment. This also was when the social practice of having a drink (or two or three) before dinner became widespread. Though the *beau monde* might well quaff Champagne, most drinkers tended to dismiss wines in favor of cocktails in what after all was called "the cocktail hour." Here women led the way, as the home was their domain and entertaining their forte. Modern etiquette guides sang the praises of cocktails, urging women not only to drink them but also to make and to serve them.

One of the best literary representations of the ascendency of cocktails at the expense of wine comes in the English novelist Evelyn Waugh's *Brideshead Revisited*, written in 1945 but with the scenes in question set over twenty years earlier. When the protagonist and narrator, Charles Ryder, spends a summer with his aristocratic college friend, Sebastian Flyte, the young men pass idyllic evenings tasting and learning about wine. In an oft-quoted passage, they talk about what they drink, their language becoming ever more colorfully exotic as the bottles empty. One wine, "little [and] shy," is likened to "a gazelle" and "a leprechaun," while another, "wise [and] old," is said to be "a prophet in a cave," and still another "a necklace of pearls on a white neck . . . like a swan [or] the last unicorn." Waugh took obvious fun in this gentle satire of pretentious wine-speak, but the real significance of the scene comes in the fact that no one else drinks any of these wines. The Brideshead cellars once held "a vast store," but only one section remains in use, and no new wine is being added to it. As the novel unfolds, the rest of Sebastian's family display little if any interest in wine, and the circle of his and Charles's friends rarely touch it. Most of the characters drink a substantial amount of alcohol. But their libations of choice rarely include wine. Instead, these upper-class men and women drink spirits or spirit-based cocktails—including Alexanders (made with brandy, cream, and crème de cacao), gulped down with relish by the foppish but fashionable Anthony Blanche, who invites Charles to dinner but refuses to allow him to order Sherry. Much like the dusty bottles of Claret from the mansion's now largely empty cellar, Sherry has become hopelessly passé. By contrast, an Alexander is declared "a delicious concoction."

In the decades following the First World War, whether depicted in novels, featured in Hollywood movies, or presented in the pages of glossy magazines, cocktails, not wines, were almost always *au courant*. This was their own golden age. Drinking cocktails marked one as sophisticated and in vogue. By contrast, savoring wine seemed stodgy. There certainly were many people, especially among the social elite, who continued to have a glass of wine with meals, but when it was time to entertain, or to be entertained, cocktails tended to be what nearly everyone wanted. New ones were being invented all the time, and old ones improved. Drinks like Daiquiris, White Ladies, and especially Martinis became all the rage in bars and clubs, and knowing how to prepare them marked one as a good host at home. At London's Savoy Hotel, Harry Craddock popularized these and others, while on the silver screen, characters like Nick and Nora Charles drank them with abandon. Put simply, cocktails were glamorous drinks for glamorous people.

Before long, some cocktails were being made with wine. Many remain popular today. The Bellini, for example, invented by Giuseppe Cipriani in Venice, combines Prosecco or other Italian sparkling wine and white peach puree, while the Kir, named for Félix Kir, a Catholic priest and longtime mayor of Dijon, blends crème de cassis and white (preferably Burgundy) wine. The most famous of these, of course, was the Champagne Cocktail, a mix of sugar, Champagne, and bitters. Regardless of the specific wine, however, the simple fact that urban sophisticates chose to drink wine in this new guise indicates how its cultural standing had changed. No longer prized aesthetically in and of itself, it now was much like gin and whiskey, a source of alcohol made delectable through the bartender's skill.

War came once more in 1939. Though the new armies did not destroy as many vineyards as their predecessors twenty-five years earlier, the conflict again disrupted both wine production and the wine trade severely. Once again, governments needed to requisition alcohol for military use. Once again, able-bodied men had to leave grape-growing jobs to serve their countries, and still again, for everyone, both those fighting and those left home, strong drink became an obvious vehicle with which to dull pain and quell fear. Owing in part to still fresh memories of the earlier cataclysm, attitudes toward alcohol tended to be less severe this time around. In England, even while new taxes raised prices on all forms of intoxicating drink, the government acknowledged that beer and whiskey were part of the national culture, and pledged to keep them flowing so as to maintain morale. In Italy, alcohol, including wine, lubricated Mussolini's army (and police force). And in France, the call to arms included a patriotic advocacy of wine as a military necessity.

In early 1940, fully a third of the French railroad's tank cars were appropriated to carry wine to the front, the rationale being that soldiers needed it more than civilians. When the Nazi blitzkrieg swept across the border later that year, some people blamed the French defeat on the army's being drunk, while others contended that the soldiers actually had not had enough to drink. No matter, under German occupation, whether directly or indirectly through the Vichy government, French wine suffered. Unlike the First World War, there now was plenty of male labor to tend the vines, but much as in the earlier conflict, sprays and pesticides were in short supply, and vineyards often fell into disrepair. This was especially true in southern regions that were sources of cheap common wine. Superior wines from more esteemed places fared somewhat better. Their market, however, was in near-total disarray, with few Frenchmen being able to afford them, and exports having to be shipped and sold surreptitiously. The only strong segment of the export market was Germany, but German bureaucrats and military officers paid artificially low prices for their favorite wines, when they didn't just commandeer them.

The Third Reich displayed a somewhat schizophrenic attitude toward all alcoholic drinks. On the one hand, Nazi propaganda often depicted them as dangerous, and habitual drunks could be sterilized or sent to concentration camps. Heinrich Himmler declared in 1938, "No German has the right to impair himself through alcohol abuse . . . such action is detrimental not only to himself, but to his family, and above all, to his people." On the other hand, Germans often drank a good deal—beer and schnapps of course, but also wine. They toasted their military successes (and then later bemoaned their defeats) with not only German wines but also all the French cuvées they shipped home. Nazi agents confiscated massive amounts of vins fins from Bordeaux, Burgundy, and Champagne, for which they paid little or nothing. They sent these home, where military officers and state officials drank them eagerly. Many French vintners retaliated by sabotaging the wines, substituting bad vintages for good ones, or relabeling cheap plonk as prized crus, or even filling bottles with dishwater. Some hid their best wines in secret cellars or hidden caves. (Some also hid colleagues or compatriots, members of the resistance, or Jews.) Nonetheless, a steady stream of wine flowed east to Berlin all during the war. And as the war went on, with fronts eventually being fought on both east and west, and bombs beginning to fall on the Fatherland, they drank more and more of it. In the last years of the war, average citizens in the Reich could get very little alcohol, as the Nazi war machine used everything for munitions. But officers and other leaders gulped it down. To them, vin fin had represented imported style and sophistication when times were good. But now that the tide had turned, it was just booze.

That ultimately was what linked wine's many separate nineteenth- and twentieth-century periods of crisis—first agricultural catastrophe, then social skepticism, economic freefall, brutal warfare, and more. Over the course of a century, distinctive-tasting fine wine had been slowly but almost systematically devalued and cheapened. The gold in the age that preceded this catastrophic era had been more mythic than real, but there can be no doubt that during it wine had acquired a new luster by being elevated above its rivals. That sheen dimmed, however, precisely when wine became like its rivals—not so much because the contents of the bottles or the barrels changed, as because how people conceived and consumed those contents did. A cultural artifact that had been celebrated as being more than its component parts was reduced to but one of those parts. To recover, and in the process realize an even greater because a more inclusive cultural value, it needed once again to be recognized as more than just alcohol.

RECOVERY AND REVIVAL
European Wine's Second Golden Age

As wine's long history makes clear, grape growing and winemaking are precarious enterprises. Nature's fickle whims can wreak havoc, as can an invariably capricious marketplace. But vintners faced particularly perilous times during the first half of the twentieth century. At the end of the Second World War, a veteran grape grower in virtually any European country could look back over a lifetime of long, hard toil and remember little more than trouble, years marked by diseased vineyards, financial collapse, commerce filled with fraud, and horribly violent conflict. And for those just starting out, youthful zeal had to be tempered by the realization that society at large simply did not value wine in the ways it had only a few generations earlier. No longer a necessity, wine now often was not even an object of desire, the winds of fashion having shifted in other directions. Many vintners, surely, longed to return to a more peaceful time, that seemingly golden era before the onset of global wars, the arrival of phylloxera, and all the pressures exerted on their trade by both antialcohol advocates and hard liquor enthusiasts. But there was no going back. The world, and wine's place in it, had changed too much. In order for wine to function as anything more than a form of either intoxication or snobbery, the wine business had to invent itself anew. And that is exactly what happened, with dramatic, even spectacular results.

Wine's revival proved so momentous that some commentators have dubbed it a revolution. Yet in Europe, unlike in New World countries, this was no radical upheaval. Rather than overthrowing the past, vintners revitalized European wine by realizing promises hinted at earlier, the first salvos in the modern wine revolution having been fired over two hundred years before. From expressing terroir in the vineyard to employing new technology in order to attain consistency in the winery and stability in the bottle, the potential intimated during wine's initial modernization began to be achieved on an astonishingly broad scale. That inclusivity is what ultimately proved most important. Starting slowly in the 1950s and 1960s, but then quickly gaining momentum in the following decades, the quality of not just exclusive, expensive cuvées but also widely available and moderately priced wines rose to previously unimagined heights.

In the decades following the Second World War, hardly anyone needed wine anymore. Most municipal water was now clean and safe, and refrigeration was bringing milk and other perishable beverages to millions. Europe's postwar wine revival thus hinged on people again viewing wine as something worth choosing for itself. Though many had thought of it in that way before the calamities described in the last chapter, the crisis years had dampened a good deal of their (or more accurately, their children's and grandchildren's) enthusiasm. Any revitalization required that more people choose to drink better wines. But that in turn depended on a significant improvement in overall quality, with the huge disparity between vin fin and vin ordinaire lessening, and on people then recovering faith in wine as a reliable so desirable product.

The first effort at revival had come much earlier in the century, with an official definition of wine itself—"the alcoholic fermentation of fresh grapes or the juice of fresh grapes." Issued by the French government in 1907 during the phylloxera infestation, this widely publicized designation formed part of the ongoing effort to combat fraud. But it ultimately had a much broader effect. By identifying what constituted, and so also what did not constitute, wine, the authorities affirmed wine's modern identity at the expense of any older one. And while the definition applied initially only to wine produced in one country, the changes it presaged gradually spread across the Continent and eventually the entire grape-growing globe.

This new definition was directed specifically at the vintners and merchants who at the time were passing off wine made with hydrated raisins as fresh-grape wine, a common practice during the agricultural crisis. Raisin shipments, many from the Near East, came into ports like Sète and Marseille, places where unscrupulous winemakers fabricated fake cuvées of all sorts of French wine, including châteaux Bordeaux. So in an effort to combat the fraud, the government decreed that true wine needed to come from freshly harvested grapes. It no longer could be made with dried fruit that might have been picked months if not years earlier, and much of which was not even French.

But as detailed in earlier chapters of this book, many older cultures had treasured wines made with grapes dried in the hot sun until they turned into virtual raisins. Of course, Roman Fallernian or medieval Romney would have tasted quite different from the counterfeit crus made in steamy *fin de siècle* dockside warehouses. For one, those old-fashioned wines had been sweet, being mixed with honey and spice; for another, the ancient ones were thick and sticky, due to the addition of pitch and resin. Their durability, coming in large measure from their relatively high alcohol levels, is what compelled many people to prize them. And they never pretended to be anything other than what they were. By contrast, the fraud that infected the wine market during the crisis years came when raisin wine was disguised as fresh-grape wine—a deception necessitated by the new tastes that had become so culturally prevalent over the past 150 years. In this regard, it is important to remember that, when viewed in the broad expanse of history, an appreciation for fresh-grape wine as anything more than cheap sustenance was quite new. As a cultural phenomenon, it had originated in a few isolated places during the Renaissance, spread among Europe's upper classes during the Enlightenment, and then become adopted passionately by the expanding nineteenth-century bourgeoisie. Now, at the start of the twentieth century, it was so common and expected that the French authorities could use it to define wine as a whole.

For most consumers at the time, distinctions between the genuine and the fraudulent were conceptual rather than sensory. Because so many wines during the phylloxera era had reverted to tasting generic, people frequently could not identify the counterfeits. They might understand the differences intellectually (and hence become suspicious of what was being offered for sale), but they could not necessarily taste them. The finest fresh-grape wines had been something of a middle-class passion a generation before, but the various vine diseases had robbed those wines of much of their individuality and aesthetic appeal. Little would change for fifty years. Despite the continued attention of some devoted connoisseurs, wine as a consumer choice fell on harder and harder times. Especially in wine-producing countries, people still drank a great deal of it, but those consumers who wanted to savor wines of the sort that had inspired newly invented tastes and traditions back in the mid-1800s were dwindling in number and graying by the year.

European wine's postcrisis revival included both a dramatic rise in overall quality and an equally striking increase in consumer appreciation. Many people who previously had not drunk wine at all, or who had thought of it as something common and pedestrian, found themselves drawn to it. The allure came because contemporary fresh-grape wines were starting to become more appealing, in the process offering more particular flavors and aromas. Legitimate vin fin had tasted distinctive for a long time. Yet even in the happy pre-phylloxera days, the amount of it on the market had been overwhelmed by tidal waves of vin ordinaire. One of the most striking aspects of the late-twentieth-century revival came in this ratio being improved significantly. Like so many of the wines themselves, it was brought into better balance.

Part of that balance involved a reaffirmed connection between a wine's individual identity and its place of origin. In 1978, when the European Economic Community adopted rules governing wine production in all its member states, the regulations began with a definition of wine that clearly echoed the earlier French one—"the product obtained exclusively from the total or partial alcoholic fermentation of fresh grapes." But these rules went further, as they also differentiated between categories, common wines as opposed to "quality wines produced in specific regions." Centuries earlier, the taste of terroir had first revealed that high-quality fresh-grape wine did not have to be a contradiction in terms. Now, as part of wine's revival, where a particular wine came from was officially deemed an integral part of its identity.

Since winemaking regions can contain many different microclimates, soil types, and weather patterns, the new laws and regulations that defined what a vintner could and could not do within any specific region did not promote the precise taste of place as the sole mark of quality. Instead, they advocated a somewhat broader sense of particularity and authenticity. Yet these regulations—really, a whole set of them, each different depending on the area demarcated—helped revive interest in fine wine across the Continent. As more particular-tasting wines entered the market, a growing number of people began to associate quality with origin. While that association was not new with a handful of prized wines from already well-known places, it had been largely irrelevant elsewhere. After all, almost all other wine-growing regions, even those with some history of quality, had been producing primarily vin ordinaire. The new laws helped to change all that, as more vin fin started to come from more places. Moreover, advances in viticulture and oenology allowed quality-minded vintners to uncover the potential of previously unexplored regions, thus radically expanding the range of high-quality wines in the marketplace. The upshot was that the generations that came of age following the Second World War had the opportunity to experience more particular flavors than ever before in history. Since they no longer needed wine for basic nourishment or sustenance, they drank less of it than their ancestors. Yet the overall quality of what they did drink was much higher than it ever had been before, allowing vinters and consumers alike to enjoy the fruits of a new, much more inclusive golden age.

—⁂—

A movement toward officially designating specific places as sources of specific wines began in France before the First World War. It then gained momentum in the 1920s and 1930s, culminating in the establishment of that country's appellation system, a complex array of rules governing both grape growing and winemaking that eventually would be imitated, with many changes, worldwide. In the second half of the century, the movement spread to other European countries, bringing an awareness of different terroirs to many new wine drinkers in many new places. The original rationale for demarcating particular regions as the source of particular wines had been a desire for authenticity. By requiring that only wines made in specific areas be identified as such on labels or invoices, the French authorities tried to halt the sale of counterfeit cuvées. New laws compelled growers to report the size of their crops to the government, thus providing a way to detect deception. (If Bordeaux vintners, for example, were augmenting their own wines with wine from the Rhône Valley or Spain, the numbers simply wouldn't add up.) The goal of this sort of differentiation was simply to help distinguish the real from the fake. Just as true wine had to come from fresh grapes, true Bordeaux had to come from a geographical entity officially mapped and identified as such. Before long, however, other goals having to do with how a particular type of wine should be made, and indeed how it should taste, became just as important. The appellation system provided a means with which to assess more than authenticity, for it institutionalized the impulse that had led to the Bordeaux classification back in 1855, providing both consumers and vintners with a legally sanctioned hierarchy of quality.

Today, any country with any sort of fine-wine ambition, whether realized or not, has some geographically based appellation arrangement in place. Many, like those in Australia and the United States, simply distinguish land. They demarcate everything from huge, politically defined places, such as the states of California and South Australia, to smaller regions whose boundaries come more from geographic and agricultural realities—Oakville, for example, or the Clare Valley. Other systems, typically found in European wine-producing countries, go farther. They not only map a region but also define the style or type of wine that can carry the region's name. By prescribing such things as the allowable grape variety or varieties, the size of vineyard yields, and the methods of both grape growing and winemaking, these systems help identify the particular tastes of the region's wines. This has the advantage of making the designation more meaningful, but the disadvantage of sometimes stifling innovation. Nonetheless, no matter what form the demarcation takes, identifying wines in terms of legally designated places has become standard practice. As a result, contemporary consumers can be certain of the origin of the wines they drink.

But wine drinkers could not be at all certain a century before, when the market was rife with fraud, and even "true" wines frequently were not what we today would consider legitimate. This was certainly the case in New World countries, where traditional monikers such as "claret," "hock," and "port" were widely used for wines that bore little or no resemblance to the Old World originals. But it was true too in Europe, where consumers often could not be certain of a wine's provenance, no matter what the person selling it might claim. Estate bottling, filling bottles on the property where the wine is made and the grapes grown, was rarely practiced. Most wines instead remained in casks until they were ready to be sold directly to the public. Merchants or shippers would buy different lots and blend them to a formula or recipe. They were supposed to use only wine from the individual estate, but in actuality they often added other wines, most notably dark, tannic reds from the northern Rhône to châteaux Bordeaux, sometimes to improve the final product, but sometimes simply to have more to sell. They were even less scrupulous with other wines, blending this with that to achieve a desired effect, no matter what would be written on the label or invoice. Some vintners chafed and fumed, but they were powerless to change the situation. With rare exceptions, they simply did not have the money to cellar, bottle, and market their own wines.

Merchants and traders controlled the market everywhere in Europe, customarily selling many different wines under their own names. Rhines, Rhônes, Riojas, and the like often came to consumers not from individual producers but from companies that bought, blended, and sold them. Even esteemed fine French wines were assembled and sold by négociants, who would purchase batches of young wine from various growers and then blend them together to make their own cuvées. In theory, they combined only single types of wine—one farmer's Volnay with another's, for example, or batches of Vouvray from various vineyards—but in practice they combined types freely. The wine in that cask of Volnay might be disappointingly thin; adding some Pommard could improve it. And if that Vouvray tasted too tart, mixing in some sweet wine from nearby Layon might help. In these examples, the merchants used only wines made from the same grape or grapes (here Pinot Noir and Chenin Blanc, respectively) that had been grown in neighboring villages or areas. But since no rules actually specified how Volnay or Vouvray should be made or taste, they often went farther afield. In Burgundy, many négociants blended southern Rhône red wines made with Grenache or Carignan with their Pinot-based Volnays and Pommards. And in Touraine, pretty much anything was fair game to be added to Vouvray, or for that matter to Layon. The resulting wines might taste good, but they were not what the people selling them claimed they were.

Even more important, during the phylloxera era, when decent wine of any sort proved difficult to locate, these wines often did not taste at all good. The quality of virtually all wines had fallen precipitously; demand and then prices followed suit, fraud proliferated, and the market became dangerously unstable. This was precisely the situation that the men who designed the initial appellation regulations were trying to correct. To their minds, the only way to raise quality was to guarantee authenticity. While they could not force vintners to make better balanced, deeper and longer-tasting wines, they at least could compel merchants to sell genuine ones. Prices might then stabilize and demand increase, giving the vintners both an incentive and an opportunity to produce higher-quality wines.

A common misconception has it that the appellation rules codified existing practices. Nothing could be further from the truth. The new system challenged rather than preserved the status quo, improving French wines by distinguishing those that displayed a genuine particularity of aroma and flavor from those that did not. Because consumers invariably considered the former more valuable (and were willing to pay more for them), vintners tried to make more of them. The system imposed controls that compelled those vintners to use certain grapes rather than others, and to follow prescribed methods in both their vineyards and their wineries. If they refused, their wines would not qualify for appellation status.

Many people played important parts in the creation of the French appellation system, but three, Baron Pierre Le Roy de Boiseaumarié, Joseph Capus, and Edouard Barthe, stand out for their especially prominent roles. They approached the problem from different vantage points and represented different interests, but their combined efforts during the interwar years led to markedly improved quality—first in areas that already were sources of vin fin, then in places where growers aspired to such, and eventually in many regions previously home only to cheap common wines. Improvement did not take place immediately, but these three men established the legal framework within which Europe's wine resurgence would occur later in the century.

Le Roy de Boiseaumarié was a World War I flying ace who moved to southern France when he married the owner of one of the larger wine estates in Châteauneuf-du-Pape, near the city of Avignon. Though wines of some repute were made there (including some from a papal vineyard first planted in the early fourteenth century), the region had been one of the hardest hit by phylloxera, and quality proved scarce. By the 1920s, most Châteauneuf was being sold in bulk for very low prices, much of it to merchants who used it to add alcoholic punch to thinner northern reds. Even those who put together cuvées to take to market would blend indiscriminately, combining wines made with all sorts of grapes from all sorts of growers. They justified their methods by noting (rightly) that the price a barrel of local wine fetched did not justify a more rigorous selection.

Then in 1923, a small group of local growers who believed that their vineyards could produce better wines approached Le Roy, asking for his help in organizing a syndicate to promote Châteauneuf-du-Pape and improve quality. He accepted, with the condition "that you [become] the first to give the example of honesty and discipline." They agreed, even though he proposed very stringent rules, limiting the area of production to rocky sites where little except lavender, wild herbs, and vines can grow, and banning the use of sugar for chaptalization. In 1926, Le Roy submitted the requisite papers to the court in the city of Nîmes. Almost immediately, a collection of local négociants and farmers raised objections. They argued that while the proposed rules might well yield more distinctive-tasting wines, the market did not expect such from

Châteauneuf-du-Pape. Following a protracted hearing, and to considerable surprise, the court ruled in favor of Le Roy. The area he had demarcated was granted appellation status, with the restrictions he proposed intact.

One has to suspect that the judge in Nîmes was persuaded less by the baron's reasoning than by his fame as a war hero. Yes, some of the oldest and best Châteauneuf vineyards occupied the rockiest sites; and yes, the better wines tended to be those with low yields and naturally high levels of alcohol. But these were exceptions to the far more prevalent rule of mediocrity in the area. In reality, when proposing restrictive regulations, Le Roy was doing what the creators of many nineteenth-century vins fins had done before him: inventing a tradition for a wine for which he and his fellow syndicate members had high hopes but little actual experience. The only difference was that he was speaking not for a single property—as, for example, Raoul de Pichon-Longueville had done at his Bordeaux château, or the Marchesa di Barolo at her Piedmont estate—but instead for a whole region, or in the language then just starting to be used, an Appellation d'Origine.

Most of the initial French appellations were simple geographical entities, without any stipulations governing methods of grape growing or winemaking. Their creation went a long way toward limiting (though never completely eliminating) fraud, but they did not go very far toward improving quality. Baron Le Roy recognized as much, which is why he insisted on more inclusive regulations in Châteauneuf-du-Pape. Joseph Capus then did much the same for the rest of the country. A senator in the French Parliament from Cadillac near Bordeaux, Capus argued forcefully that geographic designations would prove useless if growers could plant anything they wanted and winemakers could do anything they wished. In his home district, some farmers were still cultivating hybrid grape varieties in addition to or instead of *V. vinifera* ones. They also often were harvesting their crops before the grapes had ripened sufficiently, and so producing thin, vegetal-tasting wines that required the addition of copious amounts of sugar. Were these wines representative of Bordeaux at its best? Capus insisted not. He spoke eloquently for his more conscientious winemaking constituents, contending that quality needed to be part of any regulatory system. An Appellation d'Origine was not enough. In order for consumers to trust such a designation, they needed to be able to associate it with a consistent type or style of wine. Thus it had to include some form of quality control.

In 1927, Capus succeeded in getting legislation passed that required vintners to conform to "the best practices" in both their vineyards and their wineries. This, however, was only a first step. The obvious problem was that different people, even if working in close proximity, often did very different things with their wines. Who was to say which practices were best? As in Châteauneuf, decisions often had to be made by civil court judges, but unlike what had happened in that case, the courts tended to side with existing economic interests, effectively hindering improved quality. Not until eight years later, following the worldwide depression and economic collapse that threatened so many livelihoods, did Capus succeed in persuading his fellow legislators in Paris to establish a self-regulatory system. In what was sometimes called the Capus law or rule, a specially designated agency became empowered to make all decisions regarding quality. Its members, selected from the presidents of various viticultural syndicates, as well as delegates from different national ministries, were the only ones authorized to set appellation boundaries and to approve appellation rules. Since Capus insisted that they do so in consultation with top producers in the various wine-growing regions, the controls actually came from some of France's more visionary vintners. Backed by the force of law, these men and women now had the power to regulate the practices employed by their sometimes reluctant neighbors, and so to formalize their ambitions for their viticultural homes. Following the Second World War, Capus's agency became a public-private entity, the Institut National des Appellations d'Origine (INAO). Based in Paris but run by regional committees in or near the various appellations, the institute's work revitalized French, and by extension the world's wine.

Like Capus, Edouard Barthe served as a deputy in Parliament during the interwar years, in this case representing the Hérault *département* in the Languedoc. Unlike the politically conservative Capus, however, he was a socialist with little concern for self-regulated appellations but a great deal of interest in state-controlled production. Barthe represented family producers of basic vin ordinaire, essentially the only wine made in the Languedoc at the time, and he fought tirelessly for their rights. So he advocated a series of government interventions designed to regulate the bulk market and protect farmers from ruinous price fluctuations. Among other things, these required distillation of surplus wine production, set mandatory alcohol levels, taxed vintners who harvested excessive yields, and prohibited new vine planting by those who owned more than seventy-five acres. He succeeded in getting tariffs imposed on the cheap Spanish wines then used for blending, and compelled the government to purchase a significant volume of the alcohol distilled from excess wine for use as fuel. Barthe thought of all of these measures, collectively known as the Statut de la Viticulture, as ways to stabilize the market and so protect his constituents. But the new rules had an even more important long-term consequence, as they led to an improvement in the wines made by some of those constituents—or by their children.

Edouard Barthe died in 1949, so he did not live to see the Languedoc-Rousillon's quality revolution. Without the laws he had helped enact, however, that revolution would never have started, as the gap separating quality from common wine would have remained cavernous. Instead, the disparity between these two types lessened—not in all places certainly, but in enough that a new generation of wine growers was able to develop new aspirations. More carefully tended vineyards planted with more reputable grapes led inevitably to better wines, so much better in some places that in 1973 the authorities created a new category for them, Vin de Pays, roughly translated as "country wine." Wines classified as such had to be made with authorized or recommended grape varieties within designated areas. The regulations were not as rigid as those for appellation wines, but they ensured that these wines would be superior to generic vin ordinaire. Not surprisingly, growers in some of the better Vin de Pays areas soon organized and proposed stricter Appellations d'Origine Contrôlée regulations. In Barthe's home district, both Faugères and Saint-Chinian, two places that, despite their schist-laced terroirs, had been home to nothing but thin, sour, and very ordinary wines before he started his campaigns for farmers' rights, became AOCs in 1982.

From their inception, the AOC rules valorized "loyal, local, and constant" wine-growing practices. It is essential to understand, however, that such practices first had to be facilitated by those rules before they could be protected by them. Men like Le Roy, Capus, and Barthe always focused on the future, not the past. In 1934, roughly 20 percent of all French wine came from geographically designated appellations. Five years later, after those existing Appellations d'Origine all had become Contrôlée (and new ones added), that percentage had been cut fully in half. What happened to the rest of the wine, supposedly fine since from prime grape-growing locales? It had been declassified because it did not meet the new stringent requirements, being neither loyal, nor demonstrably local, nor consistent to high standards.

The mistaken idea that an appellation's rules should be loyal to old rather than the best current grape-growing and winemaking practices romanticizes and distorts the past, transforming decades if not centuries of sweat and slog into fictional bliss. This would not be a big problem—after all, everyone enjoys fairy tales—if it did not also stifle inventiveness and suppress improvement, precisely what the original AOC rules aimed to promote. By all accounts, the vast majority of French wine in the first half of the twentieth century was of poor quality. If not oxidized and vinegary, as most fresh-grape wines had been for centuries, it tasted unappealingly thin and tart. Thus to contend that the AOC regulations simply sanctioned already well-established practices is to misread history. Yes, certain places were known to produce wines of high quality. But even in Bordeaux, Burgundy, and Champagne (the three most notable such regions), grape-growing and winemaking practices varied considerably, with quality-focused vintners working beside many others who cared only about quantity. Elsewhere in France, in regions that produce highly esteemed wines today (Alsace, for example, and the Loire and the Rhône), quality was for the most part very low. Côte-Rôtie, for instance, was a wine backwater, as was Chinon—both places that, despite long winemaking histories, produced often dirty reds sold primarily in casks to local cafés. And Alsatian whites enjoyed little respect within the region, so little renown beyond it. If the AOC rules systematized anything, it was the realization, first arrived at a century before, that wine traditions can be invented as well as inherited. Clearly, the emergence of truly outstanding wines in places where few had existed previously owed much more to what the system indicated was possible in the future than what had been achieved in the past.

When other European countries began planning national appellation systems of their own in the second half of the century, the issue of how to structure any such system invariably came to the fore. Should it aim primarily for improvement, or should it protect existing reputations and standards? Nowhere did the debate prove more contentious than in Italy. The authorities there initially came down on the side of the status quo, and as a result, no European appellation system proved less effective. Almost immediately upon its implementation, many of the most visionary Italian vintners began breaking its rules with abandon.

With rare exceptions such as Barolo, Italian wine as late as the 1960s was still in its long period of *decadenza*, with the exceptional potential of the country's vineyards almost wholly unrealized. Most reds tasted old-fashioned and shrill, while few whites offered clean flavors, oxidation being the rule rather than the exception. Cellars were often dirty, and a great deal of winemaking equipment antiquated. Though the country was poised for the economic boom that would revitalize it in the decades ahead, Italy had not yet recovered from the upheaval of the two world wars. Before long, much as would happen all across the globe, a new generation of consumers would develop a taste for wine conceived of as a pleasurable cultural choice. At the time, however, many Italians still thought of it as simple sustenance. (Those looking for more distinctive drinks often opted for Cinzano and other Vermouths, or headier fruit or herb-flavored alcohols such as Campari and Fernet.) Adding to the problem, wine producers invariably valued quantity over quality, especially since the postwar national government actively encouraged growers to cultivate high-yielding vine varieties in huge, fertile sites. In 1963, the government in Rome authorized a national appellation program, the Denominazione di Origine Controllata (DOC). Widely known as "930," its number on that year's legislative agenda, it unfortunately did not attempt to improve the situation so much as perpetuate it.

The new regulations forbade experimentation or innovation, privileging old practices at the expense of new ones that might result in higher quality. As early as the mid-1960s, some Italian vintners began to object publicly. This happened most famously in Tuscany, where the

official directives mandated the use of many grape varieties of ques-
tionable quality, even requiring the use of some high-yielding whites in
many DOC reds. The authorities, being defenders of established traditions, no matter how impoverished, paid the frustrated vintners no
heed. In turn, some producers decided to break or simply to ignore the
rules. Over the next three decades, their more modern wines became
the region's standard-bearers. Tuscany is home today to many of Italy's
most distinctive-tasting wines, but it is so almost entirely despite the
DOC system, at least in its initial incarnation.

Two now iconic Tuscan red wines were the first to challenge that
system deliberately. In the process, they fired a revolutionary broad-
side at the entire world of Italian wine. The first, from an estate in the
hilly coastal region of Bolgheri, was named Sassicaia (after the *saasi*,
or stones, there). Made primarily with Cabernet Sauvignon, it was
unabashedly modeled on first-growth Bordeaux, the original cuttings
for the vineyard having come from Château Lafite-Rothschild. The Italian cognoscenti clamored for a taste of its initial commercial vintage
in 1968, and not surprisingly, the wine sold for a very high price. Yet
since Sassicaia did not come from a DOC, it had to be classified as a
simple Vino da Tavola, the lowest category of all Italian wine and a syn-
onym at the time for cheap ordinaire. The second revolutionary wine
was Tignanello, almost as expensive and named for a vineyard plot in
Chianti Classico. The brainchild of the Florentine wine merchant Piero
Antinori and the oenologist Giacomo Tachis (who also helped make
Sassicaia, which Antinori marketed and sold, this being a rather inces-
tuous rebellion), its initial 1971 vintage contained only Sangiovese in a
clear violation of DOC rules. Subsequent vintages further flaunted the
regulations by including roughly 20 percent Cabernet, and by being
aged for an extended period in small French oak barrels. Yet both Tignanello and Sassicaia sold like proverbial hotcakes (or *crespelle*). Being
fuller-bodied, richer, and more compelling than most other reds, they
introduced a new style of Italian wine. Before long, other expensive Vini
da Tavola echoing that style appeared on the market—more so called
"Super Tuscans," but also wines from Friuli, Romagna, Trentino, even
Piedmont. The men and women responsible for them were happy to

bypass the "930" laws, particularly since the marketplace seemed not to care.

That was the biggest problem with the DOC system. Consumers, both in Italy and abroad, did not trust it, so few vintners benefited from it. In the 1990s, new laws designed to give it more integrity were passed, and the designation certainly means more now than it once did. Nonetheless, many DOCs still are primarily political creations, and many rules and regulations remain unnecessarily rigid. This is equally true of wines classified as DOCG, ostensibly the highest rank in the Italian system. (The "G" there stands for Garantita, though with many wines neither quality nor authenticity is actually guaranteed.) Distinctive-tasting, high-quality wines can be found today all over Italy, but their particularities of flavor and bouquet owe little to the "930" decrees. They reflect their origins, but not necessarily as enshrined in law. That's because, as Italian wine authority Burton Anderson succinctly notes, the original DOC directives frequently protected "traditions [that were] too often backward."

Different but related problems plagued the German wine industry, which suffered from a deep depression for much of the twentieth century. Not only did the country's vineyard acreage shrink, but both the quality and the reputation of its wines fell as well. In the mid-1800s, German wines had been widely regarded as some of the finest in the world. A hundred years later, they tended to be viewed (in most cases rightly) as simple, sappy, and cheap. The two world wars had brought Germany economic hardships that only intensified after peace was declared. In the late 1940s and 1950s, many growers faced bankruptcy, and many vineyards fell into disrepair. Though some small estates did continue to make Riesling-based wines of impeccably high quality, the export market became dominated by branded wines containing multiple grape varieties and coming from more than one region. (Blue Nun's Liebfraumilch, launched by the H. Sichel Söhne company in 1923, was the best known.) Not until the 1970s and 1980s did real revival begin, with a new generation of vintners providing new interpretations of old traditions.

Perhaps not surprisingly in a country where fruit often struggles to ripen, early German classification systems equated quality with grape ripeness, typically measured in terms of sugar concentration in unfermented grape juice, the "must" that will turn into wine. In a new set of laws enacted in 1971, the government tried to marry this idea with the basic concept of appellations based on geographical origin. The result was confusion, especially for consumers. Though all German wines now had to identify where they came from, the authorities delineated both individual vineyard sites (*einzellagen*) and large wine-growing areas (*grosslagen*). They then divided the wines from both into qualitative tiers, with only one tier having the potential to contain wines displaying true individuality. It was called "quality wine with distinction," or *mit prädikat*, so superficially seemed similar to a French AOC, with rules concerning yields, harvest dates, and more. Yet at the same time, wines coming from these sites remained identified by sugar concentration, or "must weight," the riper the fruit resulting in the higher the *prädikat*— from Kabinett through Spätlese, Auslese, and the super-ripe Beerenauslese and Trockenbeerenauslese. But since the *prädikats* measured musts rather than finished wines, one producer's Spätlese could well taste drier than another's Kabinett, while someone else's could be sweeter still. The whole system proved perplexing, and German wine labels became notoriously difficult to decipher. It was a classic case of people being given too much information, more certainly than they needed or could reasonably handle.

These confusing regulations, some of which were revised or amended later, irritated quality-conscious German producers. Leading the way were a small band of Rheingau vintners, the Charta group, who beginning in 1983 adopted stricter rules for making both dry and sweet wines. The organization's fifty members merged in 1999 with the Rheingau branch of the VDP (Verband Deutscher Prädikatsweigüter), a national association of influential wine estates with strict self-imposed directives regulating quality. In 2002, after years of argument and debate, the VDP published a vineyard classification, distinguishing between "great growths" (Grosse Gewächs) and other top sites, in an attempt to introduce a true cru system. The jury remains out on the question of whether it will work. Because it applies only to members of the association, some superb wines invariably are excluded, and since the VDP is a private rather than a government organization, the classifications remain unofficial. Nonetheless, it represents an important start. More than any other previous system used in Germany, the VDP system has brought the basic idea of controlled appellations to some of that country's, and indeed the world's, greatest vineyards.

Other European appellation laws, typically coming in countries with less entrenched winemaking traditions, have been more effective in providing vintners with incentives to raise quality. Though Spanish lawmakers first created the Denominación de Origen (DO) system in 1930—inspired by what was happening in France as well as by regional classifications initiated in Rioja—the current structure took shape only after Spain joined the European Union in 1986. In it, the country's different regional governments, rather than any Madrid-based bureaucracy, regulate the appellations, drawing the boundaries, then administering and revising the rules. Each DO is controlled by an official council, or Consejo Regulador, composed of government officials, grape growers, winemakers, and wine merchants from the area. The Spanish system—more flexible than Italy's, less hierarchical than France's, and more focused on locale than Germany's—encourages innovation. Many DOs are admittedly too large, being political rather than viticultural constructs. They often contain a variety of different terroirs and produce an array of different wines, but the simple fact that decisions regarding what is and is not acceptable within them are made by people who have a vested interest in their success can only be an advantage. That advantage has been realized spectacularly in regions that only a generation ago had virtually no quality-wine traditions. For white wines, these include Rías Baixas in Galicia, Rueda in Castilla y León, and the Basque appellations in País Vasco. The list is longer for reds but contains (among others) Jumilla, Navarra, Somontano, Toro, and in Catalonia alone, Penedès, Montsant, and Priorat.

The last of these offers perhaps the best illustration of how the Spanish DO system allows for invented traditions and continuing improvement. Vines have been cultivated in Priorat, a rugged, isolated area southwest of Barcelona, since the twelfth century, but until the 1990s, unless carted to the commercial city of Reus to be distilled into brandy, the wines rarely left the local villages. In fact, an official history of Catalan wine, published by the regional government in 1990, did not even mention them. But by the early 2000s, Priorat was producing some of the most compelling, and most expensive, wines in all of Spain. What happened to impel such rapid change? First, an influx of energy and investment came to the area. René Barbier, a Frenchman inspired by the potential he saw there, had started a winery in the small village of Gratallops in the mid-1980s. He soon was joined by four other outsiders, forming Priorat's "gang of five," who together began producing intensely concentrated red wines that were a far cry from the rustic, raisiny ones typically made in the region. (The wines also tasted very different from Spain's more famous reds, both oak-influenced Riojas and Bordeaux-inspired cuvées coming from Penedès and Ribera del Duero.) But second, the local Consejo Regulador actively encouraged Barbier and those who followed him. No rules prevented experimentation; no regulations rewarded old practices at the expense of new ones. Native growers formed or joined cooperatives, which in turn hired trained oenologists to ramp up quality, while an influx of foreigners opened new wineries. The amount of land under vine doubled. And the demand for Priorat red wine exploded—in Spain, but even more internationally. In 2002, it became only the second region in the country to be designated as Calificada, a superior DO category. Priorat's traditions, then, clearly are very new. But the character of its best wines, literally rooted in the dark slate, quartz-infused soil known locally as *llicorella*, is no novelty.

Equally important change also came to Portugal. When that country joined the European Union in 1986, its old wine laws had to be brought into line with those of the other member states, and a rash of new *denominaçãos* quickly appeared on its wine maps. Based on the French AOCs, these specified the permitted grape varieties as well as allowable yields, alcohol levels, and more. But because Portugal had been isolated politically as well as geographically from the rest of Europe for a very long time, prescribing such things proved difficult. There were plenty of old traditions, but few that any ambitious vintner wanted to follow in lockstep. The country is home to a myriad of local grapes, many with the potential to produce exciting modern wines but few with any real history of having done so. Some vinters planted imported grape varieties, but more focused on these native ones, striving to learn which methods and techniques will yield the most distinctive wines. That obviously takes time, but unfortified Portuguese wine already has come a remarkably long way in a very short period. From Minho in the north to Alentejo in the south, overall quality has risen markedly. Particularly striking improvements have come in the reds from Bairrada and Dão, both regions that used to be known for aggressively tannic, rustic wines but that now are yielding much fruitier and more refined ones. And in the Douro, long famous solely for Port, dry red wine has suddenly come into its own, so much so that in less than two decades Douro *tintos* have become Portugal's most prestigious red dinner wines.

In addition to rules in individual countries, most European winemaking is governed by regulations that explicitly link quality with geographical origin in all the member states. These affect fully two-thirds of the world's wine production today. They have had the most significant impact in countries with long wine histories but few traditions of modern winemaking—not only Spain and Portugal but also (in descending order of production) Greece, Hungary, Austria, and Slovenia. Of these, the most noteworthy may be Greece, where an entire wine industry has undergone a radical transformation in less than a generation's time. The directive to distinguish quality wine from common wine, and to require that the former come from specific places, compelled growers in those places to improve their wines, many made with native Greek grapes such as Assyrtiko, Moscophilero, and Rhoditis for whites, and Aghiorghitiko, Mandelaria, and Xinomavro for reds. Most important, the implementation of the Greek appellation system, copied directly from the French one, inspired vintners to think differently about their country's wines than they or their fathers and grandfathers had before. An influx of agricultural funds from the European Union assisted the process, as the money helped modernize the country's vineyards and wineries. Today's top Greek wines taste clean and often extremely compelling, and they have virtually nothing in common with the tradition of oxidized juice that dominated the country's production for centuries. Often fashioned by young winemakers who learned their craft in France or California or Australia, they have found eager buyers both in export markets and at home, particularly in cities like Athens and Thessalonika, where a new generation has embraced native flavors.

The various European appellation laws have enabled new generations of wine drinkers throughout the continent to discover similar flavors. Coupled with the increasingly common practice of estate bottling, these laws have in some cases restored, and in many others provided for the first time, badly needed integrity to wine in general. In the process, they have given consumers new confidence—confidence not only in the wines they might buy but also in their own ability to discern and discriminate between different types and styles. Serious fraud, commonplace before the establishment of appellations, has not disappeared entirely, but it has become so rare that it occasions widely publicized scandal when it is discovered (as happened, for example, in both Austria and Italy in the 1980s). And improved quality, the initially unintended consequence of these laws, has led literally millions of people to value wine anew. In the 1930s and 1940s, many Europeans had reverted to thinking of wine simply as a cheap way to get drunk. But by the 1970s and 1980s, a new generation began to trust it to provide intellectual and emotional pleasures as well as physical ones. The idea of wine as a natural expression of the earth, and a particular piece of earth at that, was not in itself new. Its acceptance by the wine-drinking public at large, however, most definitely was. High-quality wine identified in terms of region or place was no longer the exclusive province of connoisseurs. Now even casual wine drinkers could be at least reasonably certain that the glass or bottle they purchased at a neighborhood bistro, trattoria, or tapas bar would taste not only good but also distinctive, with particular flavors coming from particular places.

—⚘—

The renewed emphasis on terroir and the particularities of place went hand in hand with important advances in both grape growing and winemaking. These compelled vintners to become more involved with the intricacies of their craft, enabling them to produce wines that better reflected natural origins. During the first half of the twentieth century, production at all but the most well-financed estates, the vast majority of which were small and family-owned, remained largely what it had been for thousands of years—a process of letting nature run its course. But beginning in the 1950s and 1960s, as the necessity of revival became ever more apparent, many grape growers and winemakers began to employ new tools, both conceptual and technical, to direct that course. These tools were not just preventative, as had been the case with the various chemical treatments used to combat vine diseases a century earlier, but also progressive, a set of specific means utilized to reach specific stylistic and qualitative ends. On the technical side, they included innovations such as temperature management and regular chemical analysis, which gave vintners greater control over their vines and fermentations. On the conceptual side, equally important was the ever-increasing conviction that human beings in fact could and should assume control. This control never could be complete, since nature always retained the last word, but vintners now believed that they could manage their work to a greater degree than their ancestors ever had dared dream possible. Enlightenment scientists like Antoine Lavoisier and Jean-Antoine-Claude Chaptal had first introduced the idea of controlling the winemaking process back in the 1700s. That idea then led to Louis Pasteur's eye-opening twin discoveries, that yeasts are necessary for fermentation, and that bacteria cause spoilage. Building on those discoveries, scientists now provided vintners with an ever more precise understanding of their enterprise. They revealed how wine's complex chemical structure changes over time, and how people can manage the change. As a result, by the second half of the century, the basic idea that men and women can "direct and master" winemaking, something that had seemed radical when Chaptal first proposed it, was becoming so commonplace as to be unquestioned.

As a modern commercial product, wine comes as much from human choice as from nature's caprice. While it is certainly true that a good wine cannot be made with bad grapes, it is equally true that grape quality is a function of both human action and natural conditions. After all, nature is responsible not only for the seductive aromas and flavors that distinguish great wines, but also for the tart smell and taste of vinegar. And without human intervention, wine always turns into vinegar. No matter how spectacular a terroir, bad decisions will yield bad wines, just as good wines can result only from choices intelligently made. Such choices begin in the vineyard and then extend into the winery. The shared job of the modern grape grower and winemaker thus consists of making decisions that will enhance the likelihood of the wine in question tasting distinctive and providing intellectual and emotional pleasures as well as sensual ones.

As detailed earlier, almost all vinters' primary focus for most of wine's history was simply on preventing spoilage. Only with the technical innovations that hastened wine's modernization could more than an occasional and usually isolated winemaker aim for particularity. But as we have seen, by the middle of the nineteenth century, in places like Barolo and Bordeaux, the Rhinegau and Rioja, Champagne and Burgundy's Côte d'Or, winemaking had at least sometimes become an artisanal if not an artistic endeavor. In their efforts to capture an elusive taste of place, the men and occasionally women responsible for the wines produced there had to make deliberate decisions. These involved determining what sort of wine they wanted to make—sweet or dry, sparkling or still, barrel-aged or young and fresh—and then deciding what steps to take to realize that goal. When should they harvest, and then how long should they hold their wine before taking it to market? Should they add sugar, ferment to complete dryness, or retain some residual sweetness? How much sulfur should they use, and when? During the 150 years since, as winemaking increasingly has become informed by scientific research and technical innovation, the number of such decisions has multiplied many times over, giving vintners everywhere more options, and resulting in many more high-quality, exciting wines.

A great deal of this research has been conducted in universities and academic institutes. The first school for wine growers opened in 1811 in Saxony, but it was not until Pasteur's analyses revealed the potential of scientific investigation that more schools began to devote resources specifically to the study of vines and wines. Some were independent entities, others departments within already established institutions. The most important were in France and Germany (or in other German-speaking countries), befitting the fact that these were nineteenth-century Europe's most important sources of high-quality wine. The University of Montpellier, where Jules Émile Planchon worked in the department of botanical sciences, established an independent school in 1872. Its mission was, and still is, primarily viticultural. (The collection of vine varieties there, started in response to the phylloxera infestation, now numbers over three thousand.) Eight years later, the University of Bordeaux followed suit. Directed by Ulysse Gayon, formerly the university's lone professor of chemistry, its faculty concentrated more on oenology, something that only intensified in the twentieth century. In Germany, the faculty at the Geisenheim Grape Breeding Institute in the Rheingau also started researching and teaching in 1872. Its most influential member, Hermann Müller (from Thurgau in Switzerland), soon developed the grape variety that carries his name, and the institute remains a leading center of research in vine breeding and physiology. Other important nineteenth-century centers of German-language research included Klosterneuberg in Austria, San Michele All'Adige in the South Tyrol (now Italy's Alto Adige), and Wädenswil in Switzerland. But regardless of location, by the early 1900s viticulture and oenology had become legitimate academic disciplines.

Though formal training often was not the norm for winemakers during the first half of the twentieth century, it was being conducted in almost every significant wine-producing country by the 1960s and 1970s, often at multiple schools. Regional needs and economies invariably stimulated the specifics of faculty research. Virtually all of Europe's academic wine centers established cooperative programs with local syndicates, and many researchers also worked as consultants, going into vineyards and wineries to oversee the methods and practices employed there. Hence it would be a mistake to characterize European winemaking practices as tradition-bound (in contrast to more explicitly innovative ones in the New World), as some commentators do. After all, Europe's wine traditions were being invented and reinvented all the time. The wines from Tuscany and Priorat that were exciting consumers by the end of the century definitely were not made in the image of old, tired ones. Moreover, news traveled fast, and recalcitrant winemakers inevitably knew about new equipment and techniques. Even if they shunned such, their sons and daughters likely did not.

The list of influential European academic oenologists and viticulturalists is very long. It includes Louis Ravaz and Pierre Viala from Montpellier, coeditors of the groundbreaking journal *Revue de Viticulture*; René Engel at the University of Dijon, who helped bring the scientific principles of winemaking to Burgundy; and Heinrich Birk and Helmut Becker from Geisenheim, pioneers in the fields of vine breeding and clonal selection. But the most prominent twentieth-century wine researcher was Émile Peynaud, a professor at the University of Bordeaux's Institute of Oenology. Peynaud conducted groundbreaking laboratory research, but his even more important work came as an adviser to over one hundred Bordeaux châteaux, as well as many wineries in Italy, Spain, and even the United States. As much as anyone in Europe, he successfully applied the principles of pure science to the practical art of making wine, devoting his long career to solving, or better eliminating, wine's mysteries.

The romantic notion that wine is a mysterious, even magical substance has a long history, but Peynaud insisted that it be given no place in a modern winery. His self-imposed mission was to help eliminate winemaking accidents by eradicating winemaking ignorance, for, as he famously said, "[an] ignoramus only makes good wine by accident." Thus beginning in the 1950s, and then continuing for the rest of the century, Peynaud consulted directly with vintners, translating seemingly abstract scientific concepts into hands-on advice. As he explained in his 1971 *Connaissance et travail du vin* (translated into English as *Knowing and Making Wine*), "It is not enough to pursue the knowledge of wine in the laboratory alone; it must be spread through the wineries in order for this knowledge to become part of daily practice. Moreover, the faster scientific progress advances, the greater risk there is of widening the gap between what we know and what we do." Many of his methods, viewed as radical when first introduced, have since become standard practice throughout the winemaking world.

The most significant challenge facing mid-century vintners concerned solving what Peynaud called "the thermal problem." This problem begins during fermentation, when heat generated by the biochemical reaction increases the risk of spoilage, retarding or even stopping the process altogether. It then extends through all the various stages of a wine's life and development. According to Peynaud, "it is vital" for any winery to have "a sufficient means of cooling, adapted to its particular working conditions." This would have been a pointless contention before the advent of refrigeration, but by the 1950s, winemakers had (or could have) equipment with which to regulate the temperature of their fermentations and, if necessary, their cellars. The technology was costly, but Peynaud argued forcefully that the results justified the expense. After all, it gave the winemaker significantly more control over both the quality and the character of the wine. Without it, he said, "the success of vinification [could] only be at best the result of a series of lucky accidents."

Equipment with which to manage temperature probably ranks as the second most important technological innovation in the entire history of wine, following only the invention of the securely sealed glass bottle. Temperature-controlled tanks are standard equipment today in all but the most primitive wineries. They are used not only during fermentation but also both before and after—before to cool the grapes or must, and afterward to stabilize the finished wine. Early models cooled wine either by running refrigerated water through metal tubes immersed in vats or casks, or by pumping the wine itself through coils immersed in cold water. The current technology is more sophisticated. Tanks, usually made from stainless steel, have cooling devices built into their walls or in "jackets" that surround them. Probes read the temperature inside the tank, and computers automatically regulate the supply of refrigerant, thus ensuring that whatever is in the tank—juice about to be fermented, must in the process of fermentation, or finished wine—remains at precisely the temperature that the winemaker has determined to be optimal.

Temperature control has had a profound effect not only on how modern wine is made but also on where it can be made—or more accurately, where high-quality fine wine can be made. More than any other technical innovation, it has enabled vintners working in warm or even hot climates to produce distinctive-tasting dry wines. The improved quality of wines from southern France, for example, would have been impossible without refrigeration. So too with the emergence of fresh-tasting wines from Mediterranean countries like Greece, Italy, and Spain. In regions where summers linger long and winters prove relatively mild, managing the temperature of the cellar itself can prove crucial. Though contemporary winemakers work assiduously to keep tanks and barrels full and sealed, some exposure to oxygen proves inevitable. Since spoilage will occur about four times as fast at eighty-five degrees Fahrenheit than at sixty-five degrees, maintaining a low cellar temperature becomes extremely important. Émile Peynaud and his Bordeaux colleagues certainly did not invent refrigeration. Nor were they the only researchers to advocate its use. But because Bordeaux remained the world's most important single wine region, they changed winemaking both there and beyond, helping vintners everywhere realize a much greater degree of control than was possible before.

One of Peynaud's most significant areas of research involved a winemaking phenomenon known as malolactic fermentation. Technically not a fermentation at all, this occurs when a specific strain of bacteria converts a young wine's harsh malic acid into softer lactic acid, giving the finished wine a smooth, supple quality. (Contrary to Pasteur's claims, these bacteria prove beneficial.) Malolactic fermentation cannot begin, however, if conditions are too cold, and it carries spoilage risks when cellars become too hot. Temperature control thus proves crucial when the winemaker wants to induce it. Peynaud called malolactic the "finishing phase" of a wine's biochemical change. Vintners long had observed it, since their cuvées sometimes would start bubbling and hissing following days or even months of apparent inactivity. Some had thought it a continuation of alcoholic fermentation, while others presumed it to be evidence of disease or infestation. But before Peynaud publicized his research, few understood it. Malolactic fermentation "promotes quality," he told them, and with red wine "may be considered the first step in improvement by aging." Again, the key is understanding and control, understanding a desired result and controlling the winemaking process so as to achieve it.

Peynaud and other twentieth-century researchers also urged control in the vineyard, notably at the time of harvest. Vines are notorious for ripening unevenly, one plant maturing before another and sometimes even one cluster before a different one on the same vine. What, then, should a grower do? The scientists recommended two things—first, monitoring and measuring the ripening process as carefully as possible, and second, practicing a severe selection, so using only the best grapes for the best wines. Deciding when to harvest inevitably entails taking risks. Pick the grapes too early, and the resulting wine likely will taste tart and vegetative. Pick too late, and the wine may turn out heavy and unbalanced. The more knowledge the vintner has, the more calculated such risks can become.

With his classified-growth Bordeaux clients, Peynaud counseled using only the most mature grapes from the best sites, and separating the rest of the crop for sale under a second label. He did not invent the idea. Second wines made from vines deemed not good enough for a château's *grand vin* had been produced in poor vintages since the late eighteenth century. Peynaud, however, argued that the fundamental issue involved the quality of the fruit, not the vintage. "[Always] using only the best grapes is a new phenomenon," he told an interviewer in 1990, adding revealingly that he considered it "the crowning achievement of my work." Since some grape clusters inevitably will be either under-ripe or overripe in even the best years, this sort of careful selection needs to be made during every harvest. Peynaud certainly recognized that relegating some grapes or wines to a second label entailed financial sacrifice, as the resulting cuvée will sell for only a fraction of the price charged for the first one. Yet even though many châteaux proprietors in the 1950s and 1960s had not yet recovered from the financial devastation of earlier decades, he coaxed and cajoled them successfully, convincing them that the highest quality results from the most carefully controlled selection. Every ambitious Bordeaux châteaux follows his lead today.

All the research conducted by Peynaud and his colleagues at the university's institute changed the stylistic and qualitative character of Bordeaux wines. The whites started to become less tart and vegetal, and the reds more supple and sensuous, fuller in flavor but less astringent. These changes invariably resulted from the practical application of scientific research. But while the cognitive advances came in laboratories, the utilization of those advances in the actual production of the wines was what made the crucial difference. As the institute's director, Pascal Ribéreau-Gayon, put it, great wines are not just gifts of nature, but "the fruit of a discipline imposed by man upon nature." No words more succinctly summarize the modern approach to winemaking. That approach was first advocated 250 years ago, but only in the second half of the twentieth century did it become accepted everywhere that people aimed to make high-quality, distinctive-tasting wines.

Many of those wines—some in the New World certainly, but some also in other winemaking parts of Europe, Tuscany, for example, as well as the different *denominacións* in northern Spain—explicitly emulated the modern Claret style that Peynaud and his colleagues helped popularize. Realizing as much, some commentators have contended that his approach was formulaic. But little evidence supports that claim. As a consultant, Peynaud always insisted that the style or character of a specific wine comes from both natural conditions and human choices. When he began his work in the 1950s, many growers were harvesting their vineyards early, and many wines, even from prestigious properties, tasted excessively green or vegetative owing to the immaturity of the grapes. Of course, the wines also often had been adversely affected by exposure to air. "The wines of yesterday were more stereotyped than today's," he insisted, arguing that "they were all similar because they shared the same defect—they were oxidized." His work definitely helped change all that. But Peynaud also cautioned against the opposite extreme, insisting that in hot years growers need to work just as hard to avoid excess maturity, disproportionate alcohol levels, and an undue lowering of acidity. The crucial thing, he wrote, is for the vintner to "know wine better in order to make it better, cultivate it, mature it, and appreciate it better too." Only when armed with that knowledge can he or she manage both vineyard and winery so as to attain a desired result.

Since a good deal of that knowledge involves chemistry, very few wineries with any significant volume of production in the world today do not have a laboratory on site. It may be located in a converted storeroom or closet, but a facility devoted specifically to chemical analysis has become a standard part of winery design. Of course, having a laboratory also means having someone on staff who possesses the requisite expertise concerning what to do with the equipment in it. Contemporary winemakers may take courses and receive diplomas, read books or study manuals, receive tutoring from neighbors or friends, but no matter how they acquire the technical information, they make use of it regularly in their craft. Not too long ago, the science of oenology was something practiced in institutes or research centers set apart from actual wineries. But oenologists today often are as much at home in a winery's working laboratory as in a university's research-oriented one.

They have become intimately involved in the actual practice of growing grapes and making wines.

By the 1980s, just about every European vintner who could afford to do so was purchasing temperature-control equipment, sorting tables, and all the other tools of modern winemaking. Those who did not have the funds or the energy tended either to abandon wine growing, to band together in cooperatives, or to sell their grapes to larger wine companies. Some small, independent growers certainly continued to cultivate vines and make wines, but for the most part they could do so successfully only in prestigious appellations, where the price they charged for the finished product justified the expense involved in modernization. All this change helped improve vin ordinaire even more than vin fin. Though the stylistic differences might remain broad, the basic qualitative gap between these two types of wine began to narrow significantly. Inexpensive everyday wine, still often sold from tank or cask, no longer had to taste unpleasantly shrill. While it probably did not display much particularity or complexity, it often tasted quite good. Modern winemaking science and technology propelled this change, as did a marketplace that simply would not put up with unpleasant-tasting, sour wine anymore. European consumers in the increasingly affluent final third of the century simply had too many alternatives. For the first time in history, no matter how low its price tag, a wine needed to taste at least decent in order to sell.

The lack of interest in cheap, generic wine led to the market becoming flooded by it. Overproduction, often resulting from misguided government policy, was the primary source of what became known as Europe's "wine lake." Agricultural ministers in all of the Continent's wine-producing countries had encouraged new vine planting in the 1950s and 1960s as a way to revitalize their war-ravaged economies. Much as had been true earlier, however, few government bureaucracies differentiated between wines in terms of quality. Hence most of the increase in volume came in regions producing inexpensive, low-quality wine of the sort that was attracting fewer and fewer customers. Over those two decades, European production increased by approximately 50 percent, the vast majority of the new wines tasting at best unexceptional and at worst nasty. Yet as noted earlier, the old vin ordinaire market already had begun drying up, impelled by changing fashions and tastes. Nothing was going to reverse the trend. Consumers neither needed nor wanted this sort of wine anymore, no matter how low-priced it might be.

Further contributing to the rising level of the "wine lake" was the fact that growers had become more proficient. Aided by advances in technology and viticultural science, they were able to harvest significantly larger crops than in decades past. Many now drove tractors, which they used not just to till their land but also to prune and spray their vines. These could deliver newly developed fungicides and fertilizers, as well as conventional copper or sulfur sprays, faster and more efficiently than individual farmers could with tanks strapped to their backs. Tractors also could cover ground faster than horses or donkeys, let alone workers on foot. They especially benefited producers who owned large plots of land, and constituted yet another reason why many small-scale growers, who often could not afford to buy such an expensive piece of equipment, were being driven out of business.

Equally important, the plant material itself had changed. Back in the 1920s, researchers at Germany's Geisenheim Institute had demonstrated the viability of clonal vine selection. This is the practice of propagating cuttings from a single superior plant. As contrasted with massal selection, in which many cuttings from many different vines are used to replicate the general characteristics of a vineyard, clonal selection allows the viticulturalist to grow vines evidencing quite specific properties—resistance to a particular disease, for example, or the propensity to deliver a desired yield. It is yet another example of human beings taking control of nature to realize particular goals. Yet while clonal selection certainly can be employed as a means with which to reach qualitative ends, most growers during the 1950s, 1960s, and 1970s used it simply to pursue increased quantity. They planted new commercial clones in order to harvest a greater tonnage of grapes than they could have otherwise. The end result was more and more wine— occasionally of higher quality but more often not. Though appellation regulations might specify maximum yields, no such rules applied to growers of generic vin ordinaire. Hence the lake threatened to turn into a veritable flood.

Two exceptionally large harvests in 1979 and 1980 impelled the European Economic Commission to act—first by mandating compulsory distillation of excess wine, and second by offering financial incentives to growers in marginal places to uproot vineyards. The distillation plan included nearly a fifth of the member states' total production, and the vine-pull program eliminated approximately 10 percent of their vineyards. By the early 1990s, the overflowing lake had been reduced to an (admittedly large) puddle. Then in 1999, the European Union launched new initiatives aimed at maintaining an appropriate balance between supply and demand. Among other things, these included a ban on new planting as well as a reconversion project, enabling growers with vineyards producing unmarketable wines to replant so as to produce ones that could sell. That, after all, was the key to all of these programs—eliminating cheap, sour wines that no one wanted to drink anymore. The EU ministers and commissioners did not speak about distinctive tastes or particular flavors, but the wines that they removed from the market were invariably of poor quality. That these wines also were the direct descendents of all the thin, acrid ones that had lubricated drinkers for literally thousands of years made no difference. For consumers, high quality, long the exception, was fast becoming the rule.

Though not as severe as in the 1970s and 1980s, surplus European wine production remains a problem today. It is aggravated not just by improved efficiency in the vineyard but also by falling consumption rates in many historically important wine-drinking countries. People in the late twentieth and the early twenty-first century simply drink less wine than their forebears. The numbers tell the story. In Italy, per capita annual wine consumption fell from approximately twenty-nine gallons in 1950 to slightly more than fifteen in 2000, a drop of some 45 percent. The decline was even greater in France, from forty gallons per person to about sixteen. And while not as severe elsewhere, no wine-producing country was immune, with German consumption falling by roughly a quarter and both Portuguese and Spanish by a third.

A closer look at these figures, however, reveals a silver lining, as virtually all the decline has been in cheap generic wine. The second half of the twentieth century brought unprecedented prosperity to Western Europe, including a socialized safety net for the poor and greater disposable income for just about everyone else. That prosperity corresponded with significant demographic shifts, as more of the Continent's population moved to cities and suburbs, and fewer people remained on farms in the country. The two mainstays of the old vin ordinaire market, lower-class urban workers and rural laborers, were losing both economic and social influence. The old practice of industrial workers beginning their day with a slug or two of wine, much as the custom of workers and farmers coming home for a noon meal that included a bottle or two, was fast disappearing. Moreover, attitudes were shifting. Factory bosses no longer condoned wine drinking on the job, and the police began to look askance at truck and automobile drivers who drank any sort of alcohol before getting behind the wheel. Even in the most remote villages in southern France, Italy, and Spain, wine no longer was something that a healthy person would think about drinking all day long. A glass or two after work in a café or trattoria was fine, as was a bottle on the dinner table, but wine no longer belonged in the workplace, or for that matter in many parts of the family home. Its role in people's lives, and so its place in the culture at large, had shifted. Wine was not used as a medicine anymore, and the availability of recreational drugs led fewer people to conceive of it as a vehicle of escape. These changes did not benefit producers of generic vin ordinaire, but they did benefit vintners, no matter whether working in historic appellations or in previously neglected regions, who had set their sights higher.

Further contributing to the decline in consumption was the fact that the generations born after the Second World War did not drink alcohol of any sort with the same kind of abandon as their ancestors. Earlier challenges to wine's cultural dominance always had involved other alcoholic drinks—everything from hopped beer in the late Middle Ages to cocktails in the early twentieth century. Even in the 1700s, when tea and coffee first entranced Enlightenment drinkers, vintners were being tested at least as much by the popularity of spirits like brandy and gin. The postwar generations certainly drank their share of beer and hard liquor, but they also consumed fruit juices, carbonated soft drinks, and bottled mineral waters. These beverages had been either unavailable or in scarce supply earlier. By the 1960s and 1970s, they were grocery-store staples.

Of course, people also could buy wine in grocery stores. The kind of wine, however, had changed. Few grocers offered their customers wine poured from a cask anymore. Instead, they stocked already filled bottles. Even had the wine in the two originally been the same, the bottled version would have offered the advantage of less exposure to air and hence less opportunity for spoilage. But in fact, the wines rarely were the same, since the producer of even inexpensive bottled wine tended to make something of higher quality than in previous generations. It might still be considered vin ordinaire, but it likely benefited from the technical advances that had so obviously narrowed the gap with vin fin. Moreover, most grocery stores, even if small, usually stocked a variety of wines, since consumers living in rural villages, like their compatriots in cities and suburbs, sometimes now wanted and could afford to buy something better. As small shops began to be challenged by supermarkets, the range of choices expanded significantly. Large chains such as Atac in France, Punto in Italy, Tesco in England, and the Dutch-based SPAR purchased wines in huge volume. They offered their customers everything from Champagne to cheap red and white, at prices that tended to be very attractive.

The general rise in Western European living standards further affected consumption. Though a smaller percentage of the population drank wine regularly, what these people did drink tended to be of significantly higher quality. People simply could afford to purchase better wines. They wanted ones that tasted special, usually meaning appellation wines, and since many of them now drank wine three or four times a week rather than every day (and rarely anymore all through the day), they had more money to spend on the bottles they selected. These were not always true vins fins, but they invariably proved superior to what had been customary a generation or two earlier. The specific choices depended on both income and situation—what one could afford to drink, and when one might do so—but people up and down the social ladder focused on quality as never before. A French lawyer or doctor might drink an AOC Côtes du Rhône at home on a Wednesday evening and then a classified-growth Bordeaux in a restaurant or at a dinner party on Saturday night, while the janitor in his office might drink a Vin de Pays during the week and an AOC wine on the weekend. So too in Italy with a simple Vino da Tavola and, say, a Chianti Classico, or in Spain with a Crianza and then a Reserva. But for all except the very poor, the movement toward buying and drinking higher-quality wines proved unstoppable.

If consumers in wine-producing European countries tended to drink fewer but better wines, consumers in many export markets were drinking more—in large measure because they now could afford to drink better too. These markets included Great Britain, where beginning in the 1970s the middle class rediscovered its taste for wine, the United States, and as the new millennium dawned, Japan, Hong Kong, and other parts of Asia. Some Vins de Pays and other non-appellation wines attracted foreign buyers, and some inexpensive European wines—for example, German Liebfraumilch in the 1950s and 1960s, sweet Portuguese rosé in the 1960s and 1970s, and Italian Lambrusco in the 1980s—found considerable success as exports, but the overall trend was toward higher quality. The already famous growths and crus continued to sell well, no matter that their prices had started to rise steeply, but the real excitement came from other regions. In France, white wines from the Loire exploded in popularity, as did reds from the Rhône. So too with wines from Friuli and the Veneto in Italy, Ribera in Spain, and to a lesser degree the Pfalz in Germany. In all these cases, increased demand led to higher quality, with the impetus coming primarily from foreigners. By the 1980s, legions of foreign wine buyers, men and women trying to ferret out new wines from new producers, were crisscrossing all of Europe's wine regions, both the famous and the obscure. Many if not most were first-generation enthusiasts whose passion for wine came from their being able to experience firsthand Europe's remarkable revival. Their work would bring the taste of that revival to the rest of the wine-drinking world.

Whether in Alto Adige or Alsace, the Nahe or Navarra, quality-minded European vintners kept making better and better wines. Many of the best wines of the late twentieth century came from relatively small properties run by artisanal vintners who brought a modern perspective to their craft. Many, like Didier Dagueneau in Pouilly-Fumé and Angelo Gaja in Barbaresco, became well known, their wines highly sought-after collectibles. Others, like Marcel Guigal in Côte-Rôtie and Miguel Torres in Penedès, grew their businesses into regional empires, their names becoming fixtures on restaurant lists and store shelves the world over. But no matter whether large or small, a single-vineyard operation or one with multiple contracts and holdings, these producers led the way as overall quality kept rising.

Were the most esteemed wines—grand crus from Burgundy, for example, and first growths from Bordeaux, Beerenauslesen from the Rheingau, and single-vineyard bottlings from Barolo and Rioja—were these definitely better than their antecedents a hundred years before? Who can say, there being no way to taste them at a comparable age. By all accounts, the best nineteenth-century examples of these vins fins had exhibited the same qualities of balance, depth, and length that continue to characterize quality wines today. Like top wines now, they apparently also displayed particularity, with a complex array of aromas and flavors that set them apart from other wines (even other fine wines). Styles certainly changed over the years, but there can be little doubt that those early modern wines were very good. There also can be no doubt, however, that the roll call of compelling wines multiplied many times over during the second half of the twentieth century. Scores of distinctive-tasting wines now displayed a multiplicity of aromas and flavors that enabled each one to taste unlike others but like itself. Some came from famed grape-growing regions, but plenty came from other places, some with a limited history of quality production, many others without any previous renown at all. And as the map of high-quality European wine became more crowded, the market had to adjust. Many vintners now competed not only with their neighbors but also with compatriots working across the Continent, and indeed all across the globe. The realities of a more expansive marketplace required them to learn about the new wines coming from new places in order to compete. As a result, a new generation of usually academically trained winemakers refined their craft less by following their fathers than by acquiring hands-on experience far from home. By the 1980s, it was not at all uncommon to find a young Frenchman or Frenchwoman fresh from university working the harvest at a winery in Tuscany, or an Italian working in France, or for that matter, both working in California or South Australia. Vin fin, once limited to a handful of regions and terroirs, was fast becoming a global phenomenon.

At all levels of this increasingly diverse market, from the most refined collectibles to the simplest quaffs, there was less and less room for dirty or spoiled wines. For thousands of years, sour wine had constituted common fare. But consumers wouldn't put up with it anymore. The combination of greater competition, lower rates of consumption, and increased incomes changed how and what people drank, just as the advent of controlled appellations, coupled with advances in research and technology, raised wine quality. In the dark days at the end of the Second World War, European wine had not yet recovered from its nearly century-long crisis. Fifty years later, it definitely had. The recovery involved how and why wine was being made as well as how and why it was being purchased and poured. By the last decades of the century, virtually everyone agreed that European wine in general tasted significantly better than it ever had before. No one looked longingly to some mythic past. Instead, millions of people were savoring the golden present.

VISIONS AND VARIETALS
The Wine Revolution Comes to the New World

Like many fine wines, this one started as an experiment. The year was 1951, and the experiment involved the seemingly outlandish idea that an Australian wine could taste as compelling as a classified-growth French cru. Australian vintners still produced mostly heady fortifieds to satisfy the national desire for strong drink, with lower-alcohol table wines little more than an afterthought. Though the country's population was changing quickly, with a rush of immigrants from Greece, Italy, and other European countries bringing a taste for dry wine Down Under, this cuvée, all of three barrels, was not crafted to meet any expectations other than those of its creator—Max Schubert, a thirty-six-year-old winemaker for the South Australian firm of Penfolds. Schubert had traveled to Europe the year before, sent by his employer to learn about fortified-wine technology. While there, he had taken a side trip to Bordeaux, where his eyes (and palate) were opened to how deliciously distinctive dry wines could be. According to his daughter many years later, it was during the long flight home that he came up with the idea for his experiment—"a truly Australian wine but able to rival the wonderful French wines he had seen." That is an especially appropriate choice of words, since the end result of this and other New World winemaking experiments during the second half of the twentieth century was a rivalry that would change wine the world over. Within little more than a generation's time, not only Australia but also the Americas, New Zealand, and South Africa became sources of wines that indeed could challenge Europe's best.

New World wines did not begin to vie with established European crus in the international marketplace until the 1970s and 1980s. Some tasted very similar to Old World prototypes, others quite different, just as some competed at the highest levels (and highest price points), and others in bargain bins. Yet they all shared the essential characteristics of any quality modern wine—balance, depth, and length, with many going even further and tasting intriguingly distinctive and complex. What separated them, and for a time made the rivalry especially intense, were competing conceptions of where those characteristics come from. The new generation of American, Australian, and other New World vintners exemplified by Max Schubert did not accept the emphasis their European compatriots placed on terroir and tradition. Instead, they stressed the significance of winemaking vision and varietal integrity, in the process significantly expanding the range of wines available to consumers the world over. And because they refused to be confined by either locale or custom, they further narrowed the gap between excellent but exclusive vins fins and more widely available and affordable vins ordinaires, thus bringing more quality wine to more people than ever before in history.

When Schubert returned home, he made a deliberate decision not to make his new wine with Cabernet Sauvignon, Merlot, or any of the other traditional red Bordeaux grape varieties. Since few South Australian vineyards were planted with these, he opted instead to use the best red grape then available Down Under—Shiraz (the local name for Syrah), often crushed at the time for Aussie "port," and in this case picked from two separate vineyards, one at the Penfolds winery and another nearly fifty miles to the southwest. With hopes of appealing to consumers who preferred to buy bottles sporting European-based designations, Schubert called his experimental cuvée "Hermitage," after France's most famous Syrah-based wine, prefaced by the name of the original Penfolds homestead, "Grange." But with so little of it produced, few people got to try Grange Hermitage. More important, and to Schubert's chagrin, virtually everybody who did try it disliked it. Being so different from anything they knew in Australia, it seemed rough and intense. "A concoction of wild fruits and sundry berries with crushed ants predominating," declared one taster, while another sarcastically congratulated the winemaker for having fashioned something that "no one in their right mind will buy—or drink." Undaunted, Schubert kept trying, but after five more vintages, none consisting of more than a handful of barrels, the Penfolds board of directors ordered him to stop.

Bottles of those initial vintages were left to gather dust in the Penfolds cellars. Every once in a while, though, somebody would open one, and gradually it became clear that this full-bodied wine, initially overflowing with tannin and extract, was softening and mellowing into something special. A new tasting with the company board confirmed as much, and production, still on a small scale, was reinstituted in 1960. (Max Schubert then confessed that he had been making the wine surreptitiously all along.) Over the next two decades, Grange Hermitage became Australia's most celebrated wine, regularly collecting medals in international competitions, the older vintages in particular receiving multiple awards. "People who have been lucky enough to see [these] wines," opined Australia's leading wine authority Len Evans, "agree that we have been treated to something quite extraordinary . . . [They] represent a new, great wine style of the world." Subsequent commentators and consumers concurred, and in the years ahead Grange (Penfolds stopped using the word Hermitage in 1990) became even more celebrated. It is widely recognized today as Australia's most iconic wine, as well as one of the best in the entire world.

The new wine style that Grange represents resulted from a philosophy or approach that focused first on the grape and the winemaker, and only second on place. It thus reversed the priorities advocated by virtually all quality-minded European vintners since the medieval Cistercian monks first cultivated vines in the Côte d'Or. "The objective," Schubert explained, "was to produce a big, full-bodied wine containing maximum extraction of all the components in the grape material used." Put another way, the fruit, not the land, was key. That's why, for sixty years now, Grange never once has depended on the performance of a single vineyard. Instead, the Penfolds winemakers always have aimed to find the ripest, most intensely flavored grapes possible, no matter where the vines grow. Grange needs to be big and bold so as to maintain its signature style and age successfully, meaning not simply endure, but actually evolve and improve over time. After all, Schubert's experiment had been from the start an attempt to replicate the allure of mature wines with a cuvée that would taste different from its French models but that would prove just as compelling.

Grange is certainly not the only wine, and it was arguably not even the first, to exemplify this new style of fine wine, but more than any other, it illustrates what sets so many New World wines apart from their European counterparts. As distinctive-tasting as the best crus from Bordeaux and Burgundy, it displays a particularity of aroma and flavor that can be recognized year after year. Yet its individuality stems less from an expression of place than from a winemaking vision. That vision does not ignore locale but focuses first on the specific qualities that the vintner wants the wine to exhibit. In this, Grange and wines like it are quite different from European terroir-based crus. The philosophy behind them holds that human beings, not simply natural conditions, determine whether a particular wine should be intense or subtle, graceful or muscular. Thus not only has Grange never come from a single vineyard, but its fruit sources have changed frequently, rarely repeating themselves even in subsequent years.

For Max Schubert and those who followed him, the crucial thing was to remain true to their vision. More than anything else, it was what showed them how a particular wine should taste. Thus they insisted that locale need not define or confine a wine's style. Precisely because some vineyards tend to produce more concentrated (or conversely, more refined) wines than others, they wanted to have the freedom to choose which grapes from which vineyards should go into which wines. And since vineyards do not perform identically every year, they also wanted to be free to make different choices in different years. This was not making wine according to a recipe. Instead, it was being faithful to one's ideas and one's self. Those ideas did not come out of the blue but were formulated on the basis of experience—in Schubert's case, his eye-opening exposure to mature wines in Bordeaux, as well as his extensive experience with many different (and often disappointing) wines at home. He did not try to emulate something already achieved, but rather looked forward to what was possible, what he might be able to achieve in the future.

This philosophy clearly depended on the scientific and technical advances that already were raising wine quality in Europe. Those same advances, and even more to the point the conviction that human beings can direct and control the natural forces and processes that for thousands of years had produced wine largely on their own, were adopted eagerly in Australian and other New World wineries. During the second half of the twentieth century, vintners from McLaren Vale to Mendoza, and Colchagua to Calistoga, came to embrace the basic idea of control, even if some might at times choose not to act on it. Scientific research circulated quickly in journals and at conferences, initially going mostly from Europe to the New World, but soon flowing just as rapidly in the other direction as well. And some winemakers jetted regularly from continent to continent, honing their craft by working multiple harvests. By the 1980s, any vintner aspiring to make high-quality wines knew all about the new science of wine and winemaking. He or she might ignore some of it, but that in itself constituted an informed choice.

While this new approach to fine wine definitely came to have adherents in Europe, it was embraced more widely and more ardently in New World winemaking countries. The reason is not difficult to discern. Ambitious New World vintners simply had to look forward. They were working in places largely devoid of quality-wine traditions, and they did not have the decades, let alone the centuries, of hands-on experience necessary to know their terroirs intimately. As we have seen already, it is a mistake to think that all European vins fins enjoyed such traditions. Many wines—upmarket Châteauneuf-du-Pape, for instance, and Super Tuscans like Sassicaia and Tignanello, and even most high-quality wines from Bordeaux's right bank—were themselves twentieth-century inventions. Yet much as had happened a century earlier, the vintners responsible for these wines adopted the time-honored approach of defining particularity in terms of locale. Whether in France or Germany, Italy, Portugal, or Spain, they claimed that their best wines displayed a distinctiveness literally rooted in specific places. The situation was very different for vintners in New World wine-producing countries. Like their nineteenth-century European predecessors, they sometimes felt the need to cloak their often innovative wines in the guise of tradition, using borrowed names and designations (including the word "château," as at Reynella in South Australia, Tahbilk in Victoria, and Montelena and Souverain across the Pacific in California). Their vision for their wines, however, invariably was futuristic. As a result, the New World's version of the wine revolution came to be marked by rebellion, not revival, with a new order supplanting the old.

—៣—

Max Schubert certainly did not usher in the modern era of Australian wine all by himself. Other important Aussie winemaking pioneers in the 1950s and 1960s included European immigrants like Caludio Alcorso (from Italy) and Wolf Blass (from Germany), as well as Down Under natives such as Cyril Henschke, Max Lake, Peter Lehmann, D'Arry Osborn, and more, some employed by large companies, others who worked for, and in some cases started, smaller ventures. They all shared a vision of quality, inspired largely by each other's often experimental cuvées. Australia, recovering from the pain of depression and war, was an isolated country, with wine playing only a minor role in its insular culture. In 1960, the country's per capita wine consumption constituted a meager 1.35 gallons, with roughly three-fourths of that amount consisting of cheap but strong "ports," "sherries," and other fortifieds. Tastes would change radically over the next two decades, owing in part to shifting demographics, and even more to the rapid upsurge in the quality of many of the country's dry table wines. By 1980, consumption had quadrupled, with the vast majority of what people were drinking being unfortified (though not always completely dry). Yet even then, Australia's wine culture remained inward-looking, with imports accounting for only about 3 percent of sales, and exports an even smaller percentage of total production. Any Aussie wine style thus needed to develop on its own, with native tastes rather than foreign models leading the way.

The inherent fickleness of such a changing market helps account not only for the fact that Australian tastes shifted quickly but also for the specifics of how they did—moving from a red wine boom in the 1960s to a white wine one in the 1970s and 1980s, and then another surge in reds more recently. Much as would happen at the same time in the United States, new wine drinkers kept looking for something new. In response, growers planted just about every grape variety in just about every locale. Some vineyards produced excellent wines, others mediocre ones. Vintners thought nothing about blending tanks and vats of wines coming from very different places, some literally hundreds of miles apart. For a time, a popular inside joke among winemakers had it that the most important source of Australian wine was "Sheppard's Creek," a fictitious site named for the country's largest tanker-truck company. The blends were varietal as well as regional—Cabernet Sauvignon mixed in with Shiraz, Sauvignon Blanc with Sémillon, Riesling with Gewurztraminer, and so on. Since many of these different grape varieties often grew side by side in the same vineyards, some invariably performed well and others poorly. Blending became widely considered a way to make the whole taste better than the sum of the parts.

That ostensibly better taste tended to be fresh and full. Along with their California counterparts, Aussie vintners in the 1960s and 1970s pioneered a flamboyant, fruit-forward wine style that, by the end of the century, would captivate drinkers the world over. The sometimes earthy or mineral-laden flavors that characterized many of the most esteemed European crus were literally foreign, so Aussie and Golden State vintners alike began to emphasize a clean style that aimed to accentuate fruit flavor above all else. Before long, young winemakers were expected to have scientific training, and academic oenology programs saw enrollments rise dramatically. The most prestigious were at Adelaide and Roseworthy in Australia, and at UC Davis and Fresno State in California. Their graduates, all of whom were taught the principles of anaerobic, or nonoxidative, winemaking, eagerly welcomed modern techniques and technology—temperature-controlled stainless-steel vats, hermetic centrifuges, antioxidant gases, filtration devices, and more. In Australia, much of the new equipment and many of the innovative ideas were imported (from the United States as well as from Europe), but some were home-grown. The Potter fermenter, for example, a patented stainless-steel tank with a conical base, allowed winemakers to monitor and adjust the temperature of their musts. Named for its inventor, a winemaker-turned-engineer named Ron Potter, it became standard equipment in most wineries in the 1970s because it gave vintners more precise control over their fermentations. Its widespread use helped fuel consumer enthusiasm for the era's clean, fresh-tasting wines—particularly the whites, which by the end of the decade could be purchased in a new type of container, another Australian invention, the "bag-in-the-box."

Many of these new wines were still labeled and marketed with generic, imported names. But before long, some of Australia's more ambitious vintners began to advocate for a more accurate and less derivative sort of identification. Bin or vat numbers began to show up on labels, as did the names of some grape varieties. Rieslings were early examples, as were Sémillons, two white wines with successful track records Down Under. The former tended to come from the Clare and Eden Valleys, where wines made with Riesling previously had been called "hocks" or "moselles"; the latter, from the Hunter Valley north of Sydney, where Sémillon-based wines had been known as "burgundies." But more than any other, Chardonnay was the varietal that changed how people thought of Australian white wine. Hardly anyone knew its name as a grape let alone a wine in 1970, but everyone with even a modicum of interest in wine recognized it a decade later. In turn, the remarkable success enjoyed by Aussie Chardonnay, first domestically and then as an export, revolutionized the country's wine industry, giving it a global focus and ending forever the days of insularity and isolation.

Chardonnay had been introduced to Australia as part of James Busby's collection of vines back in the 1830s, but it languished in oblivion until the 1970s, when a Hunter Valley winemaker named Murray Tyrrell attempted to elevate it as a varietal. At the time, the grape grew mostly in old vineyards, where it produced fruit used mainly for distillation. Since nurseries had no new vines for sale, Tyrrell and his son, Bruce, clandestinely took cuttings from a neighbor and propagated their own. Their first vintage was fashioned in what at the time was the usual Hunter manner, with a very cool fermentation followed by maturation in old, large casks. That technique left the wine tasting somewhat simple. So the next year, they tried using new, smaller French oak barrels, not only for aging but also for fermentation. The result, which debuted in 1973, was unromantically labeled as "Vat 47." Much as had happened with Grange nearly two decades earlier, it was greeted at first with skepticism if not outright rejection. Most of the show judges and journalists who first evaluated it had no experience with oak-aged white wines, so they found its rich vanilla-tinged flavors and thick, almost oily texture off-putting. At the Brisbane Wine Show, it received just six points out of a possible twenty, prompting Bruce Tyrrell to remark that even the spit bucket could have gotten a higher score. But Australian wine drinkers were eager for new experiences, and skepticism quickly turned into enthusiastic support. Vat 47 Chardonnay began to collect trophies across the country. Following the especially strong 1976 and 1977 vintages, it frequently was said to be one of the country's best wines, regardless of color.

More than any other grape or wine, Chardonnay led the New World wine revolution. Though it hardly grew anywhere outside Burgundy and Champagne before the 1960s, vintners were planting it just about everywhere else twenty years later. Whether coming from Australia or California, Chile or Argentina, South Africa or Washington State, it became the ubiquitous New World white—easy-going and fruity, sometimes creamy, sometimes spicy, but almost always pleasurable. Relatively neutral in itself, Chardonnay served as the ideal vehicle for winemakers to express their ideas and visions of how their new wines should taste. Some quite consciously emulated Burgundian techniques, aiming to produce subtly nutty and mineral-rich wines, but others wanted more power and flash. In Australia, where few French wines of any sort were available to compare with domestic ones, vintners tried to extract as much flavor as possible from the grapes. They ripened them to high sugar levels, used aromatic yeast strains to help produce tropical fruit flavors, and aged the young wines in forests of vanilla-laden oak barrels. The result was a fruit salad of flamboyant flavor. The wines often were not remotely subtle or nuanced, but they undoubtedly were fun to drink, especially when compared with the many tired, dull whites that had been made with other grapes earlier.

Two seemingly antithetical phenomena—the growth of small, so-called boutique wineries, and the emergence of mass-market brands from large wine companies—inspired Australia's love affair with Chardonnay. Those same developments took place in California (and to a lesser degree in other New World regions and countries), but they were especially significant Down Under since the rapid growth of the wine industry there led to an export boom, with Australian wines becoming new models or prototypes for many wines made elsewhere. By the close of the century, Chardonnay was being grown not just all over the New World but throughout much of Europe as well—in Spain and Italy, southern France, Bulgaria, Hungary, Romania, even England. Its popularity, both domestically and as an export, in all these places owed a great deal to the success enjoyed by the first wines made with it outside Burgundy to achieve international renown—the golden-colored Aussies, with their crowd-pleasing broad, fleshy textures and exotically rich flavors.

A small, usually family-owned and operated enterprise, a boutique winery was invariably devoted to quality and committed to customer service. The Australian boutique movement, which started in the 1960s and then turned into a frenzied rush in the 1970s, owed much of its success to the welcoming atmosphere of the wineries' tasting rooms or "cellar doors," as well as to the quality of the wines themselves. And by the early 1980s, virtually all cellar doors were featuring or were planning to feature Chardonnay. Being small, boutiques could not make enough wine to satisfy the growing demand for this suddenly trendy varietal. Their wines led the way, however, in show and newspaper tastings as well as on restaurant lists. And their owners both planted new vineyards and purchased grapes from growers sometimes far afield. As a result, what had started as a Hunter Valley specialty exploded into a nationwide obsession, with award-winning Chardonnays soon coming from small producers in every wine-producing state in the country.

The most celebrated boutique winery was Leeuwin Estate, located in the Margaret River region of Western Australia, a full continent away from the Hunter Valley. Established in 1974 by Denis and Tricia Horgan, who opened a restaurant at the winery and hosted a concert series in the vineyards, Leeuwin embodied the sort of hospitality that made the boutique movement so successful. Most important, its wines turned heads far and wide. In particular, Leeuwin's Art Series Chardonnay became Australia's most acclaimed white wine. Showing remarkable aging ability, it did for this varietal what Grange had done for Shiraz some twenty years earlier, demonstrating that an Australian rendition could hold its own with the world's very best.

An equally important development involved Australia's large wine companies, many with histories dating back to the previous century. They too were benefiting from the growing consumer interest in unfortified, or table, wine, their increased profitability making them attractive targets for corporate takeover. In the 1970s and 1980s, big, sometimes multinational conglomerates acquired firms such as Orlando, Penfolds, Seaview, Seppelt's, and Tulloch, some of which ended up being bought and sold multiple times. (The only two sizable family-owned operations that managed to hold out were Hardy's and Yalumba, though the former did finally succumb to the lure of corporate millions in 2003.) Because many Australian wines already were multiregional blends, the company names were as important to new corporate ownership as any specific piece of real estate in these purchases. Business executives and managers recognized that these names could be turned into national brands with wide consumer appeal, and no wine seemed more attractive as a branded commodity than Chardonnay. Extremely adaptable, this grape variety now was growing satisfactorily in a host of different locales. It seemed tailor-made for large-scale production.

A big question concerned where to get the grapes needed to establish and then grow these brands. The answer came not in any of the places with histories, even if recent ones, of high-quality wine production, but instead in a long five-hundred-mile swath of flat bushland in the Australian interior. Extending west to east, from the edge of South Australia well into New South Wales, this immense area would be unsuitable for farming of any kind were it not for irrigation. But the presence of the Murray River, along with many smaller rivers like the Darling and the Murrumbidgee that flow into the Murray, already had transformed its otherwise inhospitable terrain into an agricultural wonderland. Pastures provided grazing for cattle and sheep; cereal crops, including barley, oats, and wheat, grew plentifully (as did rice, in artificially flooded fields); and all sorts of fruits, including grapes, flourished in the sizzling summer sun. Most of these grapes were table varieties, good for eating but not well suited to winemaking, or at least not to making table wines. Starting in the late 1970s, however, many of the country's large wine companies began to invest heavily in the area. And while they planted many varieties, they invariably emphasized Chardonnay, a grape that adapts happily to a multitude of different soils and climates.

This vast, almost arid region supported cheap and easy viticulture across what would become three Geographical Indications (that being the Australian name, adopted in the 1990s, for the country's land-based appellations). The surrounding miles of parched red sand and saltbush made it difficult for mildew or other fungal diseases to gain a foothold, and the irrigated vines grew almost ferociously, producing an immense harvest every year. Those abundant yields helped keep costs down, as did the use of machines for pruning, weeding, and even harvesting. It made little difference whether the companies themselves owned the vineyards or growers sold grapes to them, as production grew rapidly. The wineries then grew as well, some turning into massive tank farms, with rows and rows of huge steel cylinders filled with wine and reaching toward the heavens. This wasn't romantic grape growing or winemaking, but it proved extremely efficient and cost-effective, and so helped make wine part of Australian social life.

Though this growth occurred initially to meet domestic demand, the companies responsible for these new, mass-produced wines soon started to look elsewhere for new customers. The result was an export explosion, with total sales of Australian wine overseas more than doubling in less than a decade. This proved so significant for the country economically that the national government got involved, initiating various plans to sell more and more wine, and promoting increased planting to meet projected needs. In 1980, hardly anyone outside Australia knew that the country produced wine. But over the next twenty years, starting in Great Britain and northern Europe, then moving quickly to include the United States and Canada, and before long various East Asian markets as well, Australian wine, led by Chardonnay, became an international phenomenon.

The fortunes of no company better illustrate what happened during those boom years than those of Lindeman's. One of Australia's pioneering wine firms, it had been founded in the 1840s in the Hunter Valley by an Englishman, Dr. Henry Lindeman, who promoted drinking table wine as an antidote to the spread of alcoholism caused by fortifieds and spirits. In addition to setting up shop in his main market of Sydney, Dr. Lindeman shipped wine back to England, and even won awards at a number of international exhibitions. His sons and then grandson ran the business after his death, but the domestic market remained limited, and when war, economic depression, and shifting fashions conspired to dampen enthusiasm overseas, their fortunes suffered severely. In 1930 the company was placed in receivership owing to debt. It revived as a publicly traded firm following the Second World War, with the family no longer playing an executive role, and then prospered in the 1950s by producing fortified reds and a sweet, Muscat-based "Montilla sherry." Over the next two decades, Lindeman's began to focus less on fortifieds and more on table wines. The managers bought a number of rival wineries, and by 1970 Lindeman's again had become one of the largest and most profitable wine companies in Australia, something that led to its takeover the next year by the international tobacco corporation Philip Morris. Two years after that, construction began on what would become Australia's largest winery, a facility at Karadoc in Murray Darling, capable of producing some 120 million bottles annually.

Lindeman's, which for most of its history had been based exclusively in the Hunter Valley, was all over the place by the late 1970s, with winemaking facilities in three different Australian states, and vineyards separated by up to a thousand miles. As trucks carted wines from one place to another, the company just kept growing. It made its share of award-winning fine wine, including Cabernets from Coonawarra that won the coveted Jimmy Watson Memorial Trophy at Melbourne in both 1980 and 1986, Sémillons from the Hunter, and Chardonnays from Padthaway. But it also made hundreds and hundreds of tanks of vin ordinaire, the fruit sourced near and far. The best-known example was its Bin 65 Chardonnay, a multiregional blend first created exclusively for export (to North America) in 1985. It became Australia's most successful single wine in terms of sheer volume, and was accompanied by a bevy of other Lindeman's "bins"—varietal wines like Cabernet, Merlot, and Shiraz, and blends like Shiraz-Cabernet, Riesling-Chardonnay, and many more. The word "bin" may have suggested a relatively small cuvée, the barrels or bottles stored together in a cellar, but in fact it was a branding tool and had nothing to do with quality, style, or size.

What did this wine taste like? Though neither as long on the palate nor as deeply flavored, and certainly not as complex, Lindeman's Bin 65 was modeled on the successful Australian boutique Chardonnays. It too offered ripe, fruit flavor; it too tasted rich, with a spicy, vanilla-tinged accent. But whereas the boutique wines tended to be priced for special occasions, this wine cost scarcely more than a cheap bag-in-the-box "burgundy" or "chablis." No wonder people lapped it up. Here was a mass-produced and varietally labeled wine that looked, smelled, tasted, and even sounded like a fine boutique wine.

Making inexpensive, branded wines with exclusive and expensive wines as a model was as significant an Australian innovation as Penfolds's Grange, Tyrrell's Vat 47, and any of the country's other groundbreaking fine wines. The latter certainly came first. They set the stylistic standard and reflected individualistic visions. But Bin 65 and the other branded, mass-produced wines also were made to a vision that dictated how they should taste. This one, however, focused less on individual likes and dislikes than on a broad awareness of consumer predilections. Where did that awareness come from? Not trips to Europe, or experience with famous French crus. Not a sense of history or tradition, let alone terroir. And not any single person's preferences. Instead, carefully conducted market research, combined with an awareness of which wines were regularly winning plaudits in shows and tastings, allowed the corporate directors and vintners responsible for these wines to define what they wanted well before any grapes were even picked.

By the late 1980s, it had become clear that both the domestic and the export markets wanted Australian Chardonnay to fit a specific stylistic profile. The wine should be balanced but soft, fresh but adequately long, with fairly deep fruit and oak flavors, and often a trace of sweetness from residual sugar. If priced high and made in small volume, it needed also to display individualistic particularity, while if priced low, it simply had to embody the attributes of any quality wine. Distinctive aromas and flavors were never the goal for the new Aussie brands. Instead, the challenge for Lindeman's and the other producers of massmarket wines (Hardy's with Nottage Hill, for example, and Orlando with Jacob's Creek) became how to make a wine in a consumer-friendly because a recognizable style year after year. The boutique producers could experiment with different methods so as to fashion wines with subtly different personalities. If successful, and their success would be measured by sales figures as much as by medals and awards, the large producers might well choose to emulate them. But the big brands did not want to offer consumers something new and different. Instead, the commercial appeal of these wines came from their ability to deliver just the opposite, something comfortable because reassuring and familiar.

How did they do it? Low-cost viticulture in the Murray Basin certainly supplied these companies with an abundance of raw material with which to work. Equally important were techniques and procedures pioneered by Australian researchers that enabled vintners to process this fruit so as to produce the type of wines they wanted. These techniques, many of which were being adopted elsewhere as well, allowed winemakers to remove excess water from otherwise weak-tasting wines, and excess alcohol from hot or heavy ones. If a particular wine was unbalanced because of an acid deficiency (a not uncommon problem given the intense heat in the Australian interior), the winemaker would add tartaric or citric acid. And if the searing sun had compromised the tannic structure of red grapes, he or she would pour powdered tannin into the must so as to correct the defect. All of these decisions were made on the basis of carefully calibrated measurements. The vintners in charge knew precisely the acid levels, pH balances, and alcohol contents they wanted. They thus monitored and manipulated their musts to reach already defined goals. Oak barrels, imported from France or North America, were expensive, but the flavors imparted during barrel aging could be emulated by using wood chips or even sawdust. These and other methods allowed Australian vintners to produce a reliably consistent product on a previously unimagined scale. Some commentators have criticized them for making overly processed wines, but the end results proved astonishingly successful—not simply because the wines sold well, but more important because they tasted good.

Considered historically, what was most important about Lindeman's Bin 65 and the rest of the Australian mass-market brands was not the scale of their production or even the technology that enabled it, but rather the vision that inspired them, the audacious belief that common table wine could be made on the same stylistic model as high-quality fine wine. That ultimately proved just as significant as Max Schubert's equally daring experiment a generation earlier. Bin 65 Chardonnay was not the same as Vat 47, just as Rosemount's "Diamond Label" Shiraz (a huge seller) was not Grange. Nonetheless, the branded wines clearly followed the models provided by the more individualistic ones, their being so obviously imitative becoming a form of flattery. And the people who felt most flattered were the consumers who so eagerly bought and drank them. While these branded wines lacked the complex particularities of aroma and flavor that provided the best wines with individuality, they in no sense lacked quality. After all, they were balanced, as well as satisfactorily deep and long. Given the influence of oak, they even tasted somewhat multidimensional.

The idea that wines designed for affordable, everyday consumption could exhibit characteristics that previously had been the property of the elites was revolutionary indeed. It was by no means exclusive to Australia, though it was nowhere else embraced as ardently by winemakers as well as wine drinkers. In the United States during the 1970s and 1980s, more and more low-priced wines started to echo expensive ones. And in Europe at the same time, the gap between vin ordinaire and vin fin narrowed rapidly. In France, for example, both the domestic and the international market no longer tolerated old-styled dirty, oxidized wines, regardless of price level or place of origin. So in Bordeaux in the 1980s, just when international demand for the classified-growths started to skyrocket, interest in the region's more generic reds and whites began to decline. These wines often tasted short and simple, or unbalanced and thin. Many people opted for Australian, and before long Chilean and South African, wines instead.

Australia's contribution to the wine revolution, both at the artisanal and at the mass-produced levels, thus involved style as well as general quality. No one ever claimed that the mass-market, branded wines were identical to the medal-winning small production ones. But when a newspaper writer or show judge ranked one of them only a point or two lower than its invariably much more expensive competitor, consumers definitely took note. In many cases, both sorts of wine were produced by the same company. Lindeman's, for instance, made an award-winning Padthaway Chardonnay in addition to Bin 65, just as Penfolds produced its Koonunga Hill Shiraz in addition to Grange. (And by 1990, both Lindeman's and Penfolds were owned by the same huge corporation.) The vision behind all these wines, however, was much the same, the conviction that wine style results from human choices as well as from natural conditions. As Max Schubert once said when addressing a symposium of Australian winemakers, "We must not be afraid to put into effect the strength of our own convictions, continue to use our imagination in winemaking generally, and be prepared to experiment in order to gain something extra." There can be no doubt that, at all levels of production, he and his fellow vintners succeeded.

—m—

Revolution came as well to the United States, which over the course of the twentieth century went from being a country where wine was contraband to becoming one of the world's leading consumer nations. The American version of the wine revolution displayed many of the same features as Australia's, including a reliance on new technologies, a symbiotic relationship between small, boutique producers and large, mass-market companies, and most important, a conviction that human vision and initiative are essential to successful grape growing and winemaking. Yet there also were differences. For one, American wine drinkers, initially a small minority of the population, were not as culturally isolated, and so had at least some experience with fine European wines. They tended to view these imports as models of both quality and style against which their own domestic wines needed to be measured. For another, wine producers did not need to court an export market with anything like the Aussie fervor. Their challenge instead came almost entirely at home. Finally, even more than their Australian compatriots, American vintners came to stress the significance of varietal selection. Thinking about wine first and foremost in varietal terms proved in fact to be the most significant American contribution to what before long would become a truly global transformation of both production and consumption. It changed not just the character of many wines, but as important, the ways in which millions of people, including many new consumers, identified their own tastes and desires.

Since very few European wines ever listed the names of grapes on their labels, it may seem strange that this emphasis on varietal identity went hand in hand with a desire to make American wines that tasted like well-known foreign ones, particularly the famous French crus. Yet most post-Prohibition American wines, even those labeled "burgundy," "chablis," or "claret," were made with inferior grapes—Alicante Bouschet, for example, and even that old relic of pioneer days, Mission. A crucial first step in raising quality thus entailed planting better grape varieties. And since almost everyone who cared about quality viewed the great wines of Europe as benchmarks against which domestic efforts needed to be measured, the best varieties were widely considered to be those that went into the best imports. In California, then as now the largest source of American wine, vintners aiming to raise standards looked specifically to Bordeaux and Burgundy for models to emulate. Most of the Golden State's vineyards had very different terroirs. They shared neither climate conditions nor soil profiles with vineyards in either of those French regions. Yet since those were the places where the most famous wines came from, these wines served as California's reference points.

At least they did so for the small band of visionary vintners, researchers, and merchants whose work first flamed the embers of revolution. Of these, Frank Schoonmaker, a New York–based businessman and writer, was one of the most influential. In many ways ahead of his time, Schoonmaker worked initially as an importer, bringing high-quality European and European-inspired wines to a largely middle-class American clientele that previously had no use for them. He first entered the wine business in 1935, selling mostly French imports, and setting himself apart from his competitors by actually traveling to all the estates whose wines he imported. In an era still marked by fraud and deception, the words "a Frank Schoonmaker selection" printed in green on a yellow neck label reassured wary shoppers that the wine in question was actually what it claimed to be. At that point, he had little interest in American wines. Eastern ones made with native or hybrid grapes tasted odd, and in California, the only state then planted with *Vitis vinifera* varieties, the vast majority of wines were being made with grapes better suited to eating or distilling than to winemaking. Moreover, domestic wines tended to be labeled with names such as "burgundy," "claret," or "rhine" wine that misinformed and misled consumers. To his mind, any improvement had to begin with what he called "honest labeling," wines identified by the grapes in them. When that happens, he argued, American wine drinkers will be able to buy better wines, but it cannot happen until growers plant better grape varieties.

Schoonmaker began selling American wines only when the approach of war in Europe threatened his import business. Following a trip west in 1938, he added four Golden State producers to his portfolio (Inglenook and Larkmead from Napa, Fountain Grove from Sonoma, and Wente from Livermore). "The vine," he wrote, "at long last, is beginning to receive, in the better California vineyards, the respect and study and loving care which it deserves." He opened a company office in San Francisco the following year, and expanded his California offerings, so that the catalogue of "Frank Schoonmaker selections" soon included varietals from a range of different producers. Then following the war (during which he allegedly worked as a spy), Schoonmaker became America's most recognizable wine writer, regularly contributing to *The New Yorker*, *Gourmet*, *Holiday*, and other magazines. He also authored a series of books, including his *Encyclopedia of Wine*, designed to make wine in general more understandable and more accessible in a country where millions of people still had little use for it. After selling his import business, he went to work for Almadén, a company based in Santa Clara County then beginning to produce a range of reasonably priced, varietally labeled California wines. Packaged in distinctively shaped globular bottles, they sported back labels penned by Schoonmaker (with illustrations by the artist Oscar Fabrès) that connected the varietals with their European antecedents—Pinot Noir, for example, with Burgundy, and Riesling with Germany. Though Schoonmaker's prose sometimes promised more than the wines actually delivered, these Almadén varietals presaged wide-scale changes to come.

While championing the potential of American wine, Frank Schoonmaker always remained realistic, acknowledging how far California and the rest of the country had to go. The problem was not just that many wines were made with poor-quality grapes, or even that they were labeled with misleading designations. Equally distressing, few people in the domestic wine business were able to identify which varieties were which. The U.S. Treasury Department, charged with ensuring the accuracy of commercial wine, had no way of checking whether what was in the bottle matched what was on the label. Moreover, far too many growers did not even know which grapes were in their vineyards. Schoonmaker, whose interest in wine had awakened in France during the fraud-filled 1920s, admitted that some vintners may have been deliberately deceiving their customers. He suspected, however, that many more were simply ignorant. There was only one solution. Someone needed to undertake the task of identifying the grape varieties then being grown in American vineyards.

Two University of California professors, Alfred Winkler and Maynard Amerine, took up that challenge. Viticultural research had been a small but important academic enterprise on the university's Berkeley campus at the turn of the century, but the regents had halted it in 1916, decreeing that no one on the faculty could study anything having to do with alcohol. By the repeal of Prohibition in 1933, most agricultural research had moved to the university's Davis campus, near Sacramento, but since the professors there had not conducted any research, they could offer the state's grape growers little help. To correct that situation, Winkler, the senior scientist, and Amerine, his junior protégé, went to work. Beginning in the fall of 1935, they traveled the length of the state, collecting grapes from hundreds of vineyards, and taking the fruit back to their laboratories, where they made small, five-gallon lots of wine with the harvest from each site, over 550 separate ones that year alone. Their equipment was primitive, their storage facilities virtually nonexistent, but they persisted each year—until the war eventually put a halt to their efforts. By then, however, with the experience of seven harvests and thousands of wines behind them, they had learned a great deal. Specifically, they now knew that the choice of grape variety makes a tremendous difference to the quality of the wine, and that certain varieties grow better in certain places.

This certainly was not a new idea, but Winkler and Amerine gave it a secure scientific foundation. They conducted chemical analyses on every wine they made, involving such things as acidity and pH, sugar content, tannin levels, and color concentration. They also tasted, and rated, each wine, comparing varieties grown in one region with those grown in others. Those comparisons led them to conclude that temperature plays a critical role in determining wine quality. Perhaps because they were surveying such a large and diverse geography, they saw more clearly than European scientists (who tended to concentrate on grapes and wines from much smaller and more homogeneous places) that there was a direct correlation between heat in a vineyard and a wine's chemistry. Grapes grown in cool areas take longer to ripen than those in hot ones; they also retain more acidity, have more color pigment and tannin in their skins, and so tend to make more balanced, deep, long, and complex wines. While some grape varieties will perform satisfactorily in relatively hot climes, others do so only in quite cool ones. Winkler and Amerine's crucial conclusion, then, was that California growers not only needed to plant better grapes but also needed to know precisely which varieties would perform well in which regions. The two professors called the influence of temperature on a grape's maturation "heat summation," and they identified five broad temperature zones in California. They then printed a map of the state in five different colors, so that farmers could tell at a glance where they were in terms of comparative heat summation figures, and therefore which grape varieties they should and should not plant.

In Alfred Winkler's words, all this work was conducted with just one goal in mind: "to improve quality." He spoke directly to this point when he distinguished between what he called "table" and "festive" wines, the latter being "wines which possess a delicacy of flavor, bouquet, smoothness and balance," wines so good that it will be "a privilege and a treat to set them before our guests"—so in the more traditional French term, vins fins. What gave these wines such character? Their distinguishing features, Winkler argued, had to come directly from "the principal variety used in their production," since they needed to display what he dubbed "varietal characteristics."

Unfortunately, most California growers and winemakers paid scant attention at the time. Following the Second World War, American wine as a whole was scarcely in better shape than it had been during the so-called dry years of Prohibition. The small market for quality dinner wine remained dominated by imports, and most domestic table wines tasted cheap and crude. In California, grape prices were depressed, and the only wines that sold well were inexpensive fortifieds like E & J Gallo's

Thunderbird, a white "port" blended with a dollop of lemonade. Some brave (but at times also foolhardy) souls tried to swim against the cultural current. Leon Adams was one of the most prominent. A journalist and publicist, Adams had founded a trade organization for California vintners, the Wine Institute, in 1934. As head of that organization for two decades, he wrote numerous articles and pamphlets and gave countless speeches extolling the benefits of American wine. His lifelong goal was to bring table wine to his country's kitchens and dining rooms, and in 1954 he published *The Commonsense Book of Wine*, which as its title suggests was designed to demystify its subject. Nearly twenty years later he produced his magnum opus, *The Wines of America*, a comprehensive survey of wine and winemaking from coast to coast. By then, the tide had turned. National sales of table wines had surpassed those of fortifieds, and in California the amount of acreage devoted to wine grapes had doubled. "At long last the civilized custom of dining with wine is spreading across America," Adams wrote in his preface, adding that this "meteoric rise in table wine consumption was causing revolutionary changes in vineyards and wineries."

It worked the other way round as well, since better wines helped lead to increased consumption. The Napa Valley had been the source of many of California's finest wines before Prohibition, and select wineries there led the state's slow revival following repeal. The two most renowned at the time were Beaulieu Vineyard and Inglenook, and not surprisingly, their best wines were Cabernet Sauvignons made purposely on a Bordeaux model. André Tchelistcheff, a Russian émigré who had come to California from France, was the winemaker at Beaulieu. He had brought with him the latest scientific research and was obsessed with growing the right grapes in the right places. Beaulieu's Georges De Latour Private Reserve Cabernet Sauvignon, named for the winery's founder, was his greatest achievement. It came from a vineyard in the hamlet of Rutherford in the middle of the valley, where temperatures were vaguely comparable to those in Bordeaux. Because of the success of that wine, Tchelistcheff became the self-styled "prophet" of Napa Valley Cabernet, which he counseled his neighbors to make in the image of the elite growths from the Médoc. One of those neighbors was John Daniel Jr. down the road at Inglenook. Daniel revitalized that winery in the 1940s and 1950s, bottling only the best wines under its label, while selling the rest of his production in bulk. Inglenook produced a range of reds and whites, but the company's best wine was undoubtedly its Cask Selection Cabernet. Along with Beaulieu's Georges De Latour, it set a high bar. People who tasted these two Napa Valley standard-bearers could easily recognize the debt they owed to Bordeaux's classified crus.

Efforts to emulate a French model in California were not confined to Napa. Starting soon after repeal, in the hills above what is now Silicon Valley, an ex-stockbroker named Martin Ray made pure varietal wines from Cabernet, Chardonnay, and Pinot Noir, all modeled directly on the best Bordeaux and Burgundy crus. He honed his palate by spending the then-outlandish sum of one thousand dollars each month on the finest French wines in order to recognize what he wanted to achieve, and for nearly thirty years he produced tiny quantities of those three varietals (along with even fewer bottles of *méthode champenoise* sparkling wine), loudly insisting all the while that they were America's very best. In a similar but less bellicose vein, a San Francisco industrialist, James Zellerbach, planted two acres of Pinot Noir and four of Chardonnay on his Hanzell property in Sonoma County. He built a winery there, the design of which replicated the press house as well as the façade of Clos de Vougeot, and hired a winemaker, R. Bradford Webb, with explicit instructions to make wine on a Burgundian model. This was in 1953. Webb fermented his cuvées in temperature-controlled stainless steel, inoculated the young wines with the bacteria that facilitate malolactic fermentation, and used small, expensive French barrels, aging the wines in them for an extended period so as to simulate as closely as possible the flavors of fine Burgundies. By the time of Hanzell's first vintage in 1957, James Zellerbach was serving as the American ambassador to Italy. Webb shipped over some bottles of Chardonnay, which Zellerbach then served to a group of allegedly expert tasters without telling them what it was. When they confidently declared it to come from the Côte d'Or, he knew that the ideal was within reach.

It took almost two decades, but proof that the ideal had been reached came in May 1976 when a set of California wines bested a group of prestigious white Burgundies and red Bordeaux in a professional tasting in France. This event, the so-called Judgment of Paris, was another revolutionary moment. What proved so astonishing was not just that the American upstarts won, but that the judges, all French experts, were to a person unable to tell the different wines apart. Steven Spurrier, the young Englishman who organized the tasting, assumed that trained palates could distinguish easily between the taste of France's famed terroirs and the aromas and flavors of New World pretenders. But they couldn't. The judges sampled the wines blind, with the labels concealed, and they repeatedly mistook the French ones for the Californians, and vice versa. The red that one judge insisted bespoke France's magnificent heritage turned out to be a Napa Valley Cabernet, while the white that another disparaged as "definitely California [because] it has no nose" was a grand cru Bâtard-Montrachet. On it went, to the chagrin of the experts and the astonishment of everyone who later heard about it. Yet considered from another point of view, the French might well have felt flattered. After all, the vintners responsible for the winning American wines were quite clearly imitating established French models. In this particular case, they bettered the benchmarks, but their doing so did not change the fact that high-quality red Bordeaux and white Burgundy remained their winemaking reference points.

The two winning wines in Paris, Stag's Leap Wine Cellars Cabernet Sauvignon and Chateau Montelena Chardonnay, both hailed from Napa Valley. Neither label had existed ten years earlier. They thus represented the new wave of talent and ambition that was well on its way to revolutionizing American wine. Yet it would be a mistake to think that these wines had no precedents. The winemakers responsible for them, Warren Winiarski at Stag's Leap and Miljenko "Mike" Grgich at Montelena, clearly benefited from an earlier generation's pioneering work. That work included technical innovations of the sort pioneered by Tchelistcheff at Beaulieu and Webb at Hanzell, but it even more importantly involved vision, a way of thinking about wine that emphasized before anything else the necessity of growing the same grape varieties as in the great vineyards of Europe, and identifying the resulting wines as such.

No one in the United States better articulated that vision than Robert Mondavi, who opened his eponymous winery in 1966, and for whom both Grgich and Winiarski worked soon afterward. Mondavi spent the better part of the next four decades aggressively marketing his varietally labeled wines as the stylistic and qualitative equals of the very best French wines. A master salesman, he regularly organized tastings featuring his and other California wines alongside their French counterparts—Chardonnays with Montrachets and Meursaults, Cabernets with first-growth Bordeaux. The goal was not to pick a winner so much as to prove how similar the different wines tasted. "My bit of showmanship opened a lot of eyes," he recalled later. "I was preaching the gospel as I saw it." Mondavi's good news—that the United States could produce wines of comparable quality as the best from Europe—was embodied by Opus One, the joint venture that he formed in 1978 with Baron Philippe de Rothschild from Château Mouton Rothschild. If that wine has never quite reached the heights the two men envisioned for it, the partnership behind it represented something remarkable, the tacit admission on the part of one of the giants of French wine that the American revolution was succeeding, and succeeding spectacularly.

The suddenly unleashed national interest in varietal wines was as important to the success of America's wine revolution as the emergence of domestic wines that could hold their own with top imports. Many factors contributed—the countercultural tenor of the times in general, the coming of age of the baby-boom generation, the country's increasing affluence—but the upshot was that for the first time in history a significant number of Americans were developing a taste for high-quality fine wines. Imports could satisfy that taste, and the volume of European wine offered for sale in the United States certainly increased, but now so too could domestic wines, and more and more American producers were working to satisfy it as well. Much as in Australia, big corporations such as Coca-Cola, Pillsbury, and Nestlé, their managers and accountants sensing that profits could be made, began investing in wine. At the same time, again as happened in Australia, many new artisanal or boutique wineries opened for business. Almost all were devoted to the production of high-quality, European-inspired wines.

Not all Americans took part in the revolution. Many continued to shun wine, preferring beer or spirits, or soft drinks and fruit juices. America's national per capita wine consumption rose, but it never came anywhere near the levels in the historic European wine-drinking countries. Yet even though only a minority of American consumers became interested in wine, the country was so large that their numbers made a significant difference. Moreover, unlike in previous generations, when those who bought wine often were poor and destitute, the new consumers had money to spend. They wanted to buy not just wine, but good wine. And they increasingly conceived of good wine in varietal terms. Frank Schoonmaker, who died in 1976 after a decade of illness, would have been both amazed and pleased. Alfred Winkler certainly was. He lived until 1989, and so witnessed the emergence of his long sought-after "festive wines," America's own vins fins. As for Maynard Amerine, who remained active as a writer and speaker after his retirement from UC Davis in 1974, the new era was something truly remarkable. It constituted, he said, wine's global "golden age," one in which more fine wine was being produced in more places than ever before.

No matter how golden, the last decades of the twentieth century definitely constituted a varietal age. Beginning in America and Australia, but before long spreading across the winemaking world, a new generation of wine drinkers came to identify the wines they liked in terms of the dominant grape in them. People became Cabernet or Chardonnay drinkers, even more than aficionados of wines from specific regions. Not every consumer understood that the name on the label corresponded with the name of a particular grape. They simply knew that they liked the taste of the wine. That taste, however, was a varietal one, and vintners increasingly aimed to express varietal character in their wines. Before long, this began to happen in the United States beyond California—with Riesling in New York and Merlot in Washington State, for example, and perhaps most notably with Pinot Noir in Oregon. There too, the measure of success became echoing foreign models, sometimes to the point of confusion. For example, when a Pinot Noir from the Eyrie Vineyards in Willamette Valley, south of Portland, won a prize in the 1979 Gault-Millau French Wine Olympiad in Paris, the judges confessed that they had thought it a red Burgundy. The French vintner and négociant Robert Drouhin was baffled by this, so he organized another competitive tasting. This time the Eyrie wine finished second, losing to Drouhin's own Chambolle-Musigny by only two-tenths of a point. Now Drouhin believed. Within a few years, he had purchased vineyard land near Eyrie and started an Oregon winery of his own. He still believed in tradition and terroir, but he now had faith as well in the veracity of the variety, the power of the grape itself.

—⁓—

The revolution came slightly later to what by the dawn of the new millennium would be four other important New World wine-producing countries—Argentina, Chile, New Zealand, and South Africa. But when revolution did come, its impact proved monumental, both domestically and in the international marketplace. These four quite different wine cultures were completely transformed in less than a generation's time, more evidence of how pervasive the rapid changes that swept across the winemaking world were in the second half of the twentieth century. Much as happened in many places in Europe (in southern Italy, for example, and central Spain), grape-growing regions that lacked any ongoing traditions of quality quickly turned into sources of wines sought after by consumers the world over. The most striking example came in New Zealand, both because that twin-island country began with such a limited wine culture, and because the changes there proved so radical. As late as 1980, Marlborough, at the northern tip of South Island, was primarily sheep-grazing land. Today, it is home to not only seemingly endless swaths of vineyards but also a signature wine made from a signature grape—Kiwi Sauvignon Blanc, the astonishing commercial success of which has changed how people far and near, including many in its original French homeland, understand this grape.

Indigenous to western France, where both the Loire Valley and Bordeaux claim it as their own, Sauvignon Blanc long had been considered a fairly pedestrian variety incapable of producing high-quality white wines like those made with Chardonnay in Burgundy and with Riesling in Germany. Frequently tasting green or vegetal, with sometimes searing acidity, it was a blending grape in Bordeaux, where barrel aging could mute its aggressiveness in the dry wines of Graves, and where it added freshness to the sweet wines of Sauternes. Vintners in the eastern Loire did use it as a stand-alone variety, particularly in the twin appellations of Sancerre and Pouilly-Fumé. Yet Sauvignon Blanc had become widely planted there only following the phylloxera crisis, and the wines made with it became popular outside the region only after the Second World War. Even then, they tended to be thought of as simple quaffing whites. So when Frank Yukich, the owner of New Zealand's largest wine company, Montana Wines, decided to plant Sauvignon in Marlborough, he was gambling on an experiment. This was in 1976. Ten years later, the experiment was an unqualified success, and the country's revolution was in full swing.

Montana had been founded by Frank Yukich's father, Ivan, a Croatian immigrant who brought a taste for dry wine with him when he came to New Zealand after the First World War. His new countrymen, however, did not share it. Many New Zealanders at the time were ardent teetotalers. The country had twice come within a whisker of enacting prohibition, with nearly 56 percent of the electorate voting to go dry in 1911 (when 60 percent was required for passage). Kiwis who did drink alcohol much preferred beer or spirits, with the few wines that sold decently being fortified "sherries," and later fizzy "pops," including labels such as Montana's own "Poulet Poulet." Like his father, Yukich believed in his country's potential to produce fine table wines. Yet he had to face the fact that very few quality wine grapes grew anywhere in the country. In fact, Isabella, a North American *Vitis labrusca* grape, was the most widely planted variety used for wine as late as the 1970s, even though the change in hemispheres did nothing to alleviate its annoying foxy flavor. French-American hybrids like Baco and Siebel also found their way into many New Zealand wines, which often were chaptalized to increase alcohol levels and then diluted with water to stretch volume. The overall quality was by all accounts dreadful, but conventional wisdom held that the climate in much of the country was either too wet and tropical in the north or too cold and severe in the south for more delicate *V. vinifera* grapes. Planting them anywhere was thus very risky.

Frank Yukich took the risk in 1973 not because he foresaw what would happen with Sauvignon Blanc but because he believed in the potential of a different grape, Müller-Thurgau, the *V. vinifera* hybrid first developed in the 1880s at Germany's Geisenheim Institute. High-yielding and early ripening, Müller-Thurgau had become popular with growers in Germany, Austria, and northern Italy because it could be harvested before the first autumn frosts. That's why Yukich first chose it for his new Marlborough vineyard. Though many of his initial plantings died, he persisted, this time trying some Sauvignon Blanc in addition to more Müller-Thurgau. Winemaker Peter Hubscher, inspired by a trial wine made by the small Matua Valley winery, urged him to experiment with the French grape. The first Montana Sauvignon Blanc was made in 1979, and for both the company and the country, the rest is a history of almost fairy-tale success. New Zealand, which had never before been a player in the international marketplace, was all of a sudden home to a wine that literally millions of people across the globe wanted to drink.

Delicately textured yet intensely flavored, with riveting aromas and a long, pure finish, Montana's Sauvignon Blanc compelled critics and consumers alike to sit up and take note. It tasted something like the French wines from the Loire, but with every one of their elements and attributes amplified to such an extent that it also seemed wholly new. As the English writer Oz Clarke has colorfully put it, "This brilliant, pungent, aggressively green yet exotically ripe style of wine was unlike anything the world had ever seen before. There had never been a wine with such outspoken, cut-glass purity of flavors."

The English wine press, at that point still the most influential in the world, fell in love with Marlborough Sauvignon Blanc, urging consumers to try it and other vintners to make it. The most important of these was an Australian, David Hohnen, who after tasting one of the early Montana Sauvignons, started work in 1985 on what would soon become New Zealand's most celebrated winery, Cloudy Bay. Hohnen hired a Kiwi winemaker, Kevin Judd, and together they fashioned a wine that, while just as vibrant as Montana's, displayed more complexity, with a slightly smoky undertone enhancing its lingering green melon and grapefruit flavors. Before long, Cloudy Bay Sauvignon Blanc could be found on restaurant lists from New York to Singapore, with the wine in such demand that it had to be allocated in just about every market. Before long, too, a bevy of other winemakers and investors came to Marlborough, which by the late 1990s had become the world's stylistic trend-setter for Sauvignon Blanc. Vintners in both the New and the Old World, including many in France, looked to the wines made there for inspiration.

The astonishing success of Marlborough Sauvignon Blanc soon led winemakers in New Zealand to experiment with other grapes and so make other wines as well. White varieties like Riesling and the by now ubiquitous Chardonnay led the way, with Pinot Noir showing potential in previously unexplored regions like Martinborough and Central Otago, while Cabernet and Merlot began to yield interesting wines in Hawke's Bay. The crucial developments that made all this possible came in the vineyards, where advances in trellising techniques allowed vintners to cultivate grapes in locales long suspected to be unsuitable for quality wine production. Soils in New Zealand, much of which was originally rain forest, tend to be rich in nutrients. Rainfall usually proves plentiful, so vines grow vigorously—too vigorously if left alone, because dense canopies of foliage will shade the fruit, producing unpleasantly herbaceous flavors, delaying ripening, and promoting fungal disease. (Resistance to disease is the primary reason why North American varieties and French-American hybrids had been cultivated there earlier in the century.) Led by Dr. Richard Smart, an Australian researcher who served as New Zealand's national viticulturist from 1982 until 1990, farmers learned that canopy management provided the key to growing ripe, healthy grapes. By compelling the vines to grow in specific directions, thinning unwanted shoots, and then removing leaves from around the grape clusters, they could increase and then control sun exposure. The result was less rot and mildew in warmer, wetter areas, and more rapid ripening in cooler, drier ones. Yields became better regulated, with the grapes picked only when they had reached desirable sugar and acid levels, and overall quality skyrocketed. The days of sappy plonk made out of Isabella, though only a few decades back, seemed light years away.

As important as advances in quality were shifts in public attitudes toward wine and wine drinking. In just three decades, wine went from being something cheap and *déclassé* to something widely viewed as integral to a fulfilled life. Though a great deal of New Zealand wine was exported (England and then the United States being the biggest markets), a fair amount stayed home, where a new generation embraced it. Even more than their Australian neighbors, New Zealanders loved wine festivals, cellar doors, and the so-called wine lifestyle. Books and magazines devoted to wine flew off the shelves, and the country's young winemakers became celebrities, hosting wine dinners in chic bistros where Kiwi cuisine, previously dominated by mutton and lamb, became reenergized by a new fusion of European, Asiatic, and Pacific Island ingredients. By the 1990s, in Auckland and Wellington, Christchurch and Hamilton, nearly every restaurant patron was drinking wine. And the wine they drank more often than any other was Sauvignon Blanc, an often ideal partner for fusion dishes filled with citrus, chiles, ginger, tropical fruit, and fresh seafood.

If Sauvignon Blanc became king in New Zealand, Malbec played a similar role in Argentina. Once widely grown throughout western France, this grape had been one of the most important red Bordeaux varieties in the halcyon days before the phylloxera crisis. Yet following replanting, Malbec's sensitivity to frost and susceptibility to disease caused it to fall out of favor. If used at all, it constituted only a small percentage of a Bordeaux château's twentieth-century blend. The grape did retain a more prominent position in the wines from the inland appellation of Cahors, where it went under the name of "Cot." Cahors reds, once known as "black wines" because a percentage of the unfermented juice was boiled so as to concentrate both color and sugar, had once been held in high esteem. Yet that infestation devastated the region's vineyards, and the advent of rail shipping from both Bordeaux and the Languedoc severely reduced demand. By the second half of the twentieth century, with fewer and fewer vines being cultivated, the wines were pale imitations of their former selves. All the while, however, Malbec continued to grow abundantly in Argentina. It first had come there in the 1850s, and definitely had formed part of the impressive Claret-inspired blends made by Tiburcio Benegas and other vintners later in the nineteenth century. The dry climate and sandy soils in the grape-growing province of Mendoza kept pests and diseases at bay, and the long growing season allowed the grapes to ripen fully. By the 1950s, Malbec was one of the most widely cultivated wine grapes in Argentina, with over 120,000 acres under vine.

Virtually all of the wine made with these grapes was drunk domestically. Argentina at the time was the third thirstiest wine-drinking country in the world, with a per capita rate of consumption just below that of France and Italy. Yet until the late 1980s, the advances in viticulture and oenology that proved so momentous in those countries were essentially unknown in this one, where quantity rather than quality was the rule in even the best vineyards. Since most newly fermented wines saw exposure to air through storage in old leaky casks without any sort of temperature control, they tended to display pronounced oxidative flavors. Coarse and sour, they thus resembled the sort of wines that the market in most European countries no longer tolerated. Argentineans, however, put up with the stuff because they knew nothing else. The country, run for much of the twentieth century by a series of military dictators, was isolated both politically and economically. Its vineyards may have been home to a potentially wonderful grape variety, but no one recognized it as such.

The situation changed when domestic consumption started to decline, beginning in the 1970s. Argentinean vintners then experienced their own version of the "wine lake," with the grapes in some vineyards left to rot on the vine, and gallons of surplus wine going unsold. For many, exports constituted the only alternative to financial ruin. Their wines, however, needed to improve, and improve quickly, for anyone outside of Argentina to want to buy them. Nicolás Catena, a third-generation Mendoza vintner with a PhD in economics, realized as much before most of his colleagues and compatriots. In 1981, he took a teaching position at the University of California. Surprised by the quality of some of the wines he drank there, he went to Napa Valley, where he visited with Robert Mondavi, and afterward decided to try to make something similar to Mondavi's award-winning Cabernet Sauvignon back home. As odd as it may sound, Catena's inspiration thus was a New World wine that had been crafted deliberately on an Old World model.

Catena at first thought to plant Cabernet vines in his family vineyards, but the cost proved prohibitive since he also needed to modernize his winery. So he stayed with Malbec, or primarily with Malbec, retrellising and revitalizing his vines, and by the end of the decade exporting his wines. The breakthrough came with the 1994 Catena Malbec, a wine that received kudos from the critics. Rich and ripe, it certainly resembled its California prototype, and in fact more than one experienced taster confidently declared it to be made with Cabernet.

Yet this wine was softer and suppler on the palate, with more red than black fruit flavors, and an idiosyncratic because a somewhat floral and anise-tinged bouquet. If similar to what already was in the marketplace, it also tasted intriguingly different.

Flush with that initial success, Nicolás Catena was not satisfied with wines that could merely compete internationally. He now wanted wines that could triumph. To that end, he began studying the soils and climate of Mendoza, and soon became convinced that the very best wines would have to come from vines grown high up in the Andes foothills, where the combination of intense sunlight and cool temperatures would allow the grapes to ripen while retaining both acidity and tannin. So he planted a series of new vineyards, going ever higher (the highest being nearly five thousand feet of elevation). His vineyard manager had worried that red grapes would not ripen fully there, but they did. Moreover, the poor soils in these sites, rejected by previous generations because of their low fertility, turned out to be ideal for high-quality viticulture. And the near-total absence of rain during the growing season proved an asset, as the Catena viticultural team could control vine vigor through irrigation. The result was a series of his best wines yet, called "Catena Alta." It included a Chardonnay, a Cabernet, and a Malbec.

Catena's international success rapidly inspired others to raise their ambitions. Some owned or worked at wineries that, like his, had a history in Argentina. These included Luigi Bosca, Norton, Trapiche (now corporately owned), and Valentín Bianchi. Others were newer and enjoyed the financial backing of foreign investors, including the Lurton brothers from Bordeaux and Donald Hess from Napa, as well as corporations such as Codorniu from Spain and the Champagne house of Moët & Chandon. As winemakers from Australia, California, France, Italy, and elsewhere came to Argentina, overall quality rose rapidly. People did not confine themselves to Malbec, but by the close of the 1990s it had become clear that wines made with this grape variety, largely discarded in its French homeland, constituted Argentina's principal contribution to the ongoing global wine revolution. Just as New Zealand vintners had revitalized Sauvignon Blanc, giving it unprecedented prestige and élan, winemakers in Argentina had elevated Malbec to a status it had not enjoyed for nearly 150 years. Their wines now set the international standard for what this variety could achieve. Not surprisingly, before long vintners from all over the world, including France, were coming to Argentina for vine cuttings to take home.

No single variety dominated wine production in Chile. That country's vineyards remained divided between the old colonial grape, País, still used often for brandy, and French imports, almost all of which had come from Bordeaux in the 1800s. For much of the twentieth century, the country's poor drank products made from the former, while its aristocracy and small middle class enjoyed wines modeled on the French crus. Many Chileans in all social ranks drank a good deal. Alcohol consumption reached record levels in the 1920s, leading the national government to declare it a social problem. Though wine was not the only culprit, the authorities enacted a series of laws that set limits on production levels and new plantings. Over the following decades, vintners experienced a series of booms and busts, climaxing when a military coup in 1973 eliminated the possibility of state control, something that had threatened wine production during the preceding socialist government's rule. Yet Chileans now were drinking less than in previous generations, and vintners faced a crisis of oversupply. The country was producing double the amount of wine as had been made thirty years earlier, while per capita consumption had dropped by half. Making matters worse, trade barriers blocked the importation of most foreign-made goods, and there was little if any interest in Chilean wine abroad. Exports constituted less than 2 percent of production, and without modern equipment, overall quality suffered.

All the while, some high-quality wines, invariably echoing a red Bordeaux model, were being made at some of the old family-owned wine estates. Over the next twenty years, they provided the impetus for Chile's wine revolution. Once the military junta led by General Augusto Pinochet opened the country to international commerce, outsiders had an opportunity to try these wines and, as important, to gauge Chile's viticultural potential. Many were impressed. When the economy stabilized, some even began to invest in that potential. Miguel Torres from Spain was the first. He started a new winery in the Curicó Valley in 1979, equipping it with stainless-steel tanks rather than the traditional beech-wood vats that often imparted dirty aromas and flavors to

Chilean wines. Others soon followed suit, bringing with them modern technology as well as modern ideas. Some established partnerships with old family-owned wine companies—the Australian Mildara winery with Santa Carolina, for example, and the French Marnier-Lapostolle family with the Rabats from Manquehue in a venture called Casa Lapostolle. Others struck out on their own. For instance, two high-profile Bordeaux vintners, Paul Pontallier and Bruno Prats, started Viña Aquitania in the Maipo Valley south of Santiago in 1990. And one year later, Agustin Huneeus, originally from Chile but president of Franciscan Estates in Napa Valley, planted nearly one thousand acres in the previously undeveloped Casablanca Valley with vines he imported from California and France.

Many foreign observers were impressed by the high quality of the grapes already growing in Chile. In 1984, Eduardo Tagle, director of the country's largest wine company, Concha y Toro, sent both his son and his chief oenologist to Bordeaux to meet with Émile Peynaud. They took with them samples of Cabernet Sauvignon made from grapes grown in their Puente Alto vineyard in Maipo, and asked him to assess its quality. Peynaud was not all that impressed with the winemaking, as the wine verged on excessive oxidation, but he was astonished by the quality of the raw material. Three years later, Concha y Toro released the initial vintage of its flagship wine, Don Melchor, named for the company's founder. Made with the assistance of Peynaud's partner, Jacques Boissenot, this was the first Chilean wine specifically produced to rival the world's best—not just European crus, but also the top wines now being fashioned in Australia and the United States. It would not, however, be the last. Santa Rita's Casa Real came onto the market in 1989, Montes's M in 1996, Errázuriz's Don Maximo in 1997, and both Eduardo Chadwick's Vinedo Chadwick and Casa Lapostolle's Clos Apalta in 1999. All were unmistakably world-class, Bordeaux-inspired red wines, as was Almaviva, first released in 1996 and, like Opus One in California, produced as a result of a joint partnership, this one between Concha y Toro and first-growth Château Mouton Rothschild.

All these wines were made with modern equipment in state-of-the art facilities, the growers and winemakers benefiting from the latest scientific advances in viticulture and oenology. Long cut off both geographically and politically from the outside world, Chile by the 1990s had become part of the international wine-producing community, with foreign consultants and vintners jetting in and out on a regular basis. The country also was quickly turning into a major exporter, with important markets in Europe, the Americas, and even Asia. By 1995, Chilean exports had grown to roughly eighty-four million gallons, nearly a third of its total production.

Most of the exports did not consist of Don Melchor or Chile's other expensive icon wines. Instead, more affordable, varietally labeled wines introduced Chile as a wine-producing country to millions of consumers outside its borders. There were some Chardonnays, and once vines were planted in Casablanca, some impressive Sauvignon Blancs (made very much in the style popularized by New Zealand producers), but for the most part Chilean varietal wines were made with red Bordeaux grapes—Cabernet Sauvignon to be sure, but also Merlot as well as Carmenère.

A variety previously misidentified, so misunderstood, Carmenère had come to Chile in the mid-1800s along with the various other Bordeaux grapes. Much like Malbec, it fell out of favor in France following the phylloxera devastation but continued to be cultivated in South America. Yet because Carmenère tended to be part of a multi-grape field blend, and because there was no recognizable prototype still growing in France, Chilean vintners did not know what it was. It looked like Merlot but ripened later, leading some to call it "Chilean Merlot." Only in 1994 did DNA testing reveal the variety's true identity. Since then, growers have learned how to harvest it when appropriately ripe, muting its potentially herbaceous character, and many vintners have come to claim that Carmenère is destined to become their country's signature grape variety. It's too soon to tell if that's true, especially since the very best Chilean wines remain dominated by Cabernet Sauvignon, but the savory flavors imparted by this rediscovered grape clearly do taste distinctive.

Chile's vineyards enjoy one other distinction. Unlike vines cultivated other places, those in Chile grow on their own rootstock. Phylloxera has never been able to cross the Pacific, traverse the desert, climb the Andes, or survive the perils of Patagonia, so it never has infested the country's vineyards. (Though present in Argentina, phylloxera does not survive long in the sandy soils there, and many vines in Mendoza also grow on their own roots.) It is difficult to know if the absence of North American rootstock imparts any special nuances of aroma or flavor to wines. When tasting today's top Chilean and Argentinean cuvées, however, it is not at all difficult to tell that they are very special. In both countries, the long era of inward-looking isolation has ended, and the wines are now in international demand.

A long period of seclusion and estrangement has come to a close in South Africa as well. When that country ended apartheid and moved to majority rule in the early 1990s, other countries lifted economic sanctions, allowing South African wine farms to export their wines much more broadly than before. They had to compete, however, in an increasingly global marketplace, as well as in a domestic one in which spirits and beer remained more popular. The pace of change since then has been truly dizzying, with South African wines changing and improving stylistically, and producers developing new markets both at home and abroad. As the celebrated English wine writer Jancis Robinson notes, "Occasionally wine and politics do bump into each other," with almost only positive results in this case.

For most of the twentieth century, South Africa had been plagued by overproduction, with both a grape and a wine surplus nearly every year. The market for unfortified wine was fairly limited because, under apartheid, the vast majority of the population could not afford it, and the ruling white minority tended to prefer stronger drink. Grape growing was largely controlled by a politically powerful association, the Ko-öperatieve Wijnbouwers Vereniging, or KWV. This organization, legally empowered to set production limits as well as prices, served the interests of politically influential landowners who grew grapes primarily used for distillation or juice concentrate. It did little to help the farmers who wanted to grow grapes for higher-quality wines. Most growers thus sold their crops either to cooperatives or to large companies, the largest of all being the Stellenbosch Farmers' Winery, a publicly traded corporation that, beginning with the 1959 introduction of a white wine called "Lieberstein," dominated sales in the country. Made in part with Chenin Blanc (called Steen in South Africa), this semi-sweet wine benefited from the introduction of temperature-control equipment in the winery. Its surging sales led to important changes both in the country's vineyards, where Chenin soon became the most widely planted grape variety, and in its cellars, where stainless-steel tanks, high-speed bottling plants, and large-volume grape-crushing equipment became the norm. In this regard, South Africa was somewhat ahead of many other New World wine-producing countries in terms of adopting modern production methods.

The country lagged behind, however, in terms of consumption. In the 1970s and 1980s, inexpensive sugary wines like Lieberstein sold well, as did fortifieds, and of course brandies made with the excess wine production at the large companies and cooperatives. What did not sell at all well, however, were South African versions of the new dry, fruit-forward table wines then hailing from not only Australia and California but also France, Italy, and the rest of Western Europe. These were exciting consumers all throughout the wine-drinking world, but they were largely unavailable in even the best shops and restaurants in Cape Town, Durban, and Johannesburg. Perhaps not surprisingly, those decades saw a roughly 25 percent drop in South African wine consumption, with spirits and beer filling the void.

Everything started to change in the 1990s. A nearly tenfold increase in exports went hand in hand with a new interest in wine at home. To meet the demand, vintners planted new grapes in new places, particularly in sites that benefit from a cool maritime climate. Vineyards were established in regions such as Agulhas, Elgin, Walker Bay, and Constantia (where the historic ones were replanted), while established regions like Paarl and Stellenbosch were revitalized by new investments in both the wineries and the vineyards. White grapes still outpaced reds, but more and more growers started planting varieties such as Cabernet Sauvignon, Merlot, and Syrah (commonly called Shiraz there). For decades, the high-yielding Cinsault grape had been South Africa's most widely planted red variety, but it quickly dwindled in importance. Pinotage, a cross between Cinsault and Pinot Noir, became increasingly popular domestically, while single-variety wines or blends fashioned on a Bordeaux model sold best abroad. Chenin Blanc remained the most widely planted white grape, but by the close of the century both Chardonnay and Sauvignon Blanc were fast gaining ground. Stylistically, the former tended to take its inspiration from wines being produced in Australia, while the latter followed an overt New Zealand model.

As all those changes suggest, winemaking and grape growing in South Africa were, and to a large extent still are, in a state of flux and experimentation. The political revolution that culminated with the election of Nelson Mandela as the country's president in 1994 began only slightly more than twenty-five years ago. The wine revolution is even more recent. It takes time for vintners to determine which grape varieties grow best in which locales, and for markets to adapt to the subsequent changes in production. Yet the changes that have occurred already promise a bright future, with South Africa now a serious player on wine's global stage.

Whether in the Old World or the New, the new breed of wines crafted first in Australia and California, and then in many other places across the globe, continues to delight millions of consumers. Usually identified varietally, these wines reflect a vision that applies equally well to moderately priced bottlings as to expensive cuvées, one that emphasizes the fruity aromas and flavors that come from the grapes themselves (alongside, often, the sweetness that comes from oak aging). The wines made with that vision have become wildly popular, hastening the decline of old-style vin ordinaire. Today, brownish, heavy-tasting, oxidized whites largely have become relics of a bygone era, as have thin but astringent, sour-tasting reds. That's because winemaking and grape growing virtually everywhere have been modernized, as has wine drinking. People drink less than in previous generations, but what they consume tends to be of a significantly higher quality. Moreover, they drink wine to realize different pleasures than their ancestors did, plea-sures that have intellectual and emotional as well as sensory compo-nents. In short, the revolution that started some three hundred years ago with the most exclusive wines, but that was interrupted by a full century of crisis, is finally over. It began in select, often isolated places in Europe, but ultimately transformed wine in virtually all countries and regions, ushering in a wholly new era of appreciation and enjoyment.

GLOBALIZATION AND SPECIALIZATION
Wine Moves into the New Millennium

More than any other wines from any other vintage, the 1982 châteaux crus from Bordeaux inspired change the word over. They not only reestablished this historic region as wine's global leader but also introduced a new generation of wine drinkers to a new style of (primarily red) vin fin. The best wines from 1982 tasted flamboyant, meaning showy and sumptuous because filled with rich, flashy fruit flavors. Though conventional wisdom held that young red wines needed to be hard and unyielding to mature over time, these tasted wonderfully soft and flavorful even before they were bottled. A largely unknown American writer, Robert Parker Jr., called them "liquid gold" and urged readers of his small subscription newsletter to buy all they could afford. "There may not be a vintage this great for fifty years," he pronounced. Parker later changed his mind about the uniqueness of the vintage, ranking at least six subsequent ones in the same class, but he clearly was right about both the quality and the style of these wines. They were, in some of the words he used to describe them, "opulent," "chewy," "fleshy," and "big," so very different from the tight, slow-developing reds that the top Bordeaux châteaux had been producing for over a century. Their youthful charm heralded a new era for Bordeaux's wines, one marked by lush accessibility. Even more important, that accessibility signaled a new era for fine wine in general, one in which the best examples could be enjoyed without having to defer pleasure or acquire specialized knowledge. Consumers from Stockholm to Singapore to San Francisco clamored to get hold of the most highly rated bottles, giving the 1982 vintage added cachet and sending prices soaring. In turn, many vintners elsewhere—in Australia and California, surely, but also in Italy, Spain, and southern France—began deliberately emulating this user-friendly, flamboyant style. Before long, their wines also were attracting new customers and selling for high prices.

During the last decades of the twentieth century, many people who previously had shown little interest in wine began to care about it. For the first time in history, Asia became a lucrative market. At the same time, England, the Low Countries, and Scandinavia all experienced a revival of middle-class interest, while the United States, already an important producer, became an increasingly influential importer as well. These new consumers, with money to spend but with no desire to delay gratification, particularly enjoyed wines that provided immediate, unalloyed pleasure. Since many came to wine from spirits or cocktails, they did not mind a heady jolt of alcohol. And since they often had little prior experience with wine of any sort, they did not necessarily privilege tradition. The world was their proverbial oyster, and they happily bought and drank wines from Australia, New Zealand, South Africa, and the Americas, as well as from Bordeaux, Burgundy, and various other time-honored European regions and appellations.

With so many different wines to choose from, these new wine drinkers also wanted guidance, and they soon turned to a new kind of expert to get it. Promising impartiality, critics supplanted merchants (whether at the wholesale or retail level) in providing both counsel to individuals and direction to the marketplace. They assigned allegedly objective scores or grades to wines, and those numbers, when high, propelled sales like nothing else. Moreover, though different critics influenced different markets, the global demand for wine kept growing. Acquiring, if not always actually drinking, vin fin became chic in places like Japan and Hong Kong, where few people ever had valued it before. And no wines were more in demand than the top classified Bordeaux from 1982.

Two factors combined to make this particular vintage so strong.

The first was human, the widespread application of modern science and technology. Most vintners in Bordeaux now accepted the gospel of control that Émile Peynaud had been preaching for so long. They picked riper grapes than their fathers ever had, and they carefully controlled temperatures both during and after fermentation. Better antifungal sprays reduced the presence of mildew in vineyards, just as improved sanitation in cellars led to more top-flight wines from more châteaux. The second factor was natural, specifically the weather. The summer of 1982 had been remarkably hot and dry in Bordeaux, with September especially torrid, the thermometer spiking over one hundred degrees for ten days in the middle of the month. While the year before had been warm too, steady rain from mid-September through the end of harvest had dashed prospects for a stellar vintage. In fact, Bordeaux had not enjoyed a truly excellent harvest for almost two decades, the drought year of 1961 being the last one that connoisseurs universally praised. This vintage, however, was even better. Whereas a late May frost in 1961 had led to a very small crop, mild, sunny spring weather in 1982 resulted in extensive and uniform flowering on the vines, something that in turn produced an exceptionally bountiful harvest. Vintners thus were able to make copious amounts of outstanding wine. Peynaud for one was delighted, declaring that he had never before seen "such a level of richness and quantity together."

The dry, hot growing season of 1982 did not repeat itself the next year, as Bordeaux and much of Western Europe suffered from a spate of abnormal humidity that led to rot in many vineyards. Yet 1983 was hot too, just as most summers would turn out to be over the next thirty years. The average growing-season temperature would increase by over three degrees Fahrenheit from the mid-1980s to 2010, an extension of a trend that had begun back in the 1950s, when temperatures were typically five degrees cooler than they are today. Whether caused by man-made climate change or by a quirk of fate, the rise in average temperatures meant that vintners rarely had to worry about picking underripe, vegetal-tasting fruit. This is not to say that they had no problems. Rain in September, as fell for days on end in 1993, inevitably resulted in water-logged grapes, and an oppressive heat wave, like the one that came ten years later, could lead to unbalanced wines. Yet when conditions were dry and not so hot as to be oppressive, the previously atypical but now seemingly normal high temperatures virtually guaranteed a strong, even a superior harvest.

The wines from 1982 initiated a remarkable series of vintages in Bordeaux, remarkable because there were many superior ones and very few bad ones. According to the authoritative Cocks and Féret reference guide, sometimes called Bordeaux's "Bible," well over half of the years since then can be classified as "very good" or "excellent," a record unparalleled in the region's history, or at least since Charles Cocks began assessing vintages in 1846. Vintage variation certainly still exists, but it is not nearly as pronounced as it was just forty or fifty years ago. Indeed, the combination of widely available technical know-how, warm weather conditions, and a deliberately pursued vision or idea of what constitutes vin fin means that, as a recent Cocks and Féret editor put it, "no bad wines should ever be made [in Bordeaux] these days."

Given the progress in both oenology and viticulture worldwide, it seems fair to say that no bad wines should be made anywhere anymore. The innovations in Bordeaux came as much from research done abroad as from experiments conducted there, and they soon were being echoed in vineyards and wineries all across the winemaking world. The shift toward higher overall quality was an international, not a regional, phenomenon. It benefited both expensive crus and a great many moderately priced ones, with the roll call of excellent wines getting longer all the time. As the years passed, more wines received top marks from the different critics, a sign perhaps of grade inflation, but also a clear indication that high quality was fast becoming an expected standard. Wines that did not meet that standard simply could not sell—not just at retail, but even on the bulk market, where old-fashioned, coarse-tasting ones often found their way into distilleries to be turned into industrial alcohol. Many vintners, particularly those without the capital necessary to grow better grapes and make better wines, suffered. But the increasingly competitive marketplace showed no sympathy.

The 1982 Bordeaux vintage did not by itself precipitate the global upsurge in fine wine. It did, however, signal a shift in the sort of wines people valued and why they did so. In one sense, the shift was toward something new, the recently invented flamboyant, fruit-forward style that over the next few decades would captivate wine drinkers just about everywhere. In another sense, however, the shift was not at all new, being above all toward quality. As such, it had started among bourgeois consumers hundreds of years earlier, but all the late-nineteenth- and early-twentieth-century crises had halted if not reversed its momentum. It revived slowly in the 1950s and 1960s. Then, as the new millennium neared, the demand for fine wine accelerated rapidly.

In an era of relative prosperity, consumers could afford to insist on quality, especially since more and more fine wines were being made in more places every year. Moreover, as the gap between vin fin and vin ordinaire narrowed, many moderately priced, widely available wines were fashioned explicitly to echo more exclusive ones. These ushered in today's ongoing age of globalization, the flamboyant style being its most notable feature. At the same time, however, other wines, some made with indigenous grape varieties and some with unconventional grape-growing or winemaking methods, were becoming more specialized. They too found an eager, though usually smaller, audience. Connecting both types was the inescapable realization that, whether made in an international or a local style, as a mass-market brand or an artisanal product, any wine now needed to evidence genuine quality in order to sell. The days of tart, vinegary plonk were over.

—⁂—

What, though, defines quality? The basic triad of balance, depth, and length certainly still holds sway, but many consumers today value wines that display intense concentration and power as well. Compelling, complex contemporary wines may well reflect their terroirs, but they frequently also reflect specific ideas or aspirations concerning how they should taste. Some of those ideas come from individuals, others from focus groups and market research, but regardless of the source, they demonstrate that New World winemaking can influence European production just as much as European wine can influence production in the Americas, Australia, South Africa, and beyond. The world of wine has become globalized, with style, often the product of preconceived ideas, sometimes trumping terroir in giving a particular wine its identity. What exerts virtually no influence, however, is old-fashioned ordinaire.

Early-twenty-first-century consumers will not stand for tart, thin wines, just as they won't tolerate oxidized or bacterially contaminated ones. To be commercially viable, a wine now needs to be sensually appealing as well as chemically sound. Bad wines certainly are still being made, especially in regions just beginning to experiment with winemaking, or by vintners who lack training and expertise. These, however, tend to be produced in small quantities and play no real role on the global stage. The only places producing truly poor-quality wines in any significant volume are parts of the former Soviet Union as well as eastern and southern Asia, though modern technology in countries like China, India, and Ukraine is fast raising standards and expectations even there.

Expectations already have been raised in most of the rest of the wine-drinking world, making the question of how to define quality even more pressing. In the nineteenth century, when a taste for fine wine first became a sign of cultured sophistication, the most highly regarded wines tended to be those identified as graceful or refined. Thus Cyrus Redding, arguably the era's most learned connoisseur, could praise "the modern wines of France" for their "exquisite delicacy," a quality he considered "very reasonable to believe [was] unknown two or three centuries ago." Delicacy is still valued today, but so too is flamboyance, and everything between. That's because different wines, sometimes made with the same grape varieties and coming from the same region, can embody very different styles, a vintner's ideas having become every bit as important as the particularities of place. Even in Burgundy, home to the original idea of fine wine tasting of its origin, one producer's wine may be completely unlike his or her neighbor's, no matter that they are made with grapes from vines grown right beside each other. And while delicacy long has been a hallmark of fine red and white Burgundy, some producers now deliberately fashion rich, lush, highly extracted wines. Vintners like Guy Accad, who advocates extremely long macerations in order to extract as much concentration as possible, and Dominique Laurent, who ages his top cuvées in "200%" new oak (by racking the wines from one set of unused barrels to another), make wines that, while admittedly controversial, have found an appreciative audience, turning heads and fetching high prices.

Wine's newfound ability to come in styles that can transcend both region and grape variety is the most important aspect of the current era of globalization. As such, it has been applauded by some commentators and savaged by others. In truth, however, it is not all that new, vintners ever since the emergence of the first modern vins fins having aimed for a consistency of style. The difference today is that while such consistency originally came only with specific varieties in specific places, it now can be realized in many places all at once. Globalization does not just entail an international exchange of goods—the same brand of blue jeans, for instance, being sold in Beijing as in Boston. It also involves an exchange of tastes, people in both Boston and Beijing considering those jeans fashionable and wanting to wear them. So too with wine. Part of its globalization involves the fact that more people in more places are drinking it than ever before, but part too involves many of them drinking wines that taste similar—that is, wines made in a particular style. For many consumers, a wine's ability to be true to a style even more than either a region or a grape has become a defining mark of quality.

The style most in vogue in much of the wine-drinking world today emphasizes ripe fruit flavors, lush textures, and forceful levels of alcohol—in a word, flamboyance. Many wines displaying these attributes hail from South Australia, northern California, Mendoza, and a host of New World wine-making regions, but plenty also come from France, Spain, Italy, and other European countries. As a style, then, this one is truly international, in terms of both the wines and the people who drink them. Why has it become so popular? The obvious answer is that people like it. Lavish, oak-influenced whites and extroverted, flashy reds are fashionable choices for millions of wine drinkers all across the globe. Moreover, vintners today have the knowledge and the tools to make such wines consistently. Before the advent of modern winemaking technology, including precise temperature control and scientifically informed vineyard management, it often would have been very difficult to make this style of wine—either because the grapes would begin to rot or because their high sugar levels would make fermentation hard to control and bacterial contamination even harder to avoid. Put simply, vintners today aim for this style in large part because they now can.

In the vineyard, quality-minded growers try to reduce the vigor of each plant so as to concentrate the flavor of each and every grape. They regulate yields by spacing their vines tightly, and then by cutting off a high percentage of grapes before the fruit can soften, change color, and begin to ripen. They also frequently harvest a vineyard in stages, returning two, three, even four times to the same rows, picking only the bunches that are properly mature. Moreover, their understanding of what maturity entails has changed in important ways. With premodern wines, vintners defined it solely in terms of physical taste. Since they often feared that the weather might deteriorate, they tended to harvest early, just when the grapes were beginning to taste sweet and ripe. As a result, their wines had low levels of alcohol and often seemed unpleasantly vegetal. Then in the early-modern era, once the link between sugar and ripe fruit had been established, growers at the most prestigious properties picked their grapes when the crop had matured to a certain, often predetermined sugar level. The result, not surprisingly, was more fruit-filled and fewer green-tasting wines. But research conducted primarily over the past thirty years has revealed that sugar content is not the only indicator of ripeness. A host of other factors, including seed color, pulp texture, the condition of the stems in a cluster, and the relative pliancy of the grape skins, turn out to be just as important. Taken together, these factors compose what is sometimes called phenolic or physiological ripeness (as opposed to chemical ripeness), and conscientious growers these days pay just as much attention to it as they do to easily calibrated sugar levels.

Since vintners now know that harsh, astringent wines can come from grapes with acceptable sugars but inadequate phenolics, they often harvest significantly later than early generations would have. To realize their goal of complete maturity, they monitor everything from the number of clusters on the vine, to the ratio of leaves and fruit, to the amount of sunlight that the plant receives. Some, however, go too far. They pick when the grapes are overripe, leading to possible bacterial infection and sending potential alcohol levels too high. But new winemaking techniques and technologies can help resolve those problems. Following a meticulous sorting of the just-picked grapes, many vintners will leave the fruit to soak in its juice for a few days in a refrigerated room, or in crates encased by dry ice, to extract color and perfume. (Called "cold-soaking," this technique is especially popular with thin-skinned

red grapes like Pinot Noir that otherwise can yield pale-colored wines.)
Then comes fermentation, with the temperature always being monitored carefully. With red wines, the amount of time the juice remains in
contact with the skins is often extended as far as possible so as to extract
even more color and flavor. At the top Bordeaux châteaux, for instance,
fermentations today tend to last roughly twice as long as they did a
generation ago. Moreover, in the past, when the temperature of the fermenting must could soar dangerously high, the yeasts would sometimes
die, the process halt, and the wines begin to spoil. Even though today's
harvests yield much riper grapes, these sorts of stuck or troubled fermentations rarely occur in the controlled environment of a modern,
state-of-the-art winery.

If the newly fermented wine is not what the vintner wants—perhaps
too thin or diluted because of a rainy harvest, or conversely too alcoholic because the fruit was overripe—technologies like reverse-osmosis
machines, vacuum evaporators, and spinning cones can come to the
rescue. These separate a liquid's various flavor compounds from its
base water and, in the case of wine, its alcohol. They thus can be used
for two seemingly contradictory purposes: to enhance concentration
or to reduce potency. And if the wine is too rough or tannic? A different technology called micro-oxygenation can solve that problem. It
involves introducing a carefully controlled measure of oxygen into a
filled tank or barrel, thus muting the effect of the tannins and making
the young wine softer and so easier to enjoy. Pasteur believed that oxygen leads inevitably to oxidation, but contemporary oenologists know
that small doses can prove beneficial, yielding the sort of supple textures
that previously came only from many years of aging in bottles.

The other critical winemaking advance involves an old technology,
barrels for storage and aging. In the 1970s and 1980s, when many New
World vintners deliberately tried to emulate European wines, particularly red Bordeaux with Cabernet and white Burgundy with Chardonnay, the vanilla-tinged flavors that come from a wine's having been
exposed to wood provided their wines with an obvious sensory link.
Sales of barrels, particularly those made with tight-grained French oak,
exploded. All sorts of wines made with all sorts of grapes went in them,
and many ended up tasting splintery, the wood overwhelming the fruit.

Since then, however, winemakers have learned a great deal about the science of aging and even fermenting wines in barrels. Most important, they now know how to differentiate between barrels in terms of details such as what forest the wood came from, which cooper made it, and what degree of char or "toast" was imparted during its manufacture. Small (roughly sixty-gallon) French, and to a lesser degree American, oak barrels have become standard equipment throughout the wine-making world, often replacing large, old, upright casks or tuns. Perhaps the most striking example of how they have altered wine and wine-making can be found in Italy, where, following the success of pioneer-ing Tuscan wines like Sassicaia and Tignanello in the 1970s, vintners throughout the country began using French barrels not only with wines made from imported grapes but also with those made with native vari-eties, reds and whites alike. The result was a radical change in both the style and the quality of a great many Italian wines, which on the whole became fuller-bodied, richer-tasting, and, yes, much more flamboyant.

Not every vintner aiming to produce vin fin employs all these tech-niques or utilizes all this technology. The equipment and the labor involved prove costly, so only those with deep pockets can afford the expense. In addition, some winemakers object philosophically to what they perceive to be excessive manipulation. They take a more hands-off approach, working to keep their musts clean so as to allow the result-ing wine to express itself. Yet even then, their decisions invariably are informed by science and technology. Modern wine is the product of all sorts of manipulation, or to use less pejorative language, all sorts of hands-on control. Today's tools are certainly more sophisticated than were the ones available to Chaptal in the early 1800s (or Pasteur later in the century, or even Winkler and Amerine in California in the 1940s), but the rationale behind their use is much the same. After all, there is no real difference between blocking oxygen so as to prevent spoilage and introducing minute amounts of it to help a wine soften, or even between adding sugar to raise alcohol levels and using a spinning cone to reduce them. All are examples of trying to make a wine that will match a pre-determined goal or idea—an idea of how the wine should taste, even if that idea is that it should taste of nothing so much as itself.

Modern viticulture and oenology, coupled with a more demanding consumer base, have largely put an end not only to the dismal-tasting vins ordinaires of generations past, but also to the many disappointing vins fins that came from either poor vintages or estates that lacked ambition and resources. Today, the competition between highly ranked, genuinely fine wines has become extremely intense, and a fancy name on a label (whether denoting an appellation or a producer) is not enough to guarantee sales. Moreover, the qualitative differences between vintages are far smaller than they used to be, as for that matter are the stylistic differences between many of the wines themselves. The only question worth asking, then, is whether these technical improvements have lessened differences too much—or to put it another way, whether too many wines being made these days taste the same.

Some people think they do. The American importer Kermit Lynch criticizes what he considers a herd mentality displayed by both vintners and consumers. He objects to what he calls Bordeaux's 1982 "vintage madness," describing the wines from that year as "easy," with "no mystery." Lynch also decries "the incredible power [that] wine journalists have gained in the marketplace," and laments the pervasiveness of the flamboyant (and he thinks monolithic) style that many of them have championed. Thus he rhetorically and sarcastically asks, "[Why not] have every vintage taste the same? Why not have all wines taste exactly the same?" He is far from alone in his indignation. Various writers, merchants, and other commentators (including at least one filmmaker, Jonathan Nossiter, in 2004's *Mondovino*), oppose the globalization of wine. They argue that stylistic internationalization dumbs down taste, reducing it from a sophisticated sense of appreciation to a bland because a homogeneous source of mere recreation. Often treating the issue in moral terms, they defend wine's status as an aesthetic object, and so champion originality while belittling uniformity. In their eyes, the taste of originality may stem from winemaking passion or from pure terroir (or some combination of the two), but whatever its source, they insist that it stands in stark contrast to a style that can transcend differences of locale and character. "Wine can be a bringer of mystical experience," argues Terry Theise, another American importer and one of this position's most articulate advocates, adding quickly, "but not all wine." Not badly made wine, obviously, but also for Theise not what he calls "prefab" wine—that is, wine made to a preconceived idea, particularly one that privileges concentration and flamboyance. "I have a powerful aversion," he writes, "to wines that gush and scream."

The story that Lynch, Nossiter, Theise, and other anti-globalists tells pits corporate interests against consumer choice, big against small, and commerce against art. If, as those dichotomies suggest, it often over-simplifies realities, it nonetheless does contain an important point, for a great many wines, even expensive fine wines, taste surprisingly similar these days. The question is why. Defenders of these wines point to the improvements in oenology and viticulture that have enabled contemporary vintners to achieve concentration in wines that often tasted thin and acerbic in past generations. They also note that the advent of opulent, concentrated wines has introduced literally millions of new consumers to the pleasures of wine in general. By contrast, detractors see the emergence of today's international flamboyant style as a primarily economic phenomenon. They contend that the power exerted by large, multinational companies results in boring homogeneity, whereas much of the joy of wine lies in its multiplicity. Moreover, corporate greed threatens to overwhelm anyone or anything in the way, most notably small, independent vintners whose more delicate or idiosyncratic wines may never find a place on store shelves or restaurant lists.

The anti-globalization argument relies, however, on the fantasy that there once was a time when this sort of vintner making this sort of wine enjoyed prosperity and renown. But as the previous chapters of this book have argued, such a time never existed. The marketing and sale, if not always the production, of wine long has been dominated by merchants looking first and foremost to their bottom lines. While many wine companies today certainly are larger than those in earlier eras, contemporary consumers are much more demanding, and the wines that these companies sell simply have to taste good. How "good" is being defined these days thus ends up being what the anti-globalists object to most of all. And since they cannot indict individual consumers, they reserve their severest scorn for those writers and critics who have demonstrated the ability to move the international market, and who have championed the flamboyant style.

As we have seen, writing or commenting about wine first began to interest consumers in the early nineteenth century, when the middle-class audience for fine wine expanded rapidly. Readers looked to authors as authorities who could advise them on how best to understand and appreciate wine, and so how best to refine their own tastes. For a long time, most writers acquired that authority by working as importers, retailers, distributors, and the like, their expertise coming from their experience in the trade. Nothing much changed until the 1970s and 1980s, when with a new generation of consumers turning to wine, and new wines coming into the market seemingly every day, people started looking for a different sort of advice—less how than what to appreciate, and hence what to buy. Though they did not use the seemingly old-fashioned language of taste, they too wanted to experience "the best" (or at least the best they could afford). The stage thus was set for a new sort of writer, one with expertise as a consumer, so without ties to the business and with nothing to sell save his or her knowledge, in brief a critic rather than a storyteller.

Robert Parker Jr. became the world's most important because most influential wine critic. A lawyer with a passion for wine, he appealed to readers because he seemed ruthlessly honest. Other writers would leave the trunks of their cars open when visiting wine estates, the gift of a case or two being the prerequisite for a positive story. Parker, at least at the start of his career, bought most of the wines he reviewed with his own money, and had little compunction about disparaging the high and mighty. Early issues of his newsletter, *The Wine Advocate*, pulled no punches. In the very first, he called the 1973 Châteaux Margaux "terrible," and in the second he described the 1974 Raymond Cabernet from Napa as undrinkably "crude." Indeed, in the early years, *The Wine Advocate* was noteworthy as much for what Parker panned as for what he praised. He fulminated against high prices, inflated reputations, and what he considered to be incompetent winemaking, insisting that many five-dollar wines were every bit as good as most twenty-dollar ones, and promising to identify both the values and the rip-offs. In the process, he set himself up as a consumer watchdog, someone who would, in his own words, "expose mediocre and poor wines as well as overpriced wines."

During the early years of *The Wine Advocate*, Parker's hard-hitting, consumer-oriented prose did not attract all that many subscribers. Then came his fervent praise for the 1982 reds from Bordeaux. Though some accounts hold that he was the only prominent critic to see this vintage's worth, he in fact was far from alone, the French writer Michel Bettane being equally enthusiastic, and much of the English press, though characteristically reserved, expressing excitement. In America, however, the praise Parker heaped on these young wines stood out—first, because there were not many knowledgeable wine journalists in the country, and second because a few of the better-known ones had been ambivalent in their initial reviews. The 1982 vintage was large, and the French franc relatively weak in relation to the dollar. American importers had purchased large inventories, which they wanted to move through the system as quickly as possible. They, and the distributors and retailers to whom they sold the wines, needed help getting consumers excited. They used Parker's reviews, and his grades, as marketing tools, in the process publicizing his newsletter in ways he never could have done himself. Subscriptions then poured in, and in March 1984, Robert Parker Jr. quit his job as an attorney to become a full-time wine critic.

Parker's biggest innovation was his 100-point scoring system, which in truth always was a bit of a gimmick. Since he assigned every wine 50 points to begin with, 49 was equivalent to zero, and a grade of 90 entailed earning only 40 points. (Ninety, however, sounded more impressive, particularly to Americans who were accustomed to the 100-point grading scale from school.) The numbers had clear linguistic equivalents, as he made clear from the start:

96–100: An *extraordinary* wine of profound and complex character displaying all the attributes expected of a classic wine of its variety. Wines of this caliber are worth a special effort to find and purchase.

90–95: An *outstanding* wine of great complexity and character.

80–89: A *good to very good* wine displaying considerable finesse and character with no noticeable flaws.

70–79: An *average* wine with little distinction except that it is a soundly made everyday table wine.

60–69: A *below average* wine containing noticeable flaws.

Below 60: A wine to be avoided.

Parker never had millions of wine drinkers actually reading his reviews. At the height of its influence in the early 2000s, *The Wine Advocate*, printed on plain beige paper, with no photographs, no stories, and no advertising (but always hundreds of reviews), had nearly fifty thousand subscribers—a significant number, but a mere fraction of the people who buy wine worldwide. Those who did read Parker, however, included virtually all the important producers, importers, distributors, and other people in wine's complex global delivery system, many of whom used his reviews to help them sell their wares. Moreover, as his authority grew, the marks he assigned to wines began to have a direct impact on the prices that people could charge. Since a grade of 95 invariably brought profits to a great many people, it hardly mattered if everyone agreed with him. All that counted was that his reviews and scores helped those people make money.

Because profits could be high, some producers started deliberately trying to make wines that they thought would appeal to Parker's palate. His predilection for powerfully concentrated, fruit forward wines was well-known, as was the list of winemakers and oenologists whose work he consistently praised. Michel Rolland, from Château Le Bon Pasteur in Pomerol on Bordeaux's right bank, came at the head of that list. Rolland worked as a consultant at a number of other Bordeaux properties, the wines from which consistently earned high marks in *The Wine Advocate*. Before long, his client list came to include producers much farther afield—in Argentina, Chile, Italy, the United States, and a number of other countries—all of whom hired him because they wanted their wines to display the imprint that Parker so admired. These wines did not all taste exactly the same, but they certainly shared the flamboyant style, a style that more and more vintners were aiming for all the time.

In Bordeaux, many of the most flamboyant wines came not from the Médoc but from the right bank appellations of Pomerol and St-Émilion, where Merlot rather than Cabernet Sauvignon is the most widely planted grape variety. Earlier ripening, with a softer skin, Merlot's inherent suppleness made these wines especially attractive to an audience eager to enjoy them without waiting years if not decades for them to mature. The most famous Merlot-based cru was Château Pétrus, a wine that undoubtedly benefits from aging, but that also (to quote Robert Parker's description of one 100-point rendition) tastes "magically endowed," with "layers of flavor and power" even when young. Pétrus had been regarded as the best wine in Pomerol since the early 1900s, but few connoisseurs had considered it or any wine from that appellation to be in the same league as the top classified growths. That changed in the 1980s, when the estate and its owners, the Moueix family, were almost deified by the critics, and the prices they charged started to reach stratospheric levels. Before long, Bordeaux's right bank became filled with a number of new, often small properties producing prestigious, expensive wines, almost all made in a very flamboyant style. Some of the smallest became known as garage wines, the wineries being humbly utilitarian, their proprietors evidencing little interest in the sort of ostentatious display that had characterized the first wave of high-quality Bordeaux 150 years earlier. Baron Raoul de Pichon-Longueville wanted a flamboyant *faux* castle. Jacques Thienpont at Le Pin in Pomerol and Jean-Luc Thunevin at Valandraud in St-Émilion simply wanted flamboyant wines. They produced cuvées that Robert Parker rated as "among the most ravishing, exotic, concentrated, [and] compelling" in Bordeaux. While some other commentators have since disparaged them for being untraditional, it is worth remembering that traditions in Bordeaux long have been invented more often than inherited. In this regard, these new-styled wines are in fact quite representative of the region's fine-wine history, as they share a tradition of expert care being lavished on every single vine, tank, and barrel.

Much the same is true with other so-called cult wines today, including Pingus from Spain's Ribera del Duero, Tenuta dell'Ornellaia's Masseto from Tuscany, and Guigal's "La-La" Côte-Rôties from the northern Rhône. All are the result of perfectionist grape growing and winemaking, and all taste powerfully concentrated. So too in Australia, with wines from producers such as Clarendon Hills and Noon, and in California, with wines made by consultants like Heidi Peterson Barrett, Helen Turley, and the ubiquitous Michel Rolland. Coming from high-end boutique producers such as Bryant Family, Harlan Estate, and Screaming Eagle, these Californians all have earned multiple 100-point marks in *The Wine Advocate*.

The attempt to receive high grades from Parker and other influential critics can go even further. Leo McCloskey, a chemist and former winemaker, runs a wine-quality analysis company in Sonoma called Enologix that advises customers on specific steps to take that he guarantees will lead to 90+ point wines. He does so by using complex algorithms that equate specific chemical analyses with specific marks. And vintners who have followed the steps he prescribes have seen their wines consistently score very high. Though few like to admit publicly that they use Enologix's services, McCloskey's clients have included some of the biggest names in California wine.

Robert Parker's influence is waning these days. Currently in a sort of phased retirement, he no longer writes the majority of reviews in *The Wine Advocate*, having turned coverage of most wines over to a set of other critics. Talented tasters all, none has anywhere near the effect on the market as their boss. Yet over the past three decades a host of different writers and publications have expanded the authority of wine criticism in general. Some, like the *Gambero Rosso* guide in Italy and John Platter's in South Africa, have considerable local impact. Others display a more global sway. These come primarily from England and the United States, the world's two most important fine-wine-consuming countries in terms of market influence. Most of the Americans employ Parker's 100-point grading scale, while most English writers prefer the more concise 20-point system (though since they assign half points all the time, it's not really all that different). Regardless of the scoring method they use, their reviews shape the market. Writers like Jancis Robinson in the *Financial Times* and James Laube in the *Wine Spectator* wield considerable power. Moreover, during the last ten years or so a new group of critics has emerged in various forms of electronic media, everything from e-zines to blogs and online videos. Like Parker in his heyday, these critics review and rate thousands of different wines, some from small producers, but many made by corporations with large, frequently international portfolios.

The power exercised by the large, often multinational companies constitutes yet another factor in wine's globalization. Since many seemingly independent wineries are actually owned by these companies, corporate interests invariably influence the types and styles of wines that those wineries produce. Wine production worldwide has consolidated a great deal in the last fifteen years or so. Constellation Brands, a publicly traded American firm, is currently the world's largest wine company. It owns properties in Argentina, Australia, Canada, France, Italy, New Zealand, and Spain, as well as the United States, and it sells its products in over 120 different countries. Each of its many labels appear independent (few consumers know that Robert Mondavi Reserve Cabernet comes from the same company responsible for Manischewitz Concord or, for that matter, Mouton Cadet from Bordeaux), but all are controlled corporately. Some Constellation properties make primarily value-priced, mass-market wines, while others produce expensive fine wines. But no matter the price category, each one is a brand, with a manager responsible for delivering growth and shareholders who expect profits. And while the brand manager does not necessarily tell the winemaker what to do, he or she literally cannot afford to be uninvolved with the process. Both of them know which styles of wine appeal to consumers, and both need to keep those consumers satisfied.

Corporate consolidation is far from an exclusively American phenomenon. The Pernod-Ricard company, for example, owns wineries not just in its native France but also in Australia and New Zealand (including Brancott Estate, formerly Montana, the pioneering Kiwi Sauvignon Blanc producer), while luxury-oriented LVMH's portfolio includes estates in those countries as well as Argentina. In the same vein, the Italian firm of Antinori owns wineries in the United States, Chile, Hungary, and Romania, while Fosters from Australia has a roster that includes wines from Chile, France, Italy, New Zealand, and the United States. The chief winemakers and viticulturalists at the various properties under these corporate umbrellas meet regularly to discuss their work. They taste each others' products and often visit each others' facilities. Is it any wonder that their wines display stylistic similarities? To be fair, those wines can be very good. Making fine wine requires considerable investment, and these large corporations certainly have money to spend. Moreover, the consolidation of ownership does not necessarily entail a diminution of consumer choice, since the number of brands under corporate control keeps increasing. And in a well-managed company, each brand fills a specific niche in the market, whether identified varietally, regionally, or in terms of price. Still, some people complain that too many of these wines taste too alike. "A particular idiom [has become] the prevailing idiom," Terry Theise writes, "because everyone wants the scores and the financial juju they engender."

To his credit, Theise admits that today's flamboyant idiom or style can yield good wines, meaning ones that taste balanced, deep, and long, as well as concentrated, ripe, and powerful. These, he acknowledges, provide millions of people with pleasure, and as he notes, "there are no invalid moments of pleasure in wine." Yet Theise wants more. Specifically, he wants drinkers to distinguish between what he calls "higher and lower pleasures," just as they should "delineate the distinctions among inadequate, ordinary, good, fine, and great—or between mass-produced 'industrial' wines and small-scale 'agricultural' wines." But this logic proves faulty. If the contemporary world of wine contains multiple gradations of quality, ranging from inadequate to great (or in Robert Parker's terms, "below average" to "extraordinary"), then surely it is a gross oversimplification to divide that world into two warring camps. The dichotomy of high versus low, or agricultural versus industrial, simply distorts reality.

It clearly is a mistake to assume that only one sort of winemaking or grape growing enjoys a monopoly over one sort of style. Small, family-run wineries can produce powerful, flamboyant wines. Witness, for example, the Bordeaux garage producers, the cult Californians, and many of the Australian boutiques. In the same vein, large, corporate-owned operations can produce delicately styled or nuanced wines— Chateau Ste. Michelle's Washington State Rieslings, for instance, and Ruffino's Greppone Mazzi Brunello di Montalcino, part of Constellation Brands. So too, no one form of winemaking yields one type of pleasure. In truth, artisanal wines sometimes impart little more than an alcoholic jolt, just as more technological wines sometimes provide ethereal joys. Theise and the other anti-globalists are right when they argue that some wines are capable of conveying mystical experiences. They are wrong, though, to contend that only certain types can do so.

People today choose to drink wine for many reasons. While some reasons might be considered "low" and others "high," many more fall somewhere between. Sociability, for instance, or the desire to enhance a meal, or just to relax and unwind—these are all fine reasons to enjoy a glass of wine. And since the same person can enjoy the same wine for different reasons in different circumstances, it seems clear that the various pleasures that wine provides have as much to do with the person drinking it as with the liquid in the glass. For most of its history, wine was a need, not a choice. The only significant difference then came between wines that had spoiled or soured and those that had not. Now, however, when virtually all commercial wine is chemically sound, the basic pleasure provided by unspoiled wine has become a starting point, not an end game. Millions of consumers want more, and though they do not always agree on what that might be, their desire is in no sense illegitimate.

A final aspect of wine's globalization is the simple fact that certain grape varieties, many of which until fairly recently were cultivated only in select locales, can be found seemingly everywhere today. Chardonnay, which grew almost exclusively in Burgundy as recently as the 1960s, is the best example, since vintners today make wine with it all across the globe. But other varieties, notably Cabernet Sauvignon, Pinot Noir, Merlot, Syrah/ Shiraz, and Sauvignon Blanc, have become international stars as well. While different terroirs and winemaking visions combine to prevent these wines from tasting identical, they frequently do display significant similarities. But there is little reason to bemoan those similarities. For the most part, these grape varieties have not replaced local ones used to make more specialized fine wines. Instead, they either have been part of wholly new vineyards or have gone into older ones previously planted to low-quality but high-yielding varieties used for vin ordinaire. In France's Languedoc, for example, Cabernet, Merlot, and Syrah have largely supplanted Cinsault, a grape whose principal virtue there always was its ability to deliver high yields, not compelling flavors. In turn, the wines made with these new varieties have helped raise standards in the region. In the same vein, some ambitious producers in Tuscany and Umbria have grubbed up bland-tasting Trebbiano and planted Chardonnay. Sometimes blended with more local varietals but sometimes also used alone, the resulting white wines, usually barrel-aged and definitely flamboyantly styled, are often ranked among Italy's best.

The increased volume of wine being produced with these so-called international varieties goes hand in hand with the decline in interest on the part of consumers in cheap, generic-tasting wine. Though less evident in developing countries than in industrialized ones, the demand for wines whose primary if not sole pleasure comes from alcohol is shrinking steadily. People today want to drink wines with distinct, recognizable flavors that they know they will enjoy. Moreover, they savor these wines not only with meals but also before (and after) eating, whether at bars or parties, clubs or cafés. Wine, even exclusive fine wine, does not belong only on the dining table. In fact, as even a cursory glance at its history indicates, it never really has. Good wine became linked with good food in the early nineteenth century, but even then the dinner hour was not the only time people enjoyed a glass. When the poet John Keats, writing his "Ode to a Nightingale" in 1819, called for "a draught of vintage" tasting of "Flora and the country-green / Dance, and Provençal song," he was not looking for a wine to accompany his mutton. Instead, he wanted a reprieve from "the weariness, the fever, and the fret" of the world, including the knowledge of his impending death. Again, people choose to drink wine for many reasons, and no one reason is inherently bad or poor. Wine's pleasures are wonderfully varied, and in a globalized age in which sour, spoiled wines are thankfully for the most part the stuff of memory, that variety may well be the greatest pleasure of all.

—m—

Globalization would be a more serious cause for concern if the popularity of today's flamboyantly styled wines meant that other wines coming in other styles could not find an audience. But just the opposite is true. The last thirty years have witnessed a profusion of more specialized wines, many with atypical and often delicate flavors, hailing from a host of different places. Some are made with grape varieties that have been newly discovered (or rediscovered), while others reflect new forms of viticulture or winemaking. Their advocates sometimes speak of these wines as traditional, but while the grapes may be old, and the methods of farming may reflect a return to bygone practices, the wines themselves are new. Until quite recently, wines made with varieties like Albariño and Mencía in northern Spain, and Aglianico in southern Italy, used to be available only to local drinkers. Now they can be found in restaurants and shops all across the world. And while many taste thrilling, all accounts suggest that the quality of most earlier wines made with the same grapes in the same places used to be quite poor. That's hardly surprising. Only a generation ago, such wines usually had a limited and often impoverished consumer market, and the vintners responsible for them had little access to scientifically informed methods of viticulture and oenology. Thus like so many other modern wines, today's specialized or idiosyncratic wines are the products of invented rather than inherited traditions.

Much the same is true with certain current methods of grape growing and winemaking that use old principles for new ends. Organic and biodynamic viticulture, for example, echo the way things were done in generations past, but the rationale for doing those things now is not at all what it was before. So too with noninterventionist winemaking practices, the choice of which today has to be conscious and reasoned rather than automatic or unquestioned. Globalization has not eradicated specialized wine production. In fact, specialization and globalization go hand in hand, the one being the flip side of the other's coin. That's because both fill the void left by what actually is being eradicated, truly bad because spoiled wine.

In terms of varietal choice, specialization is most evident in wines coming from Mediterranean grape-growing countries, which are home to thousands of often very local grapes. Though sometimes called "indigenous," these varieties had to have been brought to their current homes by human beings, and so actually are immigrants just like the international ones, the only difference being that their journeys took place many hundreds of years ago. Some wines made from these grapes were exported in the Middle Ages and Renaissance and so acquired some renown abroad, but once more durable and better-tasting northern European wines entered the market, they relapsed into obscurity. Plenty still remain unknown beyond the villages in which they are produced, but others are delighting drinkers these days in chic restaurants and trendy bistros everywhere from London to Los Angeles. The wines, if not yet the grapes, have become international stars, and their growing popularity gives proof that specialization and globalization do indeed go hand in hand.

Albariño, made with a grape variety of the same name cultivated primarily in Galicia in northwestern Spain, is a good example of a wine that long was unknown elsewhere but that over the last two decades has become extremely popular far from home. It definitely is not new. This grape, or an ancestral version of it, reputedly was brought to Spain by monks making the pilgrimage to Compostela back in the twelfth century, and it has grown in the damp, misty subregion of Rías Baixas ever since. Known as Alvarinho across the Minho River in northern Portugal, it is used in the town of Monção there, to make the light white wines of Vinho Verde. Galician vintners vinify Albariño so as to produce somewhat richer wines, with selective aromas reminiscent of stone fruits and spring flowers. They display an almost ethereal brightness, and so are very much the opposite of riper, heavier whites made in the flamboyant style. But very few Galician wines tasted like this in past centuries, or even past decades. The region's poverty, coupled with its isolation from the rest of Spain, meant that the various eighteenth- and nineteenth-century wine revolutions had little impact there. In fact, modern winemaking technology and expertise came to Galicia only following Spain's 1986 entrance into the European Union. The national government then began offering financial incentives to grape growers and winemakers to raise quality, and the wines started to taste cleaner, fresher, and more distinctive. New highways brought an influx of visitors to the region, including people looking to invest in the local wine as well as importers looking to buy it and sell it abroad. Change came remarkably fast, and by the dawn of the new millennium, Albariño was fast becoming Spain's most fashionable white wine.

The sudden success of Albariño has led some producers to harvest excessively high yields from what is naturally a quite prodigious variety, and some wines end up tasting disappointingly neutral. Moreover, since no single model exists to illustrate exactly what modern Albariño should taste like, vintners experiment with different techniques and technologies. Not all prove successful, and some wines taste cumbersome, their varietal and regional identities muted if not disguised by heavy-handed winemaking. Yet considering the fact that this wine's emergence as an international player happened only in the course of the last two decades, its story surely is marked by more thrills than disappointments. Those thrills can be felt in the Galician vineyards and bodegas where the grapes are grown and the wines made, for Albariño's success has helped raise the standard of living in the region. But it also can be seen in all the people living far away from Galicia who take pleasure in drinking this paradoxically new but at the same time old wine, one that at its best tastes fresh and lively, so unlike both its local forebears and its internationally styled competitors.

Plenty of other Spanish grapes are being revalued these days so as to yield modern and often distinctive-tasting wines. Verdejo, grown in Rueda, yields refreshing, zesty whites, as do Godello from Valdeorras and the tongue-twisting Basque variety, Hondarribi Zuri. And while many Spanish reds lean naturally toward richness and so lend themselves easily to the international style, some show the ability to yield more specialized wines with identities very much their own. Of these, perhaps the most notable come from the small region of Bierzo, home to the Mencía grape, another old variety that may have been brought to Spain by medieval pilgrims. For hundreds of years, Mencía made light, often vegetal-tasting reds that no one beyond the region knew or cared about. Today, it is proving itself capable of yielding intriguingly aromatic and multifaceted wines that are rapidly gaining in popularity and prestige. Alvaro Palacios, one of contemporary Spain's most acclaimed vintners, was among the first to see its potential. Famous for his dark, brooding Priorats, Palacios began in 1999 to make an entirely different sort of wine in Bierzo's slate-laced vineyards, one marked more by a dancer's grace than a weight lifter's brawn. His success led others to follow, and Mencía from Bierzo ranks today among Spain's most chic red wines, even though it often stands in stylistic contrast to the many more concentrated ones coming from elsewhere in the country.

Simply making wine with native grapes cannot guarantee a certain style. Just as using Cabernet, Chardonnay, or any of the other international varieties does not necessarily mean that the resulting wine will taste flamboyant, using a local grape does not mean that the wine will taste individualistic. That's because winemaking vision has become such a critical factor in determining how twenty-first-century wines taste. This is very evident in Spain, where vintners today produce both internationally styled wines and more localized ones, and where critics and consumers constantly debate which direction is best. Spain was for many centuries European wine's sleeping giant. Now wide awake, it is modernizing fast, with the ultimate character of its many different wines quite uncertain. In Rioja, for example, still the country's most prominent fine-wine region, plenty of wines continue to be made in the basic style pioneered in the nineteenth century. Medium-bodied and easy to drink, these display sweet but not heavy flavors made even sweeter by time spent in toasty, vanilla-tinged oak. At the same time, many contemporary Rioja reds are being fashioned in a very different style. Though made with the same grape varieties, primarily Garnacha and Tempranillo, these display far more concentration, sport much higher levels of alcohol, and entice drinkers with super-ripe flavors. As a result, high-quality Rioja today has no single identity. But since wines in both styles can be balanced, deep, and long, with real complexity, such stylistic divergence is not necessarily a bad thing. (It surely is preferable to there being one style of good wine, but all sorts of flawed or bad wines.) Much as has happened elsewhere, winemaking vision in Rioja and indeed all of Spain has become just as important as locale or grape variety.

A great many high-quality fine wines hail today from countries and regions known previously only for vins ordinaires. While the international varieties account for most of these in the New World, local grapes are every bit as important in the Old. Some are just now beginning to realize their potential. In Portugal, for example, exciting contemporary wines are being made with native varieties whose names few people outside the country recognize. These include the various Port grapes, which now are going into riveting dry wines in the Douro Valley, as well as Trincadeira, Baga, and Alfrocheiro for reds, and Encruzado, Bical, and Arinto for whites. Wines have been made from all of these for centuries, but over the past twenty years they have caught up with the revolutions in modern oenology and viticulture. Much the same is true in southern France with wines made out of red grapes like Grenache and Mourvèdre, and whites like Clairette and Picpoul. So too farther east, in the Balkans. Greece produces many of the most compelling wines there, the best almost always being made with native varieties, but vintners in other countries are now making wines that either already taste distinctive or show the potential to do so soon. The most successful to date hail from Slovenia, a small country with surprisingly separate grape-growing regions that produce very different and often very delicious wines. In Croatia, the best-known grapes, at least outside the country, are Crljenak Kaštelanski, which DNA profiling has shown to be the same as California's Zinfandel, and its close cousin, Plavac Mali. Both yield zesty, briary reds. Farther down the Adriatic coast in Montenegro, the most prestigious variety is the red Vranec, known for its berry and forest-floor flavors. Not much wine has left the country to date, but critics who have tasted it report very favorably on its character. It and many other varietal wines are just beginning to emerge from many centuries of obscurity. In the process, they are enlarging the world's fine-wine map.

Perhaps the most striking example of how that map already has changed can be found in southern Italy. Long a source of cheap, undistinguished but often quite alcoholic wine, much of which used to be shipped north to give body and substance to more prestigious wines from Piedmont, Tuscany, and the Veneto (as well as France and Germany, this practice being unacknowledged), the region is today in the midst of its own version of the wine revolution. Reform definitely has come late to the south, later certainly than to the wine-producing north, but it has accelerated with dizzying speed over the course of the past twenty years. Most of the finest wines are made with native varieties, many of which can trace their heritage back over twenty-five hundred years to when Greek sailors first brought vines to this ancient land. These include the forebears of modern Aglianico, Falanghina, and Greco, to name just three of the most popular. The Greeks, and then later the Romans, used these to make both sour everyday drink and their esteemed sweet dried-grape nectars. Some dried-grape wines, called *passiti*, still are made in southern Italy, but virtually all the wines that excite contemporary palates are vinified with fresh grapes and finished dry. Some taste quite flamboyant, the abundant heat and limited rainfall typical of the region leading naturally to high sugar levels, but others are surprisingly delicate and nuanced. The difference, quite clearly, is a matter of winemaking vision and desire.

Production in southern Italy is enormous, and a great deal of wine continues to be of marginal quality. Large cooperatives dominate in terms of volume. Some have newly raised ambitions, but many others, led by member growers who remain resistant to change, remain content to produce bulk wine. That market, however, continues to decline substantially, just as in the rest of Europe, and the future quite clearly belongs to producers who are dedicated to higher quality. Of these, the historic leader is the firm of Mastroberardino near Avellino in Campania. Founded in 1878 by a family with deep winemaking roots, Mastroberardino was for a long time the only winery south of Rome making wine that could compete with fine wines from the rest of the world. The company's patriarch, Angelo Mastroberardino, began exporting his wines to northern Europe and the United States in the 1880s, and his son, Michele, started estate bottling his best wines in the 1920s. Then in the 1960s and 1970s, the next generation raised quality even higher by applying modern viticultural science to the region's old vineyards. Antonio Mastroberardino and later his son Piero studied various rootstocks, clones, trellising techniques, and more, in the process essentially rescuing some varieties that were close to extinction. The company today is committed to preserving Campania's wine heritage, and so shuns the use of international grapes. Moreover, it shrewdly publicizes that heritage, going so far as to make a wine from bush vines grown according to old Roman methods at the foot of Mount Vesuvius at Pompeii. Called "Villa dei Misteri," this red allegedly provides a sensory link with wine's ancient past. But since Mastroberardino is equally committed to cutting-edge technology, that link is tenuous. This particular wine ferments very slowly, with an extended period of maceration designed to extract color and tannin, something made possible only by carefully managed temperature-control equipment. It then ages for twelve months in new French oak barrels, followed by more time in bottles in an air-conditioned cellar. Throughout the whole process, everything is monitored by computer in a state-of-the-art winery. Mastroberardino's approach, then, is hardly old-fashioned. Instead, it is historically inspired but modern, and very modern at that.

Of all the Campanian grapes, the most renowned is Aglianico, and Mastroberardino's Aglianicos from the commune of Taurasi have set the benchmark for the variety. The company's 1968 Taurasi wines (there were four separate bottlings) did for the family, the region, and the grape much what Ferruccio Biondi-Santi had done for Brunello di Montalcino almost a century earlier, proving that world-class, age-worthy wine could come from a place previously considered capable of producing at best only simple, everyday drink. Dark-skinned and tannic, with a high level of acidity and therefore excellent cellaring potential, Aglianico also yields exciting wines in the neighboring region of Basilicata. Ruggedly mountainous, this province lies above the arch of Italy's boot, and owing to its forbidding topography, has only one viticultural zone of note—Aglianico del Vulture, named for both the variety and the locale, volcanic Mount Vulture. Before the 1970s, most of the wines made there were shipped in bulk to be blended elsewhere, but more recently producers like d'Angelo and Paternoster have raised standards—reducing yields, for example, introducing temperature control, and harvesting late in the fall so as to render the wines balanced and harmonious. Those wines, long-lived and seductively perfumed, can prove both distinctive and delicious, with subtle flavors that become ever more nuanced with time spent in bottles.

Other impressive southern Italian red varieties are Nero d'Avola and Nerello Mascalese from Sicily, Negroamaro and Primitivo from Puglia, and the Calabrian Gaglioppo. All show considerable potential, but to date for the most part just that. With only a few exceptions, vintners use these grapes to fashion budget-priced wines. They have not yet made the sacrifices and investments required to compete at the high-est levels in today's global marketplace. But southern Italy is home to just as many exciting white grapes. These include Grillo and Inzolia in Sicily, and the trio of Falanghina, Fiano, and Greco in Campania. In the hands of capable contemporary producers, the wines made with these varieties, all of which are allegedly of Greek or Roman origin, taste very modern, being vinified in stainless-steel or concrete tanks, with continual temperature control. Just a generation ago, white wines like these were unheard of in hot grape-growing regions. Today, their nuanced flavors entice enthusiasts worldwide. As is true in many parts of Mediterranean Europe, the extraordinary rise in quality owes much to the presence of EU money, as well as to the work of a small army of well-traveled consultants. Whether red or white, wines with genuinely individualistic personalities are coming from vineyards and regions previously home only to old-fashioned common and quite often badly flawed wines. Though not fashioned in the globally flamboyant style, they nonetheless benefit from the expansion of the global marketplace, which has allowed them to find an international audience.

Specialized wines do not come automatically from certain grapes grown in certain places, since the same varieties in the same locales may well yield very different-tasting wines. Again, the more important factor involves what the vintner wants to achieve and why he or she wants to do so. Such ideas involve more than the choice of grape or even place. Decisions involving how to make a certain wine, as well as how to grow the grapes for it and manage the vineyard, can be equally important. Many winemakers today choose to use all the tools and tricks of modern oenology so as to compel their wines to fit specific patterns or profiles, usually (but not always) increasing concentration and extract while raising alcohol but reducing acid levels, thus gaining accessibility as well as power. Other winemakers, however, opt to go in a very different direction. They intervene as little as possible, their goal being to allow the wine to express itself, meaning both its varietal composition and its terroir. Yet that goal also reflects an idea, specifically the concept of how they think the resulting wines should taste. And just as the ideas expressed by more interventionist winemakers come from their sense of the marketplace, the ideas from noninterventionists originate not so much in principle or dogma as in the awareness that such wines can attract an interested, even enthusiastic audience.

That audience, smaller certainly than the one that has embraced the flamboyant style, values an individualistic taste or *goût de terroir*. And since each terroir is at least theoretically distinct, noninterventionist winemakers tend to aim deliberately for specialized wines. They use minimal amounts of sulfur dioxide, manipulate musts and young wines as little as possible (often using gravity rather than mechanical pumps to move the liquids from one container to another), and either eschew filtration devices altogether or use extremely gentle ones that will not threaten to strip a wine of textural complexity. They also frequently wait for wild yeasts to initiate fermentation rather than inducing it through the use of cultured ones. Recent scientific research suggests that yeasts, not grapes alone, are responsible for many of the flavor compounds in wine. Whether wild or grown in a laboratory, these microorganisms thus play a crucial role not just in turning sugar into alcohol but also in conveying specific gustatory sensations. Vintners who allow the wild yeasts living in a particular vineyard to start fermentation spontaneously argue that yeasts are part of that vineyard's terroir, and so an important vehicle for a wine's expression of such. Moreover, since yeast populations change year by year, they can help give each vintage its distinctive character.

Using wild yeasts can be risky, so it is worth doing only if the vision the vintner brings to his or her craft sees the wine benefiting from them. Much the same is true with other forms of noninterventionist winemaking, all of which require the winemaker to accede some control to the evolving wine itself. For example, reducing sulfur increases the risk of spoilage and infection by *Brettanomyces*, a slow-growing yeast strain that can leave red wines smelling and tasting of barnyards and Band-Aids rather than grapes. So too with wines suffering from volatile acidity and ethyl acetate, which impart an unpleasant aroma reminiscent of the smell of nail polish, or those in which the fermentations stop prematurely, since they can become contaminated with *Acetobacter* bacteria and turn vinegary. Paradoxically, then, when noninterventionist winemaking goes wrong, the resulting wines will end up tasting disappointingly similar, even though similarity is precisely what such winemaking is designed to avoid. But when it goes right, the wines can be wonderfully distinctive. Again, the vintner, armed with knowledge of the market, has to decide whether to take the risk.

There are risks in the vineyard as well. At one extreme, some come from excessive manipulation of the soil with agrochemicals and herbicides, while at the other some result from viticultural systems that can leave vineyards susceptible to rot and disease. Though there certainly are places in the world today in which vintners rely too much on spray schedules and chemical treatments, viticulture has evolved significantly over the past generation, with most growers who aim for quality trying to preserve to some degree the natural complexity of the soils, insect life, and microbes in their vineyards. This is not easy to do. Most contemporary commercial vineyards are monocultures, and so are especially susceptible to infestation by pests and diseases. Powerful chemicals can eradicate these in the short term, but they also bring many unwanted consequences, killing other forms of biological life and so sterilizing the soil. In addition, an effective treatment today may prove ineffective a decade from now, the vineyard becoming less fertile, with the pest or disease back in full force. Less invasive forms of viticulture clearly seem preferable, and a great many people are moving in that direction. These, however, can be quite expensive, and unless the grower can be certain of getting a high price for his or her crop, they may not prove financially feasible. The risks in the vineyard, then, involve economics as well as desired styles, what the vintner can afford in addition to what he or she wants to achieve.

A growing number of fine-wine producers are taking those risks. Whether in the Old World or New, they share a vision for their wines that sees individuality in the glass resulting in part from the diversity of biological life that makes each vineyard unique. In their view, such diversity constitutes an essential aspect of what they want their wines to express, and so needs to be preserved regardless of cost. Indeed, preserving ecological diversity is the rationale behind both organic and biodynamic viticulture, two new approaches to grape growing that are gaining adherents all the time.

Organic viticulture centers on the soil, the basic idea being that healthy vines come from healthy land. Rather than react to problems when they occur, an organic farmer works proactively, planting cover crops between the vines to provide a habitat for beneficial insects, as well as to serve as a natural fertilizer, returning nitrogen to the soil. He or she also likely uses compost, both in solid and in liquid form, and practices an ecological rather than a chemical approach to disease and infestation. Known as *lutte raisonnée* in French and "integrated pest management" in English, this approach combines multiple techniques to control rather than eradicate problem organisms and maintain soil quality. Instead of attacking a specific pest or problem, *lutte raisonnée* attempts to prevent it from becoming a problem—for example, by identifying natural enemies of predators or diseases and encouraging their population, or by using pheromones to cause sexual confusion and so reduce a particular pest population. Practitioners try not to use chemical pesticides, herbicides, or fertilizers. Some committed growers never use such treatments. Their vineyards then can become certified as organic through one of the nearly four hundred organizations worldwide that offer that recognition. Many others, however, resist certification, wanting to keep their options open should a disastrous growing season make the use of a certain spray necessary. Yet they too accept the basic principle of organic farming, that the entire vineyard, not just the individual vines, is a living thing.

Organic grapes do not necessarily yield organic wines. At least in the United States, the government defines the former in agricultural terms, as the product of a vineyard that has been farmed organically, but the latter in oenological terms, as a wine made without additives. These include sulfur, which results in the sulfites that are found in the vast majority of contemporary commercial wines. Some sulfites are an inevitable by-product of fermentation, but more come from the addition of sulfur dioxide during the winemaking process. Since sulfur helps to prevent premature oxidation, most winemakers are loath to give it up, especially if their wines are to be shipped and then drunk far from home. Thus while the movement toward adopting the basic principles of organic viticulture is gaining momentum worldwide, there is no comparable rush toward making organic wines. They simply prove too unstable.

The other agricultural movement attracting attention these days is biodynamic viticulture. It goes a step further than organics by focusing not just on the health of the soil but on the well-being of the entire environment. The brainchild of the early-twentieth-century Austrian philosopher and reformer Rudolf Steiner, biodynamics is not simply a method of farming. Instead, because it insists on seeing a farm or vineyard as part of a much bigger and more complex biological system, it is a way of thinking. That's not surprising since Steiner insisted that all human thought was intuitive, arguing that "just as the eye perceives colors and the ear sounds, so thinking perceives ideas." With biodynamics, the ideas in question involve elemental life forces that supposedly influence plant growth and sustain the health of the vineyard. Thus biodynamic farmers time the application of their various composts and other treatments according to the movement of the planets and phases of the moon. They view their property as part of a larger whole, not a self-contained piece of land.

The fundamental practices of biodynamic viticulture include using the raw materials from the vineyard to nourish it, treating the vineyard with various life-affirming preparations to sustain it, and harnessing the spiritual forces of the universe to nurture it. The first of these is virtually identical to organic practice, and indeed the "bio" aspect of this method of farming—the use of composts, cover crops, pest management, and the like—has become increasingly mainstream these days. The "dynamic" aspects, however, often raise eyebrows and invite sometimes severe skepticism. These include not just an emphasis on spiritual forces, but also strict requirements concerning the preparation of various biodynamic treatments—making a spray from manure fermented in a cow horn that has been buried in the ground, for example, or compost from flower heads fermented in a deer bladder and hung in a tree. Add those odd-sounding practices to Steiner's insistence on making decisions about farming based on what's happening astrologically, and it's no surprise that many people consider biodynamic farmers to be somewhat nutty. Yet what almost always tempers such criticism is the simple fact that some of today's greatest wine estates are being farmed biodynamically, and that wines coming from properties that have been converted to this system almost always taste more compelling and individualistic than they did before the change. Whether these wines have improved because of specific benefits imparted by biodynamics or because of the care and devotion to detail that this method requires is a question that occasions considerable debate. But it also is something of a moot point, since almost everyone agrees that the wines can be stunning.

Because both organic and biodynamic methods of viticulture emphasize the distinct character of individual vineyards, their adherents invariably want to produce wines that will reflect that individuality. Specialization thus becomes their shared goal. They reject chemically dependent methods on stylistic as well as ecological grounds, as they want their wines to evidence a level of nuanced complexity that will render them distinct from other wines, even those made from grapes grown a stone throw's away. Aubert de Villaine, co-owner of one of the most prestigious wine estates in the world, Burgundy's Domaine de la Romanée-Conti, stopped farming conventionally in the mid-1980s. "Being organic for years in the vineyard brings a plus to quality," he says now, because "it brings finesse" to the wines. The Domaine went completely biodynamic in 2008. De Villane is not wedded to all of Rudolf Steiner's ideology, but he clearly finds biodynamic practices beneficial. They help his wines display the grace and elegance that have made them so highly sought after the world over.

In their opposition to industrial farming methods, organic and biodynamic vintners may seem old-fashioned or traditional, even reactionary. Yet while they certainly can be dismissive of other methods, their philosophies are in fact quite new. Farmers in centuries past may well have grown grapes amid a sea of other crops, but they did not study their properties' ecosystems to determine which of those crops would best prevent dangerous insects or diseases from infecting their vines. Nor did they research which compost materials would change the pH of their soils, and then reinvigorate their vineyards through the introduction of specific chemical elements. Similarly, they may have planted or harvested at the full moon, but they did not do so while consulting Rudolf Steiner's *Spiritual Foundations for the Renewal of Agriculture*. That title gives the modern game away. Both organics and biodynamics are forms of regeneration, with something old revitalized and restored. They reflect traditions, but traditions invigorated or invented anew.

The appeal of wines made with previously neglected varieties, or with grapes grown organically, or by vintners who take a noninterventionist approach in their cellars, is just as important a part of the current fascination with wine in general as is the popularity of an international style that sometimes trumps varietal or regional identity. It is true that wines made in that style sell very well these days, with vintage variations largely eradicated, and their aromas and flavors quite predictable. Usually coming from warm locales, where grapes easily can attain high sugar levels, they often are uncomplicated, easy to drink, and inexpensive. Brands like Yellow Tail and Hardy's Crest from Australia, and Blossom Hill and Turning Leaf from California, sell in huge volume. It is a misleading oversimplification, however, to claim that flamboyant, internationally styled wines are just branded commodities created for the supermarket masses, while more specialized wines appeal to a more discerning audience. After all, plenty of expensive, small-production wines embody the flamboyant style, and many specialized wines, while not the cheapest on store shelves, sell at prices that most wine drinkers can afford. Moreover, supermarkets and chain retailers carry a wide diversity of wines these days. Many are brands sold by large corporations, but others are not. And even within those corporate portfolios, one can find a variety of styles—flamboyance, yes, but also finesse. Branded wines have not in any sense replaced more artisanal ones. Small producers who do not make enough volume to interest the large conglomerates can find their place in the market by selling to independent distributors or importers, or even sometimes directly to customers via the Internet. A generation ago, their wines, if being made at all, were for the most part unavailable except to people who visited their wineries. Today, the consumer who wants to find, buy, and drink them usually can do so.

Few people with an awareness of wine's history can dispute the fact that the world of wine is more diverse and energetic than it ever has been. As the English critic and connoisseur Steven Spurrier puts it, "Wine lovers today are spoiled for choice—proof that the present and the future are more golden than the past." Exciting wines come from more places all the time, and consumers at all price levels have choices that their fathers and mothers did not have even a generation ago. This is not to say that everything is perfect. The demand for certain prestigious wines has turned so intense that some are becoming priced out of reach of all but the richest collectors, many of whom buy these wines as investments. Some critics do exert too much influence, while at the same time other commentators over-mystify wine, treating it as an object of fetish-like desire and so alienating potential drinkers from its many pleasures. Yet all of these developments function as consequences of a single cause, the new interest in wine being expressed by millions of people all across the world. Globalization can satisfy that interest, as can specialization, and neither phenomenon should be thought of as the enemy of the other.

Regardless of what form the contemporary thirst for wine may take, anyone who ever has savored a glass of wine has to consider that thirst a cause for celebration. Not all that long ago, wine was in decline. It had only a small consumer audience beyond where it was produced, and even there frequently was considered *déclassé*. All that has changed, and the change is as important to wine's cultural status as what has happened to the contents of the glass or bottle. Though wine has existed for over eight thousand years, the beverage we drink today is relatively new, as are so many of the pleasures it provides. Those different pleasures correspond with wine's current variety and diversity, and that diversity surely is something that should occasion celebration too.

Those of us who care about wine are extremely fortunate to be living when we are. Vin ordinaire no longer tastes invariably sour and unpleasant, and the selection of fine wines grows larger with almost every vintage. Quality used to come solely from select European regions, but now it can be found all over the world. Good wine is available at every price level, enabling people up and down the economic ladder to enjoy it. There are problems to be sure, but it would be churlish to emphasize them at the expense of what has gone right. And a great deal has gone very, very right. That ultimately is the most important lesson of this account of wine's history, one that traces the evolution and emergence of modern wines in a modern world.

Such wines began to emerge in the late Middle Ages and early Renaissance with the discovery of what we today call terroir, but its story involves much more than the ongoing guardianship of select pieces of real estate. Cultivated land is just that, and the story of the cultivation of the world's vineyards includes hundreds if not thousands of decisions made by human beings. Those decisions concerned what the land produced—first the vines and their fruit, and then the wines made with that fruit. What sort of wines those would be was not dictated by nature alone, but rather was determined in large measure by the men and women who cared about them—the vintners, surely, but also all the people who purchased and then drank those wines. Why they did so changed over time, the changes corresponding with advances in grape growing and winemaking, as drinking wine slowly evolved into a cultural choice made on new because no longer necessary grounds. Though it may sound odd, the most essential aspects of terroir thus are not soil and climate but rather palates and taste buds, the human appreciation of a particular wine being what gives that particular place its value. As Jean Kressman from Château Latour-Martillac in Bordeaux once observed, "There is more history than geography in a bottle of wine." That history includes economics, since part of the appreciation of any wine is the willingness on the part of the consumer to buy it (and perhaps pay more for it than for another bottle). Yet money cannot tell the whole story. In the modern world, with modern wines, consumers choose what to buy and vintners decide what to make on the basis of expectation, specifically the expectation of pleasures received. And when all is said and done, pleasure in all its various forms—spiritual and communal, then secular, intellectual, emotional, sensual, aesthetic, and more—remains the only reason why anyone has ever cared about wine at all.

NOTES

INTRODUCTION

ix Most previous accounts of wine's past: See, for example, three otherwise excellent books: Hugh Johnson's *Vintage: The Story of Wine* (New York: Simon & Schuster, 1989), Rod Phillips's *Short History of Wine* (New York: Ecco, 2000), and William Younger's *Gods, Men, and Wine* (Cleveland: World Publishing, 1966).

x "descended from the bless'd abodes": Quotations from Homer come from Alexander Pope's melodious eighteenth-century translation. Alexander Pope, trans., *The Odyssey of Homer*, ed. Maynard Mack (London: Methuen, 1967), 323.

x "Good wine makes good blood": James Howell's *The Familiar Letters*, or *Epistolae Ho-Elianae*, was first published in the 1640s. This particular quotation is taken from a late-nineteenth-century edition published as part of a brief and limited revival of interest in Howell's work. James Howell, *The Familiar Letters of James Howell*, ed. Joseph Jacobs (London: David Nutt, 1890), 457.

xi "Only idiots take their pleasures frivolously": Gerald Asher, *On Wine* (New York: Vintage books, 1986), 202.

xiii "The role of the land": Quoted in Jean-Robert Pitte, *Bordeaux/Burgundy: A Vintage Rivalry*, trans. M. B. DeBevoise (Berkeley: University of California Press, 2008), 14.

xiv "Wine is the intellectual part of a meal": Alexander Dumas, *Dictionary of Cuisine* (abridged), trans. Louis Colman (New York: Routledge, 2005), 5.

GOD'S GIFTS

1 "The gods made wine": Probably composed in the seventh century BCE, the *Cypria* told the story of the Trojan War. Only fragments of the original text exist today. Hugh Evelyn-White, trans., *Hesiod: The Homeric Hymns and Homerica* (London: William Heinemann, 1914), 503.

1 "spontaneous wines from weighty clusters pour": Pope, *Odyssey*, 310.

4 "He it was who turned the grape": Euripides, *Ten Plays*, trans. Paul Roche (New York: Signet Classic, 1998), 407.

6 To date, the first identified by archeologists: For a detailed description of

ancient Chinese alcoholic blends, see Patrick McGovern, *Uncorking the Past: The Quest for Wine, Beer, and Other Alcoholic Beverages* (Berkeley: University of California Press, 2009), 28–59.

7 "It is a peculiarity of wine among liquids": Pliny, *Natural History*, vol. 4, trans. H. Rackham (Cambridge: Harvard University Press, 1938), 273.

8 "the color of honey": Ibid., 267, 271.

8 "It is a proof that wine": Ibid., 273.

9 "the harsh and irregular motions of the soul": Plutarch, *Symposiacs*, III, 9, available at http://ebooks.adelaide.edu.au/p/plutarch/symposiacs/chapter3 .html#section26 (accessed March 2012).

9 "Bad water is a kind of poison": Flavius Vegetius Renatus, *The Military Institutions of the Romans*, trans. John Clark, ed. Thomas Phillips (Westport, CT: Greenwood Press, 1985), 70.

12 "When a man drinks it": Quoted in Ronald Gory, "Viticulture and Ancient Anatolia," in Patrick McGovern, Stuart Fleming, and Solomon Katz, eds., *The Origins and Ancient History of Wine* (New York: Routledge, 1996), 152.

13 "in the garden of the god": Patrick McGovern, *Ancient Wine: The Search for the Origins of Viticulture* (Princeton: Princeton University Press, 2003), 102.

13 "Year Four": Quoted in Leonard Lesko, "Egyptian Wine Production during the New Kingdom," in McGovern, Fleming, and Katz, eds., *Origins and Ancient History of Wine*, 222.

15 "Do not get drunk often": Quoted in Miriam Lichtheim, *Ancient Egyptian Literature: A Book of Readings*, vol. 3 (Berkeley: University of California Press, 1980), 14.

16 "began to emerge from barbarism": A number of authorities, including Hugh Johnson in *Vintage*, 35, attribute this saying to Thucydides, the Greek historian, but whether he actually said it remains a matter of some debate.

17 "to the rich": Euripides, *Ten Plays*, 413.

17 "Greek grog": McGovern, *Ancient Wine*, 274–275.

18 "moistens and tempers the spirits": Quoted in Merton Sandler and Roger Pinder, eds., *Wine: A Scientific Exploration* (New York: CRC Press, 2002), 65.

20 "No other wine": Pliny, *Natural History*, 229.

21 "is the only wine that takes light": Ibid.

21 "Waiter, Falernian!": Charles Martin, trans., *The Poems of Catullus* (Baltimore: Johns Hopkins University Press, 1990).

23 "a sharing of earnest and jest": Quoted in Dennis Smith, *From Symposium to Eucharist: The Banquet in the Early Christian World* (Minneapolis: Fortress Press, 2003), 37.

23 "communion of life": Quoted in ibid., 38.

23 "The wine must be common to all": Quoted in ibid., 54.

24 "a libation to the god": Plato, *Symposium*, trans. Alexander Nehamas and Paul Woodruff (Indianapolis: Hackett, 1989), 6.

25 "the club banquet": See Smith, *From Symposium to Eucharist*, 87–135.

26 "dual in form": Quoted in Carl Kerényi, *Dionysos: Archtypal Image of Indestructible Life*, trans. Ralph Manheim (Princeton: Princeton University Press, 1976), 383.

27 "The son of Zeus is back": Euripides, *Ten Plays*, 395–396.

27 "I speak to you as no mortal man": Ibid., 454.

29 "From the time that the rites": Evan Sage, trans., *Livy*, vol. 9 (Cambridge: Harvard University Press, Loeb Classical Library, 1936), 255.

29 "No one is allowed to sing": Smith, *From Symposium to Eucharist*, 130.

WORLDLY GOODS

34 "if either the needs of the place": Paul Halsall, ed., "Medieval Sourcebook: The Rule of Saint Benedict, excerpts, ca. 530," Internet History Sourcebooks Project, Fordham University, New York, at http://www.fordham.edu/halsall/source/rul-benedict-excerp.asp (accessed March 2012).

35 "what the blessing consecrated": Saint Ambrose, *On the Mysteries*, trans. T. Thompson (New York: Macmillan, 1919), 67–70.

37 "nasty, brutish, and short": Thomas Hobbes, *Leviathan*, ed. Crawford Bough MacPherson (London: Penguin Classics, 1985), 198.

38 "a stoup of stronger drink": Gregory of Tours, *The History of the Franks*, trans. Lewis Thorpe (New York: Penguin Classics, 1974), 410.

39 "obsessed with wine": Pierre Riché, *Daily Life in the World of Charlemagne*, trans. Jo Ann McNamara (Philadelphia: University of Pennsylvania Press, 1978), 176.

42 "Take a dishful of wheat": Quoted in Tania Bayard, *A Medieval Home Companion: Housekeeping in the Fourteenth Century* (New York: HarperCollins, 1991), 102.

43 Yet as the cultural historian: Phillips, *Short History of Wine*, 114.

43 "To make Ypocrasse": *A Roll of Ancient English Cookery, Compiled, about AD 1390, by the Master-Cooks of King Richard II*, available at http://www.free-recipes.co.uk/a-roll-of-ancient-english-cookery/ebook-page-61.asp (accessed February 2012).

45 northern fields contained up to twenty thousand vines: Johnson, *Vintage*, 121.

47 "so completely fuddled with wine": Gregory of Tours, *History of the Franks*, 204.

49 "I want only": Quoted in Emilio Sereni, *History of the Italian Agricultural Landscape*, trans. R. Burr Litchfield (Princeton: Princeton University Press, 1997), 98.

54 "twofold operation": Shakespeare, *The Second Part of King Henry IV*, act 4, scene 3, lines 96–97, 122–125, in *The Riverside Shakespeare* (Boston: Houghton Mifflin, 1974), 912.

56 "fleas, stink, pigs, mold": "Rondeau" by Eustache Deschamps, All Poetry, at http://allpoetry.com/poem/8506985-Rondeau-by-Eustache_Deschamps (accessed March 2012).

57 "good blood, good color": Odile Redon, *The Medieval Kitchen* (Chicago: University of Chicago Press, 1998), 15.

63 "a reasonable price": André Simon, *The History of the Wine Trade in England*, vol. 1 (London: Wyman, 1906), 200.

PARTICULAR TASTES

66 "Take your Money": Richard Ames, "A Farewell to Wine, by a Quondam Friend to the Bottle," at http://www.poemhunter.com/best-poems/richard-ames/a-farewell-to-wine-by-a-quondam-friend-to-the-bottle/ (accessed February 2012).

69 Terroir is itself a modern term: For an extended discussion of terroir, see James Wilson, *Terroir: The Role of Geology, Climate, and Culture in the Making of French Wines* (Berkeley: University of California Press, 1988).

71 "under cross and plow": Ibid., 123.

75 "natural bitterness": Quoted in Rosalind Kent Berlow, "The 'Disloyal' Grape: The Agrarian Crisis of Late Fourteenth-Century Burgundy," *Agricultural History* 56, no. 2 (1982), 426.

76 "the best old Hock": George Farquhar, *The Twin-Rivals* in *The Works of George Farquhar*, vol. 1, ed. Shirley Strum Kenny (Oxford: Clarendon Press, 1988), 509.

79 "Drank a sort of French wine": Samuel Pepys, *The Diary of Samuel Pepys*, vol. 4, ed. Robert Latham and William Matthews (Berkeley, University of California Press, 1971), 100.

80 "The vine de Pontac": John Locke, *The Works of John Locke*, vol. 10 (London: Thomas Tegg, 1823), 329.

80 "fascinating": Clives Coates, *The Wines of Bordeaux: Vintages and Tasting Notes 1952–2003* (Berkeley: University of California Press, 2004), 205.

83 Protestant drinkers pejoratively dubbed it "Anabaptist": Younger, *Gods, Men, and Wine*, 310.

83 "hedge wines": Ibid.

86 "dressed in good order": Quoted in Thomas Pinney, *A History of Wine in America from the Beginnings to Prohibition* (Berkeley: University of California Press, 1989), 11.

86 "rank Taste when ripe": Quoted in ibid., 445.

87 "its healing powers on a disappointed heart": Jane Austen, *The Novels of Jane Austen*, vol. 1, ed. R. W. Chapman (Oxford: Oxford University Press, 1923), 198.

90 "Coniack brandy": Nicholas Faith, *Cognac* (London: Mitchell Beazley, 2005), 63.

91 "all the decent people": Quoted in Younger, *Gods, Men, and Wine*, 339.

92 "the sober liquor, powerfully cerebral": Quoted in Roland Barthes, *Michelet* (Berkeley: University of California Press, 1992), 190.

93 "Those who suffer from weak": Quoted in Rebecca Spang, *The Invention of the Restaurant: Paris and Modern Gastronomic Culture* (Cambridge: Harvard University Press, 2000), 34.

93 "without offending their sense": Quoted in ibid., 80.

94 "so famous in France": Arthur Young, *Travels in France and Italy during the Years 1777, 1788, and 1789* (London: J. M. Dent, 1934), 183.

BATTLING AIR AND BOTTLING STARS

96 "every morning at breakfast": Jean Anthelme Brillat-Savarin, *The Physiology of Taste, or Meditations on Transcendental Gastronomy* (New Haven, CT: Leete's Island Books, 1982), 39.

96 "some [people] any sours they get": Quoted in "Alcoholic Punch and Drink Recipe," History of Alcohol in America, 20-20 Site, at http://www.2020site .org/drinks/punch.html (accessed February 2012).

99 "one of the most striking": Quoted in Douglas McKie, *Antoine Lavoisier: Scientist, Economist, Social Reformer* (New York: Henry Schuman, 1952), 282.

99 "If it were possible": Quoted in René Dubos, *Louis Pasteur: Free Lance of Science* (Boston: Little, Brown, 1950), 119.

100 "a child who would explain": Quoted in ibid., 122.

101 "leave the impression of a child": Ibid., 135.

101 "principles [retain] their full import": Émile Peynaud, *Knowing and Making Wine*, trans. Alan Spencer (New York: John Wiley, 1984), 128.

103 "could not keep on the sea": Quoted in Johnson, *Vintage*, 187.

105 "felicitous revolution": Quoted in J. B. Gough, "Winecraft and Chemistry in 18th-Century France: Chaptal and the Invention of Chaptalization," *Technology and Culture* 39, no. 1 (1998), 103.

105 "It is for chemistry": Quoted in Johnson, *Vintage*, 313.

106 "Robert Mansell, being a seaman": Quoted in Eleanor Godfrey, *The Development of English Glassmaking, 1560–1610* (Chapel Hill: University of North Carolina Press, 1975), 16.

108 "Take thy cork out of thy mouth": Shakespeare, *As You Like It*, act 3, scene 2, lines 202–203, in *Riverside Shakespeare*, 385.

108 "a steel worm used": Quoted in Johnson, *Vintage*, 196.

111 "I love everything that's old": Oliver Goldsmith, *The Collected Works of Oliver Goldsmith*, vol. 1, ed. Arthur Friedman (Oxford: Clarendon Press, 1966), 107.

113 "sparkling Champagne": George Etherege, *The Plays of George Etherege*, ed. Michael Cordner (Cambridge: Cambridge University Press, 1982), 298–299.

115 "the effervescence of the Champagne wine": Cyrus Redding, *A History and Description of Modern Wines*, 3rd ed. (London: Henry G. Bohn, 1860), 108.

118 "sipped at leisure": André Simon, *Bottlescrew Days: Wine Drinking in England during the Eighteenth Century* (London: Duckworth, 1926), xii.

118 "the superiority of Port": Ibid., 143.

120 "small decanters of Sherry": Quoted in http://www.angelpig.net/victorian/formal_dinners.html (accessed February 2012).

122 "[The] wines in the seigneurial cellar": Quoted in Stuart Pigott, *Riesling* (London: Viking, 1991), 16.

123 "most excellent": From a 1788 letter from Jefferson to John Bondfield, the American Counsel in Bordeaux. Quoted in James Gabler, *Passions: The Wines and Travels of Thomas Jefferson* (Baltimore: Bacchus Press, 1995), 158.

123 "benefit to those": Quoted in Johnson, *Vintage*, 264–265.

126 "at its age of 115 years": Quoted in H. Warner Allen, *A History of Wine: Great Vintage Wines from the Homeric Age to the Present Day* (London: Faber & Faber, 1961), 241.

NEW TASTES AND TRADITIONS

127 "lived like gods": Evelyn-White, Hesiod, *The Homeric Hymns and Homerica*, 11.

128 "Bankers were ready to pay": Johnson, *Vintage*, 371.

129 "Whoever, having fifteen or twenty pistols": Brillat-Savarin, *Physiology of Taste*, 228.

131 "a disinterested endeavor": Matthew Arnold, *Lectures and Essays in Criticism*, ed. R. H. Super (Ann Arbor: University of Michigan Press, 1962), 283.

131 "capacity for discriminating": François-Marie de Voltaire, "Taste," in Denis Diderot and Jean le Rond d'Alembert, *Encyclopedia: Selections*, trans. Nelly Hoyt and Thomas Cassirer (Indianapolis: Bobbs-Merrill, 1965), 336.

132 "In all known languages": Ibid., 336–337.

133 "One has a taste": Quoted in Carolyn Korsmeyer, *Making Sense of Taste: Food and Philosophy* (Ithaca: Cornell University Press, 1999), 44.

133 "Some people have a foolish way": Quoted in James Boswell, *Life of Johnson* (London: Oxford University Press, 1953), 756.

134 the original *nouvelle cuisine*: For a detailed discussion of the cultural gastronomic debates and the emergence of a *nouvelle cuisine* in mid-eighteenth-century France, see Susan Pinkard, *A Revolution in Taste: The Rise of French Cuisine* (Cambridge: Cambridge University Press, 2009), 155–210.

135 "I try [a] dish": Quoted in Denise Gigante, *Taste: A Literary History* (New Haven: Yale University Press, 2005), 13.

136 "rational epicure": Quoted in Denise Gigante, ed., *Gusto: Essential Writings in Nineteenth-Century Gastronomy* (New York: Routledge, 2005), 67.

136 "an occupation neither unbecoming nor unworthy": Quoted in ibid., 57.

136 "The perfection of all enjoyment": Quoted in ibid., 62.

137 "Hosts have come to consider": Quoted in ibid., 39.

137 "The best meal without wine": Quoted in Giles MacDonogh, *A Palate in Revolution: Grimod de La Reynière and the Almanach des Gourmands* (London: Robin Clark, 1987), 218.

138 "those wines which are in the greatest vogue": André Jullien, *Topography of All the Known Vineyards, Translated from the French and Abridged so as to Form a Manual and Guide to All Importers and Purchasers* (London: G. & W. B. Whittaker, 1824), v.

139 "We possess several good volumes": Quoted in Johnson, *Vintage*, 313.

139 "an exceptionally delicate palate": Quoted in Gigante, *Gusto*, 12.

139 "statements from books and travelers": Jullien, *Topography of All the Known Vineyards*, xi.

139 "neither harsh nor sharp": Ibid., xiii.

140 "what qualities each wine": Ibid., viii–ix.

142 "very amusing": Quoted in Robert Coustet, "A History of Wine Architecture," in Jean Dethier, ed., *Chateaux Bordeaux: Wine, Architecture, and Civilization* (London: Mitchell Beazley, 1989), 74.

143 "how delicate a thing": Marc-Henry Lemay, ed., *Cocks and Feret: Bordeaux and Its Wines*, 15th ed. (New York: John Wiley, 1998), 159.

145 "the Golden Age": Allen, *History of Wine*, 225–239.

148 "There is no doubt": Redding, *History and Description of Modern Wines*, 12.

148 "wines have stood still": Ibid., 272.

149 "Ripe and unripe": Ibid., 273.

149 "the vines producing every quality": Ibid., 272.

151 "Chianti wine draws most of its bouquet": Quoted in Johnson, *Vintage*, 416.

152 "The wines of Italy": Redding, *History and Description of Modern Wines*, 269.

153 "[They] are often found": Ibid., 196.

153 "France ranks before Spain": Ibid., 194.

154 "It saddened us": Quoted in "Return to La Rioja 1844," under "Winery," then "History," then "1844," at http://www.marquesdemurrieta.com/ (accessed March 2012).

154 "The only problem": Quoted in ibid.

154 "do a good deed": Quoted in ibid.

154 "to obtain sufficient knowledge": Quoted in ibid.

157 "everybody's wine": George Saintsbury, *Notes on a Cellar-Book*, ed. Thomas Pinney (Berkeley: University of California Press, 2008), 94.

157 "*winy* wines": Ibid., 91.

158 "Wines grown so far to the north": Redding, *History and Description of Modern Wines*, 225.

158 "a small white species": Ibid., 219.

159 "the old original": Saintsbury, *Notes on a Cellar-Book*, 111.

160 "no method recommended by European science": Redding, *History and Description of Modern Wines*, 315.

162 "for the most part, healthy": John Beeston, *A Concise History of Australian Wine* (St Leonards, Australia: Allen & Unwin, 1994), 22.

165 "A taste for painting [or] music": Thomas George Shaw, *Wine, the Vine, and the Cellar*, 2nd ed. (London: Longman, Green, Longman, Roberts & Green, 1864), 48.

CRISES AND CATASTROPHES

169 "in neat, spidery pencil writing": George Ordish, *The Great Wine Blight* (London: Sidgwick & Jackson, 1987), 37.

169 "from that moment": Quoted in ibid.

171 "But what of this insect?": Quoted in ibid.

177 "the country was going to the devil": Robert Louis Stevenson, "Travels and Essays," in *Collected Works* (New York: Scribner's, 1920), vol. 7, 276.

180 "every Man [should] take Advantage": Quoted in Pinney, *History of Wine in America from the Beginnings to Prohibition*, 86.

180 "God loves to see us happy": Quoted in ibid.

180 "moral and physical preference": Quoted in Daniel J. Boorstin, *The Lost World of Thomas Jefferson* (New York: H Holt, 1948), 147.

180 "Being among the earliest luxuries": Quoted in Philip Carter Strother and Robert Jackson Allen, "Wine Tasting Activities in Virginia: Is America's First Wine Producing State Destined to Wither on the Vine due to Overregulation?" *Thomas M. Cooley Law Review* 23, no. 2 (2006), available at http://www.strotherlaw.com/Wine_Tasting_Activities_in_VA-Cooley_Law_Review_Article.pdf.

181 "more dulcet, delicious, and dreamy": Henry Wadsworth Longfellow, "Catawba Wine," in *Longfellow's Poetical Works*, vol. 3 (Boston: Houghton Mifflin, 1900), 49–51.

182 "*the* great Vineland": Quoted in Leon Adams, *The Wines of America*, 2nd ed., rev. (New York: McGraw-Hill, 1978), 222.

183 "California can produce as noble": Quoted in "Buena Vista Carneros: A Remarkable Saga," *PinotFile* 6, no. 19 (March 19, 2007), at http://www.princeofpinot.com/article/272/.

183 "bottled poetry": Robert Louis Stevenson, *Silverado Squatters* (London: Chattus & Windus, 1883), 26, 30.

184 "the evil of drunkenness": From an article by Sbarboro published in 1908 in *The Wine and Spirit Bulletin*, vol. 22, available at http://books.google.com/books?id=vQFQAAAAYAAJ&source=gbs_navlinks_s.

186 "Absolutely that is true": Quoted in "The National Prohibition Law Hearings, April 5 to 24, 1926," Schaffer Library of Drug Policy, at http://druglibrary.net/schaffer/History/e1920/senj1926/sullivan.html.

188 "a drink for skid row": Quoted in Adams, *Wines of America*, 239.

189 "The consumption of schnapps": Quoted in James Roberts, *Drink, Temperance, and the Working Class in Nineteenth Century Germany* (Boston: George Allen & Unwin, 1984), 103.

191 "for one brief moment": Quoted in Don Kladstrup and Petie Kladstrup, *Champagne* (New York: William Morrow, 2005), 212.

195 "the woes of the winegrower": Johnson, *Vintage*, 446.

196 "stimulating [liquors]": Though the origin of the word "cocktail" remains uncertain, this is the first recorded definition. It came in 1806, in a Hudson, New York, publication, the *Balance and Columbian Repository*. For more details, see the website of the Museum of the American Cocktail, http://www.museumoftheamericancocktail.org/museum/thebalance.html (accessed March 2012).

196 "the mysteries of Gin-sling": Quoted in "Cocktail Hour: Drink What Dickens Drank," Four Pounds Flour Historic Gastronomy, October 29, 2010, at http://www.fourpoundsflour.com/cocktail-hour-drink-what-dickens-drank/.

196 "to club men and men about town": "In and About the City: A Noted Saloon Keeper Dead," *New York Times*, December 16, 1885, 3, available at http://timesmachine.nytimes.com/browser/1885/12/16/P3.

197 "quickly, while it's laughing at you": Quoted in Pete Wells, "The Reformed Cocktail," *Food and Wine*, February 2001, available at http://www.foodandwine.com/articles/the-reformed-cocktail.

197 "little [and] shy": Evelyn Waugh, *Brideshead Revisited* (Boston: Little, Brown, 1946), 84.

198 "a delicious concoction": Ibid., 47.

200 "No German has the right": Quoted in Hermann Fahrenkrug, "Alcohol and the State in Nazi Germany," in Susanna Barrows and Robin Room, eds., *Drinking: Behavior and Belief in Modern History* (Berkeley: University of California Press, 1991), 315.

RECOVERY AND REVIVAL

203 some commentators have dubbed it a revolution: See, for example, Leo Loubère, *The Wine Revolution in France: The Twentieth Century* (Princeton: Princeton University Press, 1990), especially chap. 1.

203 "the alcoholic fermentation of fresh grapes": Ibid., 140.

205 a definition of wine that clearly echoed: In addition to defining what wine is, the European Community's regulations identify what it is not. Specifically, regulation no. 1493. 1999 states explicitly that "alcoholic fermentation of dried grapes cannot produce wine." For all of these definitions and regulations, see the *Official Journal of the European Union*, available at http://eur-lex.europa.eu/LexUriServ/LexUriServ.do?uri=OJ:C:2003:028E:0114:0114:EN:PDF (accessed March 2012).

210 "that you [become] the first": Quoted in "Baron Le Roy: The Man," Château Fortia, at http://www.chateau-fortia.com/baronleroy_e.html (accessed March 2012).

210 "loyal, local, and constant": This phrase was used by the French authorities as early as 1919. See Stephen Brush and Doreen Stabinsky, eds., *Valuing Local Knowledge* (Washington, DC: Island Press, 1996), 241.

217 "traditions [that were] too often backward": Burton Anderson, *The Wine Atlas*

of Italy and Traveller's Guide to the Vineyards (New York: Simon & Schuster, 1990), 20.

226 "[an] ignoramus only makes good wine by accident": Peynaud, Knowing and Making Wine, vii.

226 "It is not enough": Ibid.

226 "the thermal problem": Ibid., 165–171.

226 "it is vital": Ibid., 169.

227 "the success of vinification": Ibid.

228 "finishing phase": Ibid., 120.

228 "promotes quality": Ibid., 121.

229 "[Always] using only the best grapes": Quoted in Mike Steinberger, "The Tastemaker," Slate, July 30, 2004, at http://www.slate.com/articles/health_ and_science/wines_world/2004/07/the_tastemaker.html.

229 "the fruit of a discipline": Quoted in Harry Paul, Science, Vine, and Wine in Modern France (Cambridge: Cambridge University Press, 1996), 275.

230 "The wines of yesterday": Quoted in Steinberger, "Tastemaker."

230 "know wine better": Peynaud, Knowing and Making Wine, vii.

VISIONS AND VARIETALS

239 "a truly Australian wine": Quoted in Andrew Caillard, The Rewards of Patience, 6th ed. (Crows Nest, Australia: Allen & Unwin, 2008), 93.

241 "A concoction of wild fruits": Quoted in ibid., 94.

241 "People who have been lucky": Quoted in ibid., 98.

241 "The objective": Max Schubert, "The Story of Grange," in ibid., 12.

255 "We must not": Ibid., 17.

257 "honest labeling": For a more detailed discussion of the campaign for varietal labeling, see Thomas Pinney, A History of Wine in America from Prohibition to the Present (Berkeley: University of California Press, 2005), 118–125.

257 "The vine": Quoted in Thoms Pinney, The Makers of American Wine: A Record of Two Hundred Years (Berkeley: University of California Press, 2012), 161.

259 "to improve quality": Quoted in Pinney, History of Wine in America from Prohibition to the Present, 104.

260 "At long last": Adams, Wines of America, xii–xiii.

262 "definitely California": Quoted in George Taber, Judgment of Paris: California vs. France and the Historic 1976 Paris Tasting That Revolutionized Wine (New York: Scribner's, 2005), 3.

263 "My bit of showmanship": Robert Mondavi, Harvests of Joy (New York: Harcourt Brace, 1998), 160.

264 "golden age": Quoted in Pinney, Makers of American Wine, 193.

267 "This brilliant, pungent": Oz Clarke, Oz Clarke's Encyclopedia of Grapes (New York: Harcourt, 2001), 219.

275 "Occasionally wine and politics": Jancis Robinson, Tasting Pleasure: Confessions of a Wine Lover (New York: Viking, 1997), 333.

GLOBALIZATION AND SPECIALIZATION

278 "liquid gold": Quoted in Elin McCoy, The Emperor of Wine: The Rise of Robert M. Parker, Jr., and the Reign of American Taste (New York: Ecco, 2005), 106.

278 "There may not be a vintage": Quoted in ibid., 104.

278 "opulent," "chewy," "fleshy," and "big": Quoted in ibid.

280 "such a level": Quoted in ibid., 99.

281 "very good" or "excellent": Lemay, ed., *Cocks and Feret*, chap. 7.

281 "no bad wines": Ibid., 115.

283 "the modern wines of France": Redding, *History and Description of Modern Wines*, 85.

288 "vintage madness": Kermit Lynch, *Inspiring Thirst* (Berkeley, CA: Ten Speed Press, 1994), 171–172.

288 "Wine can be a bringer": Terry Theise, *Reading between the Wines* (Berkeley: University of California Press, 2010), 7.

288 "prefab": Ibid., 101.

290 "terrible": Quoted in McCoy, *Emperor of Wine*, 71.

290 "expose mediocre and poor wines": Quoted in ibid., 70.

291 "96–100: An *extraordinary* wine": This explanation of Robert Parker's 100-point scoring system appears on the cover of every issue of *The Wine Advocate*.

293 "magically endowed," with "layers of flavor and power": This is part of Parker's description of the 2000 Château Pétrus. Robert M. Parker Jr., *Bordeaux: A Consumer's Guide to the World's Finest Wines*, 4th ed. (New York: Simon & Schuster, 2003), 704.

293 "among the most ravishing": Ibid., 764.

296 "A particular idiom": Theise, *Reading between the Wines*, 112.

296 "there are no invalid moments": Ibid., 101.

296 "higher and lower pleasures": Ibid.

298 "a draught of vintage": Here are the pertinent lines (11–14):

> O for a draught of vintage! That hath ben
> Cool'd a long age in the deep-delvèd earth,
> Tasting of Flora and the country-green,
> Dance, and Provençal song, and sunburnt mirth!

John Keats, *The Poems of John Keats*, ed. Jack Stillinger (Cambridge: Harvard University Press, 1978), 369.

309 "just as the eye perceives": Rudolf Steiner, *Theosophy: An Introduction to the Supersensible Knowledge of the World and the Destination of Man*, trans. Elizabeth Shields (New York: Rand McNally, 1910), 6.

311 "Being organic for years": Quoted in Jamie Goode and Sam Harrop, *Authentic Wine: Toward Natural and Sustainable Winemaking* (Berkeley: University of California Press, 2011), 72.

312 "Wine lovers today are spoiled": Steven Spurrier, "Spurrier's World," *Decanter* 37, no. 2 (November 2011), 102.

314 "There is more history": Quoted in Pitte, *Bordeaux/ Burgundy*, 18.

BIBLIOGRAPHY

The following list of sources includes only books and articles that are concerned directly with wine and wine culture. Other more broadly historical or literary sources quoted in the text are identified in the notes.

ADAMS, LEON. *The Wines of America* (second edition, revised). New York: McGraw-Hill, 1978.

ALLEN, H. WARNER. *A History of Wine: Great Vintage Wines from the Homeric Age to the Present Day*. London: Faber & Faber, 1961.

ANDERSON, BURTON. *The Wine Atlas of Italy and Traveller's Guide to the Vineyards*. New York: Simon & Schuster, 1990.

ASHER, GERALD. *On Wine*. New York: Vintage Books, 1986.

BAMFORTH, CHARLES. *Grape versus Grain*. New York: Cambridge University Press, 2008.

BARROWS, SUSANNA, and ROBIN ROOM (editors). *Drinking: Behavior and Belief in Modern History*. Berkeley: University of California Press, 1991.

BASTIANICH, JOSEPH, and DAVID LYNCH. *Vino Italiano: The Regional Wines of Italy*. New York: Clarkson Potter, 2002.

BAYARD, TANIA. *A Medieval Home Companion: Housekeeping in the Fourteenth Century*. New York: HarperCollins, 1991.

BEESTON, JOHN. *A Concise History of Australian Wine*. St Leonards, Australia: Allen & Unwin, 1994.

BELFRAGE, NICOLAS. *Brunello to Zibibbo: The Wines of Tuscany, Central and Southern Italy*. London: Faber & Faber, 2001.

BERLOW, ROSALIND KENT. "The 'Disloyal' Grape: The Agrarian Crisis of Late Fourteenth-Century Burgundy." *Agricultural History* 56, no. 2 (1982): 426–438.

BRENNAN, THOMAS. *Burgundy to Champagne: The Wine Trade in Early Modern France*. Baltimore: Johns Hopkins University Press, 1997.

BRILLAT-SAVARIN, JEAN ANTHELME. *The Physiology of Taste, or Meditations on Transcendental Gastronomy*. New Haven, CT: Leete's Island Books, 1982.

BROOK, STEPHEN. *Bordeaux: People, Power, and Politics*. London: Mitchell Beazley, 2001.

CAILLARD, ANDREW. *The Rewards of Patience* (sixth edition). Crows Nest, Australia: Allen & Unwin, 2008.

CLARKE, OZ. *Oz Clarke's Encyclopedia of Grapes.* New York: Harcourt, 2001.

COATES, CLIVE. *The Wines of Bordeaux: Vintages and Tasting Notes 1952–2003.* Berkeley: University of California Press, 2004.

COLE, KATHERINE. *Voodoo Vintners: Oregon's Astonishing Biodynamic Winegrowers.* Corvallis: Oregon State University Press, 2011.

COLMAN, TYLER. *Wine Politics: How Governments, Mobsters, and Critics Influence the Wines We Drink.* Berkeley: University of California Press, 2008.

COUNIHAN, CAROLE, and PENNY VAN ESTERIK (editors). *Food and Culture: A Reader.* New York: Routledge, 1997.

DARLINGTON, DAVID. *An Ideal Wine: One Generation's Pursuit of Perfection and Profit in California.* New York: HarperCollins, 2011.

DETHIER, JEAN (editor). *Chateaux Bordeaux: Wine, Architecture, and Civilization.* London: Mitchell Beazley, 1989.

DICKIE, GEORGE. *The Century of Taste: The Philosophical Odyssey of Taste in the Eighteenth Century.* New York: Oxford University Press, 1996.

DODDS, E. R. "Introduction," in Euripides, *Bacchae* (second edition). Oxford: Clarendon Press, 1960.

DUBOS, RENÉ. *Louis Pasteur: Free Lance of Science.* Boston: Little, Brown, 1950.

DUMAS, ALEXANDER. *Dictionary of Cuisine* (abridged and translated by Louis Colman). New York: Routledge, 2005.

ESTREICHER, STEFAN. *Wine from Neolithic Times to the 21st Century.* New York: Algora Publishing, 2006.

FAITH, NICHOLAS. *Cognac.* London: Mitchell Beazley, 2005.

FERRY, LUC. *Homo Aestheticus: The Invention of Taste in the Democratic Age* (translated by Robert De Loiza). Chicago: University of Chicago Press, 1993.

FLEMING, STUART. *Vinum: The Story of Roman Wine.* Glen Mills, PA: Art Flair, 2001.

FRANCIS, A. D. *The Wine Trade.* Edinburgh: T. & A. Constable, 1972.

FREEDMAN, PAUL (editor). *Food: The History of Taste.* Berkeley: University of California Press, 2007.

GABLER, JAMES. *Passions: The Wines and Travels of Thomas Jefferson.* Baltimore: Bacchus Press, 1995.

GATELY, IAN. *Drink: A Cultural History of Alcohol.* New York: Gotham Books, 2008.

GERARD, ALEXANDER. *An Essay on Taste. A Facsimile Reproduction of the Third Edition.* Delmar, NY: Scholars' Facsimiles & Reprints, 1978.

GIGANTE, DENISE (editor). *Gusto: Essential Writings in Nineteenth-Century Gastronomy.* New York: Routledge, 2005.

GODFREY, ELEANOR. *The Development of English Glassmaking, 1560–1640.* Chapel Hill: University of North Carolina Press, 1975.

GOODE, JAMIE, and SAM HARROP. *Authentic Wine: Toward Natural and Sustainable Winemaking.* Berkeley: University of California Press, 2011.

GOUGH, J. B. "Winecraft and Chemistry in 18th-Century France: Chaptal and the Invention of Chaptalization." *Technology and Culture* 39, no. 1 (1998): 74–104.

GUY, KOLLEEN. *When Champagne Became French: Wine and the Making of a National Identity.* Baltimore: Johns Hopkins University Press, 2003.

HARRISON, BRIAN. *Drink and the Victorians: The Temperance Question in England, 1815–1872* (2nd edition). Staffordshire, UK: Keele University Press, 1994.

HENRICHS, ALBERT. "Between City and Country: Cultic Dimensions of Dionysus in Athens and Attica," in Mark Griffith and Donald Mastronarde (editors), *Cabinet of the Muses: Essays on Classical and Comparative Literature in Honor of
Thomas G. Rosenmeyer.* Atlanta: Scholars Press, 1990.

JEFFORD, ANDREW. *The New France: A Complete Guide to Contemporary French Wine.*
London: Mitchell Beazley, 2002.

JOHNSON, HUGH. *Vintage: The Story of Wine.* New York: Simon & Schuster,
1989.

JOHNSON, HUGH, and JANCIS ROBINSON. *The World Atlas of Wine* (sixth edition).
London: Mitchell Beazley, 2007.

JULLIEN, ANDRÉ. *Topography of All the Known Vineyards, Translated from the French and
Abridged so as to Form a Manual and Guide to All Importers and Purchasers.* London:
G. & W. B. Whittaker, 1824.

KERÉNYI, CARL. *Dionysos: Archetypal Image of Indestructible Life* (translated by Ralph
Manheim). Princeton: Princeton University Press, 1976.

KLADSTRUP, DON, and PETIE KLADSTRUP. *Champagne.* New York: William
Morrow, 2005.

KRAMER, MATT. *Making Sense of Wine: Revised and Updated Edition.* Philadelphia:
Running Press, 2003.

LEMAY, MARC-HENRY (editor). *Cocks and Feret: Bordeaux and Its Wines* (fifteenth edition). New York: John Wiley, 1998.

LEWIN, BENJAMIN. *What Price Bordeaux.* Dover, UK: Vendange Press, 2009.

———. *Wine Myths and Realities.* Dover, UK: Vendange Press, 2010.

LOUBÈRE, LEO. *The Wine Revolution in France: The Twentieth Century.* Princeton:
Princeton University Press, 1990.

LYNCH, KERMIT. *Inspiring Thirst.* Berkeley, CA: Ten Speed Press, 1994.

MACDONOGH, GILES. *A Palate in Revolution: Grimod de La Reynière and the Almanach
des Gourmands.* London: Robin Clark, 1987.

McCOY, ELIN. *The Emperor of Wine: The Rise of Robert M. Parker, Jr., and the Reign of
American Taste.* New York: Ecco, 2005.

McGOVERN, PATRICK. *Ancient Wine: The Search for the Origins of Viniculture.* Princeton: Princeton University Press, 2003.

———. *Uncorking the Past: The Quest for Wine, Beer, and Other Alcoholic Beverages.*
Berkeley: University of California Press, 2009.

McGOVERN, PATRICK, STUART FLEMING, and SOLOMON KATZ (editors). *The Origins and Ancient History of Wine* (volume 11 in the Food and Nutrition in History
and Anthropology series). New York: Routledge, 1996.

McKIE, DOUGLAS. *Antoine Lavoisier: Scientist, Economist, Social Reformer* (New York:
Henry Schuman, 1952).

MENNELL, STEPHEN. *All Manners of Food: Eating and Taste in England and France from
the Middle Ages to the Present.* Oxford: Basil Blackwell, 1985.

MITCHELL, EVAN, and BRIAN MITCHELL. *The Psychology of Wine: Truth and Beauty
by the Glass.* Santa Barbara, CA: Praeger, 2009.

MONDAVI, ROBERT. *Harvests of Joy.* New York: Harcourt Brace, 1998.

MONTANARI, MASSIMO. *Food Is Culture* (translated by Albert Sonnenfeld). New
York: Columbia University Press, 2006.

NOSSITER, JONATHAN. *Liquid Memory: Why Wine Matters.* New York: Farrar, Straus
& Giroux, 2009.

ORDISH, GEORGE. *The Great Wine Blight.* London: Sidgwick & Jackson, 1987.

PARKER, ROBERT M., JR. *Bordeaux: A Consumer's Guide to the World's Finest Wines* (fourth edition). New York: Simon & Schuster, 2003.

PAUL, HARRY. *Science, Vine, and Wine in Modern France.* Cambridge: Cambridge University Press, 1996.

PELLECHIA, THOMAS. *Wine: The 8,000-Year-Old Story of the Wine Trade.* Philadelphia: Running Press, 2006.

PEYNAUD, ÉMILE. *Knowing and Making Wine* (translated by Alan Spencer). New York: John Wiley, 1984.

PHILLIPS, ROD. *A Short History of Wine.* New York: Ecco, 2000.

PIGOTT, STUART. *Riesling.* London: Viking, 1991.

PINKARD, SUSAN. *A Revolution in Taste: The Rise of French Cuisine.* Cambridge: Cambridge University Press, 2009.

PINNEY, THOMAS. *A History of Wine in America from Prohibition to the Present.* Berkeley: University of California Press, 2005.

———. *A History of Wine in America from the Beginnings to Prohibition.* Berkeley: University of California Press, 1989.

———. *The Makers of American Wine: A Record of Two Hundred Years.* Berkeley: University of California Press, 2012.

PITTE, JEAN-ROBERT. *Bordeaux/Burgundy: A Vintage Rivalry* (translated by M. B. DeBevoise). Berkeley: University of California Press, 2008.

PRESTWICH, PATRICIA. *Drink and the Politics of Social Reform: Antialcoholism in France since 1870.* Palo Alto, CA: Society for the Promotion of Science and Scholarship, 1988.

REDDING, CYRUS. *A History and Description of Modern Wines* (third edition). London: Henry G. Bohn, 1860.

REDON, ODILE. *The Medieval Kitchen.* Chicago: University of Chicago Press, 1998.

ROBERTS, JAMES. *Drink, Temperance, and the Working Class in Nineteenth-Century Germany.* Boston: George Allen & Unwin, 1984.

ROBINSON, JANCIS. *The Great Wine Book.* New York: William Morrow, 1982.

——— (editor). *The Oxford Companion to Wine* (third edition). Oxford: Oxford University Press, 2006.

———. *Tasting Pleasure: Confessions of a Wine Lover.* New York: Viking, 1997.

SAINTSBURY, GEORGE. *Notes on a Cellar-Book* (edited by Thomas Pinney). Berkeley: University of California Press, 2008.

SANDLER, MERTON, and ROGER PINDER (editors). *Wine: A Scientific Exploration.* New York: CRC Press, 2002.

SERENI, EMILIO. *History of the Italian Agricultural Landscape* (translated by R. Burr Litchfield). Princeton: Princeton University Press, 1997.

SHAW, THOMAS GEORGE. *Wine, the Vine, and the Cellar* (second edition). London: Longman, Green, Longman, Roberts, & Green, 1864.

SHIMAN, LILIAN LEWIS. *Crusade against Drink in Victorian England.* New York: St. Martin's Press, 1988.

SIMON, ANDRÉ. *Bottlescrew Days: Wine Drinking in England during the Eighteenth Century.* London: Duckworth, 1926.

———. *The History of the Wine Trade in England* (three volumes). London: Wyman, 1906.

SMITH, DENNIS. *From Symposium to Eucharist: The Banquet in the Early Christian World.* Minneapolis: Fortress Press, 2003.

SPANG, REBECCA. *The Invention of the Restaurant: Paris and Modern Gastronomic Culture.* Cambridge: Harvard University Press, 2000.

SPURRIER, STEVEN. "Spurrier's World." *Decanter* 37, no. 2 (November 2011), 101–102.

STEINBERGER, MIKE. "The Tastemaker," *Slate,* July 30, 2004, at http://www.slate.com/articles/health_and_science/wines_world/2004/07/the_tastemaker.html.

STEINER, RUDOLF. *Theosophy: An Introduction to the Supersensible Knowledge of the World and the Destination of Man* (translated by Elizabeth Shields). New York: Rand McNally, 1910.

TABER, GEORGE. *Judgment of Paris: California vs. France and the Historic 1976 Paris Tasting That Revolutionized Wine.* New York: Scribner's, 2005.

THEISE, TERRY. *Reading between the Wines.* Berkeley: University of California Press, 2010.

UNGER, RICHARD. *Beer in the Middle Ages and Renaissance.* Philadelphia: University of Pennsylvania Press, 2004.

UNWIN, TIM. *Wine and the Vine: An Historical Geography of Viticulture and the Wine Trade.* London: Routledge, 1991.

VESETH, MIKE. *Wine Wars: The Curse of the Blue Nun, the Miracle of the Two Buck Chuck, and the Revenge of the Terroirists.* Lanham, MD: Rowman & Littlefield, 2011.

WALTON, STUART. *Out of It: A Cultural History of Intoxication.* New York: Harmony Books, 2002.

WEINHOLD, RUDOLF. *Vivat Bacchus: A History of the Vine and Its Wine* (translated by Neil Jones). Hertfordshire, UK: Argus Books, 1978.

WILSON, HANNEKE. *Wine and Words in Classical Antiquity and the Middle Ages.* London: Duckworth, 2003.

WILSON, JAMES. *Terroir: The Role of Geology, Climate, and Culture in the Making of French Wines.* Berkeley: University of California Press, 1988.

YOUNGER, WILLIAM. *Gods, Men, and Wine.* Cleveland: World Publishing, 1966.

INDEX